FORTY-NINERS
'ROUND the HORN

FORTY-NINERS
'ROUND the HORN

CHARLES R. SCHULTZ

UNIVERSITY OF SOUTH CAROLINA PRESS

© 1999 University of South Carolina

Published in Columbia, South Carolina, by the
University of South Carolina Press

Manufactured in the United States of America

03 02 01 00 99   5 4 3 2 1

Library of Congress Cataloging-in-Publication Data

Schultz, Charles R.
    Forty-niners 'round the Horn / Charles R. Schultz.
        p. cm. — (Studies in maritime history)
    Includes bibliographical refereces (p.   ) and index.

    ISBN 1-57003-329-3 (alk. paper)
    1. Voyages to the Pacific coast.   I. Title.   II. Series.
F865.S38   1999
910'.2'02—dc21   99-6595

Contents

Illustrations and Tables

ILLUSTRATIONS

ILLUSTRATIONS AND TABLES

Rev. William Taylor
"A Fourth of July oration"
Track chart, ship *Sarah & Eliza*
Track chart, ship *Andalusia*
"The [brig] *Osceola* in a gale off Cape Horn"
"The seaman's burial"
"Beach of Yerba Buena Cove, 1849"
"View of 'Prospect Hill' San Francisco"
San Francisco in 1849
"Post office, 1849"
"Muddy streets, winter 1849–'50"
"Parker House and Dennison's Exchange, 1849"

TABLES

Preface

I first became interested in many aspects of American maritime history when I began my work as keeper of manuscripts at the G. W. Blunt White Library at Mystic Seaport Museum, Inc., in Mystic, Connecticut, in the spring of 1963. Fortunately for me, Dr. Charles W. David, who was then head of that library, chose to seek someone who possessed the skills and expertise needed to process manuscript collections to make them readily usable by researchers and to encourage the use of them and to allow that person to learn maritime history on the job rather than to employ a maritime history specialist and permit that individual to develop the necessary archival and manuscript skills on the job. I learned rather quickly that most research and publishing in maritime history dealt with the technological aspects of designing and building vessels; famous and infamous designers, builders, captains, and owners; and dramatic events such as mutinies, speed records, and shipwrecks. Only rarely did someone research and write about economic aspects of maritime history. Even fewer people researched and wrote about social aspects of maritime history.

Early in my tenure at Mystic Seaport, I prepared an inventory of the logbooks and journals of seamen and passengers held by the G. W. Blunt White Library. In the course of carefully examining each of the hundreds of volumes to see exactly who was the author or keeper of the account of each voyage recorded in every volume, the type of activity in which the vessel was engaged, the ports entered, and the dates covered, I learned some things about how people on board lived. At that time the library had only the journals of Benjamin Bailey in the ship *Sweden* and Harry G. Brown in the bark *Selma* that dealt with individuals sailing around Cape Horn to California in 1849. A brief examination of those two volumes and hasty comparisons with the many other journals and logbooks convinced me that gold rush voyages were very different from general commercial trading and whaling voyages. Not only were the circumstances different, but also the people in gold rush vessels were different and they lived differently from those in other vessels. I knew immediately that there was a fascinating story in the lives of those adventuresome young men who left home and family to seek their fortunes in a part of the world about which they knew very little. Most of what they knew was from blazing headlines and frequently exaggerated and conflicting stories in newspapers concerning the gold discoveries made in northern California in January 1848.

Although the nucleus of the story that is told in the present volume started in my head as early as 1965, I did little toward developing that story for several years. First I had to devote all of my extra hours to completing a doctoral dissertation that I had just started when I arrived at Mystic Seaport. Increasing responsibilities at Mystic Seaport and a move to Texas A&M University in 1971 along with increased family responsibilities delayed this project for several more years. While examining issues of the *California Historical Quarterly* for articles to include in a planned bibliography of maritime and naval history I was compiling, I encountered Lynn Bonfield Donovan's article "Day-by-Day Records: Dairies from the CHS Library" in the Winter 1975 issue. That annotated bibliography of gold rush journals in the collection of the California Historical Society caused me to think seriously about undertaking this project, which I chose to call "Life on Board Gold Rush Ships." I soon made the first of a series of trips to several libraries in California and a long visit to the East Coast to visit libraries in Connecticut and Massachusetts to gather information for what I knew would one day be a monograph about how passengers lived in those hundreds of vessels in which they sailed to California in 1849.

After researching for a few years, I was challenged to submit a manuscript for the *Log of Mystic Seaport* annual essay contest. I wanted to produce a manuscript in which I could reveal the great variety of sources available and demonstrate just how different gold rush voyages were from other voyages. Therefore I chose to write about how the passengers celebrated the Fourth of July at sea while headed to the gold fields because I had, by then, encountered several detailed accounts of such celebrations in journals of passengers. My manuscript "A Forty-Niner Fourth of July" was selected as the best and was published in the Spring 1986 issue. A few years later the Maryland Historical Society and the University of Baltimore announced an essay contest on Maryland Maritime History. I decided my topic would be an account of the gold rush voyage of the ship *Andalusia* of Baltimore set in the context of all the vessels that sailed from Baltimore. The primary source for this account was the diary of Anne (Willson) Booth, the niece of Capt. F. W. Willson; but Baltimore newspapers also contained useful information. Booth's journal was the first of many journals I examined at the Bancroft Library at the University of California at Berkeley, and

Preface

I felt from the very beginning that it was certainly a rare, if indeed not unique, perspective. It is the only journal I can definitely identify as having been written by a female passenger. I later examined a series of letters by another young female passenger, but her letters do not provide as much useful information about shipboard life as does Booth's journal. The judges again selected my essay "Ship *Andalusia*: Queen of the Baltimore Gold Rush Fleet" as the best submission, and it was published in the Summer 1991 issue of *Maryland Historical Magazine*. A couple of years later I felt compelled to make better known the story of the conflict between the first class passengers and Capt. Hall J. Tibbits of the ship *Pacific*. That conflict was so severe that it led to the dismissal of Captain Tibbits by the U. S. consul at Rio de Janeiro, who was himself discharged soon thereafter. That story was first told as a presentation at the annual meeting of the North American Society for Oceanic History and was later published as "The Gold Rush Voyage of the Ship *Pacific*: A Study in Vessel Management," in the Summer 1993 issue of *American Neptune*.

It seemed to me that I would have to continue to publish small parts of the story as journal articles, as full-time employment made it virtually impossible to think of attempting a full monograph. In the fall of 1996 the Friends of the Texas A&M University Library announced the creation of the Irene B. Hoadley Professorship in Academic Librarianship and invited all the library faculty members to apply for that honor, which could be held for two years. Since the holder of the professorship could use the income from the endowment to purchase released time, I immediately chose to apply for the professorship and was fortunate enough to be chosen as the first recipient. The income from the endowment was used to purchase time to prepare the first draft of this monograph.

From the beginning of my research, I decided that I would include only accounts of voyages in sailing vessels that departed from the east or gulf coasts before December 31, 1849, and that sailed around Cape Horn or through the Strait of Magellan. The number of steamships that sailed around Cape Horn during the time period was quite small and would probably not have impacted this study even if journals kept in them could have been located. Trips between the east and gulf coasts and Panama and between Panama and San Francisco in either steamships or sailing vessels were so much shorter and so much different in nature and sometimes involved so many more people than did Cape Horn voyages that a separate study of them needs to be done. Monthly steamers between New York and Panama each carried hundreds of passengers. Monthly service was also established between Panama and San Francisco quite early. Whether or not including records from sailing vessels departing after December 31, 1849, would have made a significant difference in this monograph is problematic, but I felt the necessity early on for establishing a time frame. The calendar year 1849 seemed to be a logical time period to cover. Using information from journals kept on board later vessels might well have made a significant difference in passengers' first impressions of California, the topic of the final chapter.

From the beginning I have collected information on topics that I felt would become chapters in any monograph that I would eventually write. In fact, those topics were fixed fairly firmly in my mind from the examination of the Bailey and Brown journals at Mystic Seaport in 1965. Regular filing of notes under those topics made possible relatively efficient writing during the summer and fall of 1997.

Two earlier publications provided some early guidance even though both were broader in scope than this study, and both authors used a much smaller number of sources than I have examined. Possibly those sources were not as readily available when Octavius Thorndike Howe produced *Argonauts of '49* in 1923 and Oscar Lewis produced *Sea Routes to the Gold Fields* in 1949. James P. Delgado's 1990 *To California by Sea* is based upon a much larger number of sources than those two early volumes, but it too is broader in scope than my work. My study is based on more than a hundred original journals, a few sets of letters, nearly twenty-five published journals of passengers in sailing vessels of all sizes, and nearly seventy secondary sources. Virtually all of the vessels sailed from ports between Maine and New Jersey, but a few sailed from ports between Baltimore and New Orleans. In several instances two or three journals were found to document the voyage of a single vessel. Undoubtedly the two best documented voyages are those of the ships *Pacific* and *Sweden*. All of the accounts of the voyage of the *Pacific* were written by first-class passengers and include four original journals, one published account, a set of published letters, and a vast quantity of information in the consular post records at Rio de Janeiro. The voyage of the *Sweden* is documented in three original and two published journals as well as the papers of J. L. L. F. Warren. Such multiple sources frequently provided more complete documentation than could a single source. Voyages of several other vessels were documented in two journals or a journal and letters.

Perhaps the individual who should be recognized first for the completion of this work is the late Dr. Charles W. David, who, as head of the library at Mystic Seaport, hired this central Texas native whose only exposure to the sea before 1963 had been a few brief fishing expeditions to Rockport, Texas, during my early childhood. Placing the daunting responsibility of processing and promoting the use of an impressive collection of original source material in American maritime history in my hands was a great leap of faith by Dr. David. I hope subsequent developments justified that act. My primary credential for the position of keeper of manuscripts at Mystic Seaport was three years of part-time experience processing collections at the Ohio Historical Society under the excellent tutelage of Kenneth W. Duckett. Dr. David also had the great foresight to insist that I attend all of the sessions of the Munson Institute of American Maritime History during the summer of 1963. The institute was offered each summer with professors Robert G. Albion of Harvard University and John Haskell Kemble of Claremont College in California serving as the principal faculty. Several guest lecturers addressed a variety of special topics.

That six-week institute provided a basic introduction into the broad subject of American maritime history. The next eight years at the G. W. Blunt White Library (four as keeper of manuscripts and four as librarian) offered me the opportunity to expand upon what I had learned in 1963, and I have added to and specialized that knowledge at various times ever since through reading and research into the California gold rush, American whaling, and clipper ships.

The staffs of numerous institutions have been helpful in providing access to the many journals and publications from which the information for this work has been collected. Those at the Bancroft Library, University of California at Berkeley; California Historical Society; California State Library; Henry E. Huntington Library; J. Porter Shaw Library, National Maritime Museum; and G. W. Blunt White Library, Mystic Seaport Museum, Inc., have provided access to the majority of the sources. Lesser amounts of materials were examined at the Old Dartmouth Historical Society, New Bedford Public Library, Peabody/Essex Museum, Society for California Pioneers, New York Public Library, and New York Historical Society. Copies of journals and other materials have graciously been made available by other institutions including Rutgers University, University of Arkansas at Fayetteville, New Jersey Historical Society, Maryland Historical Society, University of Washington, and National Archives and Records Administration Federal Records Center at Bayonne, New Jersey.

My wife, Fran, has endured several absences during research trips to California and many evenings of work in the office and has been a source of constant support. She also read a draft of the entire manuscript and noted a number of spelling and grammatical errors and inconsistencies. Several former secretaries have typed or keyed in presentations about life on board gold rush ships given at a variety of meetings and manuscripts of articles that have been published out of my research for this monograph. This monograph, however, is entirely my own work, having been drafted, edited, and revised on a computer.

As is the case with many books in the humanities and social sciences, personal funds and personal time provided the majority of the resources to produce *Forty-Niners 'round the Horn*. Funding to cover portions of the cost of several research trips to San Francisco and Sacramento was provided by the Texas A&M University Faculty Mini Grant Committee and the Texas A&M University Library Research Committee. Funding from the Irene B. Hoadley Professorship in Academic Librarianship offered by the friends of the Texas A&M University Library made possible the completion of this manuscript in time for the sesquicentennial of the 1849 California gold rush. Perhaps it could not have come at a more propitious point in time.

FORTY-NINERS
'ROUND the HORN

Introduction

Gold and the acquisition thereof has been a subject of interest from time immemorial. Bits of gold have been found in Spanish caves occupied by people of the Paleolithic Age of around 40,000 B.C. Just when gold was first used to make an artifact has not been established, but perhaps someday archaeologists will yet discover items made from gold that predate the earliest items made from copper and iron as early at 2500 B.C. The ease with which gold artifacts can be melted and cast or molded into some other object because of the indestructibility of gold makes it possible that golden artifacts older than 2500 B.C. might already have been so treated. This has happened over time, as grave robbers have removed golden artifacts frequently buried with their owners in ages past. It also happened in the late twentieth century, when the price of gold rose drastically and thieves burglarized homes for gold and quickly melted the jewelry and other items in portable smelters.

Gold exists throughout the world, both on land and in the sea. Currently the great majority of the newly mined gold comes from South Africa. It has been estimated that throughout history approximately 110,000 metric tons of gold have been mined from the land areas of the world. This pales in comparison with the estimated 10 billion tons suspended on the waters of the oceans that cover two-thirds of the world's surface or the 50 billion trillion troy ounces said to exist in the sun as hot gas. In spite of numerous efforts during the past century and a half, no one has developed a way of economically extracting gold from the oceans. And no one seems to have considered attempting to approach the sun to harvest the potential gold there.

Rumors of golden cities rivaling the biblical New Jerusalem have persisted throughout the world for centuries, and explorers and adventurers have searched for them with little or no success. For thousands of years explorers searched for Ophir, the site of King Solomon's mines, and finally in 1976 geologists from the United States and Saudi Arabia reported their discovery in the Saudi Arabian desert. Spanish and Portuguese explorers scoured South, Central, and North America, seeking such mythological sites known as Eldorado, Quivira, and the Seven Cities of Cibola until 1532, when Pizarro found the golden city of the Incas in Peru. The Spanish then forced the Incas to extract the gold for Spain. Transporting the gold to Spain in sailing vessels resulted in the loss of some of those vessels and centuries of searching for the gold lost with them.

Some of the early settlers in the southeastern United States came to seek gold and achieved modest success. It has been estimated that those mines produced around fifty thousand pounds of gold by 1850. The experienced operators of the mines in this area were called upon for advice when gold was discovered in northern California in 1848. The first discovery of gold in California was made in the second half of the eighteenth century by Indians who brought gold to the Spanish missions to barter with the padres. Legendary trapper, scout, and explorer Jedediah Smith reportedly panned gold in the Sierras in the 1830s. In 1840 Richard Henry Dana wrote of gold in California in his classic *Two Years before the Mast.*[1]

On his fortieth birthday, March 9, 1842, Don Francisco Lopez discovered gold on a ranch north of present-day Los Angeles. He set out early that morning to inspect the cattle on Rancho San Francisco, gather herbs and spices his wife had asked him to find, and perhaps kill some game for the dinner his wife had planned. After eating the lunch his wife had packed for him, Lopez took a siesta under a large oak tree. During that nap he dreamed of floating in a pool of liquid gold. Then, in the process of digging up some wild onions, he discovered small flakes of gold in the dirt attached to the onion roots. He, his Indian servant, and two companions dug more of the gold in Live Oak Canyon. Lopez attempted to file a mining claim but was rejected because it was on private land. He took the gold to Los Angeles and had it sent to the U.S. Mint for an assay; the 18.43 ounces were valued at $344.75.[2] Before long others heard of the discovery and flocked to the region, where for the next six years around 260 pounds of gold were mined each year. Throughout this time his discovery remained a southern California phenomenon and was not considered of importance outside that area. Both the state of California and the Santa Clara Valley Association of Realtors have placed historical markers at the site of the oak tree, which still stands near the entrance to what is now known as Placerita Canyon State and County Park.[3]

The discovery of gold in northern California on March 24, 1848, is generally attributed to John Marshall, who found a small nugget while he was digging a millrace for a sawmill that he was building for Johann Augustus

Introduction

Sutter. Another employee named Peter Wimmer discovered a somewhat larger nugget on that day. Other employees also appear to have found nuggets. Wimmer's wife boiled the nugget with some clothes she was washing for members of the construction crew. Chemical tests confirmed that it was gold. This discovery, unlike that of Don Francisco Lopez, created great excitement worldwide, and Argonauts descended upon California in astonishing numbers.[4]

Although Sutter wanted his discovery to remain secret, that proved impossible. News of the discovery was published in *The Californian* in San Francisco in March 1848. All the workers building the mill quit and began seeking and finding gold. Others followed suit. Word spread to the East Coast and throughout the world. Official notice of the discovery was made by Pres. James K. Polk in his address to Congress on December 5, 1848, but stories of the discovery were published much earlier in newspapers up and down the East Coast, and hundreds, perhaps thousands, were already planning to make their way to California. This mania for California gold persisted through 1849 and lasted into the early 1850s. By the end of 1853 most of the placer gold had been harvested from the rivers and streams of northern California, but much more gold was extracted from California during the next half century. Some of that gold was harvested by a hydraulic method in which powerful streams of water were used to wash away hillsides in order to separate the gold nuggets from rocks and soil. Some gold was extracted from deep underground by hard-rock miners. Both hydraulic and hard-rock mining were expensive and required large amounts of capital rather than the picks, shovels, pans, and rockers used by the first Argonauts to descend upon California in 1849.

In 1849 there were three ways to reach California. One was all an all-water route around Cape Horn; one was an all-land route beginning west of the Mississippi River; and the third was a combination water and land route. Those taking the Cape Horn route could depart at any time of the year while those choosing the overland route could not leave their starting place until the grass on the plains was green and large enough to feed their animals because they could not carry feed for them. Those taking the combined land and water route were best advised to delay until regular traffic had been established between the eastern ports and Panama and between Panama and San Francisco. Once that was accomplished (the summer of 1849 for steam-vessel traffic between New York and Panama, and soon thereafter steam- and sailing-vessel traffic between Panama and San Francisco), the route via the Isthmus of Panama was the quickest way to get to

3

California. Numerous accounts have been published about the trials and tribulations of the overland route. A few publications have included a smattering of information about those who traveled around Cape Horn or down the Atlantic to Panama or perhaps Nicaragua, across land, and up the Pacific to San Francisco.[5]

This study has been undertaken to describe in detail how passengers lived on board the sailing vessels in which they traveled from the east coast around Cape Horn to California in 1849. Information for this work was gathered from upwards of a hundred original diaries located in libraries and archives on both the East and West Coasts and a few institutions in between as well as nearly twenty-five published diaries of passengers who departed in sailing vessels before December 31, 1849, on voyages that lasted between four and a half and eight months with at most two brief stops in South American ports to pick up fresh provisions and water and wood. Such stops also gave the passengers time to stretch their legs as they walked many miles to see the sights of the strange cities. Rio de Janeiro in Brazil and Valparaiso and Talcahuano in Chili were the ports entered most often. St. Catherines Island, Juan Fernandez Island (this group of three islands was consistently referred to as a single island by the journal writers of the nineteenth century and was commonly known to the passengers as Robinson Crusoe's Island), and Callao and Lima in Peru were other places at which vessels regularly stopped. Few vessels made the entire eighteen-thousand to twenty-thousand-mile Cape Horn voyage without stopping.

Topics discussed at some length in this volume include preparations for the voyages; getting underway with the associated problems of seasickness and second thoughts about the undertaking; quality, quantity, and variety of foods and drink; forms of amusement and entertainment to occupy the many idle hours; observance of Sundays, holidays, and special days such as birthdays and anniversaries; problems with the weather in both oceans and especially around Cape Horn; problems among themselves as well as with the officers and sailors of the vessels; miscellaneous problems such as sickness, death, burial, accidents, theft, drunkenness, temperance, pests (rats, mice, fleas, lice), stowaways, minorities such as women and African Americans on board; duties and responsibilities, primarily of those who were members of joint stock companies; and first impressions of California.

Up to now much of the research and publishing in American maritime history has dealt with the technology of building and operating vessels; the individuals who built, operated, or owned those vessels; a few of the most

4

Introduction

famous and infamous sea captains; and a number of dramatic episodes including shipwrecks and other disasters. In recent years researchers in Canada have begun to emphasize the economic aspects of maritime history. Throughout, the social aspects of maritime history have been largely ignored except for periodic publications about individual voyages of particular vessels. Although such publications sometimes provide information, that information is likely accurate for only that one voyage of that one vessel. Nevertheless readers and users of such accounts are frequently tempted to assume that what happened on board one vessel likely happened on all of them. It is sincerely hoped that this study will demonstrate that an account such as this one based upon a large number of firsthand accounts results in a much broader picture and that other researchers will undertake similar studies on other types of sailing vessels for other periods of time.

As one might expect in a volume that deals with the way individuals lived while sailing to California and is based upon many personal journals and letters, this volume contains numerous quotations from those sources. Many of the passengers who kept journals and wrote letters during their long voyages in 1849 had not had the benefit of education, especially in spelling. Hence they frequently spelled their words as they pronounced them, and they did not always spell a given word the same way. As a result, for example, one passenger usually spelled Talcahuano as Tuckewarner. I have retained the original spellings (including the inconsistencies) and have avoided noting any of them with the traditional [*sic*]. To have used that designation with every misspelling would have greatly cluttered this narrative.

1

Preparations for the Voyage

Well before Pres. James K. Polk made the official announcement of the discovery of gold in California during his State of the Union Address on December 5, 1848, rumors had spread the news throughout the settled eastern portion of the United States. Hundreds, perhaps thousands, of individuals had begun to make plans to go to California to seek their fortunes even though the vast majority of them had, at best, limited information of what lay ahead before they arrived at that new El Dorado or exactly how they would obtain the gold that would be the basis of their fortunes. Newspapers throughout the region contained news of the discovery of gold and of individuals and groups planning to go to California. They also contained advertisements for California-bound vessels and for implements and goods that were said to be essential for anyone going to California. Since New York was the largest port in the United States, its newspapers were an excellent representation of such news and advertisements.[1]

Isaac S. Halsey became caught up in the mania and described the situation during the winter of 1848 and 1849. He referred to the "incredible stories" of people who "were makeing themselves rich in a few days." Gold was so plentiful "that the finer particles Could be Scraped up with tin Cups" and "larger *lumps,* Some of them weighing Several Tons would be taken possession of by their lucky finders, mounting their huge proportions and thus remain astride their vast fortunes days and nights," supposedly offering amazing amounts of money for a dish of bean soup. People from everywhere "were Seized with . . . truly astonishing . . . excitement" that "grew till it attained to a frightful contagious disease, Scattering friends and foes, bringing together Strangers from all parts." Such excitement also resulted in the restoration of "valuable Old Ships that had long before been pronounced unseaworthy" and the taking of other more substantial ones "from the regular Merchant business . . . to plow a new track through the briney Ocean, freighted with human beings." He added that "this Yellow fever . . . attained Such a rageing highth, that peaceful and valuable homes were broken up, and Sold at one fourth their value, to raise funds to pay their way to California, while others were left, locked up and quiet reigned without and within." The departure of so many individuals meant that "Morning came and went, and evening too, but the accustomed Sound of the Axe and the welcome call to Breakfast and Supper, the thrilling notes of the Dinner Horn, the merry laugh and interesting Squalling of the Children, the blating of Sheep, and the Noise of the Cow, the Horse and the well known bark of the Watch Dog, all these familiar Sounds that greet the ear around a well regulated Country Home, were superseded by Solitude, and how desolate those once cheerful Homes."[2]

There were three possible routes to California, each of which had its advantages and disadvantages, based in part upon the traveler's place of residence. Many of those living on or near the Atlantic coast and some of those along the Gulf of Mexico chose to make the eighteen-thousand to twenty-thousand-mile passage around Cape Horn in either one of the numerous sailing vessels or one of the limited number of advertised steam vessels. Others from this area opted for shorter passages in either sailing or steam vessels to Panama or some other South American location, an overland trip to the Pacific, and then another vessel to San Francisco. By the summer of 1849 there were some steamers making regular runs between New York and Panama, taking hundreds of passengers on each trip. Soon thereafter there were steam and sailing vessels operating frequently between Panama and San Francisco. Many of those who lived inland chose the overland route, which required that they reach one of the jumping-off places west of the Mississippi River for an early spring departure in order to be reasonably sure there would be grass for their animals.

Those who chose the Cape Horn route spent between four and a half months and eight and a half months at sea with at most two brief visits in port for water, wood, and provisions and suffered through the vicissitudes of Cape Horn as well as storms and other dangers faced regularly on ocean voyages.[3] In spite of these dangers, the Cape Horn route was the most comfortable, but it lasted the longest. Because these Argonauts had a relatively comfortable trip, they were frequently ill prepared for the ardors of the goldfields. The Panama, or isthmian, route was usually the quickest, but the length of time depended upon the waiting period on the Pacific side for passage from Panama to San Francisco. It was also hazardous, as a great many died of diseases, either during the land crossing or soon thereafter. Those who made the trip overland had the most physically challenging trip and were therefore best able to withstand the rigors of mining once they arrived in California. Although the trek from Missouri, Arkansas, and other inland starting places was faster than the Cape Horn voyage and sometimes faster than the isthmian route, the overland travelers frequently spent a considerable amount of time getting to and waiting at the jumping-off place.

Those traveling the Cape Horn route basically had two options. They could join a company, usually a joint stock company, and be involved in the duties and responsibilities of that group as spelled out in its bylaws and rules and regulations, or they could go as individuals with responsibilities to no one. Some companies were formed in inland regions, and the members proceeded to a port and arranged passage for themselves and their supplies and provisions while others were formed in ports along the Atlantic and Gulf coasts. Octavius Thorndike Howe documented 124 joint stock companies formed in Massachusetts in 1849–1850.[4] Nearly 200 named and many unnamed companies throughout the United States are mentioned in articles and advertisements in the *New York Daily Tribune* between December 1848 and September 1849. Probably hundreds more were actually organized. Companies had memberships ranging from fewer than 10 to more than 100. Advertisements in the *New York Daily Tribune* listed company membership costs between $150 and $1,500. The cost commonly included passage to California and sometimes return passage; provisions for up to two years; and living accommodations, usually a tent although some companies intended to live on board the vessel. Some companies took houses and other structures that could be quickly assembled in California.[5] In a few instances a small number of the members remained at home to manage the business affairs there. Sometimes members appointed or hired substitutes to go in their places for a share of their profits. Members commonly were to share equally in the gold obtained by the entire company and in any profits they realized from the sale of their vessel, if they owned one, and freight. While some companies purchased vessels for the voyage, others chartered vessels or simply purchased space for each member. Members of companies and even other passengers were normally allotted a specific amount of space for personal items such as clothing, food luxuries, books, tools, and freight. Four barrels was a frequently given allotment of space for freight.[6]

One of the most unusual companies was the Ship *Sweden* Company. It apparently started as the result of a prospectus prepared by James L. L. F.

Preparations for the Voyage

Warren, a Brighton, Massachusetts, florist, who submitted it to Henry and Charles H. P. Plympton and Jesse G. Cotting, owners of the *Sweden*. Warren proposed to organize a group of up to twenty trustworthy, loyal, and hardworking men who would work their passage to California, engage in mining for a specified period of time, and return as guards and possibly as mariners. The final agreement stipulated that the men work seventy-five days in the minefields. During the voyage they were to be under the direction of Captain Cotting. While mining in California they were to work under James L. L. F. Warren. Fifteen men signed agreements with the owners of the vessel. The men promised to work to the best of their abilities to obtain as much gold or other ores or minerals as possible for a period of seventy-five days after arriving in San Francisco. The vessel owners promised to transport the men to San Francisco and back and to transport all ores and minerals to Boston. The owners also agreed to provide all the food; health care; mining tools and implements; and guns, knives, and ammunition for protection. The men each agreed to pay the owners of the *Sweden* five hundred dollars if they did not fulfill the terms of the agreement. Warren was to receive a percentage equivalent to the production of one man during the seventy-five days of mining. The remaining proceeds were to be divided equally between the owners and the other fifteen men. Two of the men failed to fulfill those terms.[7]

Another unusual organization was the California Mutual Benefit and Joint Stock Association, which was first advertised in the *Christian Advocate* (New York) on January 11, 1849, by which time they reportedly had forty members. They intended to have a hundred members, all of whom were to be members of the Methodist Episcopal Church or persons who agreed "with them in sentiment." Shares in the company were three hundred dollars each, which entitled the holder to "an equal interest in the ship, mining implements and eighteen months' provisions, together with the profits on freight and passengers." They did not permit alcoholic beverages on board. The organization purchased the 627-ton ship *Arkansas*, in which they eventually sailed on June 26 with 76 members and 36 additional passengers including 8 females and 6 children. There was a crew of 19 officers and sailors, making the entire complement 131. The company took along a large number of religious books and tracts including fifty bibles and one hundred testaments and many additional volumes given by the Tract Society, the Methodist Book Room, and Stephen Dando.[8]

Yet another unusual company was the California Association of American Women, which was organized by Mrs. Eliza Farnham beginning in

9

February 1849. The number of members in the company was never given, but they were advertised as intelligent and respectable women over the age of 25 who could provide "sufficient testimonials of character." The enterprise received the endorsement of several prominent New Yorkers including Superior Court Judge J. W. Edmonds, attorney B. F. Butler, Horace Greeley, and Rev. Henry Ward Beecher. According to advertisements, the company planned to take supplies to furnish a store to be operated by some of the women. They also planned to take medical supplies and a framed building to use as a hospital plus a quantity of cloth to make clothing for miners. Mrs. Farnham booked passage for her group in the ship *Angelique,* which sailed from New York on May 19, 1849. The list of passengers published in the *New York Daily Tribune* included the name Mrs. Farnham but did not indicate the number of members or their names.[9]

The Pilgrim Mining Company appears to have been a unique organization, as it was created and funded by a group of wealthy investors in Plymouth, Massachusetts, who fitted out and provisioned the bark *Yoeman* for a voyage to San Francisco. The young men on board were mostly from Plymouth and were not required to supply anything other than personal luxuries and their labor once they arrived in California. Some of the members were sons of the investors. The passengers were supposed to seek gold in the goldfields and give the investors half of their find until the investors had recouped their investments. Thereafter the young men could keep all the gold they found.[10]

Voyagers who did not purchase a share in a joint stock company needed only arrive at virtually any port city on the Atlantic or Gulf coast, visit the wharves, check the newspaper advertisements, and choose a vessel that suited their tastes and budgets. In large ports such as New York, Boston, and Philadelphia, there were always several vessels advertised as California bound. Choices were not as plentiful in smaller ports. The number of vessels sailing from the leading American ports to California in 1849 included 214 from New York, 151 from Boston, 42 from New Bedford, 38 from Baltimore, 32 from New Orleans, and 31 from Philadelphia. Another 250 or more sailed from smaller ports between Maine and Texas.[11]

All types and sizes of sailing vessels made the voyage around Cape Horn or through the Strait of Magellan to San Francisco. The smallest was the schooner *Toccao,* measuring only 28 tons; the largest, measuring 1,082 tons, was the ship *Memnon.* The lowest number of passengers on board any vessel was one although there were numerous vessels that carried only freight. The largest contingent of passengers on a sailing vessel was 248 in the 687-ton ship *Capitol* of Boston. Only 14 were taken in the much larger ship *Memnon*. Joint stock companies who sailed in the ship *Capitol* included the Naumkeag Company, Nashua Company, Newburyport Company, Mechanic Company of Salem, Springfield Company, Abbot Lawrence Company, Bunker Hill Californians, Lewiston Falls Company, Worcester Mining Company, Ex Bunker Hill, Duck Company, Springfield Company 2, and one unnamed company. Of the California-bound vessels in 1849, the *Capitol* probably carried the second-largest number of companies.[12]

The following sampling of the 1849 gold rush fleet provides a general picture of the ownership, size, and number and nature of passengers carried by the 762 vessels identified by John B. Goodman III. The 293-ton bark *Algoma* sailed from Philadelphia with fifty-six passengers, sixteen of whom were members of the Algoma Mining and Mercantile Company. She carried a cargo valued at $125,000. The ship *Andalusia* (772 tons) sailed from Baltimore on April 18 with seventy-six passengers, among whom were the members of the Maryland Enterprise and Mining Company; the California Company of York, Pennsylvania; a company of thirty members from Kentucky; and possibly a second company from Maryland. The previously mentioned 420-ton ship *Angelique* sailed from New York with thirty passengers; perhaps as many as nine were members of the California Association of American Women. The ship *Apollo* (412 tons) sailed from New York on January 17 with sixty-six passengers. She was one of the earliest vessels to sail and offered some of the lowest prices (which included food): $75 for steerage, $150 for cabin, $200 for cabin out and back; and $250 for cabin with board while in California. The 396-ton bark *Belvidera* sailed from New York carrying the eighty members of the Cayuga Joint Stock Company, each of whom paid $400 for his share in the company including the vessel, freight, provisions, and implements. The 198-ton bark *Canton* sailed from New York on March 29 carrying only the fifty-two members of the Island City Mining and Trading Association who owned her. The bark *Clarissa* (224 tons) sailed from New York on March 17 with the twenty members of the Excelsior Association, each of whom paid $250 for his share of the vessel and outfits for eighteen months. She also carried eight additional passengers including one female.

On January 16 the 310-ton bark *Croton* sailed from New York with fifty-four passengers, none of whom appear to have been members of companies. On January 15 *Elizabeth Ellen*, a ship of 580 tons, sailed from New

11

York with two hundred passengers, six of whom were members of the Syracuse and California Trading and Mining Company. Two new schooners, the 86-ton *Empire* and the 85-ton *Sea Witch,* both built in Mystic, Connecticut, sailed together on February 1. They departed New York bound for San Francisco through the Strait of Magellan with intentions of remaining in company throughout the voyage. The *Empire* carried fifteen passengers and the *Sea Witch* nine. Each vessel carried members of unnamed associations headed by the owners of the vessels. The *Empire* arrived on June 2 and the *Sea Witch* on June 15. The 479-ton Baltimore ship *Grey Eagle* sailed from Philadelphia with thirty-four passengers and a cargo of dry goods, groceries, provisions, hardware, cutlery, saddlery, flour, feed, boots, shoes, caps, hats, and a considerable amount of freight. One of the passengers, Theodore Dubosq, a jeweler, took the machinery for melting and coining gold and stamping it with a private mark to establish a currency in California. The *Hannah Sprague,* a 409-ton bark, sailed from New York on May 21. She was owned by the members of the New York Commercial and Mining Company, each member of whom paid six hundred dollars for his membership. There were forty-four members of the association along with three wives, another woman, four children, and fifty-two additional male passengers on board. The 409-ton Connecticut ship *Henry Lee* sailed from New York on February 17 carrying the 125 members of the Hartford Union Mining and Trading Company as well as mining implements and provisions for two years. The ship *Henry Pratt* (589 tons) sailed from Baltimore with 16 passengers, some of whom were members of an unidentified company of mostly mechanics from Baltimore and their two steam engines, an iron steamboat, a sawmill and a planing mill, a pile driver, and tools of various kinds.

The 542-ton ship *Herculean* sailed from Boston in late February under charter by an unnamed association who expected to be conveyed up the Sacramento River. They took frames of two large houses to be erected and used by the members. Each of the forty members paid three hundred dollars for passage and found, which included provisions for three months after arriving at their destination. The bark *Isabel* (237 tons) was owned by the New Brunswick and California Mining and Trading Company and carried its forty-eight members to California leaving from New York on February 7. Included among the seventy-nine passengers of the ship *Jane Parker,* which sailed from Baltimore on January 25, were the members of the Harford California Association for Mining Purposes and a company of eight who were members of the Mechanical Fire Company of Baltimore. Of the ninety-three passengers in the 714-ton ship *John G. Coster*, which sailed from New York on February 24, fourteen were in the first cabin, forty-seven in the second cabin, and thirty in steerage, including all the members of the Utica Mining Company. The 148-ton brig *Mary Stuart* sailed from New York in late January with an unnamed company of twelve members who owned the vessel and eleven other passengers. The company took with them twenty thousand dollars' worth of goods and a complete outfit for two years. Of the 102 passengers who sailed from Philadelphia in the 412-ton ship *Mason* on February 22, 21 were members of the Philadelphia and California Enterprise Association. Thirty-two passengers were in the first cabin, and 70 were in the second cabin.

The 541-ton ship *Mechanics Own* was built by the Mechanics Mining Association at a cost of seventy-five thousand dollars. She sailed from New York on August 15 with the members and some additional passengers. The largest sailing vessel in the 1849 California fleet, the 1,082-ton ship *Memnon*, sailed from New York with only fourteen passengers on April 11. There was a serious mutiny off Montevideo, Uruguay, and all of the crewmen were taken on board the U.S. sloop of war *St. Louis* in that port. The ship *New Jersey* (640 tons) was owned by the Suffolk and California Mutual Trading and Mining Association, whose 175 members owned the two hundred shares that cost two hundred dollars each. They paid twenty-two thousand dollars for the vessel and repairs including new coppering before departing Boston on May 2 with a total of 210 passengers. Capt. Hall J. Tibbits and Frederick Griffing owned the 532-ton ship *Pacific* and advertised for freight and passengers to be taken in first and second cabins. Passage in the first cabin was advertised as $300 and included all provisions and first-class service, but apparently the members of the New England Mining and Trading Company purchased a block of staterooms for only $275 each. This sale and that of more first-class tickets than advertised led several of the first-cabin passengers to sue the owners before the ship sailed on January 22. Dissatisfaction with the provisions and service and ensuing conflicts between the first-cabin passengers and Captain Tibbits led to complaints to the U.S. consul in Rio de Janeiro, Gorham Parks, who removed Captain Tibbits from command. The second-cabin passengers, who provided their own food and services, were not involved in the dispute with Captain Tibbits. The total number of passengers in the *Pacific* was 103.

The ship *Regulus* (three hundred tons) of Boston was owned by the 125 members of the Bunker Hill Trading and Mining Association who sailed in her on February 27. There was considerable conflict within this company because of alleged misconduct by some of the officers. The three-hundred-ton ship *Rising Sun* was owned by the sixty members of the Rising Sun Company who sailed in her from New York on March 30. Twenty-two additional passengers, including seven members of the Archimedes Mining Company, were on board. Cargo included a steam engine, a smelting furnace, a smith's forge, and all the essential utensils for mining operations. Members of the Albany Chemical Mining Association and others were included in the 175 passengers in the 504-ton ship *Robert Bowne* when she sailed from New York on February 6. Each member of the association paid $250 for his share in the vessel and its cargo of flour, meal, sugar, vinegar, molasses, butter, bread, rice, potatoes, beans, onions, beef, pork, mackerel, codfish, tea, coffee, and soap. This list of provisions indicates clearly the limited diet available to the passengers during their voyage of more than two hundred days. Each member was permitted to take four barrels of freight besides his baggage. A small number of nonmember passengers paid $150 for the voyage. Members of the Southampton Trading and Mining Company, who owned the 412-ton ship *Sabina,* which included seventeen sea captains and numerous officers and mariners from whaling vessels, sailed in her from Sag Harbor, New York, on February 8. The *Sabina* carried a total of eighty passengers. The 735-ton ship *Samoset,* owned by R. B. Forbes of Boston, sailed from New York on March 23 carrying 152 passengers who paid $250 for the first cabin and $150 for the second cabin. Nine of the passengers were members of the Sing Sing Company, and one was a member of the Ithaca Mining Company. The 646-ton ship *Sweden* of Boston was owned by Henry and Charles H. P. Plympton and Capt. Jesse G. Cotting and sailed from Boston on March 1 with 176 passengers, some of whom were members of the Roxbury Sagamore Company; the Mt. Washington Mining and Trading Company; the Traders & Mechanics Mining Company; the Cheshire Company; an unidentified company from Cambridge, Massachusetts; the Ship *Sweden* Company; and possibly the Granite State Mining, Trading & Agricultural Company. The new twenty-eight-ton schooner *Toccao* of New Bedford, Massachusetts, was the smallest vessel to sail to California in 1849. She carried five passengers and was dispatched to California to carry freight on the Sacramento River. The ship *Xylon* (498 tons) of New York sailed from Baltimore with 142 passengers on February 3. Her captain, John A. Brown, was removed from command by the U.S. consul in Rio de Janeiro, Gorham Parks, because of strong complaints by the passengers.[13]

Preparations for the Voyage

These examples provide evidence that a wide variety of sailing vessels was available to those desiring to take the Cape Horn route to California. Those who felt most comfortable being associated with their friends from home or perhaps with strangers could join a company and have most of their cares and concerns regarding provisions, equipment, and housing taken care of by the officers of the company. Those of a more independent nature could choose from any number of vessels and arrange for their own provisions, equipment, and housing. According to the number of vessels advertised in the *New York Daily Tribune* between December 1848 and September 1849 and the *Baltimore Sun* from January to June 1849, it appears that no more than a fourth of the vessels sailing to California in this time period were owned by an organized stock company. Most of those companies sold space to other passengers in order to fill their vessels and to recover some of their expenses. A small number of sailing vessels were chartered by joint stock companies for the voyage to California. A sizeable number of organized stock companies took passage in a vessel sent out by the owners of that vessel, and such vessels frequently carried members of more than one company along with other independent passengers. An indeterminate number of vessels carried only independent passengers. The number of vessels listed in *The Key to the Goodman Encyclopedia of the California Gold Rush Fleet* that carried either no passengers or a small number of them indicates that many vessels carried primarily provisions, building materials and supplies, and other freight to sell to the thousands who went to seek their fortunes in the goldfields.

Having made the decision to go to California, everyone, even many members of joint stock companies, began to assemble personal outfits such as clothes, special luxuries (such as jams or cakes), books, games, cards, personal hygiene items, guns, ammunition, cooking gear, and eating utensils. Many also purchased mining tools and equipment. Individuals who found themselves in New York on their way to California were offered a great variety of tools, machinery, foods, and other items by the merchants of the city in advertisements in the *New York Daily Tribune* and other newspapers. One of the most heavily advertised items was gold washers. At least nineteen inventors offered their gold washers during the first half of 1849 and gave their inventions appealing names such as Bruce's Hydro-Centrifugal Chrysolyte or California Gold Finder; Buffum's Eldorado and Scientific Gold Sifter, Separator, and Safe Depositor; Bull's Concentric Double-Acting; Burke's Celebrated Rocker; Hunt's Gold Extracting Engine; Hyatt's Buoyant Gold Washer and Life Preserver; Jenning's Alluvial; W. H. Jenison's Mercuriated Pelt Machine, Corrugate Rocker, Common Hand Rocker, and Submerged Whirling Pan; and Perry's Gyratory. The advertisements made fantastic, probably outright fraudulent, claims regarding the quantity of gold the machines could extract in a day and the ease of the process, and they frequently debunked the machines offered by competitors. Other merchants offered a wide variety of books on California, mining, minerals, medicine, and learning the Spanish language plus novels and magazines. They also offered a great assortment of foodstuffs—especially canned meats, fish, oysters, lobsters, vegetables, soups, and milk—about which they made outlandish claims regarding the quality of the products. They began advertising that the products they sold would be good quality for twenty years, then thirty years, and finally three generations. They also offered pickles, preserves, brandy fruits, jellies, jams, catsups, East and West India condiments, bread, concentrated vinegar, sauerkraut, an egg substitute called Edward's Celebrated Egg Powder, and a health food called Hecker's Farina. A great variety of medicines was offered to prevent or cure such maladies as fever, ague, pulmonary diseases, coughs, seasickness and other stomach diseases, piles, and bad breath. Other items offered were water filters, prefabricated houses of both wood and iron, bedding, insurance policies, knives, pistols, rifles, dishes, mining tools, gold, matches, fire kindler, steam engines, gold-testing equipment, chairs, gilt letters for signs, money belts, tobacco, fishing equipment, stoves, compasses, tea, photographs, passports and naturalization documents, and life-saving equipment.[14]

Between the time he decided to go to California as a member of the Salem Mechanics Trading and Mining Association in mid October 1849 and his ship *Crescent* sailed from Salem, Massachusetts, in early December, Charles Henry Harvey recorded in a journal his activities and the items he assembled. He mentioned mostly guns, ammunition, clothing, and personal luxuries made for him by his family and female friends. He also noted that his father had paid a Mr. Jones $320 for his outfit.[15] William S. Hull listed at the end of his journal all the outfits for his voyage in the ship *Jane Parker* and indicated a price paid for each item. His clothing included sixteen shirts including red flannel, striped net, checked, calico, linen, and muslin; four pairs of "drawers" including heavy twill and cotton; eight pairs of stockings; one pair of striped pants; eight handkerchiefs including silk, linen, and cotton; a black coat and pants; a leather vest; a pea jacket; a leather vest and a white vest; two pairs of boots; two hats; two caps; and a pair of suspenders. He also took bedding including a mattress, two blankets, one quilted "comfort," a pillow, a cushion, a pair of sheets, three pillow cases, and a morning wrapper. In addition he took a watch, knives, shaving apparatus, tea spoons, a hair brush, two pocket looking glasses [mirrors], paper, an inkstand, pins, needles, cotton thread, buttons, three gold breast pins, one gold heart, three gold pens, two pin cushions, tweezers, lancets, a "bead" money purse, a magnifying glass, four hundred percussion caps, a powder flask, bullets, lots of fishing lines and hooks, two boxes of cigars, pickles, preserves, a bottle of vinegar as a cholera preventive, liniment, several books, and cakes. All these items were packed into two trunks and had a combined cost of $123.72. He also took $21 in silver.[16]

Anderson Hollingsworth's personal outfits for his voyage in the ship *Daniel Webster* cost him only $56.31, and he appears to have taken along only $2 cash. The outfits included pens, two combs, two pen holders, two looking glasses, a trunk, a hat, a cap, a dozen pairs of socks, five silk handkerchiefs, four pairs of pants, two watch crystals and keys, a box of wafers, four pairs of "drawers," four vests, three jackets, a pipe, pistols and powder, a rubber cap, a bag, a blanket, and a tumbler. Hollingsworth was one of those from an unnamed company of ten who were chosen to purchase outfits for the group. Each man paid $50, and the three chosen ones purchased provisions, implements, and equipment totaling $505.99. Provisions included five barrels of extra mess beef; five barrels of city mess pork; one tierce of ham; a tierce of salt; ten barrels of Paxall flour; two barrels of pilot bread; a half barrel each of beans, peas, and sugar; a barrel of dried apples; one jar each of saleratus and mustard; two jars of cream of tartar; a keg plus twelve gallons of vinegar; ten pounds of black tea and a tea canister; two boxes of baker's chocolate; and four boxes of crackers. Cooking and eating utensils included a nest of Kamp Kettles, a dozen sixteen-quart tin pans, two dozen tin plates, a half dozen tin pans, a dozen mugs, a pepperbox, two sets of knives and forks, a dozen spoons, two frying pans, matches, and a coffee boiler. Equipment, tools, and tent-making materials included a dozen shovels, 11 pick axes, 9 hoes, a wheelbarrow, a surfboat and oars, 25 pounds of white lead, a gallon of linseed oil, 2 pounds of green paint for the boat, chain, a coil of hemp rope, 17 1/2 pounds of manila rope, 105 yards of light cotton duck, and twine. The company also paid for freight and primage on the boat.[17]

Samuel C. Lewis spent $511.60 for his outfits, but he included some things that Harvey and Hollingsworth did not. He also seems to have chosen more-expensive items. His clothing included a frock coat and pantaloons, boots, shoes, hats, overcoat, linen coat, black vest, five sea shirts, and cotton plus the making of twelve shirts. His bedding consisted of two blankets, a hair mattress, pillows, and a coverlet. Personal items included pencils, pens, ink, pen holders, combs, toothbrushes, tape, buttons, thread, soap, wafers, paper, twenty-three pounds of tobacco, an iron basin, a thermometer, a pair of eyeglasses, and a cup. He also took along several books including Andrew Ures's *Dictionary of Arts, Mines & Manufacturing,* John C. Fremont's account of his exploring expedition, "a prayer book Episcopal Service," and some novels by Sir Walter Scott. He also took one map of California and another one showing the route to California, probably around Cape Horn. In addition he took along liquor, preserved meats, syrup, and bitters. He also took an iron safe. Other expenses included $41 for a $1,750 insurance policy, fare from Pittsfield, Massachussetts to Boston, carting of his baggage to the ship, board at the Tremont House while awaiting departure, and a picture of George Washington in a gild frame, which he sent to his home in Pittsfield. The safe that cost $50 at home, was sold for $60 in California, making his actual expenses $501.60.[18]

George Dornin's journal of his 1849 voyage from New York to San Francisco in the ship *Panama* was lost when his residence burned in 1855. Sometime thereafter he prepared reminiscences of his gold rush experiences for his children and described his outfits as consisting of "several suits of heavy and coarse clothing including 3 pairs of 'stogy' boots, . . . sundry tarpaulin hats, salt water soap, and many knick-knacks and conveniences, which kind friends provided." He also mentioned several barrels of mess beef, pork, and ship biscuit, and an arsenal consisting of a double-barreled shotgun, a pepperbox pistol, and a bowie knife, all "for protection against the wild Indians, and wilder Spaniards with which imagination peopled the land." Dornin noted that cleaning and oiling the guns provided employment during the voyage but that he threw the pistol away upon arriving, as it was more dangerous to the shooter than the "shoot-at." He sold the shotgun for thirty-five dollars in California and used the bowie knife to carve his meat. He passed away many hours reading the volumes in his library of selected books, writing his journal in the blank book, and writing letters on the large quantity of paper he took along. He reported that he took the bible his grandmother had given him for his thirteenth birthday and fully intended to read through it, but he never got beyond Exodus. Viewing a daguerreotype of his mother helped overcome frequent bouts of homesickness.[19]

John Ross Browne was one of a select few who sailed to California for a reason other than to go to the goldfields to seek his fortune. He had an appointment from the federal government to attempt to keep sailors from deserting their vessels as soon as they arrived in California. Thus outfits for his passage in the ship *Pacific* were somewhat different from those discussed above. He outfitted himself "handsomely in substantial clothing at Devlin's,"[20] where he had six pairs of pants (two duck, two nankeen, one fustian, and one stout pilot cloth), a pilot cloth pea jacket, a light summer shad-sack, a fustian hunting jacket, and a short business coat made with "all of the best material and workmanship for $45." His shirts and boots cost an additional twenty dollars. He also purchased a "fine guitar for $15, case and all, and a violin for $9, together with an assortment of strings." He felt the two instruments would "add greatly to the enjoyment of the voyage" and thought he could sell them at a profit in California. The potential enjoyment was increased when he learned that his roommate in the stateroom also played "very sweetly on the violin and has a fine instrument valued at a hundred dollars." He also purchased "a lot of pencils and drawing paper, for sketching of the scenery" and expected to "make some money as an artist" because "Twenty dollars for a small sketch will be better than digging gold." Browne also had a blank book in which to keep a journal. His expenses had been so great that he doubted he would have one hundred dollars left to cover contingencies on the way and in California.[21]

Although it is not an actual list of outfits, the inventory four passengers took of their six-by-six-foot stateroom in the ship *Belvidera* seven months into the voyage gives a reasonably good indication of passengers' onboard possessions and the crowded conditions for the sixty-one members of the Cayuga Joint Stock Company who sailed in her. In the 36 square feet (216 cubic feet) allotted the four passengers were four shelves for their berths with the mattresses and bedding for each, three trunks, two India rubber bags, a barrel sawed in half, a basket, two twelve-by-eighteen-inch boxes, ten hats, a spy glass, an empty raisin box, two lanterns, a huge empty bottle, two tin pails, a box of tobacco, two small oil bottles, forty books, twenty pairs of boots, coats, vests, pantaloons by the dozen, three tin wash bowls, a twelve-by-twenty-four-inch shelf filled with small things, six canvas catchalls, an eighteen-by-thirty-six-inch board for a writing prop, ten empty quart bottles, a contribution box, a small roll of wire, four cups, two flutes, two tin boxes of matches, a ball of wicking, a small bag of sugar, four spoons, three knives and three forks, a pistol and case, a small mirror, a hatchet, pieces of burlap and carpet, a two-foot-long clothesline, a watch, two watch cases, a blacking brush for shoes and box, a bag of salt, a backgammon board, hair brushes and combs, a clothes brush, four clothes bags, a pail of "switchel," a nest of ants, and "bed bugs in droves."[22]

One of the most complete records of the outfits of a joint stock company is that provided by Charles Henry Harvey for the Salem Mechanics Trading and Mining Association, who sailed from Salem in the ship *Crescent*. The record of expenses included those for finding, purchasing, repairing, and modifying the vessel; the vast quantity of food for the sixty-one members; and plans and materials to construct a building in California. No tools or equipment for mining were included, so presumably each member supplied his own. Expenditures totaled $23,382.58, and $37.88 remained in the treasury. Income came from sixty-one shares at $350 each, $300 from one passenger who was not a member, cash from two sailors, sale of spars and old rigging, a note for half a share, a note for commission on some purchases, and money borrowed from members of the company. Thus they had a debt of $1,359.81 when they sailed.[23]

In 1849 only the packet ships that regularly crossed the Atlantic to Europe and that sailed along the Atlantic and Gulf coasts were in any way designed to carry large numbers of passengers, and they certainly could not accommodate those who wanted to go to San Francisco in sailing vessels during the early period of the gold rush. Hence most of the vessels advertised as California bound had to be modified to make provisions for passengers to sleep and eat. The way such modifications were made had a considerable effect upon the satisfaction or dissatisfaction of the passengers. Poor preparations and unannounced changes in plans by vessel owners frequently led to disgruntled passengers. Passengers of vessels owned by joint stock companies of which they were members may have fared better than those of vessels owned and operated by business firms who were interested in making a profit rather than satisfying the large number of eager gold-mining customers. It seems likely that most of the owners and shipping agents never expected to do business with those passengers again, so they did not worry about mistreating or even defrauding them.

Capt. George Coffin agreed to take command of the ship *Alhambra* shortly after he arrived in New Orleans early in 1849. He found her rigging and tackle in bad shape and her copper sheathing in need of replacement. These repairs were made, and the area between decks was cleared of all obstructions so that staterooms and other accommodations could be constructed in that area. Staterooms approximately six feet square were constructed along the port and starboard bulkheads. Each stateroom had a patent side light and a ventilator. Large draft holes were cut in each side of the bow to allow ample ventilation of the between-decks area, where the passengers lived. Wide sleeping berths were also constructed between the foremast and mainmast. Thus this area could accommodate eighty-eight individuals. Four long tables were constructed between the mainmast and mizzenmast, providing sufficient space for all passengers in this area to eat at one time. Quarters were also provided for a surgeon and servants, and a row of washbowls was installed at the bow. There were also two cabins on deck, one of which had two divisions. Captain Coffin and the super-cargo occupied the aft portion of the larger cabin, and six men who paid extra for the privilege were in the forward portion. New mattresses and blankets were provided for every stateroom along with spare bedding in a large clothes chest located near the pump room between decks. A large supply of dishes was stored in cabinets across the stern of the vessel, where there were also large windows that could be opened for fresh air. The crew, which normally resided between decks in the forecastle, occupied a large house on deck. The kitchen was also located on deck.[24]

Jacob D. B. Stillman, one of the first-cabin passengers in the ship *Pacific*, described the six-foot-square stateroom he shared with another passenger as a "filthy cell, where a dim glimmer through a deck-light, half the time covered by somebody's foot, shows the damp mold and profound ugliness of the place we call our room." On one side "were two shelves, six feet long and thirty inches wide, with an upright board in front about a foot high, making of the whole a couple of troughs, in which are moss mattresses of the consistency of a pine board, and one inch and a quarter thick, pillows of similar proportions, and a blanket. These constitute collectively what we call our berths." Pieces of old sailcloth hung above the upper berths "to conduct the water that leaks from the deck down clear of our beds." Clothing of "various vicissitudes" hung on one wall below a "shelf for books and traps." A large chest was used for sitting. A stool placed on top of his largest trunk served as a desk. "Towels and various implements of death and . . . divers boxes and clothing bags" lined another wall. The doorway took much of the fourth side of the room. On one side of the door was "a broken looking-glass, which my roommate put his hand through early in the voyage . . . and tooth brushes, other brushes, and a small box shelf containing little notions in frequent requisition." Demijohns, guns, and other firearms were stored above the doorway. That left an "unoccupied space on the floor . . . two by three feet. They called this space "our state-room; I don't know why, unless it is because it is a state-room—so the Captain called it, when we paid our passage money."[25]

Stillman did not mention that when the *Pacific* was advertised and shown to prospective passengers, her owners, Frederick Griffing and Hall J. Tibbits, who was also captain of the vessel, indicated that the first cabin would be limited to fifty passengers. But when the passengers were allowed to board the ship and bring their belongings on board, they discovered that the owners had increased the number of first-cabin passengers to seventy-two without increasing the size of the cabin. This led several passengers to file lawsuits against the owners. These passengers were left behind when Captain Tibbits slipped the ship out of New York late in the afternoon to escape further problems from the lawsuits in which passengers asked that they be refunded the cost of their tickets with an unspecified amount of interest and be compensated for unspecified losses they suffered by not going in the vessel. When the lawsuits were settled in July 1849, the passengers received only refunds for their tickets.[26]

Passengers in the ship *Argonaut* had an experience similar to those in the ship *Pacific* in that the owners modified the plans of the vessel after they began booking passengers. J. T. Woodbury wrote that the original plan shown in the office of Dow & Company in Boston indicated there would be berths along both exterior bulkheads from stem to sternpost and none down the center of the vessel, with a table down much of the center instead. Once the original berths were nearly sold, however, the owners substantially modified the plans. First they constructed a bulkhead across the forepart of the vessel at the forward companionway to create a cabin for the crew. They also constructed stairs astern of that bulkhead and extending about six feet into the passengers' quarters to provide access to the sailors' quarters. In addition they constructed single berths along the new bulkhead and a row of double berths down a portion of the center of the vessel. In all they created an additional thirty berths and removed twenty feet of table space. The passengers were thus confined to a smaller space than originally promised and had much less space to store their baggage, less table space, and reduced light.[27]

Woodbury also wrote a lengthy description of the conditions of the passengers' berth deck in the ship *Argonaut* and provided some indication of how they lived in that extremely crowded space. That account provides a vivid picture of what it was like for many passengers who chose to sail to California in 1849.

Preparations for the Voyage

The *Argonaut* is perhaps between decks 140 or 145 ft., and I should think about 28 ft. wide. There are two tier of berths, one above the other, the whole length of the ship. These berths are about 5 ft. 10 in. long and the lower ones, amidships, about 4 ft. wide—the upper ones and those fore and aft are not quite so wide. Hence the berths occupy 8 ft. of the berth deck. In the foreward part of the ship are some 30 hammocks, which during the day, are lashed up, so that they are not much in the way. The space under the lower berths is crowded with chests, trunks, boxes, bags, rum jugs, vessels which had preserves, boxes of tobacco and segars, shovels, pickaxes, crowbars, tents and tentpoles, boots, shoes, oil clothes, &c &c. Some of those chests project a foot or more beyond the front of the berths, into the aisle or gangway. In the middle of the ship is a table the whole length, except under the hatchways about 4 ft. wide and 4 ft. high. To use this table as a place to set at for comfert or convenience to take food, to a person on shore, would seem absolutely ridiculous. Under it is stowed away every imaginable kind of baggage that Yankee injenuity could devise taking to California, even to wash tubs and wheelbarrows! On either side of the table, a part of the way, are two rows of chests, parallel with it, and the side of the chests next the table, perhaps would avarage 8 or 10 in. from it; but the space is very irregular, some of the chests being longer than others. Said chests will probably avarage about 2 ft. wide on the top, many of them being tool chests; and consequently where two of them happen to be of the same height, there is a seat 4 ft. wide! This sounds extravagant for a seat; but as I have said before the space under the table is filled with every imaginable thing, so that a space for one's feet, to sit in the usual way at a table, is hard to be found. I think if man had been originally designed to sit at a table like this, he would have been made so as to shut his legs up like a jack knife, and put them into his pocket! Even if there were room under the table, it would not suit a tea party to clamber over a pile of chests 4 ft. wide to get to it. I have already stated that a part of the way there are two rows of chests next the table, but I would say that nearly all the way where there are not two against it, there is an extra row against the berths. A row of posts that support the upper deck pass through the center of the table, and about 2 1/2 ft. above it is a rude trough, part of the way, in which persons may deposit their dishes if they wish to get them mixed with those of other messes or lost. The rest of the way there is simply a strip of board nailed on to the posts, which serves to hang the lanterns and castors on; and if any person wishes to hang up a dipper or tin pot, he can; but when he goes to find it, it may not be there. The aisle or gangway between the berths and the table, when the chests are in their best possible condition, is about 2 1/2 or 3 ft. wide; but it must be remembered that chests under the berths are stowed crosswise; that is the length of the berth, so that to open a chest it must be drawn hard out against those next the table, which stops up the gangway entirely. It may easily be imagined that some of the chests are always out; and in addition to this there is constantly a number of barrels of bread standing in it. There are three companionways for passengers to descend to the berth deck, viz: one a few feet abaft the mainmast, one about half way from the mainmast to the foremast, and the other 8 or 10 ft. forward of the foremast; the last named narrower than the other two. . . . The berth deck is mostly lighted by these companionways—the remainder of light we receive from the cabin windows; three round ventilators on each side the ship about 5 or 6 in. diameter, and 4 sky lights in the deck, 2 each side; one nearly abreast the other about 8 ft. abaft the foremast: those lights are about 9 in. long and 2 in. wide. The space between decks is about 7 ft. Now to write a description of the persons and employment between decks is a hard task, and I shall attempt to do but little of it. It can be better imagined than described. When a person first descends from the middle companionway, he is first struck with the great length of the room; he looks this way and that, and can hardly see the ends! Then he is surprised to see such a host of people, and before his eyes catch them all they are attracted by the immence quantity of baggage, which is truly astonishing! It is literally a Yankee warehouse! The gangway in front of the berths is very uncertain; a man may go one third the way round the ship & meet with no obstruction, and he may not get 20 ft. before he will be "hard up" against a great chest standing across the way; and perhaps after he clambers over this he will not have gone 10 ft. farther before he brings up against another chest, with 4 persons on and round it, playing cards.

This he gets over as best he may, and perchance before he goes 30 ft. farther some one has his chest out and open repacking or overhauling his things, or to examine some of the nice fixings put up by his lady love, or it may be his eyes are fixed intently on her daguerreotype; for they seem to be very much in requisition and many carry them on their persons where they can have them handy. In going the length of the ship you will see perhaps 12, 15, or it may be 20 companies playing cards—a number playing checkers, some at gammon, some shaking dice, others playing dominos, others throwing craps [*sic*], some telling stories, and others engaged in argument, others singing songs, more or less fiddling &c. &c. &c. You may also see the following—mending especially pants, for the seats of those are exposed to unusual wear—darning stockings, making tents and cots or hammocks, money belts and sheathe belts, emptying rum jugs or kegs into smaller vessels and mixing grog, reading, sleeping, eating, picking over raisins, mixing up "duffs," washing dishes, scraping and cleaning deck and all manner of such employment that one can devise either for amusement or to "kill time." Some seem to enjoy themselves very well and others look rather forsaken. I have told what one might *see*, but shall not tell what he might *hear*.[28]

The twenty-five-year-old ship *York*, one of the oldest vessels to sail for California in 1849, departed from Boston on April 4, 1849, under the command of Capt. George N. Cheever. On board were twenty-seven associates who had paid one thousand dollars each, one man who had purchased half a share, and a carpenter in the cabin and fourteen sailors and two cooks in the forecastle. Associate Ferdinand Cartwright Ewer wrote that the vessel was 118 feet long and 24 feet wide. The cabin in which the associates and a couple of others resided reached from the stern to halfway between the mainmast and the foremast. Along each side was a row of twenty staterooms with two persons in each. The two staterooms at the stern were larger than the others, as they were occupied by the captain and the mates, and they had wooden walls and doors. The other staterooms were open to the interior of the vessel and had only blue and white curtain dividers. The boards and overhead beams were painted white, but the remainder of the woodwork was painted to resemble oak. A table was constructed down the center of the cabin except in the vicinity of the mainmast, where there were eight berths. Ewer noted that in addition to the forty-six men in this area there was "one newfoundland dog (owned by the company), a small terrier pup (a favorite with all), and two hogs, eternally under feet, and continually kicked." The chickens, which he referred to as "those nauseous hens," had all been slaughtered by the time he wrote this description. Then he listed "rats, bed bugs, hosts of black ants, cock roaches, and moths" as other occupants.[29]

The passengers in steerage in the brig *Osceola* were another group who were "shamefully imposed upon" by the owners of the vessel. When they booked passage in the vessel, there was a table sufficiently large to accommodate thirty people. It was "tolerably lighted by skylights." On the eve of the departure of the vessel, the owners removed the table and seats in order to stow cases, chests, and trunks, "a large portion of which" belonged to the cabin passengers, in that area. As a result "the steerage passengers" were "compelled to mess on chicken-coops, pig-pens, water-casks and trunks, subjected to almost every imaginable inconvenience." Passenger Samuel C. Upham concluded that "the brig has been a perfect *Hades* since she sailed from Philadelphia." He added that the steerage area was less than 650 "superficial feet" in which forty-four people resided, and he noted that there were "twelve persons more than is allowed by the laws of the United States to passenger vessels passing through the tropics."[30]

The steerage passengers were not alone in their discontent with the arrangements on board the *Osceola*, as a few days after writing about the discontent of those in steerage, Upham noted that the cabin "passengers have been growling for some time about their miserable accommodations, and to-day have declared war to the knife." They "resolved to hold an indignation meeting, and on their arrival at Rio de Janeiro to report the proceedings with their grievances to the American consul at that port, and ask his interference in the matter." They swore "by all the saints in the calendar" they would "not leave Rio until matters are adjusted to their entire satisfaction." Upham concluded that "both cabin and steerage passengers have much cause for complaint, and I sincerely hope that justice may be done to all on board before the *Osceola* leaves Rio."[31] Upham made no further reference to this matter. Likely nothing was done at Rio for fear of delaying the departure from that port and consequently the arrival in San Francisco.

Samuel W. Brown was a physician from Hartford, Connecticut, and a member of the Fremont Mining and Trading Company, which sailed from New York in the bark *Selma*. He indicated that there were twelve staterooms in the after cabin, each of which had two berths; that the forward cabin contained "temporary rough berths for 32 persons;" and that there were similar berths below deck for the remainder of the company. Two tables, one in the after cabin and one below deck, did not provide enough space for all eighty-four members to eat at one time, so one of the tables was used a second time at each meal. Although the members drew lots for tables and berths, Brown noted that the company had "kindly voted" him and Matthew L. Coe a stateroom. Perhaps this was because they were both physicians.[32]

Albert Wilson Bee was one of 170 passengers who sailed in the ship *South Carolina* from New York. Sixty of the passengers were in the cabin on deck, and the remainder were housed below deck, where "births were erected through the center and around the sides, two persons sleeping in each birth. One Hundred and ten passengers, of all ages and grades, were crowded for a five months voyage into this small place . . . far too many for the comfort, convenience, or health of any one." Each passenger furnished his own "bedding, dishes and everything else necessary for the Voyage." The passengers washed their own dishes and kept "them in our berths or trunks there being no convenient place provided for that purpose." Trunks and chests were kept under and in front of their berths and were used for seats, as no chairs or stools were provided for them. The only light came from the hatch and from lamps that were kept burning all through the day and evening, as there were no windows or skylights.[33]

Moses Cogswell, who was a member of the Roxbury Sagamore Company in the ship *Sweden*, wrote that "The greatest scene on board is perhaps about eleven O'Clock at night after all have turned in." The *Sweden* was fitted with berths along both exterior bulkheads as were many other vessels, but those in the *Sweden* were each designed for two people instead of one as in most vessels. They also had the usual table down the center of the vessel with trunks and chests stowed two deep on each side. There were "hung hammocks and clothes bags, so as completely to occupy all the space overhead and hide the timbers. It resembles a Second hand dry Goods Shop." Cogswell wrote that it was too hot to sleep two in a berth in the warm latitudes, so many of them slept on the table and chests or in hammocks so that only one would be in each berth and that it was "almost impossible to sleep until late, for each one has something to say and an occasional Dry joke will set the whole uproarious with laughter and ere that subsides another joke and reply sets the whole in motion again. It is rich decidedly."[34]

It appears that individuals wrote extensively about the sleeping accommodations in their vessels only when there was great discontent. Those who were satisfied seem not to have recorded that information. Perhaps the only conclusion that can be drawn from these examples of living accommodations is that those who sailed in vessels sent out as a commercial venture by the owners of those vessels were more likely to be abused than were those who went in vessels owned or chartered by joint stock companies. There was some abuse and discrimination within those companies as well in this and other matters, as will appear in other portions of this volume, but it seems to have been less severe than in vessels that were strictly commercial ventures of their owners.

Dudley Emmerson Jones, who sailed from New York in the bark *Nautilus,* which was owned by the Albany Company for California, was one of the few who described their living areas without complaining about the space. Seventy-five members of the company lived in an area below deck, which was about eighty feet long, twenty-two feet wide, and between five and a half and six and a half feet high, in a vessel that was one hundred feet long and twenty-five feet wide. Both exterior bulkheads were lined with trunks and other baggage. There were two tables in the center of the vessel at which thirty-eight men could sit at a time to eat. All the men slept in hammocks that were suspended about two feet apart from the deck beams. When all the hammocks were up and occupied they consumed virtually all of the space in the upper portions of the cabin. Some of the hammocks were taken down during the day to provide headroom in the cabin. There were two hatches to provide some light and air circulation. Lamps were suspended over the tables and were kept burning at night and during meals. Each person had his own hammock and was provided two blankets and a counterpane for his sleeping comfort.[35]

Accommodations for eating were also cause for some complaints among passengers. The arrangement of tables that existed in many vessels has been discussed above, but there were certainly other matters that affected the satisfaction or dissatisfaction of passengers with the way their food was prepared and served. The most common method of cooking was to have one or more cooks prepare the food in a galley, sometimes the same facility in which the sailors' food was prepared and sometimes in another facility. The more passengers there were in a vessel the more likely it was that there was more than one galley stove and more than one cook. Cooks accustomed to preparing food for a few sailors were ill prepared to provide food for the many passengers of some vessels. Many other cooks hired on vessels bound for California in 1849 had probably never even been to sea. Occasionally the original cook was dismissed, and one of the sailors or passengers was selected for that position. Some persons selected to cook for the passengers had not cooked for others before taking on such an assignment. Although the race of a cook is given only occasionally, there is evidence that some were black, as were many of the cooks on regular sailing vessels. In no case was a female cook identified.

Once the food was cooked, it was common to have stewards put it on the tables. At least that was the case in those vessels that had tables for the passengers. In vessels that tables were not provided, it was common to divide the passengers into messes of ten people, one of whom was designated to appear at the galley and pick up the food for his mess and deliver it to his fellow passengers. Those vessels carrying large numbers of passengers rarely had sufficient table space for everyone to eat at one sitting. Rather they usually had two sittings and alternated first and second sittings on a weekly basis. That way the same group did not always get the choicest pieces or the greatest portion. The quality and attitude of the stewards also had a bearing on the satisfaction of the passengers. Many of the stewards lacked the experience to carry out their duties in a manner acceptable to the passengers. In a number of instances stewards took that position as a means of earning their passage to California. The sex or race of stewards was rarely indicated, but occasionally one of the stewards was female. As was the case with cooks, stewards were occasionally dismissed and replaced by one of the passengers or one of the sailors.

The ship *Balance* out of New York seems to have had worse cooks and stewards than many of the vessels going to California in 1849. John McCrackan described these problems in letters to his mother and sisters. There was supposed to be a separate table for the passengers residing in the salon on board the ship, but for some reason it was not in operation for the first few days. Thus the salon passengers took their meals with the cabin passengers. When the salon passengers began to take their meals in the salon, jealousy arose as did problems with the stewards. McCrackan indicated that the stewards "did not know their place" and they became independent. He blamed some of this on the other passengers, who, he said, "Gave them an inch and they took a mile as the old Proverb goes." He concluded that "Our cook and stewards are wholly inexperienced & not competent to fill the situation. The result is deplorable for the best material badly cooked is not fit for food."[36] He addressed this issue again three months later when he blamed some of the problem with the stewards on Capt. E. Washborn Ruggles, who, he wrote, was a fine navigator and a good sailor but was "not the proper person to command a Passenger ship" because he was ignorant of how things should be done and he was indifferent to the conduct of the stewards. McCrackan felt the "Principal difficulty" was "a want of severity towards the Stewards. They have had their own way with none to look after them. A familiarity consequently has been encouraged between them, & some of our passengers, who are persons in the same condition in life, & the result of all this has been to make the Stewards independent and insulent." The original complement in the galley was a head steward and four stewards, none of whom "had ever been at sea before, & consequently were ignorant of their respective duties." The head steward "knew no more than they did." Each of the stewards was given a turn at the head steward's position "till he disclosed his utter inability to perform, when his place was vacated and another one substituted, when his head was cut off." He added that the cook and his assistant "were as ignorant of their duties as the stewards, & with such a condition of things what could be expected. Everything that was cooked was an experiment, but if they succeeded once, 'It could not be done a second time.'" As a result of these problems with the cooks and stewards, much of their food was wasted. He also noted that a large quantity of food had been stolen and suggested that all of these problems could been avoided had the owners of the vessel hired experienced stewards and paid them reasonable wages instead of using inexperienced people who worked for their passage.[37]

Eating order in the ship *Crescent* was determined by bunk level. Those in the upper bunks ate together, as did those in the lower ones. The former were designated "Upper Crust" and the latter "Lower Crust." One group ate first one week; the other group ate first the next week. There was a head steward who dealt the provisions for each meal to the cook. Once the cook had prepared the food he gave it to the other stewards for serving on the table. The men were divided into six divisions of ten each. Each day one of the divisions assisted the head steward in getting the wood and water, picking over beans and raisins, and performing other necessary duties. A second division was responsible for making the puddings and pastries. The stewards in the *Crescent* were paid employees rather than people working for their passage.[38]

The cooks in the ship *Argonaut* seem to have been a bit devious but enterprising and were undoubtedly overworked. There were two cooks and two stoves on board. One cook prepared meals for the cabins and the sailors while the other prepared the food for the 196 men between decks. J. T. Woodbury was adamant when he wrote, "I believe there are 196 passengers between decks, and one cook and one range to cook for them! Look at it! It is worthy of any one's consideration who has any regard for humanity. <u>One negro cook for 196 men.</u> This is abundant demonstration to the world that we do not have our food cooked as it should be." Consequently, they had to "mix our own duffs, hashes, &c." He added that the cooks understood "the catch-penny business pretty well." Their beans were always "stewed because they pretend they cannot bake them. We have scarcely had a mess of beans stewed soft enough to be fit to eat . . . but they will bake them over the next morning for a fourpence, and they generally have some to sell the morning after bean day that are baked quite eatable, for 5 or 10 cts. a plate." The cook would bake a cake or make a duff "for a fourpence" and charge extra for "any little thing that we want done." He added that the cooks "picked up a pretty good purse of money" and speculated that by the time they arrived at "San Francisco some passengers will probably have paid 3 or 4 dollars." There were four stewards in the between decks who washed the dishes, cleaned the deck, received the provisions from the commissary, carried them to the galley, and served cooked food to the passengers. They paid a fare of only seventy-five dollars and worked to pay the remainder of the cost of their voyage.[39]

Two passengers in the bark *Hannah Sprague* discussed the table manners of some of their fellow passengers. Alfred Wheeler first described the usual division into two messes who alternated eating first and second each week and mentioned that some of those assigned to eat first would gather around the table several minutes before the bell was rung for breakfast. Breakfast was usually salt mackerel, fried ham, hash, warm biscuits, corn bread, boiled Indian meal, sea biscuit, and "miserable tea & coffee, & butter soft & strong." Sometimes they had fresh fried eggs. He then described a scene at breakfast one day.

> The bell rings & over they go scaling the backs of the seats like so many steeds over a hedge. Some uncouth hog or devil has seized a plate of fried eggs & regardless of the fact that these are luxuries at sea empties half the contents into his plate & then modestly calls on his neighbor to hand him the bread, another the butter, another the salt & then growls at Sarah (the stewardess) for being so slow with his coffee. Some more genteel & less active gent, takes his seat at the table with less haste & after

31

waiting to get an opportunity to help himself to an egg or a hot roll or maybe some nicely browned & tempting fish cakes which have been passed eagerly from hand to hand with occasionally 2 or 3 plunging their own forks into them sans ceremonie at one & the same time, sees the dish set before him <u>empty</u>. "Sara" says the disappointed one "will you bring me an egg—or a roll—or" whatever the dish may be. "Ain't no more" is the quaint answer stereotyped by Sara. The modest man must forsooth breakfast from sea biscuit with a slice of ham or cold meat & a cup of exerable tea or coffee. Worse still is the fate of those who are doomed a week at a time to grace the "second table." The dishes, knives, forks & spoons used by the predecessors at the first table are gathered up & with wonderful alacrity made ready for the use of the second; that is they undergo a process of being rubbed over with a dirty, greasy rag—so I was informed by one who had seen the said rag—which leaves its mark upon the dishes in the shape of sundry greasy circles spirally winding to a point in the center of the dish & upon the knives by certain longitudinal streaks & upon the forks, which are 2 pronged steel or iron, by a kind of shiny substance on the inside of the prongs which, however, I have discovered can be removed by drawing between the said prongs a clean napkin of my own. This want of cleanliness in the steward, cook, or scullion (whoever is the culpable one) & the ill breeding of certain passengers constitute all, or nearly all, the real annoyance that I suffer.[40]

John Henry Corneilson, who noted a considerable amount of grumbling on board the *Hannah Sprague* and wrote about it at some length, gave additional insight into the nature of some of the passengers when he discussed another situation at the table and some general discontent a couple of months later.

Those at table whose appetites are strong and who generally seize upon what they can get when they first sit down grumble either because it is not well cooked or because there is not enough to suit them. Those who have moderate appetites in their turn growl at the greedy ones who help themselves so largely at first leaving but scantily for them. On the subject of eating, I may state that one day last week I was among the first at table and as

32

the gentleman opposite me was about helping himself I asked him after helping himself to help me but lo! I had hardly spoken the words when 5 forks were lunged into the dumplings with potatoes and odd scraps of chicken disappeared flying in all directions through the air for so quickly are they abstracted that the hand was invisible while the dumplings only were seen. Seeming a caricature of a bursting bomb shell of dumplings all flying in different directions, but lighting miraculously on several plates. As the gentleman was passing the plate out of reach of those [illegible word] one greedy gentleman & plates off made a dive or the fork did and carried off the remaining dumpling of about 7 inches long on which pieces of potatoes and chicken were sticking. I was perfectly bewildered by this specimen of table tactics, and looked on in speechless amazement.[41]

Corneilson went on to express sympathy for Capt. Leander Freeman because of his lack of authority to redress any of the grievances expressed by the passengers even though the captain felt they were justified.

The ship *Orpheus* was one of the vessels in which there was no table at which the passengers could eat their meals. John Taylor reported that he had been chosen to serve his mess of "ten poor starving specimens of humanity" for one week. That meant that he had "the pleasure of bringing the food from the gally" to his mess. After they had passed Rio de Janeiro he noted:

We find it very uncomfortable eating our meals on deck from the cold & added to the inconvenience to eat, & eat with, makes it more a task & less a pleasure than I ever before experienced. In the frugal outfit for this ship it seems there was just enough tin plates, cups & spoons to supply each passenger & not one over. Consequently they are now reduced more than one half, by being broken, lost over board, & I suppose a share of them stolen. We seldom have now more than three or four plates & no spoons for ten of us, so we stand up around our mess pan (which is most generally placed on the head of a barrel) & wait for each other to get through. I ate rice & molasses a few days ago with my pocket knife off from a plate with two others. The close air & want of room below present so few comforts, we eat on deck only when [not] driven below by the rain & cold, the latter not having

33

been severe enough yet to compel us to do so. The complaint is general throughout the ship but more silent than at first. As there seems to be no remedy to be had now we are fairly embarked, we make the best of it, & get along as well as we can, until the voyage is ended, when I think redress will be had sooner or later.

Taylor then related an incident that had happened when the captain was shown a piece of pork that was intended to be served to the passengers. He indicated that he "could not help laughing however the other day at the appearance of a piece of pork carried to him for his inspection by one of the passengers. It was half of a hogs head with the snouse not taken of & but half of the bristles. Its countenance being turned upwards on the plate it presented a broad grin that made a roar of laughter. Its full row of teeth & broad half scraped ear appearing quite conspicuous. The idea of its being boiled with the beans spoilt my dinner for that day pretty effectually."[42]

Thus the manner in which food was prepared and served could and did have an effect on the degree of satisfaction or dissatisfaction passengers experienced during their sail to San Francisco in their quest for riches in the goldfields. Detailed discussion of the food served to the passengers in these sailing vessels is presented in chapter 3.

It has commonly been stated that a great percentage of those who went to California for the gold rush were young men in the prime of their lives in their twenties and thirties and among the most promising and industrious citizens in the area from which they left. This has usually been stated without any real statistics, perhaps because the statistics were not systematically generated at the time. San Francisco harbor master Edward S. King maintained a record of the total number of persons and their genders who arrived by vessel in 1849 and 1850 and the areas of the world from which they had come. He calculated that 15,597 individuals, of whom 309 were women, arrived via Cape Horn from Atlantic and European ports in 1849 and 11,209 individuals, of whom 501 were women, in 1850.[43] Figures for ages of passengers exist primarily in the diaries of passengers who recorded the names of each passenger in their vessel and frequently provided ages, occupations, and places of residence. On rare occasions they provided marital status as well. The table below contains a limited record of the numbers of passengers in each of several age brackets from eleven vessels that sailed to San Francisco in 1849. These limited statistics confirm that the majority of the men who sailed around Cape Horn to California were between the ages of 20 and 29.

Name of Vessel	Teens	%	20s	%	30s	%	40s	%	50s	%	N.g.	%	Tot.	%
Bark Ann Smith[1]	3	12.5	10	41.7	7	29.2	2	8.3	2	8.3	0	0	24	100
Ship Argonaut[2]	17	7.9	144	67.3	31	14.5	12	5.6	4	1.9	6	2.8	214	100
Ship Crescent[3]	2	3.3	33	54.1	18	29.5	7	11.5	1	1.6	0	0	61	100
Ship Daniel Webster[4]	6	10.2	23	39.0	13	22.0	13	22.0	2	3.4	1	1.7	58	100
Ship Edward Everett[5]	12	7.9	101	66.9	25	16.5	12	8.0	1	0.7	0	0	151	100
Bark Emma Isadora[6]	5	8.6	33	56.9	8	13.8	11	19.0	1	1.7	0	0	58	100
Scr. General Morgan[7]	1	3.5	19	65.5	8	27.5	0	0	1	3.5	0	0	29	100
Ship Lenore[8]	3	3.4	57	64.8	21	23.9	6	6.8	1	1.1	0	0	88	100
Bark Selma[9]	9	11.8	47	61.8	10	13.2	7	9.2	0	0	3	4.0	76	100
Ship Sutton[10]	2	3.6	36	65.5	13	23.6	4	7.3	0	0	0	0	55	100
Ship Sweden[11]	5	3.2	112	71.3	16	10.2	19	12.1	4	2.6	1	0.6	157	100
Total	65	6.7	615	63.3	170	17.5	43	9.6	17	1.8	11	1.1	971	100

Analysis of Passengers, 1849.

[1]Minor, Journal, bark *Ann Smith*, 1849. [2]Woodbury, Journal, ship *Argonaut*, 1849. [3]Cross, Journal, ship *Crescent*, 1849; Graves, Journal, ship *Crescent*, 1849; and Harvey, Journal, ship *Crescent*. [4]Hollingsworth, Journal, ship *Daniel Webster*, 1849. One additional man was in his 60s and is not reflected in the numbers in the chart. [5]White, Journal, ship *Edward Everett*, 1849. [6]Stevens, Journal, bark *Emma Isadora*, 1849. [7]Lyman, *Journal of a Voyage*. [8]Hyde, Journal, ship *Lenore*, 1849. [9]Logbook, bark *Selma*, 1849. [10]Whaley, *Consignments to El Dorado*. [11]Bailey, Journal, ship *Sweden*, 1849, and James L. L. F. Warren Papers.

Previous authors have written about how men left wives and children behind as they sailed off to the West to seek gold that they hoped would permit them to live in luxury, or at least comfortably, after they returned. However, no one has provided information on the numbers or percentages of married men who sailed off to the new El Dorado. The amount of information available is limited and is found in only three of the many journals of passengers examined during this study. Of the sixty-one members of the Salem Mechanics Trading and Mining Association in the ship *Crescent* of Boston, twenty-six (43 percent) were married. In the several age brackets ten of the thirty-three (31 percent) in their twenties; ten of the eighteen (56 percent) of those in their thirties; and five of the seven (71 percent) of those in their forties were married. Both of the teenagers and the one in his fifties were single.[44] Henry H. Hyde Jr. listed in his journal eighty-nine of the one hundred members of the New England and California Trading and Mining Association who sailed in the ship *Lenore*. He reported that 31, or 35 percent, were married. James White reported that 43, or 29 percent, of the 151 members of the Boston and California Mining and Trading Joint Stock Company in the ship *Edward Everett* were married. The numbers and percentages at the various age brackets were as follows: teens, none of 12; twenties, 17 of 101, or 17 percent; thirties, 14 of 25, or 56 percent; forties, 11 of 12, or 92 percent; and fifties, 1 of 1, or 100 percent.[45] If these three examples are at all representative of the whole number, then one might conclude that perhaps between 30 and 40 percent of the men who went to California in sailing vessels via Cape Horn were married, and a larger percentage of those over 30 were married than were those younger than that. How these figures compare with the overall population of the United States in 1849 has not been determined.

It has generally been assumed that individuals from all walks of life flocked to California during the gold rush era although no one has presented any real evidence of this. Several journalists included occupations of vessel passengers. Summaries of those occupations and numbers of people in each category might help substantiate those assumptions. Among the passengers in the ship *Argonaut* out of Boston were thirty-two carpenters; twenty-three shoemakers; twenty-one farmers; twenty machinists; nine mariners; seven (each) ship carpenters, painters, and laborers; six clerks; five (each) blacksmiths, merchants, masons, and peddlers; four (each) cabinetmakers and teamsters; three (each) tailors, moulders, pianoforte makers; two (each) lumberers, artists, boat makers, undertakers, stonecutters, bakers, papermakers, shipmasters, provision dealers, and druggists; and one (each) grocer, professor, carriage maker, lawyer, brass finisher, stonemason, agent, engineer, printer, trader, buckle maker, superintendent of International Marine Works, block printer, coach maker, newsboy, brass founder, cabdriver, patternmaker, millwright, courier, soap maker, weaver, and miller. Occupations were not given for two men.[46]

The sixty-one members of the Salem Mechanics Trading and Mining Association in the ship *Crescent* out of Boston included eleven carpenters; six masons; four (each) shoemakers, curriers, and machinists; three bakers; two (each) teachers, traders, teamsters, blacksmiths, cotton manufacturers, tinmen, and farmers; and one (each) yeoman, miller, cigar maker, stonecutter, tanner, engineer, overseer on a railroad, painter, blencher, cooper, coppersmith, mariner, morocco dresser, and pump maker. The occupation of one was undecipherable.[47]

Among the occupations represented in the ship *Daniel Webster* out of New York were four (each) accountants and house carpenters; three (each) blacksmiths, machinists, ship carpenters, painters, farmers, and sailors; two (each) masons, caulkers, coopers, tailors, and cabinetmakers; and one (each) shipbuilder, millwright, iron finisher, hatter, wire worker, plumber, gold seeker, trader, dentist, jeweler, cabin boy, physician, grocer, cabinetmaker, engineer, servant, and baker. Occupations were not given for seven individuals. The cabin boy was sixteen-year-old John Finley, who was probably the son of Daniel Finley, a house carpenter of New York. It is not clear whether he was cabin boy for the *Daniel Webster* or if he had held that post in some other vessel prior to leaving for California.[48]

The members of the Boston and California Mining and Trading Joint Stock Company on board the ship *Edward Everett* included twenty-three clerks; eight (each) machinists and merchants; seven carpenters; six farmers; five (each) physicians, painters, and mariners or seamen; four (each) printers and jewelers; three (each) provision dealers, bookkeepers, bakers, teamsters, and shoemakers; two (each) clergymen, tinplate workers, reporters, engineers, cabinetmakers, iron founders, students, apothecaries, hatters, boatmen, pump makers, expressmen, blacksmiths, furniture dealers, and shoe dealers; and one (each) chemist, leather finisher, varnisher, leather dresser, lawyer, whitesmith, butcher, tanner and currier, truckman, chandler, boatbuilder, accountant, car trimmer, cotton spinner, cordage maker, geologist, produce dealer, watchmaker, manufacturer, tailor, railroad contractor, hotel keeper, gunsmith, and pocketbook maker.[49] Occupations represented within the members of the Mutual Protection Trading Company on board the bark *Emma Isadora* out of Boston included seven farmers; five carpenters; four (each) seamen, blacksmiths, and clerks; three (each) merchants and cabinetmakers; two (each) physicians and masons;

and one (each) boatman, watchmaker, daguerreotype artist, laborer, painter, brickmaker, assayer, stobbber, river driver, factory overseer, minister, papermaker, machinist, shoemaker, fisherman, marble worker, chair painter, glassblower, provision dealer, dentist, tailor, and wool paller.[50]

The members of the Fremont Mining and Trading Company, who sailed in the bark *Selma*, were nearly all from Connecticut, which might have considerably influenced the makeup of the membership. They included twenty-four farmers; nine clerks; four (each) carpenter/joiners, machinists, and blacksmiths; three (each) sailors, shoemakers, and jeweler/watchmakers; two (each) physicians, bookkeepers, stonecutters, tanner and curriers, and tailors; and one (each) marble cutter, merchant, soldier, wheelwright, manufacturer, Brittanner worker, sash and blind maker, toolmaker, tinner, edge tool maker, and mason.[51] Many of the passengers in the ship *Sweden* came from Massachusetts, but others came from Maine, New Hampshire, New York, Vermont, Connecticut, and Rhode Island. Their occupations included twenty-eight clerks; twenty-two carpenters; ten laborers; nine (each) farmers and masons; eight (each) blacksmiths, machinists, and traders; five ship carpenters; four painters; three (each) tailors, cabinetmakers, merchants, manufacturers, shoemakers, engine builders, grocers, and tinsmiths; two (each) physicians, botany physicians, teachers, teamsters, and lawyers; and one (each) piano tuner, tinplater, silversmith, coppersmith, saddler, seaman, carriage painter, millwright, tobacconist, druggist, soldier, florist, exchange broker, engineer, wood turner, musician, trunk maker, shoe cutter, mariner, lumberer, spinner, student, and shoe last maker.[52]

The members of the Bunker Hill Trading and Mining Association in the ship *Regulus* of Boston included twenty farmers; seventeen mariners or seamen (including the members of the crew); nine clerks; six machinists; five carpenters; four (each) painters, daguerreotypists, masons or bricklayers, and shoemakers; three (each) accountants, manufacturers, and traders; two (each) merchants, dyers, dentists, spinners, cordwainers, and oystermen; and one (each) ironmonger, cooper, baker, plasterer, pianoforte maker, hat dealer, paper dealer, chaise maker, harness maker, bookbinder, ballast master, rope maker, lithographer, currier, last maker, civil engineer, coachman, cabinetmaker, paperhanger, tinsmith, cigar maker, blacksmith, weaver, wheelwright, surgeon, shipwright, physician, and joiner. No occupation was given for four members.[53]

There are 878 individuals who can definitely be classified as passengers in these eight vessels. Among them there are 157 occupations identified in the journalists' lists of passengers. The identified occupations are undoubtedly what the passengers called themselves, and some (e.g., cordage maker and rope maker, silversmith and whitesmith, and leather dresser and morocco dresser) are either identical or so close that they could easily be grouped together. The occupations listed most frequently are carpenters (including ship carpenters), 105; farmers, 95; clerks, 79; machinists, 54; shoemakers, 42; blacksmiths, 29; masons, 29; mariners (including those referred to as seamen or sailors), 28; painters, 24; and laborers, 18. These ten occupations account for 503, or 56 percent, of the total. The occupations identified in these eight vessels probably constitute a fairly representative sample of the New England population of the mid nineteenth century, except possibly for the number of mariners. It is likely that the vast majority of mariners went to California as crewmen earning their passage.

It does appear from these examples that the immigrants to California were representative of American society as far as occupations in the areas from which the individual vessels sailed are concerned, but they are probably not representative of that same society in age. Because of the small sample, it is impossible to say how representative the immigrants are of overall marital status in the United States at the time, but, as is the case with age, the figures on marital status do not accurately represent American society of the time.

2

Underway at Last

In an era in which one can board a jet airliner after breakfast in New York on any given day and be in San Francisco in time for lunch, it is difficult to imagine a time when one might have to wait several weeks or even a few months to depart from New York in a sailing vessel for a voyage of four to eight months to San Francisco at a time when thousands were anxious to get to the new El Dorado before others collected all the gold. Many anxious gold seekers who had traveled to New York or some other American port found themselves in exactly that situation through much of 1849. For more than three decades there had been regular monthly or twice-monthly scheduled sailings between New York and a few other ports to Europe, beginning with the famous Black Ball Line in 1816. How disheartening and frustrating it must have been for someone eager to get to the gold-fields to arrive in New York, Boston, Baltimore, Philadelphia, or other ports and see several vessels advertised to sail for California in a matter of days and book and pay for passage in one and then experience the seemingly endless delays as the owners of the vessel waited for more passengers and more freight to fill the vessel to capacity before departing. Owners and agents were adept at convincing prospective passengers, few of whom had ever been more than a few miles from home, much less halfway around the world, as well as shippers, many of whom were eager to get their cargo to California, that only by paying at the time passage was booked could they be assured space for themselves or their freight. It had to have been frustrating to spend precious hoarded or even borrowed cash for traveling between home and port or for room and board while waiting, expecting that the vessel would surely depart soon, when all they wanted to do was be in California harvesting the gold they had read about daily in the newspapers. Nevertheless travel or wait and spend they did; there were no alternatives. Once a passage had been booked and paid for, there were no refunds. The following examples illustrate the types of delays experienced.

40

"The Beautiful new bark *Alice Tarlton*" was first mentioned on March 19, 1849, to succeed the bark *Rising Sun* from New York. On April 10 prospective passengers were assured that her accommodations were "unsurpassed," and shippers were cautioned that she would receive only "a few hundred bbls. more freight, if offered immediately." The agent promised that "a distinguished Physician and Surgeon" would "go out in the vessel." On May 17 she was announced to sail on May 19, and on June 9 her sailing date was announced for that day even though "one fine state room remains disengaged."[1]

The ship *Andalusia*, described as a "fine A 1" vessel that was copper fastened and coppered and a fast sailer, was first advertised on February 14, 1849, with no scheduled departure date. Regular identical advertisements appeared for her from early February through April 12 although on March 1 her departure date was announced as March 24. The vessel was listed as 771 tons, about 33 feet wide, 150 feet long, and 8 feet between decks. On April 16 it was announced that she would sail that day, but weather problems caused further delays. A cold northwest wind dropped the temperatures from 67° to freezing and caused a serious drop in the water level in the harbor. Then snow began to fall, causing additional problems of visibility. Finally on April 18 at 9:00 A.M. she was towed to sea by the steamer *Relief*, which then picked up her passengers and delivered them on board the *Andalusia*. The vessel "left amid cheers, mingled with the tears and regrets of those who were parted, perhaps forever. By her departure near and dear ties were broken for the time—husbands and fathers from wives and children; sons from relatives dear to them, and friends from those with whom they had often met in friendship."[2]

The ship *Angelique* in which Mrs. Eliza Farnham and her California Association of American Women sailed to San Francisco was first advertised on March 20, 1849, to sail on April 12 or 15. On April 17 it was announced she would be detained until May 1. Her accommodations were said to be "elegant and comfortable, having furnished staterooms in the poop cabins with two single berths in each, and staterooms also in the saloon with single berths." She also had patent ventilators and port lights to ensure good air in the tropical latitudes. Price of passage was $250 in the poop cabin and $175 in the saloon including "all found with the best kind of provisions and in abundance." The *Angelique* finally sailed on May 19, five weeks after she was first scheduled to depart. Perhaps her carrying only thirty passengers enabled the owners to fill her earlier than some other owners were able to fill their vessels.[3]

The California Mutual Benefit and Joint Stock Association began holding meetings in New York in late January 1849 to plan its voyage to California to engage in gold seeking and to support missionary efforts of the Methodist Episcopal Church. By mid February they had purchased the ship *Arkansas* in which their members and other passengers would sail when all preparations were complete. The first scheduled departure date was May 3, but the association finally sailed on June 26 with a complement of seventy-six members instead of the one hundred originally projected and thirty-six additional passengers including eight females and six children. The eight females were reported to be the largest number of that gender to sail in any California-bound vessel from New York up to that time. Each member paid three hundred dollars and was entitled to an equal interest in the ship, mining implements, provisions for eighteen months, and a share of the profits from the passengers and freight. They also took a large supply of bibles and religious tracts, but alcoholic beverages were prohibited. On June 25 one of the passengers was struck by a package being loaded in the vessel and was knocked into the hold, a fall of about twenty feet. He received head and back injuries, but he insisted on going to California to realize his "visions of the El Dorado."[4] This insistence in going to California at any or all costs was typical of the times. On January 25, 1849, the "superior coppered and copper-fastened, fast-sailing, live-oak" ship *Balance* was advertised to sail about February 1. Most of her passengers and freight had already been engaged. The owners would go out in the ship, and a separate cabin was to be provided for ladies. On February 6 she was advertised as ready for sea and would sail about February 15. She eventually sailed on April 1, fully two months after her first scheduled departure date, with seventy-six passengers including seven females, two servants, and one child. Five of the women were married, four of whom sailed with their husbands. Two single women and one married woman traveled alone.[5]

The Excelsior Association announced on January 26 they had purchased the bark *Clarissa* in which their twenty members and up to thirty other passengers would sail to California when the association was fully organized and other passenger berths and freight capacity had been filled. Shortly thereafter it was noted that there would be fifty members, each of whom were to pay $150 for a share in the vessel and outfit for eighteen months. They actually sailed on March 17, at which time the names of twenty members and eight other passengers were listed.[6] Presumably the competition for members, passengers, and freight was too great for all vessels to fill up, and it was better for the association to sail when it did rather than wait longer and try to fill their vessel with people and freight.

The "fine fast-sailing coppered and copper-fastened" ship *Flavius* was first advertised to sail from New York about February 1 with William Cook as master. She would take six cabin passengers and had "ample room between decks for those who wish to husband their means and go out as second-class passengers." Passengers could remain in the vessel for twenty days after arrival in San Francisco for one dollar per day. On February 5 the vessel was advertised as having been purchased by the California Mutual Benefit and Joint Stock Association and would sail on February 15 under the command of Capt. I. Thurston. She was said to have "the most airy and splendid cabin and saloon accommodation now in port," and passengers were "guaranteed privileges that no other ship will grant" upon arriving in San Francisco. Nonmember passengers would fare as well as members of the association. Later the *Flavius* was advertised as being "clean, high, and airy" and "free from all impurities," as she had never before carried passengers. At this time I. Thacher was listed as captain. As of March 7 five shares in the association were available at $130 each. The *Flavius* sailed on March 24 with nine members of the White Plains Mutual Benefit Association, five members of the White Plains Mining Company, and four other passengers in addition to the members of the association that owned her.[7]

On January 10, 1849, the bark *Griffin*, which had been constructed only a few years earlier by an old shipmaster as a yacht for his son, was advertised to sail on January 20 and was "acknowledged by all to be superior to any yet offered" for the voyage between New York and San Francisco. She was owned by an unnamed association, which planned to have thirty-three members, each of whom would pay five hundred dollars per share, for which he would be entitled to about forty barrels of freight at no extra cost, the privilege of living in the vessel in California, and return passage at no cost. Later the number of shares was increased to fifty, and each shareholder was allowed between twenty and forty barrels of freight without charge. The *Griffin* sailed on March 8, not quite two months after her first advertised sailing date.[8]

"New, Staunch, fast sailing, coppered and copper fastened" described the bark *Keoka*, which was advertised on December 28, 1848, to sail on January 5 or "sooner if passengers and freight are on board." She would "proceed as far up the Sacramento [River] as possible," and the passengers were to stay on board during inclement weather. Later she was rescheduled to depart on January 25 and actually sailed on February 5.[9]

The year-old "A 1 fast sailing, copper fastened and coppered" bark *Kirkland* was advertised on January 25, 1849, to sail on February 10 from Baltimore. Her staterooms were described as those "of the most superior order," and she was said to be "a beautiful vessel" and "one of the fastest sailers of the port" with excellent cabin arrangements. She sailed February 24 in company with the brig *B. W. Brown* and the schooner *Ferdinand*, all of which were towed out by the steamer *Relief*, and a "large number of persons were assembled on the wharves, including many ladies, relatives and friends of the adventurers, and they left amid the cheers of the crowd. The emigration, as has been all those who have left Baltimore, is composed of excellent citizens."[10]

On April 16, 1849, Baltimoreans were invited by James S. Weathered, who had just returned from California, to take passage in a vessel to sail to California as soon as one could be chartered and filled with passengers and freight. Weathered promised to give each passenger or all companies who took passage in the vessel "a complete Gold Washing Machine and implements, such as he knows to be the best in use, having seen many costly and ingenious machines thrown aside as unfit for the purpose." He promised also to give them "the benefit of his experience in mining" and to "make known to them the most productive gold placers." On May 8 Weathered announced that he had chartered the twelve-year-old Harve packet ship *Louis Philippe*, which would sail about June 1. She would have cabins for both gentlemen and ladies and was "high and roomy between decks" and "well ventilated, offering in every respect superior accommodations and comfort to passengers and freight." The *Louis Philippe* sailed on July 11 carrying thirty passengers, nine of whom were ladies. The remainder were "mostly young men of this city of excellent parentage and education." Her hold was filled to capacity with a valuable cargo. She left the wharf "amid the hearty 'three times three' given by a large number of persons who had assembled on the wharf to witness her departure, which was lustily responded to by those on board the gallant vessel."[11]

The bark *Martin W. Brett* of Baltimore was advertised on July 9, 1849, to "Sail Positively" on July 15 for San Francisco with stops at Rio de Janeiro and Valparaiso. She offered separate staterooms for ladies and gentlemen, a "Library of miscellaneous works" for the use of passengers, a stewardess to serve, and a physician to look after the health of the passengers. Each stateroom was to be furnished with "beds, bedding, washstands, &c." All this was offered at packet fare. After arriving in San Francisco the *Martin W. Brett* was to "run as a regular Packet between

San Francisco and Panama." On July 31 it was noted that the bark had been detained and would sail in a few days. She finally sailed on August 21, more than two months after her first announced departure date. She carried freight consisting of lumber, bricks, tobacco, liquors, and several houses ready to set up immediately upon arrival and thirty-four passengers including six women and three children.[12]

On May 22, 1849, the Mechanics Mining Association of New York launched their new six-hundred-ton ship *Mechanics Own,* which they had constructed at a cost of seventy-five thousand dollars at the Bishop & Simonson shipyard with two-thirds of the workers being members of the association. The association had decided to construct a vessel to sail to San Francisco. She was initially scheduled to sail under the command of Capt. Joseph Adams on July 15. All the members of the Mechanics Mining Association expected to sail in the ship and anticipated taking an additional sixty passengers, all of whom would be housed in one cabin with staterooms on the spar deck and a second amidship between decks fitted out as a saloon with berths on either side and dining tables. By the end of June, James R. Malcomb had assumed command of the vessel. Despite her advertised "elegant accommodations," passengers were slow to book passage. She finally sailed on August 14 with a passenger list that included 102 names.[13]

The "elegant . . . fast sailing bark *Rising Sun,*" having made only one voyage during her four months of activity, was advertised in early February 1849 to sail on the twenty-fifth of that month. Because she was so new, she was said to be "free from vermin or bilge odor, which cause ship fevers and other sickness on board." She was owned by the sixty members of the Rising Sun Company but would take twenty-five additional passengers. Because she was of shallow draft, she could be sailed up the Sacramento River "to the mines, which will give the party a safe and comfortable home until other arrangements can be made." On March 1 she was reported to be nearly full and would sail "in a day or two." She eventually sailed on March 30, six weeks after her first announced departure date.[14]

The bark *Samoset,* "Splendid A 1 copper fastened and coppered . . . 15 months old . . . built expressly with a view to the accommodation of . . . a limited number of passengers," was advertised on February 1, 1849, to sail on or about the fifteenth. She was said to be "amply provided with patent port holes between decks for light and ventilation, and also with Emerson's celebrated patent ventilator." As she had never carried steerage passengers, she was described as "free from all impurities." A physician and surgeon was to be employed by the ship, and a stewardess would serve passengers in the first cabin. On February 21 her departure date was given as "by the 18th of March." A steamboat was to be taken along to carry passengers up the Sacramento River to the diggings. Fare for the first cabin was $250 and for the second cabin $150. The number of passengers was limited to 150. By March 5 she was advertised to "positively sail . . . in a few days." Since she had proven in previous voyages to Hawaii and Calcutta to be a fast sailer, passengers were told they could "calculate on a passage to the Gold Region in 100 days." She finally sailed on March 23, slightly more than a month later than originally promised, with 153 persons on board. Her passage to the goldfields was 175 days, substantially longer than was originally suggested.[15]

The "first-class Liverpool packet" *Susan G. Owens,* built in Baltimore in 1848, was advertised on February 28, 1849, to "be dispatched immediately" from New York to San Francisco. In subsequent advertisements it was noted that there would be "bathing rooms," each passenger was to be in a stateroom with a single berth, and the owners of the ship promised to provide "a library of 500 volumes for the passengers' use." On April 23 it was declared that she would probably sail the next day and that she would take 225 passengers. On April 25 it was reported that she would be "delayed for a few days only to complete her extensive outfit." Finally a June 4 report was that she sailed from Philadelphia on May 15 with 174 passengers. In one advertisement the owners predicted "from her unrivaled speed passengers may safely count upon reaching" San Francisco "in four months." Her passage was 151 days, or almost five months. She departed from Philadelphia approximately three months after she was first scheduled, and her passage was a month longer than predicted by her owners.[16]

Departure delay was only one of many frustrations for persons booking passage in California-bound sailing vessels. The overall length of the voyage in number of days was another significant frustration. Those who wrote about the topic in their journals indicated that weather delays caused a considerable amount of frustration. They feared that all the gold would be removed from California before they arrived. On the other hand, a couple of days of favorable fresh winds created an instantaneous degree of optimism among the passengers. An analysis of the vessels sailing from New York during the latter portion of each month in 1849 and the length of time they took to get to California should give some indication of the potential for frustration caused by delays.[17]

The ships *Pacific, South Carolina,* and *Tahmaroo;* the barks *Axim, Eliza, Hersilia, Mazeppa, Phillip Hone,* and *Victory;* the brigs *Mary Stuart* and *George Emery;* and the schooners *Decatur, Roe,* and *William Ivy* sailed between January 22 and 29. The shortest passage, 154 days, was made by the schooner *Roe,* while the longest, 230 days, was made by the bark *Mazeppa.* Between February 16 and 25 the ships *Henry Lee* and *Sara Eliza;* the barks *Connecticut, Eliza Ann, J. A. Jesurun, Nautilus,* and *St. Marys;* the brig *Brothers;* and the schooners *Gen. Morgan, Jacob M. Ryerson,* and *Mary W.* sailed for San Francisco. The 153-day passage of the schooner *Jacob Ryerson* was the shortest, whereas the 325-day passage of the bark *Eliza Ann* was the longest. Only the ship *Flavius,* the barks *Canton* and *Rising Star,* and the schooner *Linda* sailed between March 23 and 30. The 165-day passage of the *Rising Star* was the fastest, whereas the 188-day passage of the bark *Canton* was the longest. During April 17–30 only the barks *Clyde* and *Magdala* and the schooner *Penelope* sailed, and the 199-day passage of the *Clyde* was the shortest, while the 239-day passage of the *Penelope* was the longest.

There was a slight increase in sailings between May 14 and 29, but there were problems with some of those vessels. Sailings included the ships *Angelique* and *Robert Fulton,* the bark *Alice Tarleton,* the brig *Casco,* and the schooner *Smyrna.* The 168-day passage of the *Smyrna* was the quickest, whereas the 235-day passage of the bark *Alice Tarleton* was the longest. The *Alice Tarleton* sailed a month after she was first scheduled to sail, so her passengers must have been doubly frustrated. The ship *Robert Fulton* was wrecked en route, and the brig *Casco* had no arrival date. Her fate is uncertain. During the period June 22–28 only the ships *Arkansas, Far West, Probus,* and *Tonquin* sailed from New York. The 134-day passage of the *Tonquin* was the quickest, and the 178-day passage of the *Arkansas* was the longest. Between July 21 and 27 the ships *Thomas Perkins, Queen Victoria,* and *Unica* and the barks *Adelaide* and *Charter Oak* departed. *Thomas Perkins* made the passage in 124 days, while the *Unica* took 183 days. During August 17–30 only the ships *St. Lawrence, Sheffield,* and *William Gray* sailed from New York. The 185-day passage of the *Sheffield* was the shortest, whereas the 225-day one of the *William Gray* was the longest, but the latter vessel apparently was caught in a bad storm and put into Boston from which she sailed again on October 20.

There was another increase in departures between September 19 and 29, when the ships *Russell, St. Lawrence, Susan Drew, Tarquin,* and *William*

Sprague and the schooner *Elizabeth* departed. *William Sprague* made the passage in only 118 days, while *Russell* took 163. The ships *Grecian* and *Thomas Dickason,* the bark *Mersey,* and the schooner *Fawaway* sailed between October 13 and 31. The *Grecian* made the shortest passage of 137 days, while the *Fawaway* made the longest one of 230 days. There was a large increase in sailings in November, when the ships *Hampden, Manchester, Martha, Rowena, St. Mary,* and *Senator;* the bark *Gardiner;* the brigs *Detroit, Emma Prescott, Reindeer,* and *William E. Collis;* and the schooners *Isabella* and *John C. Demarest* sailed between the twenty-third and the thirtieth. The 131-day passage of the ship *Senator* was the quickest, while the 257-day one of the brig *Detroit* was the longest. The bark *Gardiner* was reported lost in the Falkland Islands. The ships *Burlington, Diadem, Natchez,* and *Russell Glover* and the schooners *Green Point* and *Primoquest* sailed between December 21 and 31. The 135-day passage of *Russell Glover* was the quickest, and the 283-day one of the *Primoquest* was the longest. Thus the fastest voyage overall was 118 days, while the longest was 325, making a difference of 207 days.

From these records it appears that September would have been the best month to sail quick passage between New York and San Francisco, but those wanting to get to California were probably more interested in departing early in the year than in a quick passage later in the year. Although there were some glowing reports in the newspapers about how much gold was to be found in California, there were others that asserted the supply was rather limited and only the earliest arrivals would have a chance to collect a fortune in the goldfields. The month of November had the second shortest passage of 131 days, but it also had the second longest of 257 days, making a spread of 126 days between the quickest and longest voyages that month. February had the longest spread of 172 days between the shortest and longest passages.

In normal times owners frequently scheduled departure of their vessels at a time that would enable them to miss the winter season at Cape Horn although even the summer season is cold at the dreaded cape. The gold rush era was certainly not a normal time, but concern over winter weather at Cape Horn may have been a factor in the small number of sailings from New York in June and July 1849, as such sailing times put vessels at the cape during the winter in the Southern Hemisphere. Rounding Cape Horn was rarely easy, yet some vessels bound for California rounded it in a few days, while others took weeks to accomplish the same feat. A great deal depended upon the storms that were encountered and how far off course they might have blown a given vessel.

Underway at Last

As the actual sailing day for many vessels approached, owners, members of joint stock companies, families, and individuals began to prepare for the eagerly anticipated departure. There appears to have been more celebrating for the earliest vessels to leave from any given port than for the later ones as the uniqueness of the departures began to wear off, but even the later departures were of great interest and concern to the individuals leaving and to their families and friends. Celebrations and festivities connected with the departure of a vessel for California varied considerably from the simple to the elaborate. They also varied from the widely publicized to the almost clandestine. In a number of instances there were special, sometimes long and elaborate, church services for the Argonauts departing for the virtually unknown land of California. Many passengers in those sailing ships left behind their thoughts and feelings as they departed from their homes, families, and friends with serious doubts about whether they would ever see each other again. One passenger expressed a sentiment that could have been recorded by a large percentage of those who sailed around Cape Horn to California. "Yes! At sea, on my first voyage, and methinks a pretty long one too for me, never having been more than one hundred miles from home before."[18] Many other passengers joined, certainly in spirit if not in voice, those on board the ship *Panama* out of New York as they gathered in the rigging and sang "Ho for California, That's the land for me, I'm bound for the Sacramento, With my washbowl on my knee," to the tune of "Oh! Susannah."[19] A great many Argonauts had serious second thoughts about their decisions to engage in their great adventure and recorded those thoughts, some immediately and some later, after they had recovered from that much-dreaded and much-discussed malady—seasickness.

Religion, religious activities, and superstitions frequently came into play in the departure of sailing vessels during much of history and especially in 1849. Little was known about California, but there were many rumors about that distant land and the dangers the pilgrims headed there would face. An unknown passenger in the ship *Friendship* addressed these issues in one of a series of undated episodes, all of which were written during the first two months of the voyage. The *Friendship* left Fairhaven, Massachusetts, on Sunday, September 2, 1849. One passenger noted that the "old superstition, in regard to lucky and unlucky days of sailing, seems, within a few years past, to have been rapidly passing away" and added that few were "willing to acknowledge any special dread of the consequences of getting a ship to sea on Friday or that a voyage is likely to be more fortunate if commenced on Sunday." Nevertheless "the frivolous excuses often made for detaining a ship which happens to be ready for sea by Thursday night, until after Friday has passed" seemed to indicate some lingering aspects of the superstition. Although it was once a common practice to sail on Sunday "if possible in preference to all others," increasing respect for the Sabbath led to an "understanding that this day is not a day" for sailing "unless . . . the very strongest reasons can be given for so doing." Contrary winds and foul weather had detained the *Friendship* for a week. When Sunday opened with fine weather and there were definite possibilities of being "detained another week or ten days if the opportunity was suffered to pass unimproved," it "was looked upon as providential and not to be neglected." He added, "it was easy to perceive by the joy depicted upon the countenances of all, and . . . it was considered peculiarly auspicious that Providence had pointed out this particular day." The passenger felt it was fine if all they did was "getting up the anchor and making sail on a Sunday" as long as "the remainder of the day could be made a day of rest as it usually is on board ships at sea when every thing is in sea trim." He left it up to the "consciences of those more immediately concerned" to decide if the "ship was really got underweigh, as was alleged in obedience to the directions of Providence, or some less worthy motive was at the bottom of it."[20]

Activities associated with the departure of the ship *Sweden* from Boston on March 1, 1849, were among the most extensive and elaborate of any vessel that left the east coast that year. In a lengthy article about a worship service at the Seamen's Bethel on North Square for those about to depart in the *Sweden*, a Boston newspaper noted that it was "most gratifying" that "among all the excitement incident to the . . . departure of so many of our citizens and friends for the 'Gold Regions,' that there is so strong a desire . . . to gather themselves together and join in religious exercises." The program for the evening included organ music, hymns (one of which was an original composition of James L. L. F. Warren, one of the passengers in the *Sweden*), prayers, addresses by the Rev. E. T. Taylor and the Reverend Dr. Pierce of Brookline, presentation of bibles to the ship for use by the passengers, and presentation of a large white satin banner with gold fringe and trimmings by the Reverend Dr. Pierce to James L. L. F. Warren, who was the commander of a group of sixteen men who had signed an agreement to seek gold on a partnership basis with the owners of the vessel. The banner had the word "EXCELSIOR" on one side and "Ship Sweden, February, 1849" on the other. There were additional designs on both sides of the banner. In presenting the banner the Reverend Dr. Pierce urged Warren to keep it unfurled to "be your guardian and your guide in a strange country, and may it shelter you alike in storm and calm." In his response Warren addressed the meaning of each word and symbol on the banner and promised to carry it always in order "to win an undoubted title to *Excelsior!*" After the presentation of the banner, Henry Plympton, principal owner of the *Sweden* and uncle of her captain, Jesse G. Cotting, spoke about the purchase of the vessel and fitting her out for the voyage. The newspaper editor concluded that "The meeting was a most solemn one; here were husbands about to depart from their wives; parents to be separated from their children; brothers from their sisters; and friend from friend; and the sob and tear told that the heart was deeply tried." That the service "continued to a late hour" indicates it was a lengthy one.[21]

March 1, 1849, was "very mild," and "a great number of people were gathered on the wharf to witness" the departure of the ship *Sweden* from Boston at 2:00 P.M. Rev. E. T. Taylor boarded the vessel and gave the passengers "some wholesome advice which, considering the experience of the giver and the uncertain journey we had concluded to make, was listened to with much interest." He also offered a "good prayer for our Safety and that we might be wafted quickly and Safely onward to our destined Port." The Sagamores, a small company of men from Roxbury who went to California in the *Sweden,* "sang several pieces viz Sweet Home, Farewell, Good By, &c. &c." One passenger noted that the songs "took very well although (perhaps) they were not very appropriate." As the vessel cast off from the wharf, "The gentlemen cheered and the ladies waved their handkerchiefs." One passenger noted, "As the hour of parting drew nigh a close observer would notice that sadness deep and heartfelt seemed to oer'Shade each countenance," but another wrote, "We left under full sail in high glee." One passenger noted that there were "about 200" passengers; another noted that "the number of passengers was 180 mostly young men leaving their native homes to seek their fortunes in a distant country."[22]

On Sunday, February 11, 1849, the Reverend Samuel Roosevelt Johnson used the subject of California for his sermon at St. John's Church in Brooklyn. It was dedicated to the bark "*St. Mary,* and her Goodly Company, with Warm Wishes and Earnest Prayers for Their Welfare and Success." One of his sons was a passenger in the *St. Mary.* Reverend Johnson announced that the special offering for the day would go to "the extension of the Church in California" rather than to the missionary fund of the

New York diocese. He urged those going to California "to maintain ever their integrity as men, as citizens of our great Republic, as Christians, and as members of Christ's Church; to remember that pecuniary advantage though legitimately sought, is but a very secondary consideration; that principle and honor and duty stand infinitely before it;—that true gentle affection cherished in the heart of the one, and met by the heart of others, is worth more than all that can be purchased by 'treasuries of gold and silver'; that at the altar of our religion all should bow with reverence and submission, owing God and his Christ as Sovereign." Johnson also urged them "to make good temporal and spiritual arrangements of their affairs" to pay any debts they owed, to prepare wills, to pray regularly, to forgive the offenses of others, and to practice their religion in California as faithfully as they did at home. He also addressed the issue of who should not go to California. Among them he included those who already "possessed . . . great social comforts of every kind," those whose parents did not want them to go, those whose going would leave families without financial support, and those whose departure would cause great emotional suffering.[23]

As the bark *Suliote* of Belfast, Maine, and the schooner *Eudorus* of Frankfort, Maine, were preparing to sail for San Francisco in January 1849, a special worship service was arranged for the passengers at the Hammond Street Church in Bangor. Rev. Prof. George Shepard and the Reverend S. L. Caldwell of the Baptist Church were invited to speak. The Young Men's Bible Society donated bibles, and several Christian friends contributed religious books for the men to read during the voyage. A large crowd gathered at the church to participate in the service. About twenty of the passengers occupied several of the front pews of the church. The service began with the singing of a hymn by the church choir under the direction of Col. William H. Mills. This was followed by the singing of a psalm, reading from the scriptures, a prayer by the Reverend Mr. Herbert, and the singing of another psalm. The two ministers then preached their sermons, and Capt. Charles L. Wiggin, master of the schooner *Eudorus*, responded to the speeches of the two ministers.

Reverend Shepard used as his text Proverbs 16:6: "How much better is it to get wisdom than gold, and to get understanding rather than silver." He urged the men to be temperate, refrain from profaning God, refrain from gambling, and keep the Sabbath. He also implored them to take with them the principles and habits as well as the character of New England and suggested that they be kind, respectful, and courteous in all things. Reverend Caldwell presented bundles of bibles and religious books from the Young

Men's Bible Society and Christian friends before delivering his sermon. He suggested that the good books would help the men occupy their time while they were at sea and indicated that they would help "keep off the scurvy of the mind." He felt the men needed such religious literature in California, as they would be away from the influences of their New England homes and families. Caldwell noted that religion had made New England the best place in the world in which to live and that the bibles should be their personal lighthouses in the dangerous sea they were crossing and the tempestuous land to which they were going. Captain Wiggin then thanked both ministers for their words of wisdom and for the bibles and other books and promised that they would all peruse them and endeavor to profit from reading them. At the conclusion of the service everyone sang a hymn in which they asked God to guide the pilgrims in their journey to and through the barren land to which they were about to travel.[24]

Eventually all preparations for a voyage were completed, and the time for parting arrived. Passengers gathered all their belongings and baggage and boarded their vessel. As their vessel moved from the dock into the port and on to the open water, the passengers took longing looks at their families and the familiar landmarks of their homeland. It was then that the full impact hit them, and they really began to think about the potential consequences of what they were doing and what lay ahead. Many began to have second thoughts about the wisdom of their decision to seek their fortunes in the distant, unknown land of California.

Early in 1849 L. M. Schaeffer traveled to New York to seek passage in a vessel to San Francisco. He obtained a berth in the ship *Flavius,* which was towed from the wharf on March 24. He described his activities and thoughts and recorded his reactions to what was going on around him. He had breakfast with his younger brother but "had no disposition to eat" even though the "meal was inviting." Instead his mind was filled with the thought that he was "about to leave his happy home . . . to separate from a few highly regarded friends, and I dreaded the long time that must elapse ere we would meet again." As they approached the ship *Flavius,* they "saw crowds of men, women and children standing on the wharf—some were taking a last farewell, others were imparting excellent advice, which I thought was <u>listened to with one ear and rapidly passed out of the other,</u> and others again were mingling tears of love, grief and hope, for even in that hour of departure, they were anticipating the pleasure of a future meeting." Then they heard the cry "All Aboard," and everyone—passengers, relatives, and friends—rushed to board the ship. The band hired for the occasion played "Yankee Doodle," and all on board gazed "intently upon the vast Metropolitan city, as we receded from its piles of brick and stone." The steam tug towed them to the quarantine landing, where they awaited the arrival of their captain, I. Thatcher. As the tug departed with the relatives and friends, "cheer upon cheer was given and returned with a hearty will, hats and handkerchiefs were waved aloft. Good Bye and good bye was given and returned until the steamer passed out of sight." When Captain Thatcher arrived the next morning, the "'gold hunters' saluted him with cheers and sang in right good style Hail Columbia." Once the pilot left them, they felt they "were bound in earnest for California."[25]

Three passengers in the ship *Crescent*, which sailed from Salem, Massachusetts, with the Salem Mechanics Trading and Mining Association among its passengers on December 6, 1849, wrote quite different accounts of the departure. William Graves noted that they set sail after "taking a affectionate farewell of our friends and acquaintances and bidding adue to the land of our Bearth and dropping a Teer of Rememberence of the many pleasures" he had enjoyed at home, "perhaps never more to realise it was with Pain that I cast that long last lingering look upon the last outlines of that beloved shore." He also noted that since it was his "intention to keep a Journell of the voyage . . . I must commence." Charles Henry Harvey was much more excited when he wrote, "All was excitement this morning in getting ready to sail. We was all very much pleased. Fired the cannon, hollowed, and yelled, and could hardly hold ourselves." He added that they had three passengers with musical instruments who played tunes and "There was quite a crowd on the wharves to see us sail. At 11 oclock anchor was up. Sails began to be spread and we began to move swiftly away from land." William Berry Cross took a more businesslike approach when he noted that they departed after waiting for a fair wind and that on board were the steamboat *Excepter* and cargo, which included about 125,000 feet of lumber, boards, and timber; about 25,000 shingles, clapboard, and lathe board; 40,000 bricks; and provisions for twelve months. There was also a steamboat valued at $6,500, owned by Daniel R. Bowker and others that the Salem Mechanics Trading and Mining Association could sell if it were profitable to do so or they could use it to transport their goods up the Sacramento River or to haul freight for others and share the profits with the owners.[26]

George Denham's regular occupation was minister, but he went to California in the schooner *Rialto* to seek a fortune. Throughout his diary there is ample evidence that he missed his family and home. Long before they reached California, Denham was at odds with many of the other passengers, several of whom were whaling captains. Even his first entry gives a hint of what was to come, as he noted that they "cast off and set sail from Holmes Hole wharf at eleven o'clock today and the cheers of neighbors and tears of sadness of wives and children. But the hope of success gives comfort even in grief. . . . Got an opportunity to signal with a white handkerchief to my wife who was in the steamer crossing the sound on her way to her fathers to spend the time of my absence." He then added that before sunset they had lost sight of land "for a <u>long, long time</u>. Some sad faces & more sad hearts. Man was made a social being and few things on earth are dearer to any than <u>Home & Family</u>."[27]

Three passengers also described the departure of the ship *Magnolia* from New Bedford, Massachusetts, in early February 1849, two in original diaries and one in a work of fiction. The differences between the two types of accounts illustrate clearly the differences between the two modes of writing. William F. Reed noted that the steam tug *Telegraph* towed them from J. & J. Howland's Wharf at 8:30 A.M. "In fine style amid the cheers of hundreds who had collected . . . to witness our departure which cheers were returned by us heartily." He also reported that a passenger named Bates came running toward the wharf only to see the ship departing without him and that they exchanged cheers with the passengers in the bark *Pleiades* as the *Magnolia* passed her. S. Mortimer Collins noted that the weather was pleasant as they left amid the cheers of the hundreds of people on the wharf and that they enthusiastically cheered in return. He reported that four passengers were left behind but that they were all brought to the *Magnolia* by a pilot boat, which could reach them because the southerly wind drove them back within sight of the port. [George Payson's] fictional account was quite different. He wrote, "Early in 1849, the unwilling ship in which I had taken passage for California was dragged away from the wharf in the sooty hug of a remorseless steam tug, like a struggling, kicking schoolboy in the arms of a hated master. Such an event was not then so common as it has since become, and an immense crowd had assembled to witness our departure, with some such feelings as if we had been bound on a voyage of discovery to the moon, or, at the very least, in search of the Northwest Passage." According to Payson, the day was cold and gray rather than pleasant, and he added that "Everybody looked cross and out of sorts, as if he would like nothing so well as to get into a quarrel with everybody else."[28]

Some passengers described their departures succinctly, while others provided a considerable amount of detail. Two in the ship *Arkansas* illustrate this difference in style. Robert N. Ferrell noted simply that the steamboat *United States* towed them to sea shortly before noon and that they had "a Large Party of Ladys & gentlemen on board to bid their friends fair well. It was a very trying seen. I would give all I possess or ever will to have my family on Board. . . . We had singing and an address from 2 Rev. Devines." Benjamin H. Deane, on the other hand, described the activities in much more detail. He started his account with his breakfast and the arrival of passengers and friends by 9:00 A.M. Around 11:00 A.M. the steam tug arrived to tow them to sea. Deane noted that at 12:12 they "left the Pier amid the cheers of Passengers and lookers on who stood on the wharf. I chose to reserve my cheers until some future time." One passenger had been left behind. When Capt. Philip W. Shepeard saw him, he stopped the ship and waited for the passenger. Deane noted they passed the fort at 1:00 and that on the passage down they had two speeches from two ministers he did not know. Then it was "announced that the friends must leave the ship . . . and then the parting was in real earnest, some leaving friends never again expecting to meet, others expecting that in a year they would meet again." He concluded by noting that here was a large "quantity of cheering."[29]

Isaac W. Baker crammed a substantial amount of facts and feelings into his description of the departure of the bark *San Francisco* from Beverly, Massachusetts, in the summer of 1849.

> After a protracted "South Easter," and a week of foggy disagreeable weather the wind finally hauled in to the Westward in a squall of rain which proved to be the clearing up shower. This morning commences with clear beautiful weather, and a fine breeze from N. W. All the population of Beverly stirring and the streets alive with males & females, boys, girls, old & young, with ears distended and eyes "sticking out a foot," all wending their way down Cabot St. through "Ice Alley" as if for a wager towards "Foster & Lovetts" Wharf to see the departure of "us Californians." At 7 A.M. Loosed Foretopsail and hoisted all our Buntings, overhauled a range of chain & made preparations for a speedy departure. Eight o'clock. Pilot on board, wharves getting crowded. Cast off all shore fasts & hung the Barque by a stern hawser. Set topsail & main t'gallant sail. Half past Eight—cast off hawser & started exchanging cheers upon cheers with the broken hearted, weeping, unhappy shoresmen & women, who

vainly endeavoured to cheer <u>loudly</u> in reply, & followed us disconsolately along the beach. Wind hauling to Northd. Braced sharp up & shaved off the corner of Beverly Bar, then hove to & called roll. "<u>All hands on board</u>." Up helm & kept away & <u>Good bye Old Beverly. God bless your women at any rate</u>.[30]

Nelson Kingsley incorporated some new information not mentioned by any other person in his brief description of the departure of the bark *Anna Reynolds* from New Haven, Connecticut, in March 1849. He noted it was a pleasant morning and that the dock was "crowded to overflowing." They had a worship service on board featuring the hymn "Old Hundred," an address by the Reverend Mr. Floy, and a prayer by the Reverend Mr. Smith. The vessel was then "cleared and searched to prevent smuggling." The roll was called to make sure all members of the California & New Haven Joint Stock Company were on board. They then sang another song and were towed out of the harbor by the steam tug *New Haven*.[31]

Dudley Emmerson Jones also provided some unique information in his description of the Albany Company's February 23, 1849, departure from New York in the bark *Nautilus*. In addition to the usual roll call on vessels whose passengers were all or mostly members of a joint stock company, there was a moment of silence and the singing of a song composed for the occasion by William H. Carlow. Jones also noted that they loaded gunpowder on board that morning, as the law prohibited loading that commodity before a vessel was ready to sail. A few days after they sailed, the captain requested that they all bring their gunpowder on deck so that it could be stowed in a barrel or barrels at the stern of the vessel. Most of the passengers had between one and ten pounds, but one man had nearly two hundred pounds. This was in addition to the quantity taken by the company. The captain allowed each man to keep only one pound. As a result they threw overboard about 250 pounds of gunpowder.[32]

Members of the Connecticut Mining and Trading Company departed from New York in the schooner *General Morgan* shortly before 2:00 P.M. on February 22, 1849, "amid the hearty cheers of friends and spectators, which were answered from on board by our whole company, and by several salutes from our cannon." One member described it as "an intensely exciting and interesting occasion for us all" and noted that "every heart and pulse throbbed with the deepest emotions." They were called aft soon after leaving the wharf, and Captain Hanks gave them a "short but pithy speech on the nature of the voyage and the enterprise" in which they had embarked. He reminded them of the deprivations they would suffer during the voyage, urged them to "bear them patiently," and reminded them they must always obey orders of the officers of the vessel. The members then toasted the success of their venture with "three times three" cheers.[33]

Passengers in the bark *Gold Hunter* of Bangor, Maine, probably suffered through one of the most frustrating and longest-lasting departures. They were supposed to sail around October 3, but some government men who had booked passage in the vessel objected that there were too many passengers. They suggested that the number should be reduced from fifty to thirty, but the owners refused to reduce the numbers that much. The matter was appealed to an official at the customhouse who reduced the number to forty. At noon on Saturday, October 6, they were towed down the river "amid the cheers of our friends on shore, which was returned by our Company on board. At Hampton we were saluted by the discharge of a field piece which was returned by us on board by the discharge of all the fire arms on board." They came to anchor at Fort Point and remained there until Monday the eighth, when they approached Thomaston harbor and anchored again. On the ninth they got to sea, but a change of wind forced them back to Thomaston, from where they finally sailed on October 12.[34]

Passengers of the ship *Pacific* experienced departure activities different from any others that sailed from New York and quite possibly from any other port. The owners, Capt. Hall J. Tibbits and businessman Frederick Griffing, fitted the vessel out with first- and second-class cabins. They promised early ticket purchasers that they would sell only fifty tickets in the first-class cabin, where everything and every service for the comfort and well-being of the passengers was to be provided. When the passengers were permitted to bring their baggage and personal belongings on the ship a day or two before the scheduled departure, the first-cabin passengers learned that the owners had increased the number of passengers to seventy-two without increasing the size of the cabin. Several first-cabin passengers requested refunds of their passage money, as they considered the overpopulated area unsafe. They also considered the increase in the number of passengers a breach of contract. Because the owners refused to refund the passage money, those passengers filed suit against the owners and libeled the ship, which prevented its departure for several days of legal maneuvering. Early in the afternoon of January 22, 1849, the owners had the *Pacific* towed from the wharf by the steamboat *Telegraph* amid the cheers of the passengers who were on board and a crowd of people on the wharf. She was towed to a point beyond the quarantine, which one passenger reported was twenty-five miles from the city. While this was being done, the owners appeared at the court and gave security in each of the lawsuits shortly before the court closed for the day. This move prevented the plaintiffs from responding before the vessel sailed. The departure from the wharf was so sudden that several passengers did not arrive at the wharf before the vessel left. They and the owners were taken on board by the small steamboat *James Farlie* around midnight. Early on the morning of January 23, they put to sea "to avoid further proceedings at law by the much abused and disappointed passengers left behind."[35]

A passenger in the ship *America* hinted at some unsavory past among the passengers when he described their departure from New Bedford. He noted the usual cheers from shore and on board the vessel and added that they sailed up and down Buzzards Bay for two hours while they waited for the remaining passengers to arrive in the various craft that had been chartered for that purpose. He said they came "some from one place, and some from another just as best suited their purpose in avoidance of <u>Constables</u>, <u>Sheriffs, &c. &c. &c</u>." They then had a roll call during which "all answered to their names or at least, such as they bespoke their passage under." They then spoke their farewells and goodbyes, and the visitors and the pilot left the *America* for the pilot boat and departed amidst the "hurraing, shaking their hats, caps, handkerchiefs, canes, &c. &c."[36]

Isaac S. Halsey included hints of passengers departing without paying bills among his descriptions of more commonly discussed activities. He noted that nearly all of the company was on board the ship *Salem* in New York at their announced time of 7:00 A.M. on March 12, 1849. He added that the "Street was crowded with anxious Spectators and friends of those who were about to depart for California." Among those in the crowd were "men, women, Children, Husbands, Wives, Fathers, Mothers, Sons and Daughters, Uncles, Aunts, Cousins from first to forty second, besides numerous friends and acquaintances." They gathered in small groups for about an hour prior to the scheduled departure, and Halsey noted "these '<u>confabs</u>' were a Sort of Compound of Love, Courtship, Matramony, difference of opinion on various Subjects Such as would arise from unsettled accounts, board Bills, Washing Bills, broken promises, and a too free use of brandy, Gin, Wine, as well as whiskey." According to Halsey, even the president of the California Mutual Benefit Association, of which most passengers were members, "was not free from all these troubles, he being compelled to make a Jack of himself on the Start and mount the Shrouds, and hide himself in the Main Top to evade an Officer who made his appearance on the Wharf with a large unsettled Bill." Since the officer did not look up into the rigging, he "lost his man, and of course his Money." He concluded his account of the departure of the *Salem* by describing the heartrending final parting of the passengers from their families and friends: "Oh What an affecting Scene. Husbands parting with their wives. Parents with their Children, and friends with friends. A Scene Sufficient to melt the Stoutest heart and moisten the Eye, that never Shed a tear." He added that they "parted hardly dareing to hope of ever Meeting again on the earth." As the steamer got them underway, there was "loud cheering" that "continued so long as they could be heard to and from the ship." Some enjoyed the cheering "very Much," but it "deepened the Sorrow of others, and caused a Still greater flow of Tears." He chose "to remain Silent" on his own feelings although he did admit that he extended his "hand for a last Shake, and gave utterance to that last Good bye, with a palpatating Heart and a quivering Lip."[37]

The passengers in the bark *Norwich* of Philadelphia suffered through the pangs of departure twice. When they first sailed about April 23, 1849, one of the passengers, John Brannan, who appears to have been a captain prior to going as a passenger in the *Norwich,* noted that she was so heavily laden and her cargo so poorly loaded on deck that she was unseaworthy. The passengers held a meeting and decided to return to Philadelphia to remove part of the deck cargo rather than throw it overboard. They also appointed Brannan in charge of properly and safely stowing the cargo on deck. The passengers asked Brannan to take charge of all their affairs, but he declined to accept that responsibility. Captain Anthony took the *Norwich* back to sea on May 11.[38]

A great many of those who sailed away from their homes had second thoughts about their adventure, some almost immediately and others after several days or weeks or even a couple of months. Numbers of them recorded such thoughts in their journals. Experiencing seasickness, eating salt pork and salt beef for the first time, and missing the comforts and pleasantries of home were frequently occasions for passengers to describe doubts about seeking their fortunes in the new El Dorado. It is important to remember that each of these individuals was undoubtedly experiencing his first ocean voyage and probably his first extended period away from family and close friends. That alone would be cause for second thoughts about any adventure, but the unique situations in which these men, mostly in their early twenties, found themselves give increased cause for reconsidering the wisdom of their decision.

James H. Gager had serious second thoughts about his decision to venture to California as a passenger in the ship *Pacific*, which sailed from New York in late January 1849. After he had been at sea for about two weeks, he wrote, "Beyond all example is the monotonous sea, & the voyage only just begun. What fools people are for going to sea. Why cant they stay on land? There is room enough, & yet people will launch out upon the sea, expose themselves to storms, sea sickness, shipwreck, & pirates & Salt, Salt, Salt for breakfast, dinner & Tea." He had "eaten salt, breathed salt, drank salt until" he felt he was "a relation to Mrs. Lot." Gager then remarked, "How we long for things at sea which we care so little about ashore. If we only had some of this or that, how good it would taste." He longed "for soda water all day" and noted that if he could afford to go to sea again, he "would lay in Raisins, Almonds, oranges, lemons, figs, ginger bread, plum cake, sugar, nutmegs, cocoa, brandy peaches, cranberry sauce, mince pies, prunes, sugar plums, currant jelly, apple sauce, wine, brandy, lemon sugar, lemon syrup, segars, soda water, cherry bounce, crullers & every thing else of the nature." Gager vowed he "would <u>eschew</u> all salt meat, not <u>chew</u> it, save a very little once a day," and lamented there was little opportunity to "exercise at sea . . . to work off heavy food." After noting they had "fritters for desert," he remarked, "What small events do we think worthy of record at sea! even the dinner is worth a place in ones journal. But the fact is, there is so little occurs at Sea, that what does occur is of importance." On several other occasions Gager made comments about why people undertook the adventure on which he and the other passengers in the *Pacific* found themselves, and shortly before the end of the voyage he speculated that he thought "Not half a dozen"[39] would have done so if they had known what lay ahead. That seems a rather small number, considering that there were more than a hundred passengers in the ship.

Anderson Hollingsworth noted that he did not respond, as did most of his fellow passengers in the ship *Daniel Webster*, to the nine cheers given them by their friends as they left on board the steamer that had towed them to sea. Rather he "unconsciously" put his hands over his ears because "that cheer seemed to break all connection with this part of the world" and caused him to wonder "When shall I see it again." He reported that he "paced the deck till a late hour" and that his "thoughts were of home and may be more easily imagined than described."[40]

Henry H. Hyde Jr. was another passenger who had second thoughts on the first day out. He sailed from Boston in the ship *Lenore* on February 3,

1849. As he watched familiar places and landmarks recede into the distance, he began to think of the things he would miss such as "my New England Shore," his "family circle," and the "religious privileges" that were "like blessings" he was "leaving perhaps never to return." He noted that he could "imagine the good people going to their houses of worship." As he was thinking about these things, he realized that "the steady breezes are fast taking me from the view of everything but the broad deep and the sky above."[41]

George Denham recorded a feeling expressed by passengers in many other vessels when he was only four days out from Holmes Hole, Massachusetts, in the schooner *Rialto*. He wrote that many of the company were homesick and if they were back on Martha's Vineyard "with their present experience of the sea they would take a long look at their comfortable homes, wives and friends, with their fare and hard work, before they would decide to go by sea to California to seek their fortunes."[42] Ferdinand Cartwright Ewer also wrote on the fourth day out, but he recalled his thoughts of the first night at sea. He saw a bird fly toward them, and he fancied "it bore my heart 'home' to her. But alas I had left that heart and she who had it was mourning for the dear one departed." He could eat neither dinner nor supper and could not even enjoy the beautiful sunset and said "that first night was sad & long & tearful to me for I thot of all I had left behind."[43]

After he had been out from Philadelphia in the ship *Europe* for eight days, Enos Christman wrote that he could not describe his feelings and emotions of leaving his friends to go on such an expedition. He indicated that he had "left all that is near and dear" and turned his "face towards a strange land, expecting to be absent two or three years, hoping in that time to realize a fortune." His "greatest consolation and comfort" was that his friends would welcome him when he returned. He thought of his work as a printer at the *Village Record* in West Chester, Pennsylvania, and wished he were back there again. Nevertheless he would "proceed with a strong arm and an honest heart, with bright anticipation of joy and happiness in the future." Then he wondered why he was optimistic, as such "lofty castles" had often been leveled to earth.[44]

Ebenezer Sheppard, who sailed from New York in the ship *Morrison* in early February 1849, recorded the feelings of some fellow passengers as well as his own about two months into the voyage. He wrote first that "Charley Hifferd . . . is only one of many as Lockwood, Green, Bond and several others have bitterly regreted the undertaking—Joseph Castner,

John, and myself have many a time when thrown back upon the past by reflection for which sea life is admirably adopted wished ourselves back and enjoying the comforts of home." Sheppard's greatest concern seems to have been for the well-being of his elderly father whose age, "his many former troubles, his solitary situation though married, and his anxiety for me to remain at home constantly act on my mind." He added that if he had sufficient funds, he would be content to return home from Rio de Janeiro "if we ever reach there in preference to risking my life around Cape Horn or in an unknown foreign soil." Six days later he recorded, "Joseph Castner is sometimes halting between going on and returning and is rather famous for the hard epithets he bestows on himself and others for ever leaving home on such a vessel and cusses the sea in general. Sands says less but thinks to himself the more—I believe no one regrets the absence of his family more than he does." Three days later he reported that "Charley Hifferd is bemoaning the imprudence of this wild goose chase and says with the experience he now has gained $2000 would be no temptation to him for leaving his wife and child—If we ever get home I doubt not those married will love their wives better than heretofore." He added that one does "not usually duly appreciate his comforts while in the undisturbed enjoyment of them."[45]

An anonymous journalist in the ship *Pharsalia* of Boston recorded over a period of three weeks his questions about the advisability of his adventure to California. He first wrote about three weeks after sailing, "I can hardly realize where <u>I am</u>, where I am going or for what I am going." Every morning he rubbed his eyes and looked "around wondering if" he were "really awake or still dreaming" and could not "help feeling foolish when" he realized the truth of his situation. He acknowledged he was "going seventeen <u>thousand miles</u> to a Country" that neither he nor anyone else knew "hardly anything about, after <u>gold</u>, and what seems still more <u>foolish is that I expect to accumulate enough of it in a short time</u> (two or three years at most) to make me independant for life." After considering his "youth and former habits," he admitted this was "presumptous." Then he contended that a man who "(<u>risks his all</u> undertakes, and accomplishes one of the longest and most perilous voyages in the world, sacrifices <u>every</u> comfort and encounters <u>disease</u> in almost <u>every</u> form) he certainly deserves more than an ordinary recompence." Three weeks later he indicated that he was "in hopes that" when his friends see his journal "and <u>remember</u> that if in future I should (in an evil moment) (propose to take another voyage around Cape Horn with such a lot of passengers) that I am certainly <u>deranged</u> and ought

63

to have a strait waistcoat put on at once." A little more than two weeks later he indicated that the passengers are now saying "if" rather than "when" they get to California and added "That little word never sounded so unpleasantly as it does now." At the end of three months he noted that they were "three of the longest months I ever lived through and have the prospect . . . of being two months more on the salt water." He added that Neptune was certainly no friend of his and that "He is a rough old fellow and if he lets me get clear of him this time, I will sing praises of him on shore but will not trouble him soon again in person." He vowed that he would "Never! Never More . . . undertake a voyage of the same length as this one" and indicated that he thought that no "man ever made two voyages around Cape Horn as a passenger unless he was deranged."[46]

Amid the excitement of departing from Boston on January 11, 1849, in the bark *Oxford,* Cornelius Cooledge wrote that he had "never before experienced such peculiar feelings. I could laugh with pleasure, while with a tear I saw the waving of hands, and heard the cheering voice of some Father, Mother, Brother, Sister, or Friend to those who were perhaps for the last time bidding them farewell." It was a severely cold yet clear and pleasant day with bright sunshine, and they passed through much ice getting out of the harbor. As the scenes of Boston such as Bunker Hill, the many buildings including the statehouse, and "the busy and domestic smoke from the work shops . . . the whole speaking volumes for civilization" gradually disappeared from view, he began to wonder "Why should I not dread to turn from it?" Behind him were "the fruitful fields and the granite hills of the home" of his youth, the home of his heart, while ahead of him was "the barren ocean." This was the first time in his young life he was leaving home on a long journey. He had never been at sea "to be deprived of all the pleasures that a life among the hills and running steams of the country afford. It was all new and rather exciting." As they sailed farther from shore, they began to realize how cold they were. Then the sea became rough, and "nearly all began to grow sick." Then, "Before night most of the passengers might be seen leaning over the sides, imitating Jonah's whale." They all went to bed but were cold and sick. He awoke about midnight and "never felt much worse." Others were in the same condition, and he described it as "a more laughable scene I scarce ever beheld, as I saw by the dim lantern that rendered darkness visable, first one depositing the contents of his stomach into a bucket, or into the boots of some unlucky fellow, who had placed them in the way, while the others would break out in peals of laughter, but soon they would be in the same condition, and so it would go, each in his turn would have to be an object of merriment, but few escaped not one could help laughing however sick he might be. No one that was sick seemed to care for himself or any one else. This was my first experience in going to sea."[47] Cooledge and some of his fellow passengers continued to experience the symptoms of seasickness for most of the first month at sea. Later, after a stop in Rio de Janeiro, he and some of the other passengers experienced yet another bout with the disease although this one lasted only a couple of days.[48]

The condition in which Cooledge and his fellow passengers found themselves was a common one experienced by a large percentage of those who undertook to travel to California in a sailing vessel around Cape Horn. Few had ever been to sea, so it was to be expected that they would be seasick. It was also common for the forty-niners to be amused at some of the adversities of their fellow passengers. Probably it helped to pass the dull times for them to laugh at things other people might not find so amusing. Seasickness was a common and debilitating illness that one could only suffer through although many remedies were suggested and tried by those who suffered from the malady.

Multiple experiences with seasickness occurred frequently among passengers in sailing vessels bound for California. Two passengers in the ship *Pacific* recorded their experiences. James H. Gager referred to his sickness and that of fellow passengers throughout most of the first two weeks after they left New York and then noted similar problems after they departed Rio de Janeiro in early April. Charles Williams recorded similar circumstances in his journal. On January 26 he noted that his "slumber was disturbed" by "the cascading of different passengers who kept it up pretty regularly all night."[49]

Albert Lyman, a passenger in the schooner *General Morgan,* noted on their first day at sea that "so many seasick . . . makes it rather disagreeable for all," but then he added rather optimistically, "Never mind, better times coming." The next day he added, "This seasickness is surely one of the most disagreeable sensations that man can be afflicted with, rendering him indifferent to all that is passing around him." For the next couple of weeks he continued to note that two or three passengers were seasick. Then in mid April they put into Rio de Janeiro for fresh provisions. Shortly after departing from that port, they encountered a violent squall, causing "many of our company" to be "revisited with seasickness, myself among the number." The next day he noted that "Those who are not too seasick, amuse themselves by sitting around on deck, munching oranges and looking at each other."[50]

Warren Fletcher, one of thirteen people on board the bark *Elvira*, all of whom appear to have been officers or crewmen, appears to have been both seasick and homesick, a not uncommon problem. He became sick the day they sailed from Boston and remained in that condition for about a week. The second day he noted that he "thought of home all day and I wished myself there more than once." The next day he wrote that he had made up his "mind that it would be the last time I went to sea or round the Horn." A day later he "was very lonesome during the day" and "was very sorry" he had "ever thought of coming out here." The next day he "felt some better after getting out in the open air." He did not write anything more on this topic until he left Rio de Janeiro in early March, when he mentioned sea-sickness for three days.[51]

Elias P. Overton and other passengers in the bark *Keoka* of New York also experienced seasickness twice, but apparently only once was it first-hand. On their third day out, Overton wrote, "If we were not all so seasick it would be really laughable to see our vain attempts to keep our feet, crawling along slowly and holding on by the table and births, and at every lurch clinging with all our strength just like children learning to walk." Three days later he wrote that the high waves presented "a most magnificent scene to those [who] love the wild raging oceans, but alas our stomachs are so sympathetic, that spite of all we can do, they heave as well as the sea." While they were in port in Valparaiso in July, they took on board a number of Chilean passengers. The day after they sailed, Overton wrote, "our Chillians soon got sick, and we have been amusing ourselves laughing at their long-drawn phizzes; they think us very heartless, but sea-sickness is a malady which excites very little sympathy."[52]

S. Mortimer Collins, one of 127 passengers in the ship *Magnolia*, which sailed from New Bedford in late January 1849, and some of his fellow Argonauts suffered three epidemics of seasickness. He also experienced some homesickness. His first experience with seasickness is not mentioned until they had been at sea about two weeks. At that time he noted that he had never seen "anything so well calculated to destroy all of one's good feelings" and lamented, "Oh! What would I have given to have been on land, at home, where I could have a mother's care a short time." He went on to explain that he had been "very sick and vomiting most of the day" and asked the steward for some porridge, which he felt would improve his situation. The steward promised to bring him some but went to bed instead. Collins then "thought of home" but added he would not "record more of these events for it makes me homesick." This bout of seasickness lasted about a week. When they sailed out of Rio de Janeiro in mid April, Collins had his second experience with seasickness. A day out of port they encountered a storm of near-hurricane strength, and Collins said he "was very sea-sick the whole time; vomited six times during the afternoon." Three days later he was still ill, but he noted he had received better care during this bout than he had during his first one. He expressed particular concern for "the ladies" among the passengers who were seasick. For two days after they left Talcahuano, Chile, in June, Collins experienced a third bout of seasickness. This lasted at least two days on the second of which he noted that "while I write I can hardly keep from vomiting."[53]

Most California-bound passengers seem to have suffered only one epidemic of seasickness. At least that is all they wrote about in their journals. Some of their accounts, however, were graphic; some were humorous, and others were a combination of the two. Still others were simply straightforward descriptions of their experiences. The one hundred members of the New York Mining Company sailed from New York on February 2, 1849, and experienced rough weather for several days, greatly aggravating the seasickness of the passengers and causing extreme wetness throughout the vessel. Near the end of the first week, Griffith Meredith wrote that the wind blew "with renewed violence," causing the sea to be extremely rough and many of the members to be "taken again with that disagreeable and dreaded sea sickness. A great many with the 'Blas' wishing they had never saw the Barque *Strafford*." He speculated that "shares could be bought this morning very cheap" and if members could get back to New York some would choose to go to California via the isthmus, while others would not leave their homes again. About a week later Meredith wrote that "Evry member sick and all was talking about it. Some very much frightened about it." He then wished the weather would clear so they "could clear up our cabin and sweeten it for it has got to be quite filthy." He concluded by noting that "those that are well have got tired of waiting on the sick and arranging things for them and cleaning the cabin."[54]

J. T. Woodbury also mentioned the disarray caused by seasickness and discussed the things going on around those who were ill on their second day at sea. He noted that "A large number are seasick & even the Capt. has strong symptoms of said disease." The area in which they lived looked "as though a schoolmarm had not been here for half a century—some are in their berths, some setting on their chests, with a bucket by their side, some are on deck leaning over the rail as though they were very sorry they have left their friends & meditate most melancholy." He indicated he had some medication with him but was sure that "a little epicac would be no relief." As he was writing, "a fiddle, tamborin, triangle & something else" were "playing marches, dances &c about 8 feet from my left hand & within 3 feet of my right is a man with a bucket by his side. Truly we have variety."[55]

In describing his experiences in the ship *Flavius* out of New York, L. M. Schaeffer noted that although only a few passengers experienced seasickness firsthand, one could get a good idea of the "awful sufferings" they experienced if one could imagine "a fellow being utterly wretched, perfectly indifferent as to whether the ship kept straight on her course or sank beneath the waters."[56] A passenger in the ship *America* from New Bedford noted that many of the passengers were lying on the decks "Rendering up their accounts" to King Neptune and added that since "the sea is to be their mistress for some time to come, they are willing to give unto the sea that which their mistress requires of them—the contents of their stomachs."[57] A passenger in the bark *Belgrade* of Cherryfield, Maine, referred to seasickness sufferers emptying their stomachs when he noted that the vessel was bounding "away over the high tumbling billows" and that the "grandeur of the scene now began to excite in some of our stomachs peculiar emotions. . . . A sympathy for the hungry tribes of the ocean, prompted us to do what we were most inclined to do, which was to feed them from our intensely nauseated stomachs."[58] One Argonaut commented that while seasickness was "very disagreeable," it was "said to be highly conducive to health as it cleans the stomach of all bilious matter."[59] Another described seasickness as "Father Neptune administering another dose of medicine to his refractory children, much to the distress of their stomachs."[60]

A few individuals wrote of things that enabled them to overcome their seasickness. George Dornin wrote that "good old Captain Coffin" advised him to drink "copiously" of "some warm water from the ocean." This "not only aggravated the retching, but hastened the reaction and cure."[61] A passenger in the ship *Daniel Webster,* who had suffered the agonies of seasickness for six weeks, wrote that one of his companions brought him a "piece of hard bread and a pickle" and as soon as his lips touched the pickle he could feel it in his fingers. At that point he began to regain his appetite.[62] John Taylor noted that "Salt beef is the best regulator of the stomach I find of any thing I have tried during my experience with sea-sickness. After an inward scouring, a few slices of it seems to relish better than any thing else & will remain when lighter food would be immediately thrown off." He noted he "felt much relieved . . . after forcing down as much beef" as he could for supper.[63] In a long discussion of seasickness, Raymond Cazallia Davis mentioned several possible cures. The first was a "Hydropathic" cure. It was a cold-water bath in which a sufferer was hung by his feet from the yardarm and dropped head first into the sea. One immersion was usually "held to be sufficient for a cure . . . but sometimes . . . a patient [was] dropped a second time." He then noted that it was "a cruel joke, and not often perpetrated." Another was a remedy for constipation, which was often associated with seasickness. It consisted of "half a pint of slush (grease), a pint of salt water, and a pint of molasses" all boiled "thoroughly together." The patient drank as much as he possibly could.[64]

In writing his autobiography George Goodwin included an account of his 1849 voyage from Boston to California in the ship *Sweden*. Early in the account he discussed both his second thoughts about the adventure and his experiences with seasickness. His words provide a fitting conclusion to these topics.

> Who has been at sea and can not recall his first few days experience? The Gradual waking of the heart to its unhappiness, the visions of pleasure and the schemes of profit, all so bright but an hour ago, have vanished now. Memory has usurped the place of imagination, and thoughts of loved ones and scenes all too dear separated from, perhaps forever, awaken all the tenderness of regret and flood the senses with exquisite anguish.
>
> Well do I remember as the land faded from the view how plainly I could see with my heart's eyes nestling far away among the New England hills, my home; the scenes of my youth, my parents and the loved ones I had parted from. Could I have gone back to them then! But pride, so often a stumbling block to duty and common sense—so often our better angel to hold firm our failing purpose—had prevented me, had I been able to return. But the sea with its restlessness furnishes an antidote for the heart-disease, and, though as bad as the malady ministered to, effectually engages consciousness of a present as well as a Past. I well remember my first dose of it. I can afford to laugh over it now, though at the time, I assure you, it was no laughing matter. It was on the occasion of my first debut at the supper table. I had with a dignified and reasonably cheerful mien, despite my unhappiness and a certain qualmishness not clearly definable,

taken my seat at the table when Oh, my! Sick! What a pauper is the English language. How I made my escape I never knew, and I do not recollect whether the fact was consoling at all or not, that I was not the only eccentric and energetic person who proceeded in eager haste to hold profound and mighty discourse with the mysterious sea from over the ship's side. Suffice it to say that it induced me to throw up my visions of blue clay hills and their melancholy concomitants, besides inducing a violent effort to resign everything else at my command from teeth to boots included.[65]

Many passengers continued to have second thoughts about their decisions to seek their fortunes in California and to get there by sailing around Cape Horn. Once they were over their first experience with seasickness, thoughts of that malady rarely entered their minds again. Therefore they were ready for the remainder of their great adventure. First they were ready to partake of real food. While some obviously were pleased with what they had to eat, others were greatly disappointed. Some of the disappointed ones took action appropriate to their degree of dissatisfaction. Few passengers were really prepared for the many hours of nothing to do, but most found ways to amuse and entertain themselves. In many instances they attempted to live as much like they did at home as they could, except that they did not have the regular jobs or duties that they faced at home or their families or friends to comfort them. Lots of them took tools of their trade and occasionally made use of them to make things. In many vessels they had regular worship services on Sunday, at least during the early part of the voyage. They also observed most national and some state holidays or other special days in appropriate fashion. All faced problems such as weather, sickness, conflicts with the captain and other officers, and disagreements among themselves. Members of companies had meetings to attend and frequently had a variety of duties to perform, especially as they approached their destination, but those who went as independent gold seekers were normally exempt from such obligations and duties. There were frequent disputes among members of joint stock companies, virtually all of which disbanded before they arrived in California or shortly thereafter.

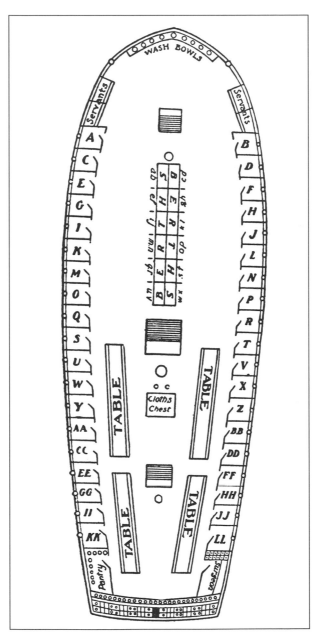

"Plan of the berth deck of the ship *Alhambra*." This is quite possibly the only surviving actual drawing of how the staterooms and berths along with the tables for eating and other accommodations were arranged in a sailing vessel bound to California in 1849. From Coffin, *A Pioneer Voyage*, facing p. 10.

"The place where you take 'Comfort!" This drawing from the journal of Isaac W. Baker in the bark San Francisco in 1849 illustrates quite well the crowded conditions under which both passengers and sailors lived on board California-bound sailing vessels. Courtesy of the Bancroft Library, University of California, Berkeley

"Passengers Tracking the Ship's Progress at Night." Many passengers took great interest in checking the track chart that was updated daily during the voyage. This scene is probably in the dining area either below deck or in a house or cabin on deck on board a California-bound sailing vessel in 1849. Only on rare occasions were there as many women and children on board such vessels as are shown here. From *California; Its Past History; Its Present Position; Its Future Prospects*, 1850, opposite page 80. Courtesy of the Beinecke Library, Yale University.

"Emigrants on Deck at mid-day." This deck scene is indicative of the crowded conditions on board California-bound vessels in 1849. Here again there are more women and children than were typically found in sailing vessels bound to California in 1849. From *California; Its Past History; Its Present Position; Its Future Prospects*, 1850, opposite page 136. Courtesy of the Beinecke Library, Yale University.

FOR SAN FRANCISCO,

CALIFORNIA!
DIRECT!!

The Elegant, Coppered, & Copper-fastened, A 1
PACKET
SHIP SWEDEN
CAPT. J. G. COTTING,

Will sail for the above Port with all possible dispatch, and can accommodate a limited number of First and Second Cabin Passengers. Gentlemen who are about proceeding to CALIFORNIA, will please call and see the accommodations.

☞ **Dr. ELLIOT,** an experienced Physician and Surgeon, goes out in the Ship, whose services will be devoted to all on board, free of charge to passengers.

The Ship is **656** tons, and her accommodations will not be surpassed, probably, by any other vessel in this or any other port in the country.

The Ship SWEDEN has lately made a remarkable voyage to California, thence completing her tour Round the World, returning to Boston, via Manilla, performing the whole voyage, in 429 days, of which 354 days were at sea, including the stoppage at five ports in the circuit, to the most entire satisfaction of all parties.

Captain COTTING is a most experienced commander, both as a nautical man, and a gentleman of kind feelings and attentions, and has made a number of India voyages. Finally, a more desirable conveyance round Cape Horn cannot be found, than that now presented in the Ship SWEDEN, lying at the end, (north side,) of INDIA WHARF.

FOR FREIGHT OR PASSAGE, APPLY TO
JOHN R. DOW & CO.,
130, STATE STREET, BOSTON.

☞ *No Ardent Spirits to be taken as Freight.*

Advertising poster for the ship *Sweden*. Posters such as this were probably quite common in 1849, but very few seem to have been preserved. It is worth noting that in spite of the announcement prohibiting ardent spirits on board as freight, some passengers did take quantities of alcohol on board. Courtesy of the Bancroft Library, University of California, Berkeley.

"The California Company going from the town of York in 1849." Local folk artist Lewis Miller prepared this sketch of the fourteen members of the California Company of York, Pennsylvania, who sailed from Baltimore to San Francisco in the ship *Andalusia* in 1849. This drawing includes many of the items Argonauts typically took with them on their adventures. Members of the company were R. C. Woodward, Dr. Henry Smyser, Henry Hantz, Alexander Klinefelter, George Rupp, Jacob Furney, Alexander Wentz, Alexander Stair, George Lanmaster, Joseph McAllier, John Miller, Ham. Hartman, McFurson Barnitz, and George B. Schmitt. Courtesy of The Historical Society of York County, Pennsylvania.

"Acknowledging a draft on Father Neptune." This graphic illustration of the common malady suffered by a great many passengers is from the journal of Isaac W. Baker on board the bark *San Francisco* in 1849. Courtesy of the Bancroft Library, University of California, Berkeley.

"Lady passengers being somewhat troubled with sea-sickness." Passengers frequently stretched their imaginations to take their minds off problems. This illustration from the journal of Isaac W. Baker on board the bark *San Francisco* in 1849 is an excellent example of using imagination to overcome seasickness. Courtesy of the Bancroft Library, University of California, Berkeley.

3

Food and Drink

Food—the quantity and quality and the way it was prepared and served—was a major factor in the satisfaction or dissatisfaction of passengers on board vessels sailing around Cape Horn to San Francisco in 1849. Early in the voyage of the schooner *Rialto,* George Denham noted that their cook was sick again and that the men had to cook for themselves. He added that this caused "some dissatisfaction as we expected to have had our food in good condition. This is an important part of our comfort and a part we can illy afford to spare." Then he turned philosophical and wrote that the idea had struck him that they were "not entirely unlike Irish Emigrants going to a country we know but little of in search of easy fortunes. We talk much of California and its gold, and set our expeditions high. It will be well for us if we are not disappointed in some way we now do not think of."[1]

Based upon passengers' journals, owners of vessels, shipping agents, and officers of joint stock companies responsible for purchasing provisions for the company, the passengers were frequently promised more and better food and a greater variety of food than was served. They were also promised better-prepared food served in a better manner than usually happened. In some instances a regular weekly bill of fare was promised. Sometimes that promise was fulfilled; other times it was not. In other instances no such promise was made, but the regularity with which the same foods were prepared made possible the construction of a weekly bill of fare. Passengers could often tell what day of the week it was by what food was served.

Variety, especially in the form of fresh foods, could have been reasonably expected only for a short time after the initial departure and the departure from any ports at which they stopped before arriving in San Francisco. It is likely that even at their homes the Argonauts did not have a great variety of fresh fruits and vegetables out of season and certainly did

71

not have the types of canned and frozen foods available today,[2] but what they were served at home was certainly better prepared and was served with more concern by wives and mothers than was done by the sometimes unskilled and uncaring cooks and stewards in some of the 1849 gold rush vessels. Virtually all the Argonauts were employed in some profession or skill or owned their own business before deciding to undertake this great adventure. Thus they were likely accustomed to eating good food prepared well.

Most vessels bound for California during the gold rush stopped at least once, often twice, to get fresh water and provisions. The number of stops sometimes resulted in a brief improvement in the quantity, quality, and variety of food, but they generally had no affect upon the way it was pre-pared and served. During those stops many passengers purchased their own fruits and occasionally other luxuries to supplement what was pur-chased for the vessel or the company. The quantities of such food that some of the passengers ate immediately after departing sometimes caused intestinal problems, as they had gone so long without fresh fruits.

The frequency of tickets and published bills of fare in the sailing ships going to California in 1849 is uncertain, but it is known that tickets were issued for the ships *Capitol* and *Crescent* and for the bark *Orion*, and copies still exist for the *Capitol* and the *Orion*.[3] A bill of fare is provided on the back of the *Orion* ticket. The ticket was for the lower cabin and cost $150 and included the privilege of remaining on board the vessel for twenty days after they arrived in San Francisco. It promised a daily ration of fourteen ounces of bread, two ounces of sugar, one ounce of coffee or cocoa, and one-fourth ounce of tea to each passenger. In addition provi-sions for each person on Sunday and Thursday consisted of one pound of beef, one-half pound of flour, and one-fourth pound of raisins or dried fruit; Monday, one pound of pork and one-half pound of beans; Tuesday, one pound of beef, two ounces of cheese, two ounces of butter, and one-fourth pound of rice; Wednesday and Saturday, one pound of pork, one-half pound of beans, and one-fourth pound of pickles or cranberries; and Friday, the same as Tuesday plus a half pint of molasses.

Three passengers in the bark *Belvidera* reported their bill of fare. J. Haskell Stearns reported that there was a considerable amount of grum-bling about the food and the crowded conditions during the first few days out from New York. Capt. Samuel Barney divided the passengers into eight messes, each of which had to choose its own steward. At that time he prepared a bill of fare that was to be in effect for the entire voyage.

Stearns noted that they were to have sea biscuit each day. The other items were Sunday, pork and duff; Monday, beef and the weekly allotment of butter; Tuesday, pork and beans; Wednesday, beef and rice; Thursday, pork and beans; Friday, beef and rice; and Saturday, beef. He added that occasionally they had codfish or mackerel as a treat. On March 29 he reported that they were to have duff on Thursday as well as Sunday. Late in March, John T. Randle indicated that they had only one meal a day, but he also wrote that they ate breakfast at 7:30, dinner at 3:00 and tea and crackers at 7:00. Apparently he did not consider what they ate at breakfast and tea to be meals. He also recorded a slightly different bill of fare for their dinners: Sunday, beef, crackers, and duff; Monday, codfish and beef; Tuesday, beef, johnny cake, rice, and molasses; Wednesday, beef and pork and beans; Thursday, beef and duff; Friday, mackerel and rice; and Saturday, beef and pork and beans. He added that they could have all the molasses and sugar they wanted and that they also had mustard, pepper sauce, sauerkraut, pickles, dried apples, and raisins. In mid April, Stearns reported that they had breakfast about 8:00 and dinner about 2:00 and that they had sea biscuit, butter, and tea about 7:00. He modified the bill of fare by dropping the fish on Monday and Friday and substituting beef, and indicating that Sunday and Thursday, Tuesday and Friday, and Wednesday and Saturday menus were identical. Isaac Shepard Jr. reported that their "repast was simple indeed consisting of but one thing at a meal which was either lobscouse, dunder-funk, duff, boiled rice, or baked beans." He also indicated that the captain had removed their large table, divided them into messes of ten each, and told them to eat wherever they could find a place. Each mess had a steward who picked the food up at the galley and divided it into equal portions.[4] Having the same menu each week for five to eight months would be bad, but to have some of the meals twice each week seems doubly bad.

Things were handled a bit differently on board the ship *Crescent*, which sailed from Boston on December 6, 1849. She was owned by the sixty-one members of the Salem Mechanics Trading and Mining Association, so it was the company rather than the captain who established the bill of fare. The company adopted a bill of fare at its semiannual business meeting. There is no record that they had one before this. They listed three meals for each day. Monday—hasty pudding for breakfast; baked beans and rice pudding with sauce for dinner; and gingerbread, cheese, and cranberry sauce for supper. Tuesday—fried ham and hard bread for breakfast; "sago" or "sego" and duff pudding for dinner; and fried cranberry pies and salt fish for supper. Wednesday—fried pork and hard bread for breakfast; baked beans and rice for dinner; and doughnuts, cheese, and sauce for supper. Thursday—soft bread, butter, and apple sauce for breakfast; baked beans, rice, and sauce for dinner; and doughnuts, cheese, and sauce for supper. Friday—hasty pudding and hard bread for breakfast; boiled ham and duff pudding for dinner; and Indian Cakes, butter and cranberry sauce for supper. Saturday—rice pudding and sour sauce for breakfast; baked beans and soft bread for dinner; and pancakes and hard bread for supper. Sunday—fried salt pork and hard bread for breakfast; boiled beef and pork for dinner; and fried cranberry pies, hard bread, and fish for supper. They could also have beef and pork at each meal if they wished and received pickles for dinner each Monday, Thursday, and Saturday.[5]

The portion of the voyage between New York and Rio de Janeiro for the ship *Pacific* was one of the most tempestuous made in 1849. There seems to have been continual conflict between Capt. Hall J. Tibbits and the sixty-four passengers in the first cabin. The quality and quantity of the food and how it was prepared and served were significant factors in this conflict. That few of these men had ever been to sea and Captain Tibbits reportedly had little or no experience in carrying passengers were contributing factors, as neither knew what to expect or how to act. The first-cabin passengers held at least one "indignation meeting" and drafted a petition to the captain. One of the major complaints was that they received only two meals per day, which were poorly prepared. Thus they received less than sailors were guaranteed by federal regulations. As a result, on February 16 Captain Tibbits posted this bill of fare for Monday through Saturday for what apparently is only dinner. Monday—beef and pudding; Tuesday— pork, beans, and apples; Wednesday—beef and pudding; Thursday—ham and rice; Friday, pork and bread; Saturday—beef, pork, and apples. Charles Williams noted sarcastically that it was "certainly enough to make landsmen mouths water." There is evidence in journals of passengers that this bill of fare was not always followed.[6]

Passengers in the ship *Sweden* also held an indignation meeting early in the voyage and complained to Capt. Jessie G. Cotting about the food they were served. One passenger noted during the first week, "we lived like Hogs, had Horse Beef, Hard bread, and Pots of swill, made of burnt Peas and Beans by the taste. That was for Breakfast. Dinner, Horse Beef, Pork, by sticking a fork into it would almost make It squeel, and hard Bread. Tea, Hard Bread, Beef, and Pots of Medicines, made of dried Cabbage leaves and Rosin by the taste. That is what they call Tea." In the second week the passengers held a meeting and sent a delegation to Captain Cotting, who said he was not aware of how badly they were being treated and promised to provide better food as long as it was available. Benjamin Bailey then listed their "hebdomadal" menu. Monday: breakfast—mush, beef, hard bread, and coffee; dinner—beef, pork, turnips, and hard bread; tea—beef, hard bread, and tea. Tuesday: breakfast—boiled rice, beef, bread, and coffee; dinner—beef, pork, and bread; tea—hard bread and tea. Wednesday: breakfast—mush and molasses; dinner—beef, pork, and rice; tea—apple sauce and bread. Thursday: breakfast—rice; dinner—duff; tea—hard bread and tea. Friday: breakfast—ham; dinner—salt fish and bread; tea—doughnuts and bread. Saturday: breakfast—mush; dinner—mackerel; tea—hard bread. Sunday: breakfast—beef, pork, and bread; dinner—preserved meats; tea—gingerbread. He noted that the duff was made without any seasoning, "not even salt, and to the taste, with a very few pieces of dried apples, and sometimes Raisons." If you cut it you "Might get 3 Raisons or 2 small pieces of apple for your part." Their mush was corn meal and water "boiled thick with molasses for sauce" and cost pennies per gallon. The beef and pork were "so tough and salty that more than half the time we cant eat it." Doughnuts were "made with out any spice and when fried are so hard and tough they are not much of a relish." Gingerbread was made of water and flour with "very little Molasses without any spice" except maybe cassia.[7]

John Taylor recorded the weekly bill of fare on board the ship *Orpheus* carrying 198 passengers from New York and indicated that they were provided so bountifully that his mess ate hardly a fourth of the one pound of meat per man they received each day. They also had tea and coffee sweetened with sugar every day. Many others had no sweetener, and some had only molasses. Taylor also noted that "most of us have our own stores," which they resorted to "when feeling dainty & particular."[8] Maria M. Child wrote her sister from the brig *Colorado* to tell her what their meals were each week. After listing the regular foods, she indicated that butter, cheese, and pickles were always on the table and that they had fresh pork, puddings, pies, and cakes "in abundance." Duff was not listed anywhere. She also informed her sister that she subsisted on "vegetables, bread, &c &c abstaining from tea, coffee, seldom eating meat or butter."[9] Josiah Griswold described a bill of fare for the bark *Salem* from New York in which everything was repeated twice each week. Twice a week breakfast was leftovers from previous days. He hoped that this routine would end when the voyage terminated and noted, "with living like this I am becoming but a shadow of my former self."[10] J. T. Woodbury recorded the weekly rotation of meals in the ship *Argonaut* and added that they got as much cheese as they wanted and had "plenty of Hard Bread with every meal" as well as pickles, sugar, molasses, pepper and mustard, "but not enough." He also indicated that "by some work & extra expense, we get some addition, such as 'lob'scouse,' (Hash,) 'Soft Tack,' (Common Flour Bread, &c.)."[11] An unidentified passenger in the brig *Forest* out of Boston recorded a fairly typical bill of fare and noted that he would not "find falt with the fair if the cabbin could be made cumfortable."[12]

Although landlubbers may have had the same meals prepared at home with some regularity in the mid nineteenth century, likely none of the passengers in these California-bound vessels had experienced such monotony in their menus and such poor cooking. Few passengers would have been familiar with a steady diet of salt-cured meat, and likely none would have had dishes such as duff or lobscouse before they put to sea. Some who lived in seaports may have heard of such foods if they knew any sailors. Fortunately for some passengers, there was more variety than appears in these weekly bills of fare. A few vessels carried livestock to provide fresh meat instead of always having salt beef and pork. Stops at places such as Rio de Janeiro, St. Catherines Island, Talcahuano, Lima, and the islands of Juan Fernandez Island (where the passengers all wanted to see Robinson Crusoe's cave) enabled the ship to obtain fresh meat, additional livestock, and a variety of fruits and vegetables. Such stops also allowed individual passengers to purchase their own supplies of fruits. In addition the sea sometimes provided bounties such as porpoises, sharks, fish, and birds.

Based upon what the passengers recorded during their voyages, pork was certainly the most frequently consumed fresh meat. Anne (Willson) Booth wrote a little over two months after the ship *Andalusia* sailed from Baltimore that they killed a pig every Saturday. Their first meal from it was "mock turtle soup, made of the head," which was "highly seasoned with wine and spices, and is really very nice." Next they had steaks and liver fried for breakfast. They later had roast, which their cook could prepare well.[13] Those sailing in the bark *San Francisco* seem also to have killed pigs regularly on Sundays during the early portion of their voyage and to have had mock turtle soup and fried pork for breakfast. They also had sea pie. On December 16, 1849, four months into the voyage, Isaac W. Baker lamented, "Didn't kill a pig—no sea pie—no Roast pork—no turtle soup today; yesterday it was toungs & sounds, and tomorrow salt beef, proba-

76

bly.[14] Passengers in the bark *Elvira* of Boston seem to have butchered, or as passenger Warren Fletcher referred to it, "murdered" their hogs on Saturday so they could have fresh meat on Sunday as long as their pigs lasted.[15] James M. Teller reported that the pig "Santa Anna," which their captain Tucker brought from Veracruz during the Mexican War, "fought his last battle" and was eaten.[16] Few vessels had pigs that survived so long. One of the pigs on the ship *Nestor* became ill, and when "all hope of its recovery were abandoned, he was dressed and cooked." Passenger Pierce W. Barker noted that he "did not taste of it, although there was quite a number that did." When it became evident that the passengers would not eat all of it, the captain gave the remainder to the sailors.[17] When some of the pigs became sick on board the bark *Maria*, the passengers decided to kill the sickest ones first "to keep them from dying, and to keep the best feeders until they get sick, then serve them like the first."[18] While most of the passengers were glad to have the fresh meat from the pigs they carried along for that purpose, that feeling was not shared by everyone. A passenger in the ship *Crescent* recorded that they had just killed the last of their pigs. He seemed glad they were all gone and sorry that they had taken them, as seven had died and portions of those killed were thrown overboard. He noted they were expensive and they took space in which they could have carried fifty barrels of provisions, "beside they made a very bad smell all over the ship."[19]

Although chickens may not have been taken on board as many California-bound vessels in 1849 as were pigs, usually larger numbers of chickens than pigs were taken in vessels that took both. Passengers in the bark *Orion* had some of their chickens for Thanksgiving and the remainder of them at the very end of the year. Since there were so few left at the end of December, they had them in the form of chicken soup and had lots of beef and pork to go with the chicken. The passenger who reported this appears to have felt sorry for the chickens, as they were cooped up in cages. When any chickens escaped the cages, it appeared to him that they had "almost entirely lost the use of their limbs, and some of their feathers." They hardly seemed "fit for anything except eating."[20] Henry Green noted that the passengers in the ship *Sabina* of Sag Harbor, New York, had twenty-four chickens for their Sunday dinner.[21] Members of the California and Thomaston Protection Company seemingly carried a large flock of chickens, as they had eighteen for one Sunday dinner and eight or twelve on several other Sundays. They also took along a few geese, as they had two for Thanksgiving and four for one Sunday dinner. On at least two other occasions they also killed pigs for Sunday dinner.[22] The passengers in the ship *Sutton* had a large quantity of livestock on board when they left Valparaiso on the last leg of their voyage between New York and San Francisco. Thomas Whaley wrote they had loaded "two oxen, six sheep, as many pigs, thirty turkeys & a hundred or more chickens." They expected to "live on fresh provisions all the way."[23] It would seem then, that California-bound passengers had chicken on Sunday at sea just as many of them likely did at home on land.

Apparently many vessels departing from the east coast took a large supply of potatoes. They also took other vegetables that would keep for a period of time to either eat or sell in California, but because many left in the winter or early spring before the fruits of that season were ripe, they had to await their arrival at a port south of the equator to purchase fresh fruit. Most acquired fresh fruit and vegetables at stops in both Atlantic and Pacific ports. The ship *Nestor* of Boston carried forty barrels of potatoes as food for passengers. Pierce W. Barker reported that they kept very well, as they found few diseased ones from the time they departed on November 30, 1849, until they ate the last of them on March 17, 1850. The same could not be said for the rutabagas, which they intended to sell in California, and the onions. Both were found to be so badly spoiled two months into the voyage that they were all thrown overboard still in their casks. During a stop in Callao the captain of the *Nestor* purchased more potatoes as well as beans, onions, and squash.[24] Those in the brig *Perfect* did not have such good fortune with their potatoes because cockroaches got into them and their turnips and ate portions of them. Apparently the passengers ate those portions of the potatoes not eaten by the roaches, as they did not want to waste good food. Alexander F. Spear noted that they had "some sport killing them as they open the barrels" and added that there were as many "as a quart in a barrel."[25] Among the vegetables they enjoyed on Thanksgiving Day were boiled onions, cucumbers, and beets. About two weeks after departing from Valparaiso, Spear noted that they had a boiled fish plus cabbage, turnips, beets, and potatoes for dinner and added that it made him "think of the old garden at home."[26] It is likely, based upon earlier entries, that they purchased all these vegetables in Valparaiso. Anne (Willson) Booth noted that they also had problems with rotten potatoes in the ship *Andalusia* of Baltimore. She reported, contrary to what many others did in other vessels, they were worse off after leaving Valparaiso than before they entered port for provisions. Before that time they had beets, parsnips, and carrots in addition to potatoes. After they left Valparaiso they had pumpkins virtually every day. She did not like them, but the other passengers seemingly ate them with relish and reported they tasted much like the sweet potatoes they had at home in Maryland.[27] When the bark *Anna Reynolds* of New Haven stopped at the island of St. Iago for provisions, vegetable purchases included sweet potatoes and yams.[28]

Apples were the one fruit that could be carried from the East Coast in the winter and early spring of 1849, and many vessels seem to have had large quantities on board when they departed. A variety of other fruits were purchased or harvested free at various locations on both the Atlantic and the Pacific coasts. Alexander F. Spear noted when they divided a barrel of apples among the passengers of the brig *Perfect* and how many each one received. When they entered Rio de Janeiro, however, he seems to have overindulged in fresh fruit, as he ate twenty oranges, seven bananas, six papayas, and part of a watermelon on Christmas Eve. He added that the members of the company had a meeting and decided to buy four thousand oranges. Later he noted they picked over the oranges daily and ate them as fast as they could because they rotted quite fast. When they stopped at Valparaiso, they ate as many peaches, pears, and apples as they could and probably took some with them.[29] Captain F. W. Willson purchased oranges, apples, grapes, and other unnamed fruits and "a good supply of nuts" when he stopped the ship *Andalusia* in Valparaiso.[30] The bark *Orion* made stops in Rio de Janeiro and the island of Juan Fernandez. She left the first place "with a plentiful supply of fruit of all kinds" and the second with an undetermined quantity of quinces and "no less than one hundred bushels" of peaches.[31] The brig *General Worth* of Newburyport, Massachusetts, was at Juan Fernandez a few days earlier than the bark *Orion* and left that island with "fully fifty bushels of fine peaches on board."[32] Charles Henry Harvey noted that when the ship *Crescent* stopped at Juan Fernandez, they picked large quantities of quinces and peaches. They made preserves from some of them, but they ate lots of them fresh over the next two weeks.[33] Several other journalists noted the large quantities of fruits, especially quinces and peaches, that grew wild on the island and were available to anyone who wanted to pick them. Both the ship *America* and the bark *Helen Augusta* stopped at St. Catherines Island. C. W. Haskins noted that they took "on board a good supply of tropical fruits of various kinds, with bananas in greatest abundance." When they departed, they had so many hanging in the ship's rigging that the vessel "had the appearance of a banana plantation going on an excursion."[34] George W. Young noted that the passengers in the *Helen Augusta* had so many oranges they could not eat them as fast as they rotted.[35] The passengers in the ship *Magnolia* left Rio de Janeiro with "upwards of thirty thousand" oranges. They gorged themselves to keep the oranges from rotting. About three weeks after departing, William F. Reed reported his stock of oranges was reduced from 350 to 20. It seems, then, that he ate more than a hundred oranges a week.[36] Although virtually all the vessels that stopped on the Atlantic did so at Rio de Janeiro or St. Catherines Island, the bark *Anna Reynolds* put into St. Iago, where the fruits purchased included oranges, lemons, bananas, cocoa nuts, plantains, tamarinds, and casaba.[37]

Desserts constitute a significant part of many meals in the late twentieth century, but they seem to have been a rarity for passengers sailing to California in 1849. Occasionally a passenger noted having doughnuts, but on the few occasions on which they were served, they seem to have been considered the whole meal. Commonly, when the passengers celebrated significant holidays such as George Washington's birthday, Fourth of July, and Thanksgiving, they had special desserts, but on most days they had salt beef and/or pork, rice, beans, and bread for their main meal during the middle of the day. Duff, a food to which many passengers looked forward on either a regular or an occasional basis and which some others disdained as being too heavy, would likely be considered a dessert today because of the sweet sauce that was sometimes poured over it. In some vessels it was served in addition to the meat and other foods, but in others it was the only thing served at some meals. Nevertheless passengers in some vessels occasionally enjoyed desserts and other rare sweet treats.

Passengers on board the ship *Tahmaroo* composed this song about duff that expresses well the feelings some had about that delicacy.[38]

> Gold hunters listen to my song
> A story I'll relate
> Which hapened on board the Tahmaroo
> On her voyage round the Cape
> Down in the second cabbin
> They eat all kinds of stuff
> I always chawed the harder
> When I got my hardy duff
>
> *Chorus*
> O that heavy duff

Food and Drink

I never get enough
Some like salt junk
Some dandy funk
But I'd rather have my duff

They put a chunk on each mans plate
I wish they'd give me more
It's a great deal better
Than dumpling hard ashore,
Then upon deck I Started
Lick the lasses off my thumb
And wait with all the patience
For the next duff day to come

Chorus
Down in that second cabbin
Whare the beems they hang go low
The bed bugs in their blankets play
And the rats they keep below
Oh there is the spot
Where the duff it tasts so sweet
And when John rings the bell
We tumble down to eat

Chorus
Down in that second cabbin
We sat for many an hour
And the smell of pork and beans
and hard bread rather sower;
Oh that heavy duff
I'll mourn when thou departest
I'll give my lips a farwell smack
And up on deck I started

Anne (Willson) Booth reported one occasion on which the passengers in the ship *Andalusia* had plum pudding. She also noted one instance in which the steward had made taffy for a portion of the passengers and one case in which she made puffs filled with preserves for two of the male passengers after the steward's attempt to do so was a failure.[39] Pierce W.

Barker noted one instance in which every passenger and sailor in the ship *Nestor* "had quite a luxury" of fried turnovers for dinner. They were such a treat that he did not eat any of their "Common fare after I had eaten such a sweet morsel" and added it would have "been almost madness to try to eat anything else."[40] Albert Lyman indicated two occasions on which they had desserts in the schooner *General Morgan*. Once it was "apple pies with two crusts," and the other time it was "some with no under-crust," which the steward called "Tarts."[41] H. F. W. Swain, a passenger in the bark *Belvidera* of New York, reported that contrary to the popular notion that "nice things are to be had only on shore . . . we the Cabin Mob did eat, Swallow and inwardly digest apple pie which circumstance I presume will forever prove their ideas incorrect." A few days later he reported some of the ladies were "preparing to make mince pies," which "also gives considerable satisfaction."[42] Griffith Meredith documented more desserts more often in the bark *Strafford* than did any other passenger. From the middle of February to early June 1849, they seemingly had frequent desserts including apple or peach pies; current, peach, or plum puddings with brandy, rum, or wine sauce; and "Role Poles."[43] Perhaps the most unusual dessert was served in the ship *Sutton*. Thomas Whaley recorded two instances of having ice cream during the passage between Rio de Janeiro and Valparaiso, probably near Cape Horn. On one of those occasions he noted, "Indulged in the luxury of ice cream, all very fine, excepting the cream."[44]

The Atlantic and Pacific Oceans provided the California-bound Argonauts a variety of foods with which to supplement their usual fare of salt meats, bread, rice, potatoes, beans, and occasional fresh fruits and vegetables. Porpoise and an occasional dolphin were the food most frequently harvested from the sea. Also caught and eaten were several kinds of fish, sharks, turtles, and a variety of birds. Catching them also provided a form of amusement or entertainment for the passengers, few of whom had ever seen any of these species before their adventure to California. Also the species of birds and fish in the Southern Hemisphere were different from those in the Northern Hemisphere from which the gold hunters came.

John McCrackan's description of the catching of a porpoise by the ship *Balance* is typical of the excitement caused by such an event on a gold rush ship.

> Just after dinner the cry was given of "Porpus, Porpus." A general rush was made for the bow of our vessel around which were some half dozen very large ones playing in great glee, throwing

themselves some six feet into the air. . . . A harpoon was soon thrown & fastened into one. He was drawn out of the water. Then a rope was fastened around him, when he was drawn upon deck amid the loud huzza's of all the passengers. He proved a young one twelve feet long & a most unprepossessing subject, I do assure you. It had a long snout like a hog, indeed it is called & very properly, the Sea Hog. . . . Its anatomy is like the Hog in every particular. We waited impatiently for breakfast when we would pronounce a verdict upon the Porpus. Some were very much prejudiced by its appearance & "nothing would induce them to taste a bit of anything so unnatural." When breakfast came many were induced to eat from it who thought "they would not be hired to." I relished it very much. It is much like a number of dishes viz. Calf liver, venison, black duck, & cooked in ragout form for dinner, was very much like Hare, however I thought it more like liver & black duck. . . . The meat is black but very tender.

In a later letter he reported the taking of another porpoise and indicated that the people who would not eat the first one "were as delighted as any of us," as one who has not been to sea before "can have no idea how grateful anything fresh is after our 'salt junk' and hard tack." They had porpoise "meat balls" for breakfast and a "french dish" made from porpoise meat for dinner.[45]

Three passengers in the ship *Sweden* all had different thoughts on the taste of their porpoise. Benjamin Bailey noted it "tasted like Liver very much, has not any Flavor of Fish," but Moses Cogswell felt it tasted "much like Beef Liver" and added, "Let it taste ever so bad, it was a <u>change</u> from the regular routine" and "it relished well." John Tolman agreed that it did not taste like fish but felt it "tasted very much like ham."[46] Passengers in other vessels agreed that porpoise tasted like beef steak and commented that it "was quite palatable," "was quite a luxury," or "relished very well." J. L. Akerman noted that the sight of their first one "sickened me from eating it" but agreed the second one tasted like beef and "was very good indeed."[47] A passenger in the ship *Plymouth* felt that when porpoise steaks were baked, "you could not tell it from beef that is well done" but that the heart and liver tasted exactly those of a pig. Willard C. Childs, a passenger in the ship *Reindeer*, agreed the liver "tasted like hog liver" but added he did not think much of the meat. Ferdinand Cartwright Ewer also agreed with others about the liver, reported the brains tasted like hog brains, but felt the steaks "tasted like a cross between venison & liver with a dish of fish in it."[48] Two other passengers had quite different opinions. Alfred Wheeler in the bark *Hannah Sprague* felt that porpoise cooked "into steaks & a hash tasted like wild pigeon, being quite tender & sweet, & free from any fish taste. I ate a little & only a little for the idea of its being Porpoise meat made me too qualmish to have relished it even though it had tasted like Ambrosia." Enos Christman, on the other hand, ate "it with a hearty relish" even though it resembled "horseflesh very much."[49] Two of the few passengers who recorded the taking of dolphin noted how the dolphins changed colors as they died and indicated that the meat was "a good fresh bite" or "was a delicious variation of our regular bill of ship diet." A third felt the flesh tasted "very much like halibut." On several occasions passengers mentioned trying out small quantities of oil from the porpoises.[50]

Nothing from the sea seems to have created as much excitement on board a gold rush ship as the catching of a shark. Anne (Willson) Booth described catching one by those on board the ship *Andalusia*.

> Just after dinner some one sang out "Sharks, Sharks" when such a rushing on the quarter deck, I never saw. They threw out bait, attached to large iron hooks & chains, but they swallowed both bait & hooks, besides large pieces of the chain. They then threw the harpoon & succeeded in striking one, which they hauled on deck amid the shouts and hurras of the men. After maiming him in such a manner as to prevent him from injuring any one, they kept him awhile for exhibition & then dissected him—& had him prepared for supper. If any one had told me of a shark being eaten I should have been rather incredulous & was therefore much surprised to see it prepared for the table. It was cooked in different ways, some parts being fried very brown & other parts made into a kind of stew, highly spiced. When it was brought to our table I felt a little curiosity to taste & try, but must confess no little difficulty in sufficiently divesting myself of prejudice, to partake of it. I did, however, conquer my aversion enough to put a piece in my mouth & was very agreeably surprised at its rather pleasant taste. Some profess to be very fond of it & declare an intention of being on the alert for more sharks.[51]

Ferdinand Ewer noted the catching of one shark by the passengers in the ship *York* and cutting steaks to fry for tea time and added that the "scene was exciting and reminded me of Old Isaak Walton." Thomas Whaley reported that the tail of the shark was the only part fit to eat and was served to the steerage passengers for tea time. Elias P. Overton noted only that the shark they caught "Tasted very well." J. T. Woodbury reported their shark "tasted better than it smelt." Charles Henry Harvey, however, reported that the flesh of a shark "was not good to eat." Those in the bark *Belvidera* caught three sharks but simply killed them and cut them up and tossed the remains overboard. On one occasion, however, they took the pilot fish that always accompanied sharks and sometimes was attached to them. It "furnished a dainty meal for the ladies in the cabin. The meat was very white and was said to taste like the whitefish."[52]

Skipjacks, albacores, flying fish, and bonitos were among the types of fish caught by passengers bound for California in 1849. All but the flying fish were caught with lines held or suspended over the sides of the vessels. Flying fish frequently landed on the decks of sailing vessels. Some passengers noted that skipjacks and bonitos resembled mackerel except that skipjacks were much larger and bonitos were thicker and their flesh resembled beef more than fish. Another passenger reported that flying fish were about the size of trout but tasted like smelt. He took the wings of flying fish and put them in his journal. All these fish were welcome changes from the normal foods. Rather than catch their own fish, passengers in the bark *Hannah Sprague* purchased several groupers from some Brazilian fishermen.[53]

One passenger implied that turtles were taken only when they went on land to sleep and described at length how they captured sixty turtles and took them on board their vessel, where they enjoyed turtle steaks and other turtle dishes. Other passengers, however, reported catching turtles as they swam in the sea. One reported they had turtle soup made from the two-hundred-pound loggerhead turtle taken from the sea into one of their boats and brought on board. Another passenger reported the turtle they had harpooned from the bowsprit of their vessel provided "a fine lot of good fresh meat and a considerable quantity of oil."[54]

Catching and shooting birds in the colder regions of the Southern Hemisphere provided considerable amusement and entertainment to the passengers as well as some new foods to experience as alternatives to their usual fare of salt meat, rice, hard bread, and whatever they still had in the way of provisions. Albatross, occasionally called gooney birds, were among the favorite to catch, as they were the largest and perhaps most interesting. The sailors usually told passengers that albatross were not edible, but that may have been because sailors held a superstition that seabirds carried the spirits of lost seamen and killing the birds would therefore bring bad luck. Some sailors and possibly some of the passangers might also have been familiar with Samuel Taylor Coleridge's poem "Rhyme of the Ancient Mariner."[55] Passengers in the ship *Europe* caught and killed several albatross, or gooneys, some of which weighed more than twenty pounds and had wing spans of twelve feet. In one instance they were boiled in salt water and then baked, but in another they were cooked in some undisclosed manner and eaten with stewed apples. Even though the sailors told passengers they were not edible, the birds "furnished a very good meal." A passenger in the brig *Osceola* reported one albatross was cooked and served to "Steerage Mess Number 1" and commented, "Thank God, I don't belong to that mess! I can eat albatross, but I don't hanker after it." An albatross caught by passengers in the bark *Daniel Webster* was made into a sea pie. A passenger in the ship *Pharasalia* caught and ate an albatross with a wing span of nearly eleven feet and was estimated to weigh between twenty-five and thirty pounds. Passengers in the brig *Oriental* also caught several albatross and "had a fine meal served up from them." A passenger in the ship *Plymouth* echoed the opinions of the sailors when he wrote that albatross were not fit to eat, as they were "nearly all wings & feathers." In many instances passengers saved feet, beaks, wings, and skins of albatross for souvenirs or to make items from them.[56]

A passenger in the ship *Panama* described the method of catching numerous cape pigeons or speckled haglets and had them made into pigeon pot pies after "sufficient parboiling to take away the fishy taste." On board the brig *Osceola* they stuffed several cape pigeons with pork and onions and baked them, but they ate only the pork and onions and threw the pigeons overboard.[57] Passengers in the bark *Anna Reynolds* undoubtedly killed more birds than those on any other vessel, but they did it while in the vicinity of the Falkland Islands, where they were seeking to replenish their food supplies. They killed more than six hundred geese and unknown quantities of ducks as well as foxes, wolves, and seals.[58]

Passengers traveling to California in sailing vessels took advantage of numerous opportunities to supplement their monotonous diets of salted beef and pork, rice, beans, and hard bread with occasional fresh fruits, vegetables, and meats available after stops at South American ports and islands in the Atlantic and Pacific by harvesting a variety of animals, fish, turtles, and birds from the sea. They defied the superstitions and advice of the sailors in killing and eating albatross, but no vessels seem to have had difficulty because of these actions by some passengers. In addition the passengers seem to have thoroughly enjoyed themselves while engaging in those activities through which they supplemented their regular diets.

One might well imagine that passengers who expected to be fed better and more abundantly than they seem to have been would have complained about the monotonous fare even if the foods were of above average quality and were well prepared. Many complaints about the quality and quantity of food seem to have been made between the point of departure and the first stop, which most often was Rio de Janeiro. In some instances there may well have been a lack of understanding on the part of the passengers as to exactly what they were promised when they took passage in a particular vessel. When this occurred, it was likely because few of the passengers had ever been to sea and might well not have fully understood what was told them about what they would be served and how much and how often it would be served. In other instances, however, owners, shipping agents, captains, and even officers of joint stock companies simply took advantage of the gullibility of prospective passengers who desperately wanted to get to California to make their fortunes.

A passenger in the ship *Tahmaroo* expressed sentiments about a week after leaving New York that was echoed over and over again by people in other vessels: "From the time we left New York thare has bin a great deal of dissatisfaction about our living. We all think our fare miserable. It is not as it was represented to us." He added one unique thing, however, when he included a song composed by a fellow passenger that included the complaints that were uttered over and over again—insufficient quantities of food that was frequently poorly prepared and badly served.[59]

> The ship Tahmaroo left one day
> The D. C. Pell towed us down the bay
> When we got out ware we could not be seen
> They dish us up some Pork an beans
>
> *Chorus*
> O get along John! You hungry son
> O get along John! You hungry son
> ant you glad when your duff comes
>
> The passengers growled and to the Capt did say
> We cant stand this every day,
> They dove round to the gally house
> and down came Adams with a pan of scous

Chorus

The beans was burnt most every time,
And the sugar tasted of turpentine,
They thought they'd give us something nise
And down came John with some raw rise,

Chorus

Now bout every twise a week
They thought they give us a mighty treat
They sent John down with a pan of duff
But neither man got half enough

The first-class passengers of the ship *Pacific* felt so strongly about being misled and abused that they engaged in perpetual conflict with Capt. Hall J. Tibbits during the entire passage between New York and Rio de Janeiro. Within the first two weeks at sea, these passengers held a meeting and "adopted a respectable remonstrance" in which they claimed that they were to have the same food as the captain and his family, but instead they "were fed on food that was coars, badly cooked, and no better than that fed to the crew." Captain Tibbits refused to receive the petition and told them that if the passengers caused any more trouble, "he would fire the magazine and blow us all to h—l together." Another passenger reported that the captain threatened to put in irons and confine below deck any passengers who caused more trouble by complaining about the food. Soon thereafter the captain posted a bill of fare that left a great deal to be desired in the opinions of the passengers. The quality of the food and the way it was cooked continued to decline so that one person noted the rice pudding "was hardly heated in the inside and not quarter done." He added, "Our tea and coffee are most horrid and although we have so much that is salt yet I never drank so little" and the water was getting so "villainous" that he had to hold his nose while drinking it. The complaints were not addressed to the satisfaction of the passengers, and they decided to take them to the U.S. consul in Rio de Janeiro. They selected a committee of three to prepare yet another petition to Captain Tibbits, and later they prepared a set of charges against the captain and presented them to Consul Gorham Parks. Captain Tibbits prepared countercharges against the passengers. Many rumors floated about the city, and the situation on board the *Pacific* seems to have been the talk of the town. Mr. Parks conferred with U.S. minister David Tod and decided to remove Capt. Hall J. Tibbits from command of the *Pacific* and appointed another person in his place. While the quantity and quality of food and the manner in which it was prepared and served were, of course, mentioned in the complaints to the consul, the most significant charges the passengers brought were that Captain Tibbits was habitually intoxicated and mentally deranged. Complaints about the food and how it was prepared and served to the first-class passengers ended with the removal of Captain Tibbits.[60]

Passengers in the ship *Sweden* of Boston also had confrontations with their captain, Jesse G. Cotting, about the quality and quantity of their food and how it was prepared and served. As soon as the passengers began to recover from seasickness, they began to complain about the food. By the end of their first week at sea, they sent a petition signed by fifty or more asking for better food. Captain Cotting posted a notice that he would deal with the passengers only through the commissary, a Mr. Wixwill, but the passengers declined to go that route and determined to go directly to the captain the next time they became upset over their food. In mid March a half barrel of pork was opened to be cooked for dinner. The passengers proclaimed it was unfit to eat, but they later learned it had been cooked anyway and served to them. They took some of the meat to Captain Cotting. After smelling the meat he promised to look into it when he finished his dinner. By the time the captain came below to inspect the meat, the passengers had thrown it overboard. He told them he would thrash anyone who threw food overboard. The passengers all confirmed that they were dissatisfied, and the captain promised to provide better food in the future. Some passengers felt Captain Cotting was afraid that passengers would send letters of complaints to the newspapers in Boston and endanger his reputation and the reputations of the other owners of the vessel. One passenger even asserted that the captain had said he would rather give a thousand dollars than have such news get back to Boston. One item promised them was preserved, potted, or canned meats every Sunday, but they did not get them on a regular basis. Another passenger, however, had quite regular reports in his journal of having preserved meats on Sunday.

In June the passengers once again sent a petition signed by more than 150 passengers to Captain Cotting expressing dissatisfaction with their fare and suggested that to continue to provide such poor-quality food and service would adversely affect the reputations of Captain Cotting and the owners, but giving them good food well prepared and served would enhance their stature. Captain Cotting again expressed regret that the passengers were dissatisfied and promised to remedy it. One passenger recorded a one-word response to the captain's statement—"Gas!" A few days later Captain Cotting replied in writing to the passengers reminding them that he had posted, and many of them had copied into their record books, a record of the provisions taken on board the *Sweden* and that he would continue to provide them with the best available food even to the extent getting into that which had been taken as freight to be sold in California.

Late in July one passenger, who was a member of one of the several joint stock companies on board the *Sweden,* noted that their "victuals grow worse and worse" and the "Bread is mouldy and wormy, and the Molasses sour." When they arrived in San Francisco in early August, that same passenger noted that they unloaded everything by nightfall and "cooked a *good* supper and eat it with a better relish than any meal since we left Boston." Then he added an intriguing conclusion: "We find on inquiry that we . . . lived like kings in comparison with other Ships from Boston."[61] From this statement one might conclude that the passengers who felt they were mistreated by the captain and owners of the *Sweden* were actually treated a great deal better than they thought they were even if that might not have been treated as well as they would have liked to have been treated. This probably was because few of them had ever been to sea, either as passengers or sailors.

This process of grumbling, holding meetings, drafting and presenting petitions to the captain (or in a few instances to the commissary or supercargo who appears to have represented the owners), and the captain's denial of any knowledge of the way the passengers were being treated and his promises to provide better provisions—either from what was already in the ship or from what would be purchased when they arrived in a port such as Rio de Janeiro, Talcahuano, or Valparaiso—was repeated in numerous vessels. In some cases the petitions were signed by nearly all the passengers in the vessel and in others by only those in one class or cabin of accommodations. Passengers in the ship *Reindeer* of Boston complained that their beef was "unfit for wholesome sustenance of human life," their coffee was made from bad water and "neither comfortable, wholesome or palatable" because of "the miserable nature of the sweetning," neither the beans nor the rice was cooked in sufficient quantity, and the utter negligence of the "whole administration of the commissary department" resulted in "injurious consequences to the health & safety of all of us." They asked that meat, beans, flour, meal, bread, and other provisions of good quality be provided in sufficient quantity; they be given "moderate portion of either butter or cheese" every day; they be given enough sugar

90

"each day to sweeten our tea and coffee"; they have rice three times each week; they have soup made from existing salt meat twice a week; and they have bread or cornmeal made of good ingredients once each day. The captain responded that he would have the supplies examined in Valparaiso and replace any bad food with good.[62]

The second-class passengers in the ship *Tahmaroo* prepared a petition in which they complained that the vessel sailed two weeks late, causing the passengers to spend extra money on food and lodging in New York; the distributed rations "fell short of there allowance by the use of a fals balance [inaccurate or rigged scale]"; their provisions were not "cooked in a proper and palitable manner" and proper attention had not been given to "clanlyness" in serving the food or in the utensils in which they were cooked; they had not been given the rations listed on the agreement card shown by the agent of the vessel; they were promised everything would be done for their health and comfort, but the area between decks was cluttered with boxes, barrels, and packages so as to prevent access to their staterooms until they moved them themselves; and the between-decks areas "have been and still are in a filthy and stinking condition covered with greas and dirt." The journalist did not record the captain's response.[63]

Passengers in the ship *Euphrasia* first became upset then they did not receive any cheese during the first month of the voyage, and each successive mess on December 10, 1849, shouted as loudly as they could for that commodity. They chose a committee to prepare a resolution demanding that they be given the provisions "allowed by the United States Government," but they later dropped that requirement and sent a different statement. The captain's response came in two days. One passenger commented, "He does not yet come up to the mark, but seems to keep off, but as far as he did go he talked like a gentleman." They decided that if they did not get satisfaction they would take their claim to the U.S. consul in Rio de Janeiro. Since there had been no substantial improvement by their arrival in Rio, they did meet with the consul with a petition signed by one hundred passengers. Capt. Charles Buntin was called to meet with the passengers and the consul. The passengers felt the consul sympathized with them and told them that they had sufficient power of their own to get what they wanted. They did get a promise of soft bread every day as well as pepper and mustard. Presumably they also got other provisions to their taste, as there were no more such complaints after they left Rio.[64]

Within the first two weeks of the departure of the ship *Capitol* from Boston on January 22, 1849, some of the passengers began to express discontent about the food. They held meetings and chose a committee to draft resolutions to be presented to Capt. Thorndike Proctor. The resolutions were more aggressive than those of passengers in other vessels in that they were mostly in the form of demands. First they demanded "the fulfilment of the promises made" by the owners prior to their departure. Next they asserted that no "feeling of harmony & peace" could exist under the current bill of fare since what was allowed was not sufficient "for our sustinence," and they pledged "to act mutually in defense of our rights" to obtain what was promised them. Third they claimed that they were exposed to "deseases of the most appaling nature" and they needed their food to be properly cooked and "every percaution should be taken to remove every thing in the nature of a nucence or of a contagious quality." Fourth they contended that they were men of feeling, submission, and contentment, and they would be completely satisfied if they would be provided the U.S. Navy rations. Finally they said they knew there were ample provisions available to provide each passenger with U.S. Navy rations and stated emphatically they would "submit to no other arrangements." The petition was reportedly signed by 123 of the 248 passengers. The captain responded that he could not do anything about what they said they were promised by the agents or charterers. He was bound by the written orders given him by the charterers and that what they instructed him to provide was more liberal that the U.S. Navy rations. He added that it was the charterers who arranged for two cooks, and he had no power to change that. Captain Proctor concluded with the usual disclaimer that this was the first he had heard that anyone was unhappy with the food or the way it was prepared and served and assured the petitioners that he would do all in his power to promote harmony and satisfaction.[65]

Probably the worst food and most victimized passengers on any vessel were on board the bark *Sarah Warren* of Portland, Maine. Despite unfavorable conditions, passengers did not hold indignation meetings to prepare petitions and demands to the captain. This might have been because there were only nine passengers. The owner of the vessel, George Warren, instructed Capt. Ruben Curtis to stop at no port before he reached Valparaiso. The passengers viewed this as evidence that he knew the provisions he put on board were poor and were certain that he was afraid that permitting a stop in Rio de Janeiro would provide passengers too easy of an opportunity to forward complaints to Maine newspapers and endanger his reputation. Passenger A. Bailey noted eight days after their departure, "We find out to-day that we have been greatly cheated by Mr. Warren in his not putting on board articles of <u>groceries</u> which are always done, especially where there are <u>Passengers</u>." He then added, "We have no Spices of any kind, No Lard—Nothing but Brown Sugar—Poor Butter Miserable Tea—and miserable Coffee—Miserable Flour &c." In several following days he mentioned the meanness of George Warren and the showering of curses upon him. He contended that although the pork was supposed to be the best-quality mess pork, it was actually "the meanest <u>Prime, and Southern</u> at that." When it was fried it curled up in the "Shape of a <u>half moon</u>, and the fat part is about 1 1/2 in. Thick, and the rind about 3/4 inch thick, and black as your hat." He added that their bread had been out on a previous voyage and was "full of Wevels!" On another day he reported that their flour, which Warren said "was the best, is old & full of <u>worms</u>! We found some in the biscuit this morning 3/4 in. Long with <u>black heads</u>!" He then added somewhat incredulously, "It is said he belongs to the church! Can it be Possible?" Next he said that they had some mackerel that was supposed to be "<u>good ones</u>," but they "proved to be very poor no. 2 and what was worse yet, very <u>rusty</u>! almost impossible to eat them—They made me sick—I shall eat no more of them except to save live." Later he reported that one of the passengers made a sieve by punching holes in a large pan so they could sift worms out of the flour. Next he noted they opened a barrel of beef to make boiled beef for dinner but found it "<u>smelt so bad</u>" that they threw it overboard. He then asked about George Warren, "Now, what can be too bad to say of a man who would provide a vessel for a long voyage with such provisions as this?" Five weeks into the voyage a passenger named Connor asked the captain to go into Rio de Janeiro so he could get provisions to restore his health. Captain Curtis called the passengers together and asked them to vote on whether they should go to Rio, but they refused to vote. Rather they told the captain that it was entirely up to him if they went to that port. They wanted all the blame to be upon George Warren for ordering Curtis not to go to Rio. Later, Connor offered to pay all port charges if Captain Curtis would take them into Rio so he could purchase provisions for his health. Bailey made comments about what he perceived to be actions by Curtis to purposely sail away from Rio and was angered because this would lengthen their voyage. In early December he wrote about some boiled beef that had "been put upon our table <u>10 times</u> and was never touched by any one except the Capt., and this morning the Steward threw it <u>overboard</u>." Later he made more references to worms in the flour and weevils in the rice and lamented that they had paid "175 dollars for a passage and live on worms." Late in November, Bailey discussed some things that were done to avoid going into Rio de Janeiro to save the owner "<u>a few dollars harbor fee</u>! This too is the vessel which charged <u>25 dollars extra passage money because the passengers were promised by said Warren better fair than common vessels</u>! on board of which we had not a pound of <u>Lard</u>—nor an ounce of <u>spice</u>—nor a pound of <u>raisons</u>—only 3 small <u>Hams</u>—Miserable Rusty Prime Southern Pork—Stinking Beef . . . Pooi Buttcr, and half enough of it—only <u>2 cheeses</u>—poorest kind of Fredericksburg Flour—Poorest kind of <u>Tea</u> & Coffee." They finally reached Valparaiso and got some fresh provisions, but they nevertheless continued to be served some of the old ones until they reached San Francisco in April 1850.[66]

It is doubtful that any sailing vessel carrying passengers around Cape Horn to California in 1849 made the entire passage without complaints about the food and how it was prepared and served. Those discussed above are samples of the worst. References to the milder complaints abound in journals of other passengers in other vessels. With so many individuals wanting passage to California in such a short time, there was a tremendous strain on the available experienced cooks and stewards. As a result, many vessels had inexperienced individuals, or ones whose only experience was cooking for a small number of sailors, as their cooks and stewards. Some people with no experience signed on as cooks or stewards to work their way to California, as they did not have the funds or any other way of raising them to pay passenger fees.

As was the case with food, there were complaints about the drinking water (and also the tea and coffee made from it) because of both the quality and the quantity of it. In this era of abundant and readily available clear, cold, and pure drinking water, it is sometimes difficult to understand that such was not always the case. Passengers on California-bound sailing ships in 1849, when there were no regulations and inspections as today, were sometimes forced to drink water so awful that one cannot even imagine it today. They were also put on occasional short-water rations, at times because some of the barrels leaked, resulting in less water than the captain thought there was. Other times there were not the usual opportunities to supplement the original water supply by catching rainwater. In some instances passengers who had never been to sea and were therefore unaccustomed to conserving water probably used more than they should have. The taste or quality of the water was affected by the source from which it was obtained, how long it remained in the wooden casks, how clean the casks were when the water was put into them, what had been in the casks before they were used for water, and what foreign matter might have gotten into them.

Two vessels with the worst water were the ship *Regulus* of Boston and the infamous bark *Sarah Warren* of Portland, Maine. The *Regulus* suffered from a great infestation of rats that the sailors said was the worst they had ever seen in a sailing vessel. One passenger noted that the rats chewed holes in the water casks and fell into them in such great numbers that whenever a cask was opened, there were "so many putrified rats in the water casks, it is thick with hair and slime the very stench of it is sickenin, leave alone drinking it, the way I manage it is by holding my breath, while drinking, which is the only way to get along with it." The water was so bad that he said, "I have almost wished for a drink of water, called sink water at home."[67] A. Bailey, one of the nine passengers in the ship *Sarah Warren*, reported that they caught water during rain showers in order to avoid having to go into Rio de Janeiro for that commodity. The water that was caught on "top of the <u>cabin</u> is quite good because it is <u>clean</u>, but that caught from the <u>quarter deck</u> is a very different thing. It is where we <u>walk, spit tobacco Juice</u> and carry the <u>filth</u> on our feet from the <u>Pigs pen & Hen coop</u> &c, and is thick with <u>dirt & filth</u>."[68] Rainwater was caught in a variety of ways. The method for catching the greatest volume in a hard rain was to plug the scuppers and collect the water from the main deck. This was frequently done for purposes of allowing the passengers to wash their clothes and even bathe in fresh water, but it was occasionally done to catch drinking water. Water was also caught in lesser quantities from the roofs of any structures on deck. Another method was to suspend horizontally a piece of sailcloth from the rigging to catch the water and then drain it into casks on deck.

Many passengers in the 1849 California-bound sailing vessels would have concurred with what three passengers wrote in their journals. One in the ship *Pacific* wrote, "Oh for a drink of cool water" from the "iron bound bucket at home." Another in the bark *Canton* recorded, "Oh, what joy it will be to get good, fresh water, such as you drink in the city!" and also, "Oh, for a glass of cool, fresh water to cool my parched tongue!" A third in the ship *America* wrote, "Oh! For a handful of Ice! O! For a draught of pure water!"[69] Thus it seems that the quality and quantity of drinking water was yet another factor contributing to at least some fleeting second thoughts not only about seeking fortunes in the California goldfields but also about getting there in sailing vessels around Cape Horn.

Virtually the only times passengers commented upon how good their water tasted were those instances when they had caught fresh water during a rain or had obtained new water in some port after they had been drinking bad water for many weeks. A passenger in the bark *Canton* said that a pitcher of their water "smells as bad as bilge-water" and "will have one third of filthy sediment at the bottom, with a horrid smell" and that the only way he could drink it was to hold his nose. Many passengers had the same comment about holding their noses to drink. A passenger in the bark *Midas* wrote that their water, tea, and coffee all tasted "as though impregnated with Sulphuric Gas." Walter Balfour Gould in the bark *Marlu* noted that their water had absorbed a bad taste from the casks, which had previously held oil "or some such stuff" and was "dirty as Mississippi water." Passengers in the barks *Velasco* and *Elvira* reported their water had been "mixed with Oil" and that "It stunk and was thick with oil." Raymond Cazallia Davis recalled that the water on board the ship *Hampton* became "ropy" and explained that "It would string up on a stick like molasses." The passengers also had to hold their noses and close their eyes to drink it. He added that "thirst would overcome the disgust" over the bad water. One passenger reported the water in the ship *Magnolia* "tastes worse than dead clams." Some passengers made their bad water drinkable by mixing vinegar and molasses with it to make a drink called switchel.[70]

A number of the vessels sailing toward California in 1849 experienced water shortages and had to put the passengers and the sailors on an allowance. From the passengers' descriptions of events on board, it appears that the captain and other officers often did not know the quantity or quality of their ship's water, how much had been used, and exactly where all the water was stored. Passengers wrote of the joy of suddenly finding a cask of excellent water after they had been drinking bad water for several weeks. When the captain saw that it was taking longer to sail from one point to another or when it was discovered that some of the casks had leaked, he usually cautioned the passengers about conserving water and warned them that if the level of use continued he would put them on an allowance. The quantity allowed each person included what was used in cooking meals and making coffee and tea.

When passengers were first put on an allowance of water, it was usually two quarts per person per day, but sometimes it was three quarts. Unless they were fortunate enough to add to their supply by catching a considerable amount from rains, the daily quantity was frequently reduced to three pints and perhaps even to one quart. Passengers in the ship *Europe* were in such a position. They lost fourteen hundred gallons from a large square tank and were subsequently given only one quart per person per day. One passenger reported standing "nearly an hour in the rain and cold until my fingers were quite benumbed, holding a tin cup to catch water as it dripped off one of the small boats." After they had been on the one-quart-per-day allowance for about three weeks, he wrote that "A good drink of water is much more eagerly sought after by us than brandy by the most devoted followers of Bacchus." Because of the time span between mentions of water rationing on the brig *Osceola*, it is difficult to determine if it was in effect continuously from January through July 1849. In January a passenger noted each person was allowed three quarts a day, in February five pints, in May two quarts, and in July one and a half quarts, which was soon increased to two quarts because of a favorable wind. If that rationing was continuous, it was certainly the longest one discovered in this study. Passengers in the ship *Hopewell* also experienced a decrease from three quarts to two. John Taylor, a passenger in the ship *Orpheus*, reported April 20, 1849, that each passenger was allowed three quarts per day, reduced to two quarts three days later. The two-quart-per-day ration seems to have lasted until June 28, when it was increased to three for only one day, and then it was reduced to two for one day, and increased to three again on June 30. He noted that the increases were the result of favorable winds and concluded that "wind creates water truly." Passengers in the bark *Emma Isadora* seem to have discovered quite suddenly near the end of their voyage that they had only two casks of water for sixty men. They were immediately put on a ration of one quart per person per day, and that included the usual proviso that it included what was used for cooking and making coffee and tea. To complicate matters even further, all they had to eat were salt meats and hard bread, which tended to increase their thirst! Passengers in the ship *Magnolia* became inventive when they were reduced to one and a half quarts per day. They set devised a "coal pit" that would filter salt water and produce several gallons of good water per day. They also had the fortunate of receiving a large cask of water from the ship *Helena* and another cask of water from the ship *Memnon*.[71]

When the amount of water per person was reduced, there was usually a change in what was cooked or how it was cooked. The salted meats were usually boiled in fresh water, but when rationing was in effect it was boiled in salt water, increasing the saltiness and also the desire for more drinking water. Preparation of rice was frequently halted, as it had to be cooked in fresh water. Baking of bread required fresh water, so it was discontinued. Thus water rationing created a sometimes vicious cycle, but the only alternative was taking the risk of running completely out of water. Considering all the problems that passengers experienced with food and water, perhaps the frequently recorded sarcastic expression, "Who wouldn't sell a farm and go to sea!" is a fitting conclusion for this discussion.

4

—✦⫘————⫘✦—

Amusement and
Entertainment

With anywhere from one to nearly three hundred passengers in vessels sailing around Cape Horn to San Francisco in 1849, one can imagine that those passengers, most of whom had few if any responsibilities other than to find ways to occupy themselves during their waking hours, devised a variety of ways to amuse and entertain themselves. Where there were only a few passengers the opportunities for participating with other passengers were more limited than when there were large numbers of passengers. Those who traveled with friends and acquaintances probably had greater opportunities to participate with others than did those who traveled alone, at least early in the voyage; but before many days had passed most passengers became acquainted with fellow Argonauts and developed new bonds of friendship. Plans and preparations made by forward-thinking passengers to bring games and cards and dominoes and the inventiveness of other passengers contributed greatly to how well or how poorly the passengers succeeded in amusing and entertaining themselves.

One passenger in the ship *Henry Lee,* in which the members of the Hartford Union Mining and Trading Company sailed from New York, described the many activities in which passengers were engaged on one afternoon. His sampling provides a summary of the kinds of things passengers did to amuse and entertain themselves during their long voyage to California.

> To give our friends a more life-like view of the mode of passing our time at sea we will here insert a sketch taken at the time faithful in every particular, which may be regarded as a fair specimen of things occurring daily. Five o'clock, P.M.; there are on the hurricane deck, at this moment, twenty-five persons, four of whom are playing back-gammon; two, chess; four, checkers; one,

99

reading the "Outlaw's Bride;" one at his side is sleeping soundly; two are on their backs, and three on their faces, musing; one is whittling; two are a little separated engaged in conversation; three are overlooking the plays; and two are sitting cross legged, looking at me while writing this note. Just on a level with the deck and seated on some spars . . . are seated the minister and lawyer engaged in conversation apparently on Shakespeare which one holds in his hands; a third is lying close by, reading "Morrell's Travels;" [Capt. Benjamin Morrell, *A Narrative of Four Voyages . . . from the Year 1822–1831*] at one side in the long boat, two are stretched at length reading, one a "Waverly Novel," the other a "New Englander;" two are in the same boat, bothering each other by pulling legs &c.; sitting on the rail, between the deck and boat, are three persons, one reading an old newspaper, one telling yarns, and the other listening. Just under us, at the wheel, is a passenger, and on the potato bins, each side of the wheel, are six persons; on one side guessing ages; on the other, one is reading a novel while a second is looking over; a little back on the stern a man is polishing a dirk knife, while three are superintending the job. Casting our eyes aloft there can be seen six persons in the mizzen top, one half engaged in playing cards and the other half "helping Saul." Immediately forward the wheel, a game of checkers is on the tapis, which twelve others, including the 1st mate, are watching with intense interest. Our Doctor is figuring with a pencil on a new pine box recently made as a covering for the turning lathe; seated on the rail each side of the quarterdeck are seven more, looking over the side or aloft, or at the passers by, further forward, T——A. is scuffing with one of the Sailors—there goes a new straw hat overboard as the result. Deacon M. has just lain himself cornerwise across a trunk to rest after the labors of the day at the forge. By the main mast is one pouring over a "Waverly Novel," while close by, at the forge, the fire of which is dying out, one is hammering steel, and three others are casting bullets. The waist, at present, is unoccupied. Forward are eight seamen on deck; one is engaged in making a miniature ship, and a second, in fastening a knife handle, while the rest are talking to each other and three or four passengers who, having nothing else to do, have seated themselves near them. Now comes on supper, and the immediate rush of the first side to the saloon breaks up the scene on deck. The seamen, however, keep their position and partake of the supper over the forecastle at random, one of their number acting as waiter to the others.

After supper they assemble on deck, standing in groups along the waist and are either discussing the prospects awaiting them, or some subject more immediately connected with themselves as a company, or listening to the songs of some one near them; others go further forward where they were summoned by the bell to supper, and others resume their old places on the hurricane deck. Thus, and in various other ways, the evening passes off until the hour of rest.[1]

Activities in which passengers engaged during the long voyage can be divided into three broad categories—intellectual pursuits, physical activities, and general activities. Intellectual pursuits included reading; studying (especially Spanish); attending or participating in lectures, debates, and discussions; publishing newspapers; writing journals and letters; and observing and commenting upon nature. Physical activities included swimming and bathing, rowing, walking, boxing, dancing, gymnastics, general exercises, and military exercises or marches. Some of the most strenuous exercises came while the passengers were on shore during stops to obtain fresh provisions. General activities include Neptune's visits or crossing the line ceremonies, catching and shooting birds and sharks, playing jokes on each other, conducting mock trials, gambling, speaking and visiting other vessels, making things, celebrating the rounding of Cape Horn, smoking and chewing tobacco, listening to music, and singing and dancing.

Reading was one of the major ways passengers occupied their time. They read the Bible, novels, histories, biographies, narratives of travel and adventure, works about California, Shakespeare's plays, and seafaring stories. Ferdinand Cartwright Ewer, a passenger in the ship *York,* was certainly one of the most avid readers. Nearly four months into the voyage he reported that he had read so much that he strained his eyes and the doctors told him not to read anymore. He then listed what he had read up to that time. "Dickens's Dombey & Son; Lamartine's Raphael; Irving's Sketches, Columbus, Lives of Columbus's Companions; Life in California; Nichol's Architecture of the heavens, Contemplations on the Solar System; Dana's Two years before the Mast; Cause & Cure of Infidelity; Talford's final memorials of Chas. Lamb; Elia; Parts of Byron & Pope; Coleridge's Anc. Mariner, Christabel; Shelley's Alastor; Keat's Lamia; Consuelo—Countess of Rudolstadt; Melville's Typee; Chesterfield; Cheever's Journal at the Feegees;

101

Leigh Hunt's Indicator; Hazlitt's Table Talk; Macauley's History of England, 2 vols. all that were published when we left; Smyth's Lectures on Modern History; Irving's letters of Jonathan Oldstyle; The Idler; Fremont's Journal, &c. &c."[2]

Alexander F. Spear was also an avid reader. He reported about two and a half months into his voyage that he had read all of the New Testament and the Old Testament as far as Proverbs, five histories, seven biographies or adventures of travelers, twenty-five novels, four magazines, and some newspapers. Between March 10 and 25 nearly every entry in his journal includes the name of an author or a title he was reading. He mentioned books about Nero, Pompeii, and Caesar, others either by or about (without specifying which) Homer and Cato, and a book by Lord Byron without giving a title. He also mentioned several authors without providing their full names or any hints of titles. They are Thompson, Conway, Hampden, Evans, Hershal, Rodney, and Elder Baker. He also mentioned Ned Buntline dime novels. In addition, he noted *Macbeth* by William Shakespeare, *Rose of Thistle Island* by Emilie Flygare-Carlen (translated from Swedish to English by G. C. Hebbe and H. C. Deming), *Narrative of the Life of David Crockett* by David Crockett, *What I Saw in California* by Edwin Bryant, *Life on the Ocean* by George Little, *"Twelve Years Whaling"* (probably *The Wanderings and Adventures of Ruben Delano: Being a Narrative of Twelve Years Live in a Whaling Ship* by Ruben Delano), *Bel of Prairie Eden, a Romance of Mexico* by George Lippard, *Helen Howard*, or, *The Bankrupt and the Broker* by Professor Ashby (pseudonym?), *"The Secret Crimes of New York"* (probably *City Crime; or, Life in New York and Boston. A Volume for Everybody; Being a Mirror of Fashion; a Picture of Poverty; and a Startling Revelation of the Secret Crime of Great Cities* by Greenhorn, pseud. for George Thompson), *The West Point Cadet, or, The Young Officer's Bride* by Harry Hazel, one or more books by John Milton, and the Bible. He also mentioned *Rose of Somerville*, but no author has been located for that title.[3]

Warren Fletcher, a passenger in the bark *Elvira*, also appears to have read abundantly. He mentioned more than thirty times throughout the voyage that he had spent at least part, if not most, of a day reading. The frequency with which he mentioned reading increased as the voyage progressed, so it is possible that he read many more days than is indicated in the journal. Only on one occasion did he mention what he had been reading and that was newspapers purchased in Rio de Janeiro. He never indicated the name of an author or the title of any book he had read. [4]

In describing Sunday activities, many passengers mentioned that they and others were reading the Bible at various times during the day. Several others indicated they read their Bibles every day. William Edgar Randall reported that he read two chapters every morning. S. Mortimer Collins noted on February 19, 1849, that he had started reading the Bible and on May 20 that he had finished it and added, "I consider my time well spent in reading that book." George K. Goodwin indicated that he had read the entire Bible between May 27 and July 25, 1849. Thomas Whaley also appears to have read his Bible regularly, as he reported in April and May 1849 that he had finished reading the books of Joshua, Judges, and Ruth, and had read part of Samuel. He also mentioned reading *The Conversion of St. Paul*, by John Lettice which had been given to him by another passenger "Who desired to make a convert of me" and a tract on the seventh commandment by Rev. Timothy Dwight.[5]

Several passengers mentioned reading books about California and mining. A passenger in the brig *Osceola* read Edwin Bryant's *What I Saw in California*. Benjamin H. Deane found Furman's *Travels in California and Oregon* (probably Thomas J. Farnham's *Travels in California and Scenes in the Pacific Ocean*) "more a history of the Jesuits than anything else, but on the whole interesting." J. Haskell Stearns was "much pleased" with what he read in *Tour of Duty in California* by Lt. Joseph Warren Revere. James H. Gager, a passenger in the ship *Pacific*, found "that men in the Wilderness think just as men at sea do in all matters relating to meat & drink" and "know what it is to be deprived of small comforts & how important they are to our happiness" while reading John C. Fremont's journal (probably his *Notes of Travel in California*). Cornelius Cooledge read "accounts of California Life" during his voyage in the bark *Oxford*. Walter Balfour Gould found Andrew Ure's *Dictionary of Arts, Manufactures, Mining, &c.* "a very valuable and interesting work."[6] Considering the amount of reading done by passengers and the great interest in California and its mines, it is likely that other passengers read these and other works without mentioning them in their journals.

Numerous passengers read books of voyages and travels and other seafaring works. Richard Henry Dana's *Two Years before the Mast* seems to have been quite popular, as an anonymous passenger in the ship *Pharasalia*, Walter Balfour Gould in the bark *Maria*, and William Berry Cross in the ship *Crescent* mentioned reading it. Charles Williams found "a most awful account" of "trouble getting around the Cape in the same month as ourselves" in reading Lord Anson's *Voyage around the World*. J. Haskell Stearns found the account of Pitcairn's Island and its inhabitants in Amasa Delano's *Voyages* "particularly interesting." Cornelius Cooledge found Richard J. Cleveland's *Voyages* "interesting." William Edgar Randall read *The Wreck, or the Buccaneer's Bridal* by William H. Williams and *The Wrecked Vessel* (for which no author has been identified), but he did not comment upon them.[7]

Biographies and autobiographies of both Americans and Europeans were also read by many passengers. William Berry Cross read *Washington and His Generals* by either Joel T. Headley or George Lippard. They had both written books with that title by 1849. Charles Henry Harvey, another passenger in the ship *Crescent*, read *Life of Napoleon* by Sir Walter Scott. James H. Gager found Jonathan Trumbull's *Autobiography* "rather interesting for such an egotistical work." Cornelius Cooledge read *Napoleon and His Generals* and *Memoirs of W. E. Channing.*[8]

History and travel books were also read by many passengers. An anonymous passenger in the ship *Pharasalia* completed Lytton Bulwer's *Harold the Last of the Saxon Kings.* Charles Williams found much of interest and "derived much profit" from reading William H. Prescott's *Conquest of Mexico*, was "much interested" in reading a book about Marquesas Islands. He also read a volume he referred to as *Letters from Europe*, probably by Nathaniel Hazeltine Carter. Jacob D. B. Stillman, another passenger in the ship *Pacific*, also read William H. Prescott's *Conquest of Mexico*, which he thought "ought to be in every man's library." Prescott seemingly was a popular author, as S. Mortimer Collins in the *Magnolia* found his *Conquest of Peru* "very interesting." An anonymous journalist in the ship *Plymouth* spent several days in reading both volumes of George F. A. Ruxton's *Adventures in Mexico.* Thomas Whaley read the *History of the Sandwich Islands* by Rev. Ephriam Eveleth. William Edgar Randall turned to local history and learned of the early settlers and their hardships in the *History of Vermont* by Hosea Beckley. James H. Gager found "a world of wit & philosophy & learning" in William Beckford's *Spain & Portugal & Italy.*[9]

The passengers also read a great variety of literary works of the United States and Europe. Benjamin H. Deane read *Thadeus of Warsaw* by Jane Porter, *Parson's Daughter* by Anthony Trollope, and *Scottish Chiefs* by James Porter. He found the latter "a very interesting work." John McCrackan found both *The O'Donoghue* and *Knight Gwinne* by Charles Lever "very good" and urged others "read them should you have an opportunity." He also found the *Marrying Man* by Harriet Maria Smythies "another very amusing one to read aloud." Moses Cogswell, a passenger in the ship *Sweden,* read *Don Quixote* and unnamed works by Lord Byron, Charles Dickens, George Lippard, and Alexandre Dumas. Charles Williams and Addison Clark, two passengers in the ship *Pacific,* read plays by William Shakespeare, *Knight Gwinne* by Charles Lever, *The Fright* by Ellen Pickering, *The Whim* by George P. R. James, *The Wandering Jew,* by Eugene Sue, *Typee* by Herman Melville, and an unnamed volume by Lord Byron. The last is the only book Clark mentioned in his journal. Ebenezer Sheppard read unspecified works by William Shakespeare and Lord Byron, *Constitution of Man* by George Combs, *Ship and Shore,* by Walter Colon, *Indian Cottage* and *Paul and Virginia* by Bernardino de Saint-Pierre, and Earl Chesterfield's *Letters to His Son.* He found that the last two were "very interesting and well portray the blessings of simple uncorrupted nature, a heart undefiled and a blameless life." William Edgar Randall remarked after completing *Pilgrim's Progress,* "I esteem it high." He also read *Essay on Man* by Alexander Pope. An anonymous passenger in the ship *Plymouth* read novels titled *Shirley* by Charlotte Bronte, *Forest Days* by G. P. R. James, *The Spy* by James Fenimore Cooper, and *Vanity Vain* the author of which has not been identified. He also read Benjamin Disraeli's *Curiosities of Literature* and a "little" of Henry Ward Beecher but said he "cannot agree with him entirely." George K. Goodwin read *Ivanhoe, The Betrothed,* and *The Talisman,* all by Sir Walter Scott, but did not comment on any of them. An anonymous passenger in the bark *Gold Hunter* read Alphonse de Lamartine's *Les Confidences.*[10]

From the depth and breadth of the reading done by these passengers one might readily conclude that passengers sailing to California in 1849 appear to have been well educated and had a great interest in California, history, biography, and literature of both the United States and Europe. Their reading seems to confirm the general feeling that the men in these vessels were among the best educated in their communities.

These passengers knew that California natives spoke Spanish. Thus many attempted to learn Spanish during the long voyage. Some studied on their own and others in groups under the leadership of someone familiar with the language. A passenger in the bark *Canton* noted that three or four men were learning Spanish. He had obtained a good book and thought he could learn as well as the others. He felt that even if learning the language did no good, it would do him no harm. Moses Cogswell noted that he did "not make much headway" in learning Spanish, as he found the pronunciation difficult. Although Joseph Augustine Benton admitted that he did "not advance rapidly" in learning the language, he did undertake to translate

Pres. Zachary Taylor's inaugural address from Spanish to English, probably from a newspaper acquired in Rio de Janeiro. [George Payson] reported that "a few of the bolder spirits" in his vessel had "the hardihood to attempt 'Spanish without a Master,' but they got no farther than the story of the three travelers, and the ominous moral, 'Desgraciado el que aspira a riquezas,'—miserable is he who aspired after riches." Passengers in the ship *Andalusia* seem to have been more fortunate than those in other vessels, as they had someone on board who was willing to teach a group of them "in return for the use of the cabin" as a classroom. Although there was not enough interest to start such a class, some of the passengers began studying on their own. Within a month they were able to "hold short conversations in the language." One passenger reported, "It is often amusing and always interesting." She later wrote that she spent an hour or two each evening studying Spanish or reading. The study of Spanish seems to have been halted for a couple of months, but then several of the passengers formed a class among themselves without an instructor although one of them had learned some Spanish during a stay in Rio de Janeiro. They corrected each other, "making it quite amusing as well as instructive." The language study was soon interrupted again, as the weather turned cold and some of the "gentlemen in the Cabin . . . preferred not to join in the exercises." Ferdinand Cartwright Ewer, who was an avid reader, also studied Spanish as well as navigation so that he could calculate the ship's position. Robert La Motte studied both Spanish and German, and his brother Harry studied navigation and the use of the sextant and chronometer. Passengers in the schooner *General Morgan* studied arithmetic, geometry, and trigonometry in learning the art of navigation. Chester Joseph Snow noted about a month after the start of his voyage that within a single week he commenced classes in geography, arithmetic, philosophy, and "Watts on the mind." William M. Hatch reported that a Mr. Williams taught arithmetic on a regular basis to "his scholars."[11] The study of these subjects indeed provided some way of filling the many hours at sea and may even have provided some amusement and entertainment, but they probably proved of little value or use in California, as there were so many more English-speaking Americans than Spanish-speaking Spaniards or Mexicans in San Francisco and in the mining areas that there was little use for a foreign language.

Lectures, discussions, and debates were other forms of learning as well as amusement, entertainment, and instruction for passengers. Lectures and debates were held less frequently than discussions, or arguments, as some passengers referred to them. Moses Cogswell noted that in the ship

Sweden they had "arguments on every variety of question imaginable" that sometimes became "rather personal and come very near producing serious arguments." They provided "relief to the monotony of the voyage," and he "occasionally" put "in a word to keep up the excitement." A passenger in the ship *Plymouth* mentioned three specific arguments—"Who was Cain's Wife?," "Is a funnel a tunnel and vice versa" (to which he added "See Webster's <u>unabridged</u> as the <u>infant</u> would say"), and "some question which I have now forgotten, for we are great people for argument." Several days after mentioning the first topic he wrote that they had "finally come to the conclusion to drop argument never coming out of the fight with any different convictions from what we went in." Joseph Augustine Benton noted a "dispute about the weight of a cubic foot of gold" in the ship *Edward Everett*. The captain, mates, and several passengers in the bark *Yoeman* had "a very spirited and animated discussion on the subjects of slavery, equality, and the rights of man, Universalism." Cornelius Cooledge reported that slavery was the theme of discussions one day in the bark *Oxford*. Thomas Whaley noted that the passengers in the ship *Sutton* discussed politics, religion, whether there was "an abundance of gold in California," "whether a pound of feathers weighed more than a pound of gold," "whether a man weighed more with his hat & boots on, than off," and "the right a person has to take the life of a robber upon one's own premises." Henry H. Hyde Jr. reported a lengthy discussion in the ship *Lenore* on "to what extent should a Christian mingle with the world, and whether in his business affairs, he should contrive to make his associates after his own turn of mind, or mingle without any foreselection." He added that they "finally settled on the latter as being more in accordance to Christian duties." A passenger in the ship *Tahmaroo* mentioned arguments on religion and politics. Passengers in the bark *Belvidera* had "a discussion . . . on Philosophy, which helps to drive dull care away." Passengers in the ship *Andalusia* carried the matter somewhat further by forming political parties, writing a constitution for the territory of California, and electing a governor and senators. The Whig candidates won, as there was a majority of that party on board the ship. They had a formal inauguration ceremony, and in his inaugural address the new governor "pledged himself to the support of pumpkins and cabbages, recommended improvement in relation to Duff as the late importations have been rather heavy."[12]

Several journal keepers mentioned that they had listened to lectures by one of the passengers. In most vessels there was one or two lectures, but passengers in the ship *Andalusia* held a meeting and appointed a committee to organize a series of lectures to be held each Monday, Wednesday, and Friday beginning in mid August. The first lecture on August 17 was by S. B. Marye, a lawyer from Virginia, who spoke on the "physical formation of man" and was "listened to with marked attention by all." He "fully realised our expectations in regard to the ability and talent." Colonel F. H. Hyer presented the second lecture on August 20 on "The powers of the mind." It was characterized as an "eloquent lecture" by one who "evinced a culture of his own mental powers, besides an intimate knowledge of the capabilities of the human mind generally." On August 22 George Gibson, a young Englishman who had resided in Baltimore for about a decade, spoke on "The Anglo-Saxon race" and confirmed the passengers' "previously high formed expectations" of his abilities as a lecturer. W. C. Chapman, a lawyer from York, Pennsylvania, spoke on August 24 on "The characteristics of the Age." He handled his topic "in a most beautiful and scientific manner" and spoke at some length on "the religious apathy of the age." James Reese, possibly one of the passengers they picked up in Valparaiso, presented a "very lengthy" lecture on August 27 that neither "edified or entertained . . . but it certainly did excite our surprise." It was rambling and consisted of disconnected sentences and included some personal remarks characterized as "a fulsome tirade of flattery upon several of our Shipmates" that were not appreciated even by those about whom they were made. On August 30 Dr. Buckner lectured on "knowledge" and "acquitted himself with much credit and was highly complimented upon his happy effort to instruct and entertain." The next day Dr. Thomas Hardy of Ohio spoke on "the ignorance of the human system and the encouragement generally given to the common quackeries of the day." He was severely critical of the quacks and also of those who patronized them. The Rev. Robert Kellan, a "regular Yankee" from New Hampshire, who was picked up at Valparaiso after he left the *Piedmont* because of a dispute with the captain, lectured on "Music" on September 3 and treated the subject "in a most beautiful manner and elicited much applause during its delivery." On September 5 the Reverend William Taylor, who was on board as a Methodist missionary to California with intentions to establish a church in San Francisco, gave the final lecture on "the moral dignity of man." Unlike the other lectures, his was an "extemperaneous discourse. Accompanied with so many gestures and such a thorough religious strain as to make it appear much more like a sermon than a lecture."[13]

Passengers in other vessels apparently had only one or two lectures, and they were not nearly as well organized as those in the ship *Andalusia*. In the ship *Sweden* a Dr. L. B. or T. B. Elliot lectured on March 12 on health. One passenger commented that Elliot was "not much of a lecturer." On August 2 he presented another lecture on the same topic at which another passenger noted he "gave some good advice." John Alexander, a geologist of Portland, Maine, gave lectures on geology on board the ship *Edward Everett* on June 6 and 20, 1849. The first was reportedly a "very good lecture." He concluded the second with "poetry of his own." The physician on board the ship *Lenore* presented lectures on "Anatomy" and "Physiology" during May 1849.[14]

Not all of the lectures were so well received. One passenger in the bark *Belvidera* mentioned lectures on several occasions but did not give names of lecturers or their topics until the middle of July. At that point he noted that "the long expected lecture from Revd Grove K. Godfrey came off to day on non resistance." The speaker indicated that the Bible supported the concept and any failure on his part to prove it was because of the confusion and noise in the ship while he was writing it. The passenger felt the failure was because of the lecturer's ability and added it reminded him of a merchant who was asked to pray before a meal. He went on and on in a rambling manner and finally concluded the way he usually ended his communications, "yours respectfully, Johnson Top and Compy." Godfrey ended his lecture "by saying he had clearly proved the subject." A. Mr. Pettibone from Ohio and a member of the Sacramento Mining Company in the ship *America* lectured on "Geography." A passenger commented, "He is also a nincumpoopian."[15]

Forming debating clubs or societies and holding debates seems also to have been popular among passengers sailing to California. In some instances only the formation of the groups was mentioned, but in others debate topics were mentioned and commented upon. John Brannan wrote that they had debating parties once a week on Thursday in the bark *Norwich,* but he did not report any topics debated. John Ross Browne noted that he was elected president of the debating society in the ship *Pacific,* but did not mention the organization again. Benjamin H. Deane reported the organization of the Arkansas Debating Society and mentioned its second meeting but said nothing about topics discussed. William J. Towne noted the formation of a debating society and the election of its officers in the ship *Capitol* but did not report any other activities. John Van Dyke reported a "strong debate on the poop deck between our friend J. W. Stout and H. Talmadge of Brookline on the question of slavery" but never indicated they had a club or a society. Henry Green noted that a debating society was formed on board the ship *Sabina* and they debated the question "Will the Discovery of the Gold Mines of California prove a Blessing or a Curse to the United States and the world" and decided it would be a blessing but made no further mention of the group. Passengers in the bark *Emma Isadora* organized a debating society during their first month at sea and debated "whether the acquisition of California to the U. S. Would be an advantage or not" and decided it would be an advantage. They held a second debate near the end of the voyage on "wheather Capital punishment is productive or more evel than good" and decided in favor of punishment. Passengers in the ship *Henry Lee* formed the Henry Lee Debating Club and elected officers. The only topic mentioned was whether the "government should restrict the free gathering of gold in California, by foreigners" and decided it should. A debating club was formed by passengers in the ship *Reindeer,* and they debated whether "whipping ought to be abolished in the American Navy," "is the Capt. or owners responsible for damages sustained by Pas. While at sea," and "ought Slavery to be abolished in the U. States." On only the second was a decision recorded and that was "the Capt. was & there was some hard talk against the Capt. how he had used the pas." The most active debating was in the bark *Anna Reynolds,* which held six debates during May and June 1849. Topics debated included "Are early marriages conducive to happiness or productive of general good," "Was the manner in which our forefathers treated the Abroiginees justifiable," "Will the discovery of Gold in California be beneficial to the United States," "Which exercises a greater influence on the mind of mankind wealth or women," "Are any of this company justified in private speculation," and "Does the abolishment of Capital punishment, tend to abat crime." No decisions were reported for the first and fourth. The third was decided in the affirmative, while the second, fifth, and sixth were decided in the negative.[16] It is perhaps interesting even today that the two groups who debated the efficacy of capital punishment disagreed with each other. Since no general agreement has ever been reached, that issue is still being discussed today.

Producing newspapers seems to have been a popular diversion on California-bound sailing vessels even though they were not published in the usual sense; they were always handwritten documents. Sometimes they were posted in a prominent place on board the vessel, and other times they were read aloud during one of the meals. Reading aloud was most practical when all the passengers could be seated at the same time. *Life in the Orion* was started on board the bark *Orion* in late November 1849 and was supposed to appear weekly on Thursdays, but it was abandoned after two numbers "for want of competent editors and contributors." The *Golden Budget* was produced twice on board the bark *Anna Reynolds* and was "read with considerable laugh." Benjamin H. Deane reported the first (and apparently only) appearance of the *Arkansas Courier* but could not comment on it, as he had not seen it. Sophia A. Eastman reported that she was secretary and furnished articles every week for the *Boston & California Pioneer* produced by passengers in the brig *Colorado*. The *Barometer & Gold Hunter's Log* first appeared on board the ship *Edward Everett* in February and was to appear "semi-weekly when the weather will allow." It continued in production through the issue of June 16, which was reported to be the "valedictory of the Editors." This newspaper was read aloud after tea by different passengers, possibly those involved in its production. The May 19 issue contained Joseph A. Benton's English translation of a Spanish version of Pres. Zachary Taylor's inaugural address. Issues were generally considered entertaining. On February 9 John Ross Browne, on board the ship *Pacific*, started the *Pacific Daily Journal* and produced at least two issues. On February 15 two other passengers came out with the *Pacific Evening Herald* of which they produced at least two issues. Both issues were intended for the amusement of the passengers and contained "witticism, jokes, puns, & poetry" as well as news of what was going on in the ship. Four issues of the *Morrisonian* and one issue of *John Clewlines* appeared in the ship *Morrison* in June 1849. Capt. George Coffin produced four issues of *The Emigrant* on board the ship *Alhambra* during August and September 1849. As has been the case with other activities, the passengers in the ship *Andalusia* outproduced passengers in other vessels. It was decided on August 13 to produce a series of daily bulletins that would include news, poetry, and short essays, but politics and personal remarks were to be excluded. Female passengers were encouraged to submit either prose or poetry. Some issues included satiric advertisements. The first issue of the *Gazette* appeared with much fanfare on August 16 and was continued on a regular basis through August 25. A second newspaper, *The Fler*, appeared for one day on August 20. Two competing newspapers were issued on August 23 and were described as being "pretty much in the abusive style." The *Gazette* was revived on September 6 with the new title *Whig Gazette*. One passenger noted that the newspapers were usually posted at some prominent place on deck and that the female passengers read them only after they were first screened by a male passenger and brought to the females. Two sets of newspapers issued on California-bound vessels during the gold rush still exist. Seven of the eight issues of *The Petrel,* produced in the ship *Duxbury* between March and July 1849, have survived. In the first issue the editor described the newspaper as "our weekly budget of fun, fact, and fancy, for the particular edification of amusement of the passengers." Eight issues of *The Barometer* were produced on board the ship *Mary Waterman* during her voyage to California in 1850; seven issues have survived. Issue number four is missing for both newspapers.[17]

Writing in their journals or writing letters to loved ones at home occupied some time for many passengers. Some of those who faithfully kept journals seemingly recognized that the adventure they had undertaken was a truly significant part of their lives as well as the lives of their families and even the nation and would continue to hold that importance in the future. Others faithfully wrote about their experiences and thoughts as a record for their parents, children, or spouses as well as for their own future use and enjoyment. Occasionally they noted how tedious it was to write when nothing was going on or when they were along the equator and making very little headway. Sometimes passengers wrote about how hard it was to write because of the motion of the vessel in stormy weather. Possibly the number of passengers on board was a factor in how much was going on. When there were large numbers of passengers, it was at times difficult to find a space to write, especially a quiet one where one could contemplate upon what was being written. According to what some people wrote, a great many more started journals than kept them up throughout the voyage. Some journals contain frequent gaps of a few days. About a month after the ship *Balance* sailed, John McCrackan wrote his sister that although most of the passengers started out keeping journals, there were then only about three who continued doing so. The general feeling was that there was so little to write about other than one's thoughts and "few are vain enough . . . to think the thoughts worth writing down." Anne (Willson) Booth wrote after a month at sea that a great many in the ship *Andalusia* were keeping journals and that nearly all the passengers were keeping a record of some kind. She also noted that her father had asked her to keep a journal. Walter Balfour Gould indicated about a month into his voyage in the bark *Maria* that he was "scribbling for the benefit and use of friends at home and future generations. I hope that they will derive both amusement and instruction from these pages, for they are confounded dull to me, and I am afraid will be to all who ever look at them." Near the end of the voyage of the ship *Plymouth,* a passenger noted that his was a "record written without care as intended only for the eyes of those to whom my character is well known, and who will therefore know well how to excuse the faults and errors of the writer." He noted it was his first, and would be his last, effort at keeping a journal and wished he could have made it more interesting but was thankful that he had "no tale of <u>shipwreck, fire, or starvation</u> to relate for howe'er interesting they may be to the reader, they are anything but pleasant neighbors." He added that there was "more pleasure in the <u>imagination</u> than in <u>reality</u>." John Taylor perhaps summed it best when he described why he and others persisted in their journal writing.

> Having taken upon myself the duty of chronicleing the events of this voyage, I wish to make them as plain and true to their occurrence as I can that in after years when in referring to them with my relations and friends we will not be feeding our imaginations with fancy sketches. In addition to my fully realized inability to write easily and gramatically, I find that to note day after day the wind, weather, &c. on a long sea voyage is exceedingly dull and monotonous work. So it seems and has since a month out to me. But I am gratified with the hope that when time dims them in my recollection they will read and sound different. Trusting also that my friends (for whom is the main cause of my perseverence) that see the accounts I am writing for the first time, will take some interest knowing that each days scenes were viewed by me. So I persevere in writing a journal among the few that are now doing so. Most of the passengers left N.Y. with books & writing materials for this object but gave it up saying it was too dull and too little to record to pay for the trouble.[18]

Observing nature was both entertaining and enlightening. The vast majority of those sailing to California in 1849 had never seen a sunrise or sunset over the open ocean nor had they seen moonlight over the ocean or a sailing vessel under sail on a bright moonlit night. They had never seen whales, the many different varieties of birds and fish in the Southern Hemisphere, the Magellanic Clouds (or Magellan Clouds, as the passengers called them) and the Southern Cross that can be seen only south of the equator, among numerous other things. In addition they certainly had not experienced such things as waterspouts and storms at sea. Many of the passengers wrote about these things although most of those who did so declared that they were incapable of capturing the beauty of what they saw. This was especially true of sunrises and sunsets. A passenger in the ship *Plymouth* wished for the "poetic mind of the much lamented Keats or the descriptive prowess of a Charles Lamb or a Wilis" so that he could give "a faint idea of the beauty" of such occurrences as sunrises and sunsets.[19] Some noted that not even a painting would present the beauty accurately and completely. A vast array of images could often be seen in the clouds at sunset.

"Magellan Clouds" and the "Southern Cross" seemingly were familiar terms to most passengers as they neared the equator, and they looked forward to viewing them for the first time. Many described them, but none did so with the clarity and detail as a passenger in the brig *Forest*.

> There is a phenomena in the southern sky which those astronomers which we have read have made no mention of. This is the Magellan clouds. They are three in number. One of them is black, while the other two are a bright golden color, and are on the opposite side of the south pole from that of the dark one. These two are on the meridian at 9 o'clock in the evening, on or about the 20th of December, and the other about the 30th of January. They may be seen from any position south of the equator on a clear night. They are situated—one near the head of Borado (a swordfish). The dark spot is situated near the Southern Cross, and is near the meridian about the 15th of May each year. The Crux (or cross) is on the meridian about the 15th of May, and 28 degrees from the South Pole.
>
> When we had crossed the equator and came in sight of the bright clouds, we heard the sailors' stories surmising what the cause of these bright spots might be. One had heard that it was caused by the ice in the southern region; but the most common cause assigned was that they were the reflections from some minerals in the bed of the sea casting bright rays on the sky among the stars.
>
> But we have come to this conclusion: That they were the reflection from burning craters in the newly discovered lands around the South Pole. However, not being satisfied with the opinions of others, nor with my own convictions or conclusions, I watch them closely in my rambles among the stars.[20]

A passenger in the bark *Maria* wrote that the light spots in the Magellanic Clouds were "collections of suns and planets, apparently concentrated within a narrow compass" and that the dark clouds appeared "to be a boundless vacuum or cavern, or space without bounds." Another Argonaut wrote that they were either "a mass of luminous vapor, or a cluster of celestial bodies like our own universe. The Southern Cross, said to be the brightest constellation in the universe, consists of four very bright stars in the shape of a cross and is visible just above the Magellan Clouds. At the equator these constellations are just above the horizon, but off Cape Horn they are almost directly overhead."[21]

John McCrackan wrote his sister Lottie about the appearance of the sea and the ship *Balance* on a bright moonlit night in the South Pacific. He reported, "It was very mild & nearly a full moon, (without a cloud) reflecting upon the water, & you could see by its mellow light the white crested wave coming in such majesty & beauty, while in the immediate rays, the sea was illumined giving it the appearance of silver sheen upon which our vessel glided so gracefully. O my dear Lottie! There is no sight so grand & beautiful, as a ship under full sail on a moonlit sea. There is a sublimity, a grandeur about it, that the foamy battlements of Niagra, never can inspire. You feel all spirit, so light & joyous is it. It seems as if you 'could take up yourself wings, & flee away.'"[22]

In late July 1849 several large sulphur-bottom whales were playing around the ship *Balance*. They swam around the ship, dove so deeply into the ocean that their bodies—which were about sixty feet long—appeared to be only five or six feet long, rose to the surface again, and spouted. Some of the passengers wanted to harpoon one or more of the whales, but the captain would not permit it because sulphur-bottom whales had stove one ship and crashed down upon another after rising out of the water at great speed. The whales were at times so close to the ship one passenger noted he could have touched them from his window with a short stick and added, "You can have no idea of the beauty of the sight. Here were these immense creatures, these 'Leviathan's' playing about us in great glee, & quite as familiar as we cared to be with them. This was a great treat for after seeing a 'whale' a distance from you, (& some you can see six miles off), you naturally feel a desire to get a better view, & this was a rare chance indeed."[23]

It was for the sunrises and the sunsets at sea, however, that the passengers reserved their best and grandest descriptive abilities even though many of those who described them noted that words could not adequately portray the wonders and beauties of what they saw on many occasions. A passenger in the bark *Maria* had this to say about a sunrise in the tropical regions of the Pacific:

> To what on earth can I compare this morning's sunrise, and how can I describe this terrestrial scene? At six o'clock, lying in my berth, and looking out of my little window, it facing the east, while our ship was ploughing her way through the agitated waters, caused by the storm through the night, towards the N.N.W., I beheld all along the horizon as far as I could see one heap of dark gray clouds, rolled and piled one upon another, to the height of two degrees above the horizon, sending forth vivid lightning and peals of thunder that shook the ocean to its very centre. Directly before the great luminary, rose one immense black cluster as dense as the pit of night. The sun's rays penetrating through every opening, above and in the distance, is the clear crystal azure, with clouds presenting a lake here and there an island, its waters of pearl and shores of gold. At this moment, I arose to gaze and mingle my emotions with my fellow passengers, a part of whom were already on deck, standing gazing at the scene, and like myself were enchanted with its beauty. Having now a view of the whole horizon, and casting my eye to the west, there too, all was beauty, the sun in the morning gilding the west, as it does the east at sunset, giving the clouds such a diversity, that for me to attempt the description would be nonsense; then the promised bow stretching double across the west, each seemingly trying to outvie each other in the display of their gorgeous tints. Just look at this picture, the sun gilding the clouds in the distance, while others dart forked lightning and mighty roar, with awe and admiration, presenting lakes and islands, with the bow of promise stretched double across the heavens, while all over one's head is the clear transparent blue. I could but make these few remarks, as I shall soon leave the tropics and nowhere else have I seen any thing to compare with these scenes.[24]

A passenger in the ship *Pacific* described a tropical sunset with equal enthusiasm, awe, and wonderment.

> Oh! These far surpass anything of the kind I ever beheld. The clouds assume so many shapes and forms, and when receiving the strong rays of the setting sun upon their different angles and densi-

ties, through one and upon another, a scene is produced almost overpowering. This afternoon we had one different in some respects from any that I witnessed in the Atlantic. A large black cloud lay across the western horizon rising about fifteen degrees above it. A clear narrow streak at the bottom and near where the sun was about to set was all that attracted attention until the sun appeared beneath the cloud and sunk about one half its size in the deep ocean. The change was almost instantaneous and electrifying to our senses. Near the sun the clouds looked like molten gold running in veins in all directions, then other colours would appear mingling and blending their various hues, one with another, and all continually changing in colour as the clouds changed their positions with the sun, and when at last the sun's face had completely disappeared, its rays still lingered with us (as if reluctant to withdraw the splendors that afforded us so much delight) tinging the whole heavens with a beautiful pink. Long will the scene be remembered but can never be perfectly described.

John McCrackan also described an amazing sunset viewed from the deck of the ship *Balance*. Among the shapes he saw in the clouds were a Roman chariot attached to four prancing steeds, a traveling caravan of elephants and camels with huge wagons, mounted marshals, boys on their knees playing marbles, an upside down jackass, figureheads, snow-capped mountains, tall pine trees, and "The Wandering Jew" standing on one leg.[25] Raymond Cazallia Davis in the ship *Hampton* discovered that he could view those wonderful sunsets three times. He saw them first from the deck. As soon as the sun was below the horizon, he climbed up in the rigging until he could see the sun again. When it was once again below the horizon, he climbed still higher until he could view the sun a third time.[26]

Passengers in two vessels recorded viewing a lunar eclipse in March. One simply noted that "it was a beautiful sight at sea," but the other reported that they witnessed a dark spot on the full moon about 9:00 and recorded it as "a phenomena that surprized us not a little" until they looked at their almanacs and read that a lunar eclipse was to occur March 8. By 10:30 the eclipse had reached its extent, and "only a small crescent of the moon was visible, about as much as is seen in a new moon."[27]

Normally active men, most of whom were in their twenties, simply could not be perpetually idle during the voyage of several months. They found a variety of ways to be active because they knew that they faced hard

117

work ahead in the mines or in any other work they undertook after they arrived in San Francisco. Among the many activities were boxing, military marching exercises, walking, gymnastics, climbing around in the rigging, jumping rope, rowing around the ship or to other vessels or distant islands, swimming in the tropical waters of both the Atlantic and the Pacific Oceans, snowball fights in the colder regions, and pillow fights in the cabin. They also did a great deal of dancing on deck in the evenings, but their dancing certainly was not the traditional dancing of their era. Instead it was a much more freewheeling, individualistic type of physical exertion to relieve the boredom and monotony of the voyage and to release some of their pent-up energy.

Most journalists seem to have recorded boxing only when it first occurred in their vessel and then did not mention it again. Thus it is difficult to determine whether it was a onetime or an ongoing activity. Three passengers in the ship *Sweden* mentioned boxing in early March, within two weeks after they departed from Boston. One of them reported that he accidentally broke the nose of another passenger. Three passengers in the ship *Pacific* also mentioned the sport, and again it was during their first month at sea. One of them noted that the boxing delighted their captain "to see the passengers pound each other" since the first-class passengers and Capt. Hall J. Tibbits were in a constant conflict over food, living conditions, and treatment of passengers. One of the passengers also mentioned boxing twice and a mock fight "in which 50 or so were engaged" and noted that "Any quantity of pants and coats were torn and a great deal of fun produced" in late April. Boxing was also mentioned on board the bark *Velasco* in both April and August and on board the ship *Orpheus* in February, when "one bloody nose" was "the extent of the injuries received," and again in April. Passengers in the bark *Belvidera* had their dinner disrupted one day by a "tremendous shouting & laughing on the bow of the vessel" and found that two passengers were engaged in a boxing match in which they "were belaboring each other most <u>unscientifically</u>," but one did give the other a "terrible black eye."[28]

Moses Cogswell provided reasons for the creation of military drill groups on vessels sailing to California when he noted "we don't know but we may be obliged to fight in California before we return, if not on our arrival." Such groups were often formed shortly before July 4 so that they could parade in the celebration activities of that national holiday. Others seem to have started for exercise and amusement. Harry G. Brown in the bark *Selma* noted the drilling was "good exercise" and was "beneficial for our health." Two passengers in the ship *Crescent* reported an occasion on which the marchers drilled to only a drum for a while and then they roused a large pig and forced him to precede them around the deck, squealing and grunting with the drummer trying to keep in rhythm with him. The pig made an attempt to escape and dashed down the stairs to the captain's and mates' cabin. Passengers in the ship *Daniel Webster* marched "over hogsheads, boats, the cooks gally" to the accompaniment of "one fiddle one tryangle the privates Whistling." Joseph Augustine Benton reported that the "Ann Street Corps of fantasticals paraded under Capt. Dyer, & made a very comical appearance." While there was undoubtedly some seriousness in the military exercises, they were also a great deal of fun and amusement for both the participants and the spectators. The participants benefited from the exercise.[29]

When sailing vessels were in the vicinity of the equator, they often made little progress because of the lack of wind. On those calm days captains sometimes took, or allowed passengers to take, boats to row around the ship or to row a distance from the vessel to allow those who had never seen a large vessel with all its sails set to get a full view of that sight. Sometimes passengers rowed to another vessel that was nearby; other times they had rowing races in which they occasionally pretended to be engaged in attempting to harpoon a whale; and other times they rowed to an island in the distance. Benjamin Bailey said he had never seen "anything look more beautiful" than the ship *Sweden* with all her sails set. Thomas Whaley reported two days about three weeks apart on which they rowed around the ship *Sutton* and then went swimming at the conclusion of the second rowing expedition. Charles Williams described racing from the ship *Pacific* to a vessel two and a half miles away. They had almost collided with that vessel two days previous. Williams indicated that a second expedition was planned for the next morning. Alfred Doten wrote about two crews, one headed by the first mate and the other by the second mate, racing toward an old flour barrel that had been thrown overboard. They pretended it was a whale, and each crew harpooned the barrel and then raced back to their bark, the *Yoeman*. The longest rowing expedition was undertaken by several passengers in the ship *Pacific* when they obtained permission from the captain to row to the island of Juan Fernandez, which was estimated to be fifty or sixty miles away. The men promised to return by night but failed to do so because it was nearly dark by the time they reached the island. In addition they were too tired to attempt the return trip. Bad weather forced them to remain on the island. Captain Easterbrook sailed the *Pacific* toward the island to search for the men and the boat. They eventually were reunited after a delay of four days. Those who remained on board the *Pacific* were greatly upset by this delay.[30]

Various forms of gymnastic exercises were arranged on board a few vessels. William H. Dougal simply mentioned gymnastics in brief daily notes of his voyage in the bark *Galindo*. A passenger in the schooner *General Morgan* noted that for several days "all hands" had been amusing themselves with "gymnastic exercises, and various feats of agility." He added they also "had some performances on the slack rope." John Taylor wrote of how they had lashed a "gymnasium pole . . . about seven feet high across the quarter deck" of the ship *Orpheus* and added that it was "frequently occupied with much perseverance, most generally just before dark, sometimes mornings."[31]

Many passengers wrote about walking on deck, mostly in the early morning before breakfast, for exercise. Few were as dedicated to this activity as a passenger in the ship *Plymouth*, who seems to have walked a mile every day that the weather permitted. He calculated that walking across the deck 310 times equaled a mile. At that rate it seems he could walk only between seventeen and eighteen feet across the vessel. It must have taken considerable persistence and concentration to keep track of the number of crossings. He also mentioned jumping rope and climbing in the rigging for exercise.[32]

In order to pass the time, passengers played a variety of types of games. Board games included chess, checkers, draughts, and backgammon. Many also played dominoes. A great many journalists simply reported playing cards, but others specified euchre, whist, old maid, poker, monte, bluff, and "brag" (a game similar to poker). Others mentioned "caseina" (casino?), "Fox and Geese," "rattle and snap," "pins," and "all fours." Solving puzzles, pitching pennies, and flying kites were also mentioned. Griffith Meredith was certainly one of the more active card players. He mentioned playing whist on seventy-five days between February 9 and August 28, 1849.[33] One passenger reported a superstition about playing cards in sailing vessels. The captain had established a rule against card playing, but some of the passengers in the forward house played anyway. After a week of headwinds the captain told those passengers that card playing would have to stop if they wanted to have favorable winds. The passengers stopped for the time being but resumed their card playing after they left Valparaiso. The captain seized their cards and threw them overboard. Captain Hammond of the brig *Sea Eagle* also was of the opinion that cards and backgammon were responsible for unfavorable winds and said "the cards had better be thrown over-board." A passenger in the ship *Henry Lee* noted that they had favorable winds after a pack of cards were thrown overboard.[34]

Nearly all the passengers in sailing vessels bound for California in 1849 seem to have been aware of the long-standing custom of inducting green hands, or greenies as they were sometimes called, into the kingdom of King Neptune when their vessel crossed "The Line," as the equator was commonly called among seafarers. There were induction ceremonies on board thirty-one of the vessels from which journals were examined during the course of researching this study. On another twenty-seven of the vessels from which journals were examined there were no traditional shaving and dunking ceremonies although King Neptune either appeared or otherwise made his presence known. In some he was deterred from performing the traditional ceremony by sufficient contributions of liquor. In one vessel the captain's wife sponsored a banquet and dance when they crossed the line in an effort to establish a new tradition.

In a couple of the vessels on which Neptune did not appear, the passengers "dunked" those who had not previously crossed the line or doused each other with water. Passengers in the bark *Anna Reynolds* celebrated the event by toasting Neptune's health with "a pail of Lemonade." Others noted that there were too many greenies in their vessel or that Neptune was probably up wind of them on another vessel, as there were so many fools crossing it at the time. Some of those in the brig *Osceola* put an invitation to Neptune in a bottle and threw it overboard, and he replied that he would board the vessel but could not remain long because of the "ill health of Mrs. Neptune." Another passenger noted that they had thirty-seven who had not previously crossed the line and only twelve who had done so and also that it was raining hard when they crossed it. A passenger in the ship *Plymouth* speculated that another vessel had crossed just ahead of them and had supplied Neptune with so much "50 percent above proof New England Rum" that he had gone to "bed with a headache." Isaac W. Baker surmised that Neptune did not visit them because he was "getting <u>Old</u> and not overfond of working at his trade."[35]

In most cases in which there was a visit by King Neptune and a traditional ceremony of shaving and dunking, the majority of the passengers submitted to it in good humor, but on some vessels a few passengers armed themselves with knives and guns and strongly resisted being shaved, and they usually succeeded in their efforts to avoid the traditional induction ceremony. In the ship *Reindeer* those who did not want to be shaved could be excused by treating Neptune's company with liquor or paying fifty cents. Most of the large group of Chileans who joined the bark *Keoka* in Valparaiso submitted to shaving, but a few paid two dollars to avoid it. When the *Keoka* previously crossed the line in the Atlantic, it cost the passengers a bottle of liquor or three dollars to avoid being shaved. Passengers in the bark *Canton* could avoid a shaving by contributing a bottle of brandy. Captain Nickerson of the bark *Elvira* received a note from Neptune on January 30, 1849, announcing that he would visit on board that evening. Actually two Neptunes appeared. The first was someone referred to as Old Buckley. He was given a half pint of brandy laced with four tablespoons of an emetic powder. Then the "real" Neptune announced his presence and Old Buckley took off his costume. He was later shaved and was invited to have a drink with the "real" Neptune but soon became sick from the emetic and vomited and remained sick for two hours.[36]

John McCrackan provided a detailed description of the visit on board the ship *Balance* in which he included all of the elements traditionally included in the induction ceremonies plus one or two extra elements suited specifically for the situation in that vessel.

> The old fellow came on board on Saturday night in all the pomp & circumstance that attends his visits. It had been considered doubtful if his Magesty would visit the "Balance," & many were much surprised when he hailed us about ten oclock with a huge trumpet, in a sonorous voice, commanding all hands to meet him at the Ship's bow. The rush & excitement was tremendous, the knowing ones to meet him while those who feared to be victims made strait for their rooms. His Magesty stood upon the bow sprit with his attendants, two small boys, & that you may better recognize him let me describe his dress & appearance. He was six feet, looked seven. Some swore he was ten after a hurried glance. A hair mask face, & head & body gave him a very ferocious appearance to speak mildly, bare legs, with hair hanging in strips, his feet marked with tar in imitation of sandals, over all he wore a white robe, as also did his two pages. He wore false eye brows & lashes & I must say presented a very imposing appearance. We were sailing along very quietly. The moon was full & shown very bright, lending to the whole scene a very strange & unnatural effect. His Magesty took his seat on the windlass after

he had been received by the first mate of the Ship. I may as well state that the Capt. on such occasions is supposed to be asleep. It would be rather undignified & besides he is responsible in case anything unpleasant happens. Old Neptune called for vinegar, a bottle being brought he tasted and asked how we come to have such miserable stuff. He was told it was bought for good & that the person who sold it was on the Ship. On hearing that he inquired his name & called upon him to come forward. This as you will see was preconcerted. The person who sold it was a fellow from Stratford by name of Chamberlain, & plain country looking & acting fellow, he had been very much of a butt, being too timid & cowardly to resent an insult, though he talked very large. Chamberlain was brought trembling from his berth & placed by the side of Neptune. The interview was very short & ended in making him drink a quart bottle of it. He was then lathered with slush & tar & shaved with a broad axe. This was done with all the dignity of a marriage ceremony. He was then sent forward to bail out old Neptunes boat, & here a pail of water saluted him drenching him from head to feet. He had been very quiet till now but bursting out he became insulting & disrespectful, & he was ordered to a repetition of the ceremony. This was rather hard for poor Chamberlain, & such a figure as he cut the next morning was truly rediculous, his hair being cut close on one side. We were all called up in turn, some paying the forfeit of a bottle of wine & others standing the operation of shaving & shaking hands. Neptune's hand was greased with slush after which was a coating of tar & when he took their hand he was very pressing in his salutation, & he left the hands completely covered by transferring all the tar from his hand onto theirs, & then another very unpleasant trick was, when his page was lathering the subject, Old Neptune would ask the subject some question & when he opened his mouth to reply, the brush found its way into the throat, causing the subject to cough & swear most heartily. After the ceremony had all been accomplished he formed a procession & heading it he marched all, by the Galley, stationed on top which were four persons with pails of water & as the procession passed they were all ducked in fine style. Old Neptune administers an oath most of which I have forgotten. One is "never to eat brown bread when you can get white unless you prefer the brown," "never to kiss the maid when you can the mistress," & such like. These are administered with great solemnity. It seems like wasting paper to write more though but half is told. The whole scene was very fine. . . . Most of the sailors got drunk which lasted two days. Neptune departed at midnight, but it was near day break before the Ship became quiet. His Magesty was personified by an old Sailor & one who well knew the responsibility of his position.[37]

George P. Coleman described an effort at establishing a new tradition for celebrating crossing the line on board the bark *Russell* from New Bedford, Massachusetts. As they approached the line, they were all expecting a visit from Neptune. At 6:00 the passengers received an invitation from Mrs. Francis B. Folger, wife of the captain, to meet on the quarterdeck at 8:00. They were all washed and dressed at the appointed time and were ushered into a tent that was lined with the American flag. A table "groaning under the weight of all the luxuries that could be found at home" awaited them. They were surprised to see Mrs. Folger rather than Neptune standing before them. They were formally introduced to the hostess, and the president of the Nantucket Mining and Trading Association spoke to them about "the Practice of Green Hands crossing the Line" and added that since "Reform was the order of the day," Mrs. Folger was carrying out "her desire to introduce a new method" of celebrating crossing the line. Therefore she had "prepared a Levee" for them. Captain Folger then spoke briefly and told them to help themselves to the food. As soon as the captain completed his remarks, they began "doing justice to the good things." After they finished eating they drank toasts and gave cheers to "our <u>Hostess, Captain, Officers, Crew</u>, and old Neptune."[38]

Playing practical jokes on each other and conducting mock trials, some of which were in themselves practical jokes, were popular ways of passing time and providing amusement and entertainment. Occasionally the practical jokes related to crossing the line. There was a lady (sometimes referred to as young and other times as old) named Miss Marchant, possibly the daughter of Abiah Marchant, both of whom were passengers in the ship *Magnolia* of New Bedford. Jokes were sometimes played on Miss Marchant. One such occasion occurred as the *Magnolia* approached the line. A cabin passenger was looking through his telescope and remarked that he could see the line. Miss Marchant expressed a wish to look, and the wish was granted. As she gazed through the telescope, another passenger stretched a silken thread across the other end of the telescope. Miss Marchant "was perfectly satisfied that she had glimpsed the line although at a great distance and said she supposed that it would show plainer . . . as we drew nearer to it." A passenger in the ship *Andalusia* had not previously crossed the line and stationed himself on the forecastle to be sure he saw it. Others told him to be sure to keep his head "very low" so that he would not "run against it and be knocked overboard."[39]

Most practical jokes and mock trials were relatively simple matters and were described briefly in journals, but one occurrence in the ship *Pacific* was quite different, as it was a combination of a trial and a joke. A passenger from Brooklyn named Gay had been the butt of several jokes, in part because of his "good nature and unsuspecting innocence." A group of individuals decided to organize a court "for all sorts of minor offences such as spitting on deck, and the like" and elected officers including a judge, district attorney, and sheriff. They decided to try Gay for some alleged offence in Rio de Janeiro. Of course, they found him guilty and sentenced him to "Punches for the crowd." He refused to pay the sentence. They then took him below and seized lemons, sugar, and alcohol from his room and began to mix the punch. Unknown to these passengers, there were some on board, including a Dr. Beale, who thought the jokes played on Gay had gone too far. Dr. Beale produced tartar emetic, but it is uncertain if he or an accomplice added it to the punch. The members of the court and their accomplices "partook freely of the beverage and unanimously pronounced it <u>very good</u>—<u>most excellent</u>." Later the bell was sounded for tea and all rushed to eat. Soon after those who had partaken of the punch began to drink their warm tea the emetic began to take effect, and one by one they rushed on deck to the rail and emptied their stomachs into the sea. They soon suspected that the punch had been spiked with something and asked Gay if he had put "ipecac in that punch." He replied that it was "not my wine that disagrees with you, but it is justice that don't set well on your stomachs. You are not accustomed to it; you will do better by longer practice." Most of the affected ones realized that a joke had been played upon them while they were playing one on another person and took the matter in stride although some of them attempted to discover and perhaps punish the supplier of the emetic.[40]

Combinations of music, singing, and dancing were popular amusement and entertainment. Much of the dancing was also quite good exercise. There was hardly a sailing vessel bound for California that did not have passengers who could and would sing, some well and others badly, and play a variety of instruments. Music with singing and sometimes dancing was also popular among the sailors, who occasionally participated with the passengers. Many of the passengers could also dance all the popular dances of the day as well as various improvisations. On board many vessels music with singing and/or dancing was enjoyed nightly on deck during good weather and on occasion below deck during bad weather. Much of the music and singing seems to have been impromptu, but occasionally it was provided by organized bands or singing groups. There were a few exceptions. The California Tin and Wood Band played on board the schooner *General Worth.* One passenger noted that "music sounds sweetest coming <u>over</u> water" but "the only thing that would have made the discords of this . . . band sound sweet was to hear it going <u>under</u> the water." The El Dorado Band played for the entertainment of the passengers in the brig *Osceola,* and the San Francisco Melodeon Band played on board the bark *San Francisco.* One passenger in the ship *Pacific* referred to the "Pacific band," but it may not actually have been an organized group. Those in the ship *America* were entertained on many occasions by a group called simply the Glee Club. The Andalusian Harmonists performed occasionally in the ship *Andalusia,* and the Sagamores sometimes sang on board the ship *Sweden* although it is not certain that they were really an organized singing group. They were members of the Roxbury Sagamore Company and were frequently referred to as Sagamores.[41]

Traditional instruments mentioned in journals included violin, fiddle, post horn, piano, banjo, fife, Jews harp, flute, guitar, French horn, bass drum, kettle drum, cymbals, tambourine, bells, and accordion. Nontraditional instruments included tin pan, plate, bells, dipper, barrel, tub, bucket, handspike, and "anything that is hollow." Passengers in the bark *Yoeman* made "capital horns, trumpets, and whistles" form several bunches of kelp they picked up while rowing around their vessel. One passenger noted that they all played their instruments at once, "each one trying to make more noise than the other. They sounded very much like the horns which were blown before Jerico." Titles of songs played or sung were rarely mentioned in passengers' journals other than at Fourth of July celebrations and occasional Sunday worship services.[42]

Traditional dances included cotillion, polka, quadrille, waltz, "contra," and "Irish jig." Pierce W. Barker noted that in the ship *Nestor* they also danced "fore and afters, a regular muster dance, and in fact, we cut all manner of capers. I think our antics sometimes would compare with 20 or 30 boys on a hollow day." On another occasion he referred to their dance as "a regular break down." One passenger in the ship *Morrison* noted that "owing to the absence of the fair" men "of heavy mould, coarse features, and heavy whiskers and moustache" acting the "part of the ladies destracted from the poetry of the scene." Usually some of the men simply danced the female roles, but occasionally they dressed for the part. Sometimes there were disputes over which passengers would dance the female roles. On some occasions on board the bark *Strafford*, "several of the members <u>dressed</u> themselves up in long morning <u>gowns</u> and fixed themselves as much as they could like a <u>woman</u>, which created quite a <u>laugh among the members</u> and made it quite interesting." Griffith Meredith indicated that he assumed the female role at their dance on Washington's birthday and wished that "some of our New York friends could only take a peep on our deck and see the young gents dancing as '<u>ladies</u>' showing off in their different attitudes" and indicated that he thought his sisters "would <u>laugh heartily</u>" if they "could see me dancing as a lady and waltzing too." On another occasion a single male in the *Strafford* named A. W. Potts

> put on a long morning gown and buttoned it up all the way to the top, than lasted it up on the waist tight, then filled it out in the (b___m) like a woman, then folded a handkerchief like a cape and put it on then took a broad brimed hat and turned it up behind and brought it down before like a straw bonnet and put on a pair of white linen drawers over his pants to serve (as a pair of pantelets) then a pair of linen gloves and a <u>fan</u> in his hand and then came on deck which created repeated roars of laughter from members. He was a good dancer and moved light and took them off well (<u>lady</u>) took hold of his dress when he moved forward just as a great many do dancing. He had good music. This woman (<u>gent</u>) was treated like a lady by all members introduced to her with all formality and gentility usual in society, all of which passed off in good style and perfect harmony with all. A woman would be quite a curiosity to us here on the broad Atlantic Ocean.

As part of the celebration of George Washington's birthday, the passengers in the ship *Jane Parker* had a dance at which "seven Ladies of our own manufacture" apparently were a great hit. These men had "shaved off their whiskers and moustaches for the better personification of the female character." Some made their own dresses, and others borrowed dresses from the captain's wife. A passenger wrote that it was a scene that would not "be easily forgotten to see the tall ladies all good dancers gracefully moving in the dance."[43]

Catching and shooting at birds provided considerable amusement and entertainment in the colder regions of the Southern Hemisphere. As noted in chapter 3, passengers sometimes ate the birds that they caught, but they certainly caught a great many more than they ate. Many more birds were caught than shot. Shooting either flying birds or those floating on waves from a rolling and pitching vessel was an extremely difficult feat. When a passenger succeeded in killing a bird with his gun, the bird invariably fell into the water rather than onto the deck, and it was certainly imprudent, if not impossible, to lower a boat and try to retrieve the dead bird. John Ross Browne commented upon the marksmanship of passengers in the ship *Pacific*. "All the sportsmen on deck popping away with their rifles and shot-guns. Terrible destruction of gun-powder. More than a hundred volleys fired, and the birds badly frightened, but only one or two killed. We have a marksman on board who might possibly shoot the side of a house at ten paces. One shot a hole in the mainsail, another hit the main-top-mast studding sail yard. Phil Walden in attempting to shoot a goney came within six inches of killing the man at the helm but missed him providentially, and only shot a hole through the roof of the roundhouse—on which it happened fortunately there was nobody standing at the time."

Catching birds was generally accomplished by baiting a fishhook with a piece of pork, throwing the baited hook over the side or stern of the vessel, and allowing it to float on the surface of the water. Birds would seize the piece of pork in their beaks and be caught by the hook. They could then be hauled onto the deck. Various things were done with those birds caught. A small number were killed, skinned, cooked, and eaten. Others were killed and parts taken by passengers for souvenirs. Usually someone took the beak or the head; some took feet or legs; a few took wings or at least wing feathers; some took other feathers for stuffing mattresses; others took wing bones; and a few took breast bones. Some passengers skinned the birds with the intention of preserving and stuffing them later. Hollow bones were occasionally used as pipe stems. Some of the birds were marked by having a piece of leather or light board attached to their necks with the date, name of vessel and sometimes the captain, the port from which they sailed, the date they sailed or the number of days out, and the latitude and longitude noted on the leather or board. Other birds were kept on deck for a time and examined and studied by any interested passengers and then let go. Sometimes the birds on deck got into fights with the passengers and the occasional pet dog. The passengers were always surprised that the albatross and some other birds they caught could not take off from the deck although they could do so from the water. Occasionally, rather than catch birds, passengers attached a piece of pork to each end of a string and threw the entire thing into the water and then watched as two birds swallowed a piece of pork each and then tugged and fought each other, attempting to get free. All of this seems to have entertained and amused the passengers greatly in spite of how cruel it might have been to the birds.[44]

Catching sharks, or attempting to do so, in the warmer waters of both the Atlantic and Pacific Oceans, occasionally provided exciting amusement and entertainment. When sharks were sighted, preparations were usually made to attempt to catch one or more. Shark hooks made of heavy iron were baited with large pieces of pork and thrown overboard in hopes that the shark would swallow the bait and be caught by the hook. It was normally a long and difficult fight to get a hooked shark alongside the vessel and to haul it on board, but many groups were able to accomplish it. Frequently one of the sailors or officers harpooned a shark before it was hauled on deck. Many times they fastened a line around the shark's tail to provide a second fastening. Some captains would not allow the shark to be brought on deck because of the offensive smell the carcass would cause. Usually the sharks were killed either immediately or after some examination and experimentation. Many passengers were afraid of them even after they were on board because of the multiple rows of large, sharp teeth. When a shark was definitely dead, passengers collected items for souvenirs and for practical use. The skin was a good substitute for sandpaper. Teeth and backbones made good souvenirs. Only on rare occasions did a single passenger get the entire backbone. It was usually divided into individual sections with each passenger receiving only one piece. Passengers in the ship *Balance* made checkers out of the backbone of one shark they had caught. In some instances passengers removed many organs such as the liver, heart, brain, and entrails and examined them carefully before disposing of the carcass. Sometimes part of the meat was cut off and cooked.[45]

Gambling provided some amusement and entertainment for some passengers in a few vessels and likely some sorrow for the ones who lost money or whatever else was used in the gambling. Much of what might be called gambling was in the form of small wagers on when the vessel would arrive in San Francisco or one of the other ports entered en route or on the number of miles sailed in a day or since the original departure. Wagers were commonly small and included such items as oranges or other fruit, nuts, or desserts. Conducting lotteries was another form of small-stakes gambling. Chances in lotteries were frequently a quarter or a half dollar with prizes such as a watch, a watch chain, knives, a chess set, and a spy glass. Poker and a similar game called bluff were played in a few vessels. In the bark *Midas* passengers played poker for English walnuts, but one passenger felt that could last but a short time, as the winners would eat all the winnings. Probably the worst vessel for gambling was the brig *Osceola* in which some passengers set up a faro bank and later a keno game. They also played poker and bluff. Captain Fairfowl ordered that the gambling be stopped. If it were not discontinued, he would lay the vessel to. Some gamblers who lost all their money cut the buttons off their coats, vests, and other garments and played bluff for buttons. Faro was ultimately discontinued when one person won three hundred and broke the bank. Many passengers expressed opposition to gambling of any kind, and some of them wrote disparaging comments about their fellow passengers who gambled. One in the ship *Morrison* felt gambling "really betokens no good to us" and thought it was "the height of madness and folly" and was sure the gamblers "would be shamefully mortified to be seen by their friends at home." A passenger in the ship *Pharasalia* commented, "Such are the puritanical New England men away from home" that they would gamble on shipboard but would not do so at home.[46]

A variety of pets were taken on board vessels and provided some amusement and entertainment. They also caused a few problems from time to time. Types of pets included dogs, cats, pigs, doves, a pigeon, a monkey, and a crow. As one might expect, dogs were the pets most frequently taken in the vessels. In most vessels there was only one dog, but some had several dogs. In a few instances there were multiple types of pets in a vessel. Several of the dogs became ill during the voyage, and a number of them did not survive. A dog named Jack on board the schooner *General Morgan* "was taken with the dog distemper, and was killed and thrown overboard." One of the passengers on board the ship *Arkansas* ordered the sailors to wash her dog. When they finished, they released the dog to shake herself dry. In the process of doing so she fell overboard and drowned "to the joy of all on board except her master, who would not be comforted and mourned the balance of the day upon gruel." The two dogs on board the ship *Sweden* died of unknown causes. The dog belonging to Mr. Devine on board the ship *Europe* "was taken with a fit as if mad." When Mrs. Devine noted this, "she seized her by the throat and threw her overboard." One dog in the bark *Gold Hunter* was "sick for several days with a kind of scurvy," but his fate is uncertain. Leo and Jacob, the two dogs in the bark *Yoeman*, fought regularly and frequently had to be tied at separate ends of the vessel to keep them apart. On occasion they were muzzled. The frequent fights of the three dogs on board the bark *Anna Reynolds* created so many disturbances that the passengers "almost wish the dogs overboard." One of the dogs died before they arrived in San Francisco. The two dogs on board the bark *Canton* were sometimes "set to fighting." One passenger thought it was "a cruel sport." There were five dogs named Lion, Tiger, Plato, Zack, and Sport in the ship *Magnolia* early in the voyage, but while they were in Talcahuano they added four more plus a cat. Zack and Plato fought each other from time to time. The ship *America* also had five dogs on board, but only one seems to have been well liked. The captain reportedly commented that "if they were all lost overboard but Tige he should be glad," but he "wouldn't loose" Tige "for anything." One of the dogs, Prince, died during the voyage.[47]

Cats seem to have been the second most frequently carried pets. Sammy, the cat that boarded the ship *Plymouth* in Boston, climbed into the rigging, went out on the end of the davit, and generally went everywhere in the vessel. She fell overboard twice; after the second episode one passenger indicated, "next time she will have to go for it." The passenger indicated that he had taught the cat tricks including sitting in the corner and jumping through his hands when he held them about three feet from the deck. The cat on board the brig *Oriental* was lost overboard off Cape Horn. The one on the ship *Florida* was rescued after she fell overboard, presumably in warmer waters. William Ives Morgan in the bark *John Walls* noted, "Our Female died last night, & was buried with the Honors of War. It was the only Female on Board—the death was felt all over the ship. it was the cat." He was not the only passenger to include a bit of mystery in his writing. A passenger in the ship *America* noted that "a young Brazilian, the only female on board," fell over board, but she was saved by quick action of some of the officers and sailors who reached her "before she went down for the last time and just in time to save her from the sharks!" The next day, however, the young and inexperienced Brazilian caught the favorite pigeon on board only to be caught herself by the dog Tige. Passengers interfered to free the young Brazilian from the dog. Finally the passenger identified the young Brazilian as their "kitten of direct Brazilian decent."[48]

A great many vessels carried pigs to butcher for fresh meat, but occasionally one of the pigs became a pet. Old Dick was one such in the ship *Plymouth*. He was the only survivor from the pigs taken on board in Boston and was so fat that he could hardly move; he was "in every body's mess and no body's watch." The last of the seven pigs in the bark *Canton* became "quite a pet" and would "follow any of us when called, and lie down and roll about like the dogs." He was also "very fond of nuts." One of the sows in the ship *Plymouth* gave birth, thereby increasing the number of livestock on board to twenty-three, and another was expected to give birth soon and raise the number still more. One passenger commented, "If we only had a horse & cow should have an imitation of a barn yard in miniature."[49]

The ship *San Francisco* had on board a mischievous crow named Moses, a cat named Katy Baker, and a dog but lost them all within about a month's time. The crow loved to pick up stray pipes, jackknives, and "any other small articles left in his way" and at times attempted to be "a third hand at a game of checkers." Moses "committed an involuntary suicide . . . when foolishly endeavoring to fly when he knew he couldnt, he lost his balance when alighting, and we lost his company from this date." A few days after this incident, a passenger named Wyman "gave his Dog a dose of bricks (six around his neck) and offered him up as a sacrifice to Father Neptune!" No reason was given for this act. A month later, Katy Baker simply disappeared, and her owner could not determine if she fell overboard or "whether she made too free with somebody's berth & bedding, and was thrown over, as a sort of experimental curative."[50]

When the brig *Osceola* of Philadelphia was in Rio de Janeiro, two of the passengers purchased a monkey that created problems between them and the officers because of the monkey's devilry. After one episode the first mate threatened to decapitate the monkey. The owners concluded that the monkey was neither an "agreeable companion nor as profitable investment as they first imagined" and decided to hold a raffle to get rid of him. In an odd quirk of fate, he was won by the first mate. The monkey soon developed a chill and a fever. He was treated with hot drops, quinine, and burnt brandy, all to no avail. He died and "was sewed up in a duff-bag and cast overboard."[51]

The passengers in the bark *Gold Hunter* took along a number of carrier pigeons when they sailed from Bangor, Maine, on October 3, 1849. When they had been at sea a little more than two weeks, they recorded their latitude and longitude on linen, fastened the notes to six of the pigeons, hoping the birds would go to land and the information would be relayed to

Bangor. One of the birds fell into the water and drowned, and the other five returned to the vessel. Their having been confined for so long apparently adversely affected their ability to fly. By the time the vessel reached Rio de Janeiro, all but two males and one female had died. The remaining female had to be separated from the males because they pecked at her and chased her around the vessel. The men nursed her back to health, and when they got into warmer waters, they released her. Then the two males fought over her, but one won out and began nesting with her. The male who had lost attacked the nest and carried away the first egg the female laid. Unfortunately, nothing more was written about this, so the final outcome of the battle for affection and companionship is unknown.[52]

A variety of performances including magic shows, impersonations, minstrel shows, and others were enjoyed by passengers in several sailing vessels. A passenger in the brig *Sea Eagle* simply noted that there had been two or three theatrical performances "which served to while away the evening." Ferdinand Cartwright Ewer of the ship *York* noted that "Capt. Drew got on one of his old coats and a tremendous high dickey (which by the way would make two splendid flying jibs) and went on deck as large as life to amuse the associates by acting the part of a village lawyer which he succeeded in doing to the satisfaction of all." William M. Hatch reported that M. Keniston had been "personifying Johnny Booker, Jo. Mellus a drunkard & Daniel Mellus a countryman who they call Silas" in the schooner *Damariscove*. The "Minstrells amused with a few select negro songs" in the bark *Selma*. Capt. Francis Folger reportedly remarked "A little nonsense now & then Is relished by the best of men" after he, Mrs. Folger, and passengers and crew enjoyed the first performance by the California Minstrels in the bark *Russell*. At the second performance the group sang three original songs written for the performance by a passenger named Goldsmith. Elijah Johnson, known as the Doctor, appears to have given a one-man performance consisting of "negro extravaganzas, extempore Speeches, Songs, dances etc., concluding the whole with a burlesque upon the Italian opera" on board the ship *Sutton*. He was said to be "a tall genius, and one of his kind." A couple of evenings later Johnson "gave us an exhibition of Keen, Hamblin, Forrest etc. . . . imitating the various characters very well." "Siognor Tom Davis Blotz the California magician" presented "a specimen of his art by swallowing pistol balls with his eyes, nose, and ears, and spitting them out his mouth" on board the bark *San Francisco*. It was a grand performance with much laughter according to one passenger. Stephen Fellows, performing in the vein of "Potter, The

133

Magician" of New Hampshire, presented several magic shows in the ship *Sweden*. Included in the shows were "sundry tricks in necromancy such as folding a roll of Paper so as to form a great variety of articles, various feats with eggs, goblets, coin, cards and other articles." The shows "made much sport, and served very well to while away an evening." Two assistants called "Old Cram" and "Moore the Pilot" assisted him "and made more fun than 'Old Potter' himself." A group of passengers performed "Macbeth" in the second cabin of the ship *Europe*. The crowded house, including many passengers from the first cabin, provided "thunders of applause." A farce titled "The man who saw the Fight" was presented on board the bark *Belvidera*. Reverend Mr. Godfrey "coming up the hatch feet forward attached to a ropes end was a masterly effort & drew down thunders of applause" according to one passenger. The passengers in the ship *Pacific* enjoyed "an excellent burlesque . . . presented by half a dozen characters, which brought roars of laughter as at all the stopping places we would bring out all the New York cries." The passengers in the ship *Andalusia* appear to have produced the grandest show of all, as it included a minstrel show, music by the band and the singing group known as the Andalusian Harmonists, and a juggling act, all of which were performed in the "Steerage Hall" below deck. There was also a "performance on the slack rope" on deck, as there was not enough height between decks.[53]

Based upon how much passengers bound for California in 1849 worried about getting around the dreaded Cape Horn and the difficulties some of them experienced in getting past that obstacle, one might have assumed that there would be many grand celebrations of the event. Thus it is surprising that few passengers made mention of any celebrations. Perhaps they were too exhausted to celebrate, or the weather situation did not permit a celebration. In every case in which there was a celebration, alcohol was a major ingredient, and it appears that most of the passengers experienced some amusement and entertainment, albeit part of it was watching the antics of those who consumed too much alcohol. Passengers in the ship *Crescent* voted to allocate five gallons of molasses to be made into candy for their party to celebrate rounding the cape. They spent the better part of a day making thirty-eight pounds of candy divided into eighty pieces. Thus each of the sixty-one passengers and each officer and sailor could have nearly a half pound of candy. There were also cigars and plenty of brandy so that they "all had a good time." Some celebrated until midnight. A passenger in the brig *Osceola* wrote that "several of the after-cabin passengers had a jollification which lasted all night and part of this forenoon" when they learned they had passed the cape. He added that the "participants were as drunk as Bacchus and as merry as lords." Because of the roaring elements typical off the cape and "the carousing of the revelers, the night was rendered hideous." When the passengers in the ship *Europe* learned they were around the horn, they "determined to celebrate the event in a suitable manner; the punch bowl and 'old apple-jack' had to suffer in consequence and a right jovial night was had." One passenger noted that "Many had to be put to bed; one became raving and had to be tied down; some spouted, others swore, and others again fell into the meal barrel and had to be helped out." He compared their celebration to "the close of an election" at home and concluded that "Many were rather worse for the frolic and spent the next day in bed."[54]

As many of the California-bound passengers had skills such as painting, jewelry making, silversmithing, dentistry, hat making, blacksmithing, seafaring, and others, it should not be surprising that there were many things made to while away the long days. A number of passengers wrote that they had drawn or painted pictures of scenes they had viewed or portraits of people in the vessel. Others made rings out of ten-cent pieces, powder horns, pin cases, palm-leaf hats, pipes, goblets, dice boxes, compasses, pistol belts, knapsacks, cloth caps, knives, cups of coconut shells, and locks. One enterprising passenger constructed a spinning jenny to make fishing lines. A few made ship models.[55] Many of those who were part of joint stock companies made a great many other things to be used in the mines and are discussed in chapter 9.

Use of tobacco, either chewing or smoking, was quite prevalent among passengers. Many of the men found considerable enjoyment in smoking pipes and cigars after meals while others enjoyed chewing tobacco at various times. In spite of enjoyment, some passengers made serious efforts to stop smoking during their voyages, as they recognized it was harmful to their health. At least one acknowledged that it was quite addictive. Warren Fletcher, in the bark *Elvira*, made frequent references to smoking during the first two months of his voyage but never mentioned it after March 10. He gave no indication that he planned to stop, so perhaps he simply stopped mentioning smoking. Griffith Meredith mentioned smoking only once but indicated that most of the members had resumed smoking their pipes and cigars once they got into warmer regions. Smoking was usually allowed only on deck because of the risk of fire. Passengers stayed below most of the time in cold regions. One passenger in the bark *Chittenden* indicated that others regularly smoked a cigar or pipe after breakfast and implied that he opposed it, adding that they "suck away for pastime and amusement upon this stinking smoke chimney of disipation." J. Haskell Stearns was surprised on one occasion when he witnessed passengers using plugs of chewing tobacco in their pipes and expressed some disgust when he noted, "Oh! What a fall was their my country men!" Within two weeks of departing from Thomaston, Maine, John T. Howard reported that he had "concluded to diminish the quantity of tobacco" and hoped to "abandon the use of it altogether as I am fully confident that its use is injurious to me." He later entered into an agreement with Capt. George Jordan to stop using tobacco, but he expected to do it gradually. About three months into the voyage he noted, "one after another of our passengers abandons the use of tobacco and soon after acknowledge that they are better without it" and added that he was satisfied they would "never indulge in its use again." Six weeks later he reporting smoking a single cigar that he enjoyed "for a while but it soon made me so sick that I vomited very freely." He promised to "remember this whenever I attempt to smoke again" and admitted that he paid severely for his "transgression." Because someone set fire to one of the sails of the schooner *Damariscove* by allowing a spark from a pipe to escape from the windward side of the vessel, the company made a rule that they had to smoke their pipes on the lee side of the quarterdeck. William M. Hatch wrote a little over a week after that decision was made that he had reduced his smoking to one pipe before breakfast and one after each meal. In early June he reported that he and several others had decided to "abstain from the pipe for one week." He attempted to stop smoking twice during the voyage and found doing so was good for him—"useing tobacco freely is injurious to any ones health benumming to the head"—but he confessed that "a dirty troublesome habit I have long been adicted to is hard to brake off."[56]

Whenever passengers sailing to California sighted another sailing vessel in the distance, they became excited at the prospect of seeing and possibly speaking with new people and with the possible opportunity of sending mail via the other vessel in hopes that it would reach family and friends sooner than would mail sent after their arrival in California or from one of the ports they might visit. The "proper" procedure to follow in speaking and visiting other vessels throughout the world had been established over time. When vessels were close enough that the captains could hear each other when they spoke through speaking trumpets, they exchanged information by voice. The established ritual was for the captains to ask each other a series of questions to identify the names of the vessels and the captains, the port from which they sailed, the destination, and sometimes the date sailed or number of days out. Occasionally they asked the position to check their own reckoning or to determine the accuracy of their chronometers. When the vessels were too far apart to be heard, all the information was exchanged by signal flags. The procedure for visiting necessitated an invitation extended by one of the captains. The protocol called for the captain and certain other men to visit in one vessel and for the first mate and certain other men to visit in the other vessel.

With the large number of vessels carrying passengers to California in 1849, the procedure was modified slightly as the passengers became involved. Their involvement consisted largely in exchanging a series of cheers and sometimes exchanging musical performances. Most of the time the passengers in one vessel offered three cheers to those in the other and received three in response. This was usually repeated twice. From this came the expression of exchanging "three times three." There were some variations in this so that sometimes there were fewer cheers and other times more cheers. Occasionally the passengers fired guns in salute of those in the other vessel. Passengers in the bark *Elvira* gave those in the ship *Albany* "a broadside of oranges," as they had only recently sailed from Rio de Janeiro and had a large number of oranges on board. In some instances during the gold rush passengers were also involved in the visitation process. The visits sometimes lasted many hours, depending upon how calm the seas and winds were and whether the two vessels were sailing in the same direction. Visits were seldom made when the vessels were bound in opposite directions.

When a vessel was first sighted, passengers quite often started letters, or completed ones begun before, to family and friends at home in hopes that they could be transferred to that vessel if they came close enough to each other to carry the mailbag to that vessel and if that vessel was bound for a port from which the letters could be posted. When there were large numbers of passengers on board, they could have hundreds of letters to send. It was a great disappointment to the passengers when the mailbag could not be sent to the other vessel.[57]

The passengers in the ship *Crescent* of Boston had an unusual, perhaps unique, experience in visiting another vessel. They encountered the ship *Charles,* also from Boston, in the South Pacific, and the two vessels drew near enough to visit. A passenger named W. Hardy asked Capt. John Madison for permission for a group of passengers to visit the *Charles,* as his sister was on board her. Permission was granted, and the boat was made ready and departed for the *Charles*. The captain of the *Charles* wore ship and stood toward the *Crescent*. Despite efforts of both captains to avoid a collision in a moderately heavy sea, the two vessels collided, causing slight damage to both. The *Crescent* also lost an anchor. This collision caused a great fear among passengers in both vessels, as they thought they might sink and many lives would be lost. Fortunately, that did not happen. They both proceeded on their voyages although the passengers in the *Crescent* made a slight modification in their plans in that they went to Juan Fernandez Island rather than Valparaiso for fresh provisions because they feared the customs officials at the latter would require them to replace their lost anchor, and they did not have funds to purchase one.[58]

Thus it appears that passengers found a great many things to do to pass away the many, many tedious hours, days, and weeks as they made slow progress toward the new El Dorado, where they expected to seek their fortunes. Some of their activities were intellectual and some were physical in nature. Others followed long-standing maritime traditions or modified those traditions slightly. Many of the passengers seem to have made use of their occupational skills to make things while many also learned new skills in catching fish, birds, porpoises, and sharks. Others used their professional or recreational skills to amuse and entertain fellow passengers with their musical and theatrical talents. They also enjoyed playing a variety of games and engaged in discussions and debates on a wide array of issues of their time. In these ways they partially eliminated the boredom of long sea voyages in sailing vessels.

RATIONS.

Daily Bread, 14 oz.: Sugar 2 oz.: Coffee or Cocoa, 1 oz., or Tea ¼ oz.; and on

SUNDAY.	MONDAY.	TUESDAY.	WEDNESDAY
Beef, 1 lb. Flour, ½ " Raisins, OR Other dried fruit,¼ "	Pork, 1 lb. Beans, ½ pt.	Beef, 1 lb. Cheese, 2 oz. Butter, 2 " Rice, ¼ lb.	Pork, 1 lb. Beans, ½ pt. Pickles, OR } ¼ lb. Cranberries,

THURSDAY.	FRIDAY.	SATURDAY.	
Beef, 1 lb. Flour, ½ " Raisins, ¼ "	Beef, 1 lb. Cheese, 2 oz. Rice, ¼ lb. Molasses, ½ pt. Butter, 2 oz.	Pork, 1 lb. Beans, ½ pt. Vinegar, ½ " Pickles, OR } ¼ lb. Cranberries,	

Bill of fare for the bark *Orion*. Several passengers included records of their weekly fare in their journals, and a few others noted that a bill of fare had been posted for everyone's information. This published bill of fare on the back of the ticket is a rare document. Courtesy of J. Wells Henderson, Philadelphia.

Boston, *Nov 6* 1849.

Received of Mr. *Francis D Lawrence*,
One Hundred fifty Dollars in full for
Lower Cabin Passage in

BARQUE ORION,

——For San Francisco.——

(The dangers of the Seas excepted.)

In Berth N°. *66* and *allowed twenty days on board after arrival*

Henry Smith & Co

Ticket for the bark *Orion*. Just how common printed tickets were for passengers booked on sailing vessels bound for California in 1849 is uncertain. Few of them seem to have survived. Note that passengers in the *Orion* had both their cabin and their berth number assigned and recorded on their tickets and could remain on board the vessel for twenty days after their arrival in California. There is no mention of responsibility for bedding or taking personal possessions without further charge. The price quoted was typical for the specified service. Courtesy of J. Wells Henderson, Philadelphia.

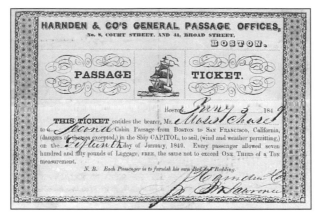

Ticket for the ship *Capitol*. Note that passengers in the *Capitol* could take up to 750 pounds of possessions without extra charge so long as they did not exceed one-third of a ton in measurement. Passengers in the *Capitol* had to supply their own bed and bedding. Note no price is given although the second cabin is specified. Moses Chase Papers. Courtesy of the Bancroft Library, University of California, Berkeley.

"Taking advantage of a Squally day." When the supply of water was short or when the water in the wooden storage casks became unfit to drink, passengers took advantage of every rain shower to catch fresh water for drinking and also for washing clothes. From the journal of Isaac W. Baker on board the bark *San Francisco* in 1849. Courtesy of the Bancroft Library, University of California, Berkeley.

"Plum Duff in Danger—Christmas Dinner at Sea." This drawing by J. M. Burns illustrates quite well the difficulties passengers occasionally had eating their meals when the sea was rough during their trip to California. From *Harpers Weekly*, December 22, 1883.

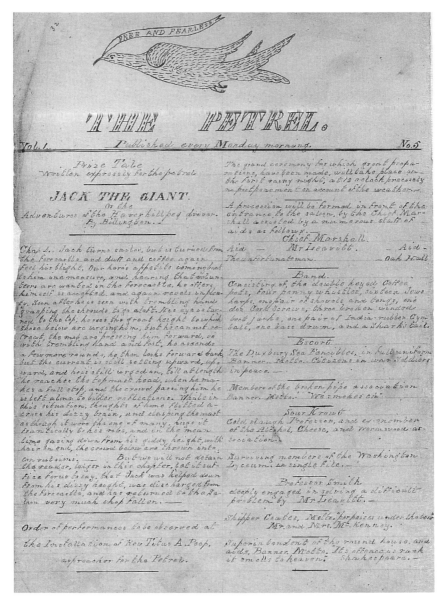

The Petrel. Producing newspapers was a popular form of amusement and entertainment for passengers bound to California in 1849, but few examples of those publications have been preserved. Eight issues of the *Petrel* were produced on board the ship *Duxbury* from Boston. The front page of issue 5 contains a short prize essay and a number of brief notes. Courtesy of the Bancroft Library, University of California, Berkeley.

"Topgallant Forecastle, Barque *Galindo,* 1849." Passengers engaged in a variety of forms of amusement and entertainment both on and below deck. Here passengers in the bark *Galindo* of New York appear to be reading, playing games, and observing those engaged in such activities. William H. Dougal Papers. Courtesy of the Bancroft Library, University of California, Berkeley.

"Sailors skylarking." Boxing was a popular form of exercise and entertainment among some of the young male passengers. Sometimes the bouts were scheduled in advance; other times they were impromptu events. From *Century Magazine,* June 1882.

"Leaving the ship." Rowing around the vessel during calms in the tropics for exercise and entertainment was quite common for forty-niners. This drawing illustrates passengers rowing away from the ship *Pacific* to Juan Fernandez Island, about fifty miles away, on May 19, 1849. It was a rather controversial event because it delayed the ship at least three days. From Browne, *Crusoe's Island*.

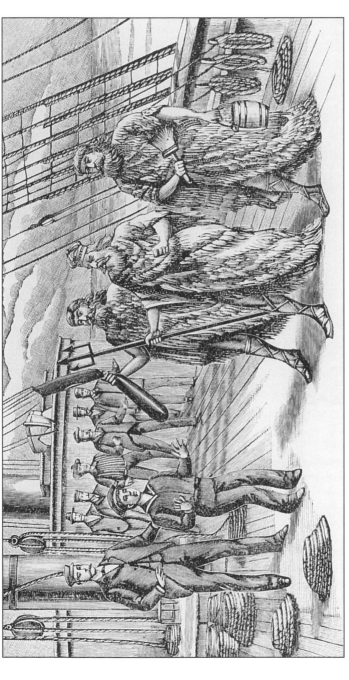

"Neptune boarding the ship." Many passengers described the visit of Neptune to their vessels in great detail. Although this drawing is from a published account of a gold rush voyage, the illustration appears to be more suitable for a voyage of the 1890s, when the book was published. The passengers shown here are not at all typical of forty-niners. Nevertheless the depictions of Neptune and his assistants are in keeping with the descriptions of 1849 passengers. Since the author of the book presented a somewhat exaggerated account of his experiences, including false names of vessels in which he sailed and of characters, perhaps the illustration is in keeping with that concept. From E. I. Barra, *Tale of Two Oceans*.

THE ORCHESTRA.

"The orchestra." Most sailing vessels had a variety of musicians among their passengers, and those individuals performed regularly for evening dances, concerts, and special events such as Fourth of July celebrations. From *Harper's Weekly,* August 7, 1858.

5

Sundays, Holidays, and Special Days

According to what the passengers recorded in their journals, many of those who went to California in sailing vessels in 1849 appear to have been regular churchgoers at home and wanted to be able to attend worship services at sea as well. The few extant copies of constitutions and bylaws or rules and regulations of the many joint stock companies specified that there would be worship services on Sunday and that all members should attend. The members were also to conduct themselves as Christians at all other times. Many of the companies had a chaplain as one of the members for the purpose of presiding at religious services. A few ministers were among the thousands of men who went to California to seek their fortunes just like men from other walks of life. Most commercial sailing vessels of the gold rush era did not operate under these principles.

It was the stated, but not always practiced, custom or policy in many American sailing vessels of the time to consider Sunday a day of rest in which only the most essential tasks of steering the vessel and setting and furling the sails as needed were performed. Sailors were expected to take baths, shave, and dress in clean clothes on Sunday and spend as much of the day as possible in reading, contemplating, or resting from their hard labors of the week. At least voyages started out this way. Many times they changed so that Sundays became workdays like any other day of the week. One might readily understand how a captain of a vessel bound home with a valuable cargo might easily be tempted to make all possible sail on Sunday as well as other days in order to get home to his family more quickly and also perhaps receive higher prices for his cargo than if he allowed the sailors to rest on Sundays. It is also understandable that the captain of a whaling vessel in which no whales had been seen for many days, or even weeks, might well decide to lower for whales sighted on a Sunday in hopes of taking one or more and thereby filling the hold with casks of oil sooner than if he ignored the whales on Sunday.

In many California-bound vessels in 1849 there were indeed regular worship services, sometimes conducted by an ordained minister, sometimes by an appointed or elected chaplain who may or may not have been an ordained minister, and sometimes on a rotating basis by passengers. Most of the time all went well, but in a few instances there were varying degrees of controversy over a variety of issues. In many vessels, particularly those that were crowded with people and heavily laden with freight, all worship services were discontinued in the coldest regions of the Southern Hemisphere because most often all services had to be conducted in the open on deck in such vessels. In a few vessels there was space for worship services below deck, but even there it was extremely cold in the vicinity of Cape Horn. The experiences of passengers in a number of vessels provide a sampling of situations regarding Sunday observance on board sailing vessels bound for the new El Dorado in 1849.

In describing the initial worship service on board the brig *Triumph*, Charles L. Badger contrasted their new surroundings with those of "our highly decorated and fashionable New England Churches." He noted that at sea they had "no splendor displayed, either in costly furniture, lifelike paintings, varigated stained glass windows, or rich and powerful toaned organs." On board the *Triumph*, "all hands, Captain, Sailors, and all off duty" gave rapt attention to the scripture readings and singing. Badger thought that many of their "minds would have been wandering" in their churches at home. He thought the singing was excellent in spite of the rough seas and the extent of seasickness among the singers.[1]

Members of the New Haven and California Joint Stock Company had morning worship services and evening prayer meetings on Sundays whenever the weather permitted as they sailed from New Haven to San Francisco. Capt. John Bottom, who was replaced by Mr. Ford in Talcahuano, read some of the sermons during his tenure as master, and Mr. Ford read some after he assumed command. Several of the passengers also read sermons. One of the passengers hinted that Captain Bottom had prevented their having services on some occasions, as the journalist noted after they sailed from Talcahuano, "Things go more pleasant now, as I think the one who has been the means of preventing exercises of this kind is left behind." A little later he reported that "A sabbath now seems more like Sunday than it did around the vicinity of Cape Horn, but still there is a difference between a sabbath here and at home."[2]

One of the prominent passengers in the ship *Andalusia* of Baltimore was the Reverend William Taylor, who was sent as a missionary by the Methodist Church of Maryland to establish a church in San Francisco. He carried with him all the materials to construct that church. Because San Francisco already had a Methodist church when he arrived the church Taylor took was sent to Sacramento. Although Taylor did have a church building for services, he became well known for his street preaching. Capt. F. W. Willson seems to have been a strong supporter of religious services in his vessel. He regularly had the sailors set up a temporary pulpit and benches covered with white sailcloth whenever the weather permitted having services on deck. According to one passenger, Reverend Taylor was an aloof person who did not get along with the passengers. One example she pointed to was Reverend Taylor's strong opposition to Captain Willson's decision to work on repairing the *Andalusia* on a Sunday after her mast and rigging were severely damaged in a storm. She contrasted this behavior with that of Robert Kellan, another minister who had joined them in Rio de Janeiro, who actually participated in the repair work and regularly visited the passengers, something that Reverend Taylor never did. During the latter portion of the voyage, Taylor and Kellan alternated preaching, one in the morning and one in the afternoon. According to Booth, the passengers preferred the preaching and the personality of Robert Kellan.[3]

George Denham was a minister who went to California to seek his fortune and may well have made a poor decision in choosing a vessel and joint stock company. He went in the schooner *Rialto* as a member of the Rialto Mining Company in which all members seem also to have been members of the crew. As he had no previous seafaring experience, he was a green hand in a crew that included sixteen whaling captains. For the first two months Denham held worship services in the cabin, but by the mid April few men attended his services. In mid-May he gave reasons for discontinuing services. The cabin was so "very much lumbered up with every thing" that it was inconvenient to worship there. He had so little time to prepare to preach "So as not to disgrace my office and make religion appear weak and comtemptable in the eyes of sensible but wicked men." His station as a green hand reduced him to the level of the lowest sailor and made it difficult for him "to stand up before them as a religious teacher." Because of these factors, he had "no practical influence over their lives." Later, Capt. Charles Downs asked if they were not going to have more worship services. Denham replied he did not know and added that "Some things have transpired which have made it very unpleasant to me to engage in any such

141

exercises." Soon after that exchange Denham noted on a Sunday that "little respect is paid to" the day and "almost all" the men "seem to think most of amusing themselves in some way pleasing to the carnal mind. Alas!" Near the end of the voyage he indicated a longing to be away from "the ignorant, coarse, vulgar and profane ribaldry of the company" and to "return to my loved employ as a pastor and stand in my capacity before my people to plead for the sacred name and cause of God."[4]

The Boston and California Mining and Trading Joint Stock Company, who sailed in the ship *Edward Everett* of Boston, conducted two worship services every Sunday that the weather permitted. Their chaplain, the Reverend Mr. Bradbury, preached at one of them, and Joseph Augustine Benton, a recent graduate of the Yale Divinity School, preached at the other. Benton entered full-time ministry when he arrived in California. He regularly recorded the scriptural basis for and gave a subject for each sermon but said little about what was discussed. The services were normally well attended during good weather. During extremely bad weather no services were held. Near the end of the voyage Benton mentioned that the services were disturbed slightly by "boisterous noisey laughter forward."[5]

Soon after the ship *Euphrasia* sailed from Boston, two passengers, Chester Joseph Snow and Deacon Merrill, asked Capt. Charles Buntin if they could hold a meeting on board. Captain Buntin gave his approval, and they had two meetings virtually every Sunday. Various passengers seem to have taken turns in reading from collections of published sermons, lectures, and essays. Several were read from Ansel Doane Eddy's lectures or sermons to young men. Others were read from *Names and Titles of Christ* by James Maple, William Dowling, or Charles Spear (each of whom authored a work of that title) and *The Sabbath Manual* by Justin Edwards. Snow reported that he received some criticism from fellow passengers for reading one of Ansel Doane Eddy's lectures about "the sinful amusements of young men" in which "there was a very close rebuke of the habit of dancing, drinking and other kindred evils." His attempts to explain that he did not intend the sermon as a "rebuke of their dancing here on board" were in vain. At the end of 1849 Snow noted that they "Had a Universalist sermon today." This seems to have been an unknown precursor of problems to come, as he later noted that they were "subjected to the necessity of associating . . . with those, whose principles exhibited as they are by profanity and obscencnes [obsenities?]" and added that "Universalism has ruined or is ruining more than one on bord this ship. Infidelity is also doing its work" because "any thing is embraced but the truth of God by the most." He also noted the deadly and deceitful "principle of cold Morrality is not idle." Later he indicated some opposition to their meetings by Universalists and reported they had given up the meeting rooms to the Universalists on one occasion, but that group did not have a meeting.[6]

Early in their voyage the passengers in the ship *Morrison* had a meeting and selected officers, including a chaplain, although there is no indication that they were members of any sort of organized company. Reverend Mr. Bullock was chosen chaplain, but he presided over only four services. He was ill or the weather was bad on several of the Sundays between New York and Rio de Janeiro. After they left Rio one passenger noted that Bullock was on deck and appeared to be in good health, but still they "had no preaching." A few weeks later, after saying nothing of worship services, he mentioned Bullock had bronchitis and could not preach. By the end of the voyage he still had not mentioned worship services on any Sunday and noted "But little attention is paid to the Sabbath."[7]

Members of the New England and California Trading and Mining Association, who sailed from Boston in the ship *Lenore*, had worship services conducted by their chaplain virtually every Sunday from early February through the first of July 1849. On some Sundays they had two services. One of the sailors usually rang the bell to announce it was time to start, and the passengers seated themselves around the after hatch. The chaplain stood on the first step that led below. Early in the voyage the sermons seem to have pleased the passengers, but after four months one passenger noted "His sermons, as a general thing, are not very interesting." This comment came after a sermon in which the chaplain told them "how societies and individuals ought to make sacrifices to . . . make peace." There had been some disagreements within the company in which harsh words and ill feelings came out. Henry H. Hyde Jr. usually gave the text for and a brief summary of each sermon but stopped making references to services on July 1, two and a half months before the voyage ended.[8]

There was more than one joint stock company on board the ship *Pacific*, but N. D. Morgan, president of the New England Mining and Trading Company, seems to have led most of the services. He appears to have used an Episcopal service from the Book of Common Prayer. Some other person usually read a sermon from a volume of collected sermons. Morgan sometimes offered a prayer. Charles Williams reported that he and Phil Walden read the service the first Sunday at sea, but James H. Gager implies that there was no organized service, as he noted that he "Thought of the peaceful Sabbath ashore & of St. Barts & the Sunday

School" and that he read sermons by Benjamin Franklin Stanton and Henry Clay Fish. He also felt the day was "respected more than I expected to see." Early in the voyage everyone seems to have been happy, as passengers from all parts of the vessel participated in the worship services that were made better by a "very good choir." By the end of the first month, however, some discord arose as Capt. Hall J. Tibbits requested the passengers in the forward cabin not "to frequent the after deck" and they therefore "declined . . . to come aft to service." Gager resented this because he felt that "The gentlemen forward are just as good as those aft" and the conduct of Captain Tibbits was "brutal & in direct violation of the contract." More discord developed after they left Rio de Janeiro, where Captain Tibbits was discharged by the U.S. consul Gorham Parks at the insistence of the first-class passengers. Gager reported that many passengers objected to N. D. Morgan continuing to be the reader because of some of his activities in the process of getting Captain Tibbits removed. He accused Morgan of "duplicity." At the end of May, nearly two months after they left Rio, Morgan "expressed his penitence for his bad example & resigned the chaplaincy." Gager thought he would be reappointed, and he seems to have been, as he led other services before they arrived in San Francisco. Early in July, Gager complained about a religious group of some sort whom he called "The Pilgrims," who sang very loudly and very badly on Sunday evenings. He said they "don't like Episcopacy."[9]

The members of the Cayuga Joint Stock Company in the bark *Belvidera* had worship services every Sunday when weather permitted. Services in the first part of the voyage usually consisted of one or more hymns, a prayer, reading from the bible, and a sermon read by one of the members from some volume of collected sermons or some other source, some of which are identified. On April 22, 1849, Capt. Samuel Barney introduced an Episcopal service, and it seems to have been used thereafter. On some Sundays they also had a prayer meeting in the afternoon, and on some others they had lectures on such topics as temperance, nonresistance, and moral obligation.[10]

Members of the Salem Mechanics Trading and Mining Association seem to have had two identical services every Sunday the weather permitted. They consisted of scripture reading, prayer, singing by the choir, reading of a sermon apparently from a volume of published ones, more singing, and a closing prayer with various members of the company participating each Sunday. They apparently did not have a minister on board and did not elect a chaplain within their company. Early during the voyage

William Graves contrasted a Sunday at sea with one at home. "A Sabath spent on Ship Borde is far diffrent then it is to spend a Sabath on Land. We cannot tak our shocial walks an cast our eye upon thoes serrounding objects which we have always been acoustum too and to here the singing of the Berds and everything that tendes to vigerate the sistum of men." Graves later indicated he was pleased that they had "some Professor of Religon on Borde which are very Candid sort of men which is a grat constraint to the action of the more unruley Members of the Company which are few." The members had at least two unique situations during their voyage. The first occurred March 9, when they had a minor but scary collision with the ship *Charles* while a passenger named W. Hardy was attempting to visit his sister on board that vessel. The second was on March 24 while they were at Juan Fernandez Island obtaining fresh provisions. There they had a joint worship service with the passengers of the bark *Belgrade* of Cherryfield, Maine. That service was identical to the usual one in the *Crescent* and was only the second service held by the members of the Sacramento Navigation and Mining Company in the *Belgrade*. Graves's belief near the end of the voyage that the passengers in the *Crescent* were then more respectful of the Sabbath than they were at the beginning of the voyage and that the Bible was read more than any other book in the ship seems to run counter to what happened in other vessels.[11]

Passengers in the bark *Strafford,* all of whom were members of the New York Mining Company, had Episcopal worship services every Sunday the weather permitted. Joseph Webb Winans and F. B. Austin seem to have taken turns reading the service from the Book of Common Prayer and a sermon from a volume of collected sermons. On one occasion near the end of the voyage F. B. Austin delivered an original sermon. Griffith Meredith did not particularly like the Episcopal service, but as it was the only one offered he was satisfied to attend it. He felt, however, that some of his "young lady acquaintances in New York would laugh heartily if they knew he had to attend servases of that persuasion," for he would "as soon attend the Catholic Church as the Episcopal." Sunday was frequently a day for passengers to sit around and talk or think of home and family and to examine mementos brought with them. Meredith described the situation better than most when he wrote that "Members all around on deck and elsewhere" were "reading and talking about home and their friends and acquaintances that they have left and are thinking of them and some are over-hauling their trunks and chests and examining their presents and trinkets, letters and Dagarotypes &c." He added that "All these little things are valuable things to a man at sea, and perticularly on a six months voyage on the mighty ocean with out the sight of any of our dear Friends and relatives." Meredith noted that someone who "has not been at sea can not immagin anything about it, how valuable they are." He indicated that without female passengers the men needed these mementos to soothe their natural "raging fierce and angry disposition." Warmth, he thought, exercised "the greatest Influence on man in any sense of any other being."[12]

Religious services began in a seemingly promising form in the ship *Sweden* of Boston and seemed to pick up right where the lengthy and elaborate predeparture service left off. John Tolman reported that they were supposed to have a clergyman accompany them and preside at services, but the clergyman was "an unfortunate deacon who was a few weeks previous expelled from an Orthodox church" and did not sail with them. The first few Sundays, Rev. A. Belknap, an ordained minister from Bridgewater or Framingham, Massachusetts, presided at the services on deck at which original hymns by James L. L. F. Warren, a florist from Brighton, Massachusetts, were sung. Warren seemingly began to write prayers as well, but Belknap declined to participate under those circumstances. Warren seemingly was disliked, so passengers would not attend if he officiated. Warren wrote at least six hymns, the words of which are recorded in a few journals. Some passengers, including members of the Roxbury Sagamore Company, held their own services below deck. The last service on deck seems to have been on April 8 although Charles Herbert Fuller recorded words to original songs, apparently by James L. L. F. Warren, in his journal as late as May 6. The last services mentioned below deck were held on April 29. Moses Cogswell noted in mid May that the only way one could tell it was Sunday was that "Cards and backgammon . . . are thrown aside for one day."[13]

An anonymous passenger in the ship *America* frequently was critical of some fellow passengers, both white and African American, for their hypocrisy. He pronounced them "full of vanity, vanishod [vainglory?] and wickness, disagreeabe to live with, and painful to the sight. Humbugs!" He was particularly critical of a man he referred to as Old Ward, whom he identified as "the vain and nimble tongued leader of our band of white and black fallen angels, the man of many words, with rouges phiz and air and another of whose good fortune it was that our ship sailed on Sunday." He also called Old Ward an "old coxcomb" who was "as flippant . . . as a Connecticut clock, notion, and nutmeg pedlar." After leaving Callao he referred to some fellow passengers as "thrice fallen angels, and daily conversers with God!" who "made no demonstration towards mocking the Christian religion today but studiously kept themselves out of sight. <u>White-haired pharasees!—hypocrites! Vagabonds</u>!" He continued writing in this vein for several days.[14]

In a few instances there was little or no evidence of any form of public worship during entire voyages. H. W. Chittenden wrote something every Sunday during the entire time the bark *Croton* was at sea but never mentioned any type of public worship. He regularly had private devotions and did a great deal of thinking about "home, youth, happiness, & domestick enjoyment" on Sundays. As they neared San Francisco, Chittenden compared their difficulty in getting into that port with that of the Jews in the wilderness who were permitted to see their promised land but were kept from entering it for a long time. Two passengers in the bark *Elvira* mentioned two instances of religious services and some singing on Sundays. Perhaps the fact that there were only eleven passengers on board was a factor. William J. Towne was a passenger in the ship *Capitol,* which had 248 passengers, but he never mentioned that any day was Sunday or that anything other than ordinary work went on. Elias P. Overton mentioned going to churches in Rio de Janeiro and in Valparaiso but never mentioned any religious activities in the bark *Keoka* during his entire voyage. In the first entry of his journal in the bark *Oxford,* Cornelius Cooledge contrasted a Sunday at sea with one at home. "The scene here presents a great contrast with that around a village church. No congregating round the altar of devotion. To be sure we have music, but it is any thing but church psalmody." Two weeks later he mentioned that all the sailors were given testaments but he did not "see any great acts of piety." That is the closest he came to mentioning worship services.[15]

It appears, then, that there were Sunday religious services on board a large percentage of the vessels that sailed to California in 1849. Quite often no services were held on the first Sunday at sea, as many of the passengers were still suffering from seasickness. In some cases the services were held only during the first part of the voyage between the departure point and the colder regions of the Southern Hemisphere. Sometimes the services were resumed in the warmer regions of the Pacific, but many times they were not. In a few cases there were conflicts or other factors that caused the services to be discontinued even before the vessel reached the cold region. Occasionally services were canceled even in the warm regions because of a sudden storm. Sometimes they were only postponed from morning to afternoon or evening. Many of the vessels seem to have had ordained ministers on board to conduct the services or at least participate in them. In other vessels people without the formal training in the ministry conducted all of the services. A few groups of passengers had men with excellent voices who formed a choir. Other groups had the entire complement of worshipers do all of the singing and chanting. Overall, it seems, the Argonauts of 1849 made serious attempts to live at sea much the way they did at home in their religious practices even if some were unable to participate in the denomination of their choice. Instead, they had to worship through an Episcopal service rather than the one to which they were accustomed at home.

In most sailing vessels of the time, holidays and other special days of the calendar were considered regular workdays, but then only a small portion of those vessels carried passengers who might have the time or the inclination to organize a special celebration for any holiday or special day. There might occasionally be a special meal or treat on the Fourth of July, Thanksgiving, or Christmas for the sailors, and sailors who kept personal journals often recognized the start of a new year and wrote philosophically about their situations. Occasionally they included a small sketch of some sort on the first day of a new year.

Situations for passengers in sailing vessels going to California in 1849, however, were quite different from those in other sailing vessels. Few of the Argonauts had ever been to sea and were unaware of nearly all of the customs and practices in commercial sailing vessels. They were in the habit of celebrating every holiday and other special days at home. Thus they usually planned and carried out some form of celebration for every such occasion that arose while they were on their great adventure.

Celebrations for New Year's Day 1850 varied greatly among the few that were recorded. A number of the passengers followed the custom of sailors in reflecting on their past lives and looking to the future. Some also described special meals. Others wrote about the celebratory partying and drinking on board. A few simply recognized the day without further comment although one in the bark *Gold Hunter* did not even note that January 1, 1850, was the start of a new year. Some compared their first New Year's Day at sea with their previous ones at home. Pierce W. Barker in the ship *Nestor* recalled the sleigh rides he had enjoyed at home but now had to be satisfied "with bobbing up and down day after day." Passengers in the brig *Perfect* had a ball on New Year's Eve and continued the celebration into the next day, when they had a fine dinner and then a shooting match. Two musicians played fiddles and one a tambourine for the dance. Those in the schooner *St. Mary* also had a dance at which musicians played a fiddle, a guitar, and a "dub-a-dub-and squeak-sqwak" and produced "multifarious numbers that it set many who was half seas over to scuff and stamp the deck." The captain and the supercargo supplied cigars and wine "which maketh glad and also <u>mad</u> the heart of man." The music "gradually died away as the band got too drunk to play and the systematic dancing turned into jumping bellowing and halloring." J. T. Woodbury in the ship *Argonaut* noted that he wished all his friends "throughout the world Happy New Year before he arose" and added, "Some passengers to day were Silly drunk,—a fine sight!" A few passengers in the ship *Europe* obtained a half dozen old muskets and fired a volley "off the aftercabin that made the welkin ring" and then wished each other a Happy New Year and drank "the same to our sweethearts and wives." Before he left Thomaston, Maine, John T. Howard had been given a bottle of brandy from a friend, and they both agreed to drink a toast to each other on New Year's Day, but by that time Howard had concluded an agreement with the captain to stop drinking. Thus he did not drink, but he ate the "last piece of a bundle of cake" given him by a "much valued female friend." He also wrote that he was "anything but happy" on this day, as he always felt sad when anything occurred to remind him of home and to cause him "to compare my present with my past situations." J. L. Akerman in the bark *Daniel Webster* also wrote extensively of his thoughts of home, "loved wife, Parents, and sisters," and wondered if he would ever see them again. He thought of his future and wrote that if he should be successful in finding the riches he hoped for in California and return home, "let no selfish soul envy me the pittance that I have earned by hardship, privation, and toil." Finally, he reported they had preserved green peas and black beans for dinner along with "Goney soup" served in his "private mess." Passengers in the bark *Belgrade* had a dinner of turkeys and chickens "served up in the best style."[16]

Valentine's Day was noted by several of those en route to California in 1849, but the men in those sailing vessels neither sent nor received any cards as they had done in previous years when they were at home among their friends and families. One noted that the day "was talked of by most all that ever lived in a city." Another commented "very few Valentines will be written on our Ship." Thomas Whaley noted it was "a great and glorious anniversary among the juveniles at home." A passenger in the ship *Edward Everett* lamented that "<u>we</u> have received & sent no little perfumed missives" on this "notable day in our Calendar." Another in the bark *Isabel* reported a discussion about Valentine's Day in which one "supposed they were very busy at the Post Office" and others surmised "who would receive valentines and who would be disappointed" among their friends at home. One person in the ship *Plymouth* noted he would "leave it to Frank to open" all his valentines.[17]

The birthday of George Washington was the second most celebrated holiday or special day for passengers bound for California in 1849 although a passenger in the brig *Mary Stuart* did not mention on February 22 that it was Washington's birthday, and the passengers in the ship *Edward Everett* voted on the twenty-first not to celebrate the next day. Still one of them recognized both Washington "First in war, first in peace & first in the hearts of his countrymen," and Zachary Taylor, who had "fought himself into the Presidency" and would soon be inaugurated. The decision not to celebrate probably stemmed from the extreme heat they suffered at the time. Members in the Salem Mechanics Trading and Mining Association in the ship *Crescent* were just rounding Cape Horn at the time and voted to use five gallons of molasses to make candy to celebrate the day. On board most of the vessels the passengers raised the American flag, decorated the vessel with appropriate bunting, fired a salute to Washington with any guns they had on board, sang some patriotic songs and listened to other songs played by any musicians on board, offered toasts, listened to speeches, ate special meals, and had dances to celebrate the day at sea in much the same way they did at home. In many cases a committee had been appointed to plan the celebration.[18] Passengers in some vessels provided much more detailed descriptions of the festivities than did the majority of those who wrote about the celebration in their vessels.

The members of the New Brunswick and California Mining and Trading Company appointed a committee on February 21 to plan the celebration of Washington's birthday. Their plans called for starting the day with a prayer meeting, something that apparently was not done on board any other vessel. The next planned activity was a meal at noon followed by toasts and speeches. Nearly a week later one of the members reported that the celebration began when "the Captain had all hands mustered at 10 o'clock in the Cabin." They then sang "While Shepards watch their flocks," and a passenger "read the chapter in one of the Evangelists, descriptive of the birth in a manger of our Saviour, and then attempted to draw a comparison and run a parallel between John the Baptist and Washington. John as the forerunner of Christ, and Washington as the forerunner of the republican movement in the world, and particularly as it has developed itself in Europe during the last year." They then had dinner of "salt junk," hard biscuit, potatoes and turnips mashed together, and duff, which was difficult to chew and made some of them sick. After dinner they went on deck for the remainder of the program. He noted that "the ship was dressed in holiday garb with all her colors up." They " had toasts drank out of tin cups with water—an attempt at an exhortation from Johnny Dunham, a speach from Dentist Kellum, and a talk by the President, in which he took up the facts that are generally known of Washington's youth, and the hardships and training that he underwent to fit him for the position that he was afterwards called upon to occupy in the World's History, and enjoined upon all present patience in the training which they were now submitting to, for a preparation for something in California." The speaker reminded them that "some of them be called upon to lead armies, or take their <u>turn</u> (<u>trick</u> as the sailors call it) at the Wheel of State in the new State of California."¹⁹ That concluded the celebration with everyone apparently surviving the day totally sober.

Passengers in the ship *Orpheus* selected a Mr. Smith, a recent graduate of Yale, to be their orator for the celebration of Washington's birthday, but he did not prepare for it. Thus they canceled that activity and decided that everyone would celebrate as he saw fit. First a group of about twenty people formed a band and dressed in "grotesque military costume" and marched

to the tune of Hail Columbia with drum & fife, and preceded by two very valient pioneers with a pail of punch suspended between them. The stars & stripes were hoisted to the breeze amid the prolonged cheers of nearly every person aboard the ship. A gentleman from Pittsburgh, A Lieutenant in the Army at Mexico was appointed Captain of the squad, who commenced his duties as a thorough drill master late from the field of action ought. He commenced exercising his command with zeal & soon had them marching, counter marching & wheeling across the quarter deck in grand style, frequently charging up to the enemy, who would most generally repulse them, & cause them to beat a retreat under a shower of <u>grape punches</u>. Before they could be ralied again by their commander the enemy would have time to reload, & would be sure to thin their ranks the next charge, however valient they might be. The <u>battle</u> was still raging with much furry although nearly night, when news came into camp that a detached portion of the Army, occupying the <u>castle</u> in front, had

151

met a small stragling party of the enemy, and were repulsed, leaving four apple jacks prostrate with their wounds. This very disheartning news seemed to have a very sudden effect, causing a cessation of hostilities, which the valient little Army profited by retiring quietly, carrying their dead and wounded with them, leaving the field in possession of the enemy. The evening passed off quietly, with the exception of the party in the castle forward, the turbalencey of which it took some little time to suppress. Thus passed the glorious 22d.

Some passengers realized later that it had been a mistake to give alcohol to the sailors. Although perhaps amusing at the time, it could have ended in disaster, as the vessel and all of the 174 passengers on board could have been in dire straits had a sudden storm come upon them with all of the sailors drunk and likely incapacitated. The captain told the journalist later that he considered it dangerous to have such celebrations at sea, as they tended to create divisions among the passengers and lead to disastrous results.[20]

The passengers in the ship *Jane Parker* of Baltimore also appointed a committee on February 20 to plan the celebration of Washington's birthday. They planned for the day to start at 10:00 A.M., when James C. Wilson would chair the exercises. The band played the "Star Spangled Banner," which was followed by the reading by B. Bayles of a poem written by Issac Withers. Next a Mr. Barret delivered "some excellent Introductory remarks" and then read "Washington's Farewell Address." Next the band played "Hail Columbia." Then C. Schulze read an address composed by Isaac Withers, followed by more music by the band and a recitation by Schulze. The exercises concluded with more music and an invitation to the ball in the evening. They then enjoyed "a bountiful repase" including boiled and roast chickens, roast ducks, chicken and sea pies with pies and duff "in profusion" for dessert. The ball was in the forward cabin, but those in the after cabin were also invited. They cleared all the trunks from the center of the cabin to create a space large enough "for four Cotillions." The berths on the sides of the ship were covered with American flags and bunting. The dance began at 7:00 P.M. and lasted until 11:00 P.M., but probably would have gone on longer had it not been so warm in the cabin. Included at the dance were "seven Ladies of our own manufacture," some of whom had even "shaved off their whiskers and moustaches for the better personification of the female character." These seven men either made their own dresses for the occasion or borrowed dresses from the wife of the captain. One passenger described the scene as "a novel one when the four Cottillions were formed, and the musick struck up." He added, "It was not one to be easily forgotten to see the tall ladies all good dancers gracefully moving in the dance."[21]

A committee also met on February 21 to plan the celebration in the ship *Pharasalia*. They began the celebration at sunrise with the raising of the American flag. One passenger thought the sunrise that morning was the "most beautiful . . . I remember to have seen in my life. The colours of the clouds were beyond description." At the appointed time a Mr. Derby assumed the chair of the celebration. He and the speakers were seated on a platform that had been erected abaft the capstan and was festooned with the American flag. The order of exercises were: a song by the company "America;" a prayer by Mr. Fowle of Boston; singing of the "Star Spangled Banner" and "Peaceful Slumbering"; a poem by Mr. Reed of Boston; an oration by R. H. Pierpont, the son of the governor of Vermont; and singing of "Homeward Bound Whaleman." Then they had six toasts, each of which received three cheers, to: our country; Washington, its father; president of the United States; president elect of the United States; officers and crew of the ship *Pharasalia*; and the ladies, amended to sweethearts and wives. They then adjourned for dinner, which one passenger described as "one of the best dinners I ever ate, or at least it seemed so," but he realized that it "would hardly go down at'all on shore." It was considered good because it included the first fresh meat they had had for a long time. The ball started at 7:00 P.M. and continued until "quite late making night hideious!" One passenger sincerely hoped there would be "no more Washington's birthdays on the voyage."[22]

The one hundred members of the New York Mining Company on board the bark *Strafford* started celebrating Washington's birthday with a bang. Gen. H. L. Twiggs fired the cannon, and they raised the flag to half-mast at sunrise. At 10:30 A.M. they assembled on deck to hear "Washington March," a reading by F. B. Austin of Daniel Webster's elegy on the life of Washington, "Hail Columbia," and an original address and elegy by Joseph Webb Winans about "the great and glorious man! Gen. George Washington!! The father of his country!!!" Winans spoke for three quarters of an hour about Washington's "great and superior judgment" and drew comparisons between Washington and other military men, including Napoleon Bonaparte, but concluded that none were equal to Washington. Winans then talked of Washington's private life. He compared the present situation of the members with the time they left New York and pointed to Washington as their guide through life as they pursued their great adventure of leaving friends and family at home to "seek after gold." The band then played the "Star Spangled Banner," and the members gave a rousing salute of nine cheers. At noon they had a sumptuous dinner of roast pork, roast beef, boiled ham, macaroni soup, homemade bread, apple dumplings, wine sauce, claret wine, and "lemon aid." One passenger noted that he enjoyed this anniversary more than any other he had experienced. After dinner the fiddlers began to play, and they danced quadrilles until every man had an opportunity to dance and made note of "the young gents dancing as 'ladies' showing off in their different attitudes."[23]

Passengers in several sailing vessels bound for California in 1849 celebrated the inauguration of Zachary Taylor as president of the United States on March 5. Those in the bark *Croton* hoisted their colors "to the limit of the gallant mast" but seemingly did nothing else to celebrate. General Taylor was given three cheers, the country nine cheers, and James K. Polk three groans on board the bark *Strafford*. Later the fiddlers played while the passengers danced on deck for two or three hours. More than three months later they obtained newspapers containing President Taylor's inaugural address from passengers in other vessels at Juan Fernandez. Griffith Meredith noted that the address was read and was "received with great applause." Joseph Augustine Benton lamented that they could not celebrate in the ship *Edward Everett* since at least half of the passengers were Democrats "or at least not Taylor Whigs." Nevertheless he asked God to "give him abundant wisdom!!" Two passengers in the ship *Magnolia* from New York described happenings on board their vessel. S. Mortimer Collins reported that some passengers from the *Magnolia* visited on board the bark *Drummond* of Boston and some from the *Drummond* visited on board the *Magnolia* and that "They had a great time celebrating in honor of Z. Taylor." William F. Reed reported the two vessels had been visiting for nearly four hours and then separated. At nightfall the *Drummond* stood toward the *Magnolia,* apparently seeking another visit, but Capt. Benjamin Frank Simmons asked the captain of the *Drummond* to come the next day if the weather was calm.[24]

Passengers in the ships *Henry Lee* and *Lenore* and the bark *Maria* had somewhat more elaborate celebrations of the inauguration of Zachary Taylor. Those in the *Henry Lee* had "a grand inauguration dance upon deck" that may not have had "the brilliancy of that in the Capitol," but probably the hearts in the *Henry Lee* were merrier and the limbs lighter. At the start of the dance there were two sets of dancers on the quarterdeck and one around the forecastle. Even the sailors eventually joined in the dance, and the "mere lookers-on" appeared to enjoy the evening. Before turning in they gave "Old Zack" many cheers even though they recognized they were the only ones who would hear them. The passengers in the bark *Maria* turned to the proverbial committee to plan their inaugural festivities. The committee called upon all passengers to contribute private stores for the "sumptuous collation" they planned. The cabin was decorated with "all the flags and streamers belonging to the bark." During dinner they had "about a dozen and a half of champagne" and "any quantity of ale &c." There were two toastmasters, one for the sentimental toasts and one for the personal ones. Most of the sentimental toasts were national in nature, but the personal ones "were mostly puns on the names of the different passengers and some of them were excellent." Many of the men stayed up most of the night. Most of those who went to bed early were summarily pulled out again. The members of the New England and California Trading and Mining Association on board the ship *Lenore* also called upon a committee to plan the inaugural celebration. They kept both stoves busy for several days, making cakes and pies for the inaugural dinner. At noon on March 5 they fired a thirty-gun salute and gave "three hearty cheers" after each volley "for the men who rule over us, also our worthy captain and ourselves and along down not excepting the sailors in the forecastle." They then gave three cheers for themselves. At 2:00 they had a dinner of prepared soup, puddings, pies, and cakes. After dinner the toastmaster presented his regular toasts including ones for Capt. H. H. Greene and the church. Then many of the passengers offered toasts, most of which were "of good sentiment" although there were "some few of a low desire which plainly told the character of the deliverer." In the evening the dancers appeared, some of whom had spent some hours preparing "their dress representing the character which they were to act." There were twenty in all in costume, but the passenger who described the festivities mentioned only some of them, including an Indian, a moor, and six or eight ladies "with flowing white drapery." These were certainly men dressed as women. The captain wore "a good representation" of "military dress." The vice president of the association appeared as "the Captain's lady dressed in an old maidish dress." Passenger Hyde noted that "the excitement and the exercise did much in relieving our minds of the dull sameness to which we were accustomed."[25]

Perhaps one of the larger celebrations outside of Washington was in Rio de Janeiro, where a group of Americans issued written invitations to all Americans stationed there as well as to all passengers of vessels bound for California who happened to be in that port at the time. There was a five dollar charge for the dinner at the hotel Pharoux (sometimes spelled Faroux). An evening of "festive entertainment" was planned after the dinner. One passenger in the bark *Elvira* had received an invitation but did not "feel disposed to go," as he knew money "didnt grow on every bush." It appears that they had a celebration of some sort on board the *Elvira* that evening.[26]

As passengers were always looking for some entertainment or amusement, they did not miss the opportunity of playing tricks on each other on April Fools' Day. Griffith Meredith in the bark *Strafford* expected "there would be a good deal of skylarking with each other April fooling" but seemed pleased "there was only a few that undertook it." S. Mortimer Collins in the ship *Magnolia* reported "very little April fooling, as it was Sunday" but noted that one passenger had fooled a few in the morning, when he sang out "Sail Ho!'—a vessel in sight, homeward bound." Alexander F. Spear seemed pleased that he had fooled the passengers in the brig *Perfect* by announcing that "one of our sows had pigged." He said they "all ran forward to see the pigs and found nothing but the first day of April." Charles Herbert Fuller in the ship *Sweden* said a great many were fooled by someone crying out "sail ho!," or "whales!," or "sharks!" or "some other thing to make them look and be laughed at." Ebenezer Sheppard in the ship *Morrison* admitted that he had been the victim of an April fool joke. The grandest joke seems to have been in the brig *Osceola*, where the steward told the steerage passengers they would have "fritters" for dinner. They ate light breakfasts in anticipation of that favorite meal. At dinnertime that same steward called the steerage passengers to the meal, and all hastened below deck only to find the table empty. The passengers made all sorts of noise and called for their fritters whereupon the steward asked them if they had forgotten that it was the first day of April. Some thought it was funny to have been fooled, but others did not. The steward soon redeemed himself by providing plenty of fritters "well slicked over with molasses."[27]

The seventy-third anniversary of American independence was certainly the biggest day for celebrating on the sailing vessels bound for California in 1849. Celebrations were planned to be as much like those at home as possible given the limited space and facilities available on board the vessels. Activities typically included in the celebrations were firing of salutes at the beginning and end of the day in connection with raising and lowering of the flag, mostly comical military parades, several patriotic songs by both musical and vocal groups, reading of the Declaration of Independence, an oration, special meals, offering of many toasts, and dances. Sometimes excessive amounts of alcohol were consumed by some of the celebrants. In many vessels committees were appointed anywhere from one or two days to two weeks in advance to plan the celebrations. The plans ranged from the simple to the grandiose. Most of the journalists who described the celebrations indicated that the celebrants enjoyed excellent weather although those in the vicinity of Cape Horn and a few others suffered heavy storms on July 4.

The celebration on board the ship *Pacific* out of New York was probably the best planned and most encompassing in its activities and is also one of the best, indeed perhaps the best, documented celebrations in any vessels at sea. An account of their celebration may serve as an example of such celebrations in sailing vessels in 1849. Perhaps the planning done by those residing in the first cabin to have Capt. Hall J. Tibbits removed and their working together to accomplish that in Rio de Janeiro gave them practical experience. Their celebration planning and execution included passengers from all parts of the vessel as well as the officers and sailors. It began at a called meeting of passengers on June 19, at which a committee was chosen to make the arrangements for the day. James H. Gager was named grand marshal, and Gen. J. J. Jones was chosen orator for the day. On June 21 Grand Marshal Gager issued an order giving many members military titles and responsibilities including the uniform they were to wear and outlining the various activities for the day, all of which seem to have been carried out as instructed and planned. The general orders for the day were copied into the journals of several passengers.

July 4, 1849, opened as a beautiful day "as fine as could be wished with a gentle breeze to cool the tropical sun" for the passengers in the ship *Pacific*. At 7:00 A.M. they fired the first salute of thirteen volleys as they raised the American flag while the regimental band played a national song. Then three cheers "from all on board hailed the glorious day." At 10:00 A.M. the military brigade consisting of between seventy and ninety persons of the New England Regiment commanded by Col. N. D. Morgan, the Easterbrook Guard under Captain Benton, Captain Sulgar's Company, Captain Cartwright's Company, and the Hartford Battalion under Maj. John Ingalls, where each man was armed with a pair of Colt pistols. They were all dressed in black pantaloons, red flannel shirts, and California hats and assembled according to the orders of Grand Marshal Gager and marched around the deck in prescribed order to the accompaniment of a

157

fife and a drum made by Mr. Stout out of a water bucket and the skin of a sheep that they had killed for meat two days earlier. Also included in the procession were police guards dressed in black pantaloons, blue flannel shirts with a star on the left breast, and beaver hats, each carrying a large club. They were followed by several in citizens dress, four physicians, two veterans of the Revolution, and one man in his uniform as a foreign minister. The grand marshal, members of the committee on arrangements, the orator for the day, and readers of the Declaration of Independence and of a special ode prepared for the day assembled in the upper cabin at 11:00 A.M. and marched around the ship to the quarterdeck. Following the singing of an appropriate song by the choir, J. W. Bingham made a few appropriate remarks before reading the Declaration of Independence. Gen. J. J. Jones then presented a brief but beautiful oration. The band then played "Hail Columbia," and everyone was dismissed until dinner was served at 3:00 P.M. In between, however, the passengers were entertained by two characters, Mose, played by second mate Douglas, and Sikesy, played by J. S. Sunham, from the play "New York as It Is." Sikesy was caught in the act of picking someone's pocket and was arrested by the police but cried out for help, and Mose came to his rescue. The police attempted to arrest Mose, but as he was one of the most nimble of the sailors, he easily avoided the police by going up into the rigging although one account has Mose being captured as well. Sikesy was handcuffed but was released when he promised to amend his ways. At 3:00 P.M. a dinner of turkey, pies of preserved meat, sweet potatoes, and pastries was served to everyone in one of the cabins from which all of the baggage had been removed. During the dinner thirteen toasts were offered but "were not very good, lacking in condensation & force." John Ross Browne had been assigned to present an appropriate poem or ode but surprised them with "an inappropriate address in which the foibles & pecularities of the passengers were alluded to with great indelicacy & consequently much offence was taken." When dinner was over, one or more large tubs of alcoholic punch were brought in, "and the company grew merry." A few drank too much, but they did not disrupt the general good feelings of the day. Entertainment in the afternoon was provided by some sailors who devised costumes of a bear and a rhinoceros. The latter consisted of two men leaning over with their heads faced in opposite directions with a board across their backs covered with a cloth that reached nearly to the deck. A person in female attire rode the animal, which was led about by a keeper who told about the capture of the animal, its docility, and its characteristics. Anyone who lifted the cloth at the rear of the animal to see if it was a real rhinoceros got a swipe in the face from the ship's swab that represented a tail. The festivities concluded at sunset, when the brigade again mustered and fired thirty volleys as the flag was lowered. Grand Marshal Gager noted that he believed "every man in the ship has declared that he never spent so pleasant a fourth on land!" The orders issued by Grand Marshal Gager called for a court-martial to be convened on July 5 for any of those who defaulted on their duties on the fourth, but there apparently was no need for this group to meet, as there is no indication in any of the accounts of the voyage of the *Pacific* that it was ever convened.[28]

Journalists who documented celebrations on other vessels included a few more details or incidents that exemplify the fervor with which the Argonauts celebrated Independence Day at sea in 1849. There were frequently two types of toasts offered. Some were referred to as regular, and were prepared by a committee and commonly consisted of thirteen tributes to such things as independence, the nation, the flag, the president of the United States, the vessel, the captain of the vessel, California, the joint stock company, the ladies or the wives and sweethearts left behind, the army and/or navy, and others. The others were volunteer and were offered by individuals. These toasts were tributes to just about anyone and anything one could imagine. Those in the ship *Henry Lee* offered seventeen such toasts. A passenger in the brig *Osceola* reported they had fifty volunteer toasts, "many of which were rich, rare and racy, and called down thunders of applause." Most journalists mentioned drinking alcohol after each of the toasts, but a few drank water. The passengers in the bark *Yoeman* had only potato whiskey made of fermented potatoes and molasses, which one called "vile stuff." On board the ship *Andalusia* they fired a swivel gun after each toast as a signal for "drinking and cheering." Griffith Meredith recorded eighteen of the toasts offered on board the bark *Strafford* and added, "there were a great many toasts that I could not get which were very good!!" There were only seven regular toasts and an additional twenty-four volunteer toasts, which had been written down and handed in to be read by passengers in the bark *Hannah Sprague*. Passengers in the bark *Canton* offered fifty-three volunteer toasts, and Richard Brown Cowley recorded each one along with the name of the passenger who presented it.[29]

Among the songs frequently mentioned as parts of ceremonies are "Hail Columbia," "Star Spangled Banner," "Yankee Doodle," "Home Sweet Home," "Our Native Land," "Land of our Fathers," "America," and "My

Country Tis of The." The last two may actually be the same song, given different titles by the journalists. Many of those who described the celebrations simply noted that they sang or played "National Airs." In a few vessels passengers composed special songs for the day. J. N. Sweezey composed one for the ship *Brooklyn*. It related to celebrating Independence Day. Two untitled songs were written and sung on board the bark *Oxford*. Both were sung by Hiram Brownell, and one was also composed by him. That one was sung to the tune of "King and Countrymen." Both contained references to their experiences during the voyage. Asa H. Snow recited his twelve-stanza poem about winning freedom and independence and seeking gold to the passengers in the bark *Oxford*. Joseph Augustine Benton wrote and presented a long poem for the celebration on board the ship *Edward Everett*.[30]

In rare instances the weather was uncooperative, and the celebrations had to be postponed or canceled. Although they were in the vicinity of Cape Horn early in July, the members of the Bunker Hill Trading and Mining Association made plans for a grand celebration on the Fourth of July. They selected an orator and a reader of the Declaration of Independence, chose the music to be played and/or sung, assigned a committee to prepare regular toasts, and encouraged others to present volunteer toasts. They also killed the last two hogs they had saved and collected "a great many other rarities" that passengers had kept for the occasion. Great was their disappointment when a gale blew in during the night of the third. They ate their special dinner on the fourth, but the weather remained so bad that they had to lay to under close-reefed main topsail nearly three days and could not have their celebration until July 10. In spite of the delay, one passenger noted, "as a whole it was a day never to be forgot by the Bunker Hill Company, there was nothing but harmony and good feeling throughout." He added, "it was the best celebration" and "the most lively and spirited of all Jubilees" he had "ever attended." Passengers in the ship *Morrison* made equally detailed plans for their Independence Day celebration and likewise awoke on the fourth to a "terrific gale from the North East" that "continued with great violence all day." By 9:00 in the evening "the pent up spirit of frolic burst forth . . . and the old tamany or fifth ward opened the ball." Wine, gin, and brandy "began to circulate freely and in common and the Bachanalian shout of inebriety resounded through our cabin." The passengers "caroused a while in the cabin" and then went up to the quarterdeck "to drink toasts where they were helped by the Captain." They drank and ate eggs and eventually "wound up being very sick." Some of the passengers "stood aloof" from the drinking and "were happily free" and saved their "name and health." One passenger concluded that it was "truly a hard way for a man to show his patriotism and thus were our bright anticipations lost in the midnight gloom of a severe ocean storm."[31]

Thanksgiving was celebrated on board fewer vessels than were Washington's birthday and the Fourth of July. Perhaps that was because fewer vessels sailed at times that would keep them at sea during Thanksgiving. A couple of passengers who described their Thanksgiving festivities wrote of the contrast between the weather they had had in the tropics and the weather they would have experienced at home in New England. Neither was particularly pleased with the meal they were served, as they had no turkeys as they did at home. Hence the weather was their only luxury for the day. One noted that they had music and singing on deck, and they danced and marched. In the bark *Orion* they chose special cooks to prepare their Thanksgiving meals in order to give the regular ones a day off. The Thanksgiving meal consisted of boiled ham, stewed chicken, potatoes, turnips, applesauce, barberries, warm bread, and pies. The four lady passengers in the *Orion* made mince pies. After dinner they raised the flag and gave three cheers and a vote of thanks to the cooks. At sunset they fired a salute and cheered to make "the very air resound" and fired guns as they lowered the flag. Then they had "a very fine address from the surgeon." The captain of the ship *Arkansas* issued a proclamation a week before Thanksgiving, and members of the California Mutual Benefit and Joint Stock Association began to make plans for their celebration. One passenger noted they had two parties, "one for God and one for the deveil" and added that "the later Belongs to the Captain." They had a worship service in the morning presided over by their chaplain, Reverend Mr. Willing, and an address in the afternoon by Dr. Fish. Their dinner was mince pie, boiled ham, mashed potatoes, and five small chickens for forty-five diners to which one passenger commented "nuf sed" whereas another passenger referred to their meal as "the first luxciarys we have resieved on Board sinse we left New York." In the evening Capt. Philip W. Shepeard "assembled his tigars on the quarter deck to clowse the day with negrow songs and dansing." The passengers in the brig *Perfect* had been to sea only a little more than two weeks, so they still had some fresh provisions. Their Thanksgiving dinner consisted of "two geese and two chickens baked . . . well stuffed and well cooked . . . three large boiled plum duffs with sauce, boiled onions, cucumbers and beets, pickels, cranberry sauce, catsup and horseradish, prepared potato and turnip sauce, bread, butter, cheese, kraut, cayene and black pepper, vinegar and mustard." "Gruel, apples, figs, grape sauce, pop corn, mince pie, chestnuts, plum sauce, Duff, beef & pork, home cakes, Lemonade" were included in the Thanksgiving dinner for the passengers in the ship *Reindeer,* which had been at sea only a week. By contrast, the people in the ship *Euphrasia* had fresh pork from the two pigs they had killed, but there was "Tremendious growling about dinner. Did not have enough was the complaint from all quarters." Isaac W. Baker included a proclamation ostensibly from Neptune about Thanksgiving in the bark *San Francisco.* They too had fresh pork, both fried and roasted, along with applesauce, pickles, duff, nuts, oranges, lemons, and figs, but they greatly missed the turkey and other luxuries they were accustomed to having at home. A sermon was preached on the theme "'Tis all for the best." Baker did not think very much of it. He included an untitled poem for the day relating to their meal.[32]

> The morning was pleasant and fair
> the breezes were gentle and free
> All hands were heard to declare
> 'Tis a peasant Thanksgiving at sea.
>
> The decks were "washed down" nice & clean
> No labor at all was required—
> (That is nothing but cooking, I mean,
> And that sure was all we desired!)
>
> The unfortunate Pig that was killed
> To our appetites was not denied,
> Our plates and our stomachs were filled
> with his porkish remains, roast & fried
>
> we've apple sauce; pudding with plums—
> (No Turkey or any such trash
> Stuffed with Herbage and pounded bread crumbs
> With which people ashore cut a dash!)
>
> O no! We'd substantial fresh meat
> (And salt too) to suit each one's mind
> More than that, we have something to treat,
> Should any one feel so inclinded!

Figs and oranges also abound
Nuts and lemons as fresh as you please.
We're clear of all cold snowy ground,
With weather guaranteed not to freeze!

Then the firing of targets! Don't tell!
No <u>poultry</u> to shoot at, 'tis true.
<u>Mother Carey</u> has witnessed right well
What revolvers and rifles can do!

Californians 'll ever remember
Should they live to a venerable age
The scenes on the day of November
Which I now inscribe on this page.
                              Novr 29th 1849

Christmas was celebrated much differently in the middle of the nineteenth century than it is in the late twentieth. Thus it is logical that passengers on their way to seek gold in California would say little about the day or the exchanging of gifts or even the fact that December 25, 1849 was Christmas day. Only one person mentioned gifts. John McCrackan wrote to his cousin five months before the holiday and asked him to purchase specific gifts for his mother and sisters. For his mother he wanted "two dozen bottles of 'Scotch Ale,' of the best quality" and suggested it be purchased in New York, where he could obtain "the real article," rather than in New Haven. Price was no consideration for this gift. He wanted "the prettyest 'jewel box' you find for five dollars" for sister Mary. Sara was to have "the most <u>elaborate work box</u> available for the same price." Lottie must have been his favorite sister, as she was to receive a one- or two-volume set of Shakespeare, estimated to cost eight dollars, plus a copy of "Women of Shakespeare" or "Shakespeare's Women," also estimated to cost eight dollars. Most of those who kept journals of their voyages either failed to mention that December 25 was Christmas or wrote primarily about the weather and what they had to eat with food being more popular than the weather. Pierce W. Barker in the ship *Nestor* reported "a little addition to our bill of fare today . . . it being Christmas." They had a pig pie and Indian meal duff. He also wrote that "some had a piece of the (striped) pig for supper if not a piece, they certainly had a fair sight at him." This appears to mean they had too much alcohol to drink. There was a big difference between what the steerage passengers and those in the cabin in the ship *Europe* were served on Christmas. Steerage passengers had chicken and turkey with two small potatoes each, but they "all arose from the table with appetites still craving." What was put out for the cabin was more generous. One of the steerage passengers took one of the cabin dishes and brought it to the steerage, where it soon disappeared. The captain attempted to find out who had committed the theft and even threatened to set fire to the powder magazine and blow up the ship, but he still did not find the culprit. One passenger noted, "With this exception the day passed without any unusual occurrence." Passengers in the ship *Crescent* spent December 24 "picking over Apples & Raisons and paring Squashes &c." in anticipation that they would "have something more then ordinary for Crismas Supper." They had "warm Buisquets, Budder and fride Turnovers and Aplesaus which went first rate." J. L. Akerman in the bark *Daniel Webster* recorded they had something "seldom eaten for a Christmas dinner . . . stewed Beans very highly seasoned with salt and pretty well burnt." They also had albatross pot pie. He indicated it was made by parboiling the bird in "salaeratus water" and mixing the albatross meat "into a pie with potatoes, onions, and a plenty of flour dumplings and then boiled" and felt "all hands" thought it "to be the best dinner that has been eaten on board since we left Boston" three months earlier. Passengers in the ship *Argonaut* had "a mammouth pudding" estimated to weigh twenty-five pounds, made of "a little boiled rice left of diner" mixed with "a heap of hard bread" pounded up, spices, molasses, and shortening "what is here called 'slush.'" It was considered "a grand Christmas pudding." William Edgar Randall emphasized the "Rowing and carousing and fighting and jawing" by the "drunk and crazy" on board the ship *Hannibal* on Christmas but noted that "our victuals are something else" without saying how bad they were. He asked to be delivered from "drinking and profanity." Passengers in the bark *Belgrade,* who were said to be a "band of happy fellows," had roast turkeys, chickens, chicken pies, plum puddings "and other good things" to which they "did justice" for Christmas dinner. In the evening they had an enjoyable dance on deck. Robert Hutchinson noted, "We called it a Christmas ball—Some would call it a sailor breakdown." They were just north of the equator, and the temperature was eighty-two degrees. Passengers in the bark *San Francisco* also had "warm and pleasant" weather "exactly the reverse as regards weather from what it is in Beverly," but those in the brig *Oriental* and the barks *Sara Warren* and *Midas* were not so fortunate. George Osborne Wilson wrote that they were in a storm and spent "A very uncomfortable night for Christmas" in the *Oriental*. The *Sara Warren* was off the coast of Patagonia and had such a gale that all sails were taken in except the double-reefed main topsail. A. Bailey wrote, "This is <u>Christmas day</u>! And, O God! I shall never forget this day." He went on to describe a fierce storm they experienced that day on the coast of Patagonia. The bark *Midas* was off Brazil near the river La Plata on Christmas day. The weather was cold and cloudy with thunder and lightning, and they were making no headway. John T. Howard called it "a mean kind of Christmas" and said he would attempt to describe the gale but assumed they would encounter worse in the future near Cape Horn that would be "more worthy" of describing.[33]

There were a few other days that were special to a small number of people, primarily those from a single state or to individuals directly involved, that might be mentioned. Passengers in the bark *Emma Isadora* and the ship *Pharasalia* both made mention that May 1 was May Day. Members of the Hartford Union Mining and Trading Company in the ship *Henry Lee* and members of the Connecticut Mining and Trading Company in the schooner *General Morgan* held their own elections in recognition of election day in Connecticut, and both gave a majority of their votes for governor to Thomas H. Seymour. Passengers in the ship *Pharasalia* celebrated the anniversary of the battles of Palo Alto and Resaca de la Palma in South Texas near the Mexican border on May 9 with decorations in the cabin, an oration, songs by the glee club, toasts, a ball, and a theatrical performance. There were a number who drank too much alcohol, and many of them "went to bed without knowing how they got there." Why passengers in a ship from Boston should observe this day is a mystery. Perhaps some passengers were veterans of the war with Mexico. Perhaps also, from the result of the celebration, some passengers wanted an excuse to drink to excess. Bunker Hill Day was observed by passengers in several vessels out of Boston. There was what might best be described as a theatrical exhibition in the ship *York*. A passenger in the brig *Sea Eagle* imagined that he could hear the cannon roaring at home and his little boys "standing at the door looking at the smoke." The last pig in the bark *Elvira* was killed for a pork dinner. Passengers in the ship *Plymouth* fired their four pounder and small arms. Cornelius Cooledge in the bark *Oxford* mentioned that they were "reminded of the sufferings of those who struggled for *freedom* on Bunkers Hill." Moses Cogswell indicated that those in the ship *Sweden* also remembered the day that was "dear to all Americans" and indicated he knew they would celebrate in Boston with "booming of the Cannon and the merry Peal of Bells." Marylanders in the ship *Andalusia* celebrated on September 12 to recognize the day that Baltimore was saved from being desecrated by an invading army in 1814 by listening to an oration in which the speaker gave a historical account of the battle, a march around the ship, firing salutes at noon and 6:00 P.M., and music and dancing.[34]

Birthdays and wedding anniversaries were occasionally celebrated on board vessels bound for California in 1849. Birthdays of ship officers were usually more special than those of passengers. Capts. Benjamin Frank Simmons of the ship *Magnolia* and Suchet Mauran of the bark *Oxford* both had birthdays during their voyages. Captain Simmons was 29 on May 31 and celebrated by "treating a select company to liquors and cake." He also had "a big gingerbread" made for the crew that was a "great luxury for poor jack." Captain Mauran had a pig killed and served for his special day on April 3 and sent a bottle of brandy to the crew in the forecastle. First mate Mr. Dunham of the ship *Sarah & Eliza* and the second mate of the ship *Mount Vernon* had birthdays during their voyages. Edward Floyd Jones noted that Mr. Dunham's birthday had been long anticipated. He reported that it was Dunham's "great desire . . . to get all on board tipsey & as many drunk as would get so" and added that this "peculiar manner of celebrating ones birthday was new" to him. Passengers also noted their own birthdays and occasionally those of others as well as how they were observed. Alfred Doten reported his twentieth birthday and lamented that he had nothing with which to treat. In order to avoid having his ears pulled, he promised to treat his friends when they got into port. Earlier he had noted the birthday of Edward Morton and indicated they pulled his ears a little because he had nothing with which to treat. Samuel Curtis Upham noted that a steerage passenger in the brig *Osceola* celebrated a birthday on May 3, and "at least a dozen of his companions retired to their berths in a state of inebriation." William Ives Morgan, a passenger in the bark *John Walls*, noted, "I got drunk" on his birthday while they were in Rio de Janeiro. He appears to have been greatly disturbed that they had been in port for forty-eight days. Benjamin H. Deane simply noted he was 28 on September 24. On his forty-sixth birthday Samuel C. Lewis became contemplative about his past and present as he sailed to California in the ship *Charlotte*. William McKendree Carson celebrated his birthday in the ship *Jane Parker* by providing some good beef, hominy, and potatoes from his "own resources" for his mess, and a friend, W. E. Steward, provided "some excellent mince pie." John McCrackan and a few of his friends in the ship *Balance* had ham and plum pudding and "three kinds of wine &

166

enough of it" for his birthday, and he shared some of his wine and brandy with passengers in the second cabin. Mr. Frye, a friend, provided a basket of champagne. Charles Herbert Fuller reported having "a good glass of Lemonade" to celebrate his twentieth birthday "on the wide Atlantic Ocean" on board the ship *Sweden*. James H. Gager reported his ninth wedding anniversary on board the ship *Pacific* but made no mention of any celebration. John McCrackan reported the first wedding anniversaries of Mr. Frye and Mrs. Reed on board the ship *Balance*. Their party of four had salt beef, rice, macaroni, cheese, crackers, champagne, and brandy for lunch. At tea they had rice fritters and brandied peaches. He noted they drank toasts and gave "many kind wishes" to the honorees.[35]

It seems, then, that passengers on long and frequently tedious voyages to California in 1849 usually had formal worship services on board those vessels whenever the weather permitted and that they took advantage of every possible holiday or special day to have a celebration. In some vessels there was conflict over Sunday worship, but the only conflicts or dissatisfactions concerning celebrations centered around the matter of passengers drinking excessive amounts of alcohol. The bylaws of joint stock companies generally required worship services and forbade alcohol consumption. Both provisions seem to have been violated at times in some vessels.

6

Weather Problems

Weather of all kinds was a significant factor in the living conditions for passengers sailing around Cape Horn to California in 1849. It played a major role in determining how short or how long their voyage was, their comfort and satisfaction, their morale, the quantity and quality of drinking water, whether they received hot or cold food on a given day, the amount of clothes they had to wear, where they slept or otherwise spent their time, their ability to get about the vessel, the activities in which they could engage, and even their amusement, entertainment, and enlightenment as they witnessed ocean storms, sunrises and sunsets over the oceans, bright moonlit nights, both sun- and moon-induced rainbows, previously unseen constellations, waterspouts, and other natural wonders.

Passengers wrote about all these things in their journals. They described the elation of heading for the goldfields in the unexplored regions of the distant West, second thoughts about leaving home and loved ones, frustrations with calms, which slowed progress to California, exhilaration and elevated morale resulting from favorable winds, tediousness and boredom of a long voyage, pleasure of catching water when it rained to provide fresh water for drink and for bathing, sleeping on deck in the tropics, being cold in the frequently unheated cabins and in their berths around Cape Horn, frightening and life-threatening experiences during storms as well as the stark beauty they witnessed in some of them, bleakness of Cape Horn and the terrible storms there, wonders of snow and ice at a time they usually experienced summer, rapid seasonal changes as they sailed south and then north again, and the anxieties and hopes as they neared, and then arrived at, their destination. The time of the year at which the Argonauts departed the east coast sometimes determined how quickly they experienced storms and other weather situations that affected them. Those who left in the height of winter in the east often faced storms almost immediately as they quickly reached the area at which the warm

Gulf Stream and the colder waters of the North Atlantic came into con-tact with each other. Such early departures also meant rounding Cape Horn during its spring or perhaps early summer. Summertime departures could occasionally result in encountering hurricanes in the Atlantic Ocean and also rounding Cape Horn during fall or early winter. The weather was always bad, and the winds were usually dead ahead at Cape Horn. By stark contrast, however, whenever the passengers reached the tropics in either the Atlantic or the Pacific, they described the water and air temperatures as hot and reported that the heat caused considerable discomfort, espe-cially since the winds were generally calm.

Weather affected the abilities of passengers to perform even the most routine things such as eating, sleeping, writing, and moving about the ves-sel. These difficulties sometimes brought out humorous responses to their own or each other's adversity. Nearly three months into the voyage of the ship *Andalusia* from Baltimore, Anne (Willson) Booth noted that even though they had a rack on the table in which all of the dishes were to fit, there were problems with the dishes sliding across the table and spilling during bad weather. During gales the vessel would lay far over to the lee-ward, causing the dishes to slide in that direction, and sometimes the con-tents spilled out. Passengers "who undertook the soup put the greater quantity of it on their clothes" during one dinner. Sitting was impossible, so the passengers "picked up a mouthful as we could," wrote Booth. On another occasion she noted that "these accidents are rather amusing than otherwise" and "at sea one's personal appearance is not much regarded." A passenger in the bark *Canton* described their situation during a storm. "The sea ran very high and caused the ship to rock and pitch to and fro in a frightful manner. . . . at dinner two or three heavy seas struck her . . . and completely capsized nearly every article including meat, rice, molasses, tea, water, sugar-pots and butter—everything hurled from one side to the other, covering and smearing all of us more or less" and break-ing nearly all the dishes. Passengers seated on the starboard were either tossed on their backs or thrown under the table. The berth of the man who reported this incident was on the leeward, so his rug was "covered with every kind of grease." Nevertheless he was "so tickled" amidst all of the "shouting and laughing" that "as if I myself should have died." Chester Joseph Snow reported that a storm encountered by the ship *Euphrasia* caused such pitching and rolling that it created "a perfect shower of sea beef, biscuit, and other things, throwing those who were eating . . . spralling and making a complete heap of trunks and men. In some cases the men were top, in others the trunks." John McCrackan reported that the table in their cabin was originally not lashed down. Hence in an early storm the table started moving, as did the chairs on which they were seated. During one pass across the cabin much of the food ended up in the lap of Captain Ruggles while on the return passage more of it landed in the lap of the first mate. This scene was repeated several times. McCrackan indicated that "a more ludicrous & amusing scene cannot be imagined" and that he was "nearly dead with laughter though the danger at the time was imminent." They later lashed the table but could not do the same with the chairs, so the passengers continued to slide away from and back toward the table during gales.[1]

Sleeping could be difficult for one unaccustomed to the motions of a sailing vessel even in good weather, but doing so during bad weather could be a real challenge. Moses Cogswell wrote on his second day at sea in the ship *Sweden* that he did not sleep well, as he was not used to sleeping on a vessel. After he became accustomed to the sounds and movements, he had no trouble sleeping in good weather. Chester Joseph Snow noted that the "considerable wind heaving us about in our berths" was "a sure pre-ventitive of sleep or rest." He added that one person who slept in a ham-mock "was suddenly awoke from a sound sleep" when the rope fastenings at both ends gave way and dropped him "some 5 ft. to the floor of the deck." John T. Howard was disturbed that the weather prevented the cook from furnishing their usual rations and added that it made for "an unpleas-ant night to sleep, or even rest." He "had to try & sleep with one eye way open & the other good half way." He felt he was "lucky not to be thrown" from his berth even though he held on with both hands and braced him-self with both knees. Anne (Willson) Booth wrote that she was "entirely raised up above the board that fits on the side of my berth" every time the ship gave a "heavy lurch." She was "compelled to hold on with all my might." Yet she thought "It was really amusing to see ourselves pitching and tossing about as we were." She feared that the heavy seas dashing over the top of the cabin would smash it at any moment.[2]

Judging from what several people wrote, there must have been thou-sands of passengers who started keeping journals of their voyages to Cali-fornia. Some of them wrote about the difficulty in writing during heavy weather and how they solved the problem. A. Bailey noted that the bad weather at the outset made writing harder than it ever had been for him before. The "continual <u>roll</u> & <u>pitch</u>" of the vessel made it necessary for him to put his paper in his lap and "dodge the motion of the vessel about every letter." He claimed that if his journal ever reached his family, they would "be lucky if they can find it out." A passenger in the bark *Strafford* listed several problems in finding a time to write. When the wind was "on the quarter," causing the vessel to lean "way over on her side," it was "almost impossible to sit on a chair or anything else." When it rained or the weather was cold, so many members were down in the cabin that they disrupted concentration by their "crowding back and forth from one place to another." In addition the cabin was "so dark that it" was "impossible to write." A passenger in the ship *America* also referred to the darkness, passengers in constant motion within a few feet, and the uneasiness of the ship but added that "salt atmosphere destroys the finish, the sizing," of the paper so that whatever he wrote became "a perfect mop . . . in a few moments!" In addition he noted with "much truthfulness" his "<u>inexperience</u> and a <u>dull brain</u>." Anne (Willson) Booth partially solved the problem by sitting "on the floor between two large chests that are fastened down, with my ink in one hand & pen in the other" with her book presumably on her lap. She hoped that no one other than her family who were "perfectly familiar" with her handwriting would see her journal because the motion of the vessel kept her from having control over her pen.[3]

A large number of journalists mentioned that most of the male passengers grew beards during the voyage. One can easily understand how much danger there might have been from attempting to shave with a straight razor, the only kind available in 1849, when the vessel was pitching and rolling sufficiently to throw sleepers from their berths and to cause dishes to slide off the edges of tables with lips around the edges designed to prevent such calamities. Even the seemingly simple task of washing oneself at the sink could be not only challenging but also dangerous. A passenger in the ship *America* described one case in which he was at the sink on the starboard side when the ship was "low down on larbourd." The legs of the sink were made fast, but the top was not. As the ship moved lower and lower, he leaned farther and farther to compensate. Eventually he was at a forty-five-degree angle to the deck. Then all of a sudden the ship straightened very quickly, and his "heels flew up like a spring trap," and his "poor nose, forehead and chin made an intimate acquaintance with the deck in the shortest time imaginable." The top of the sink, "half full of dirty water," as well as his soap dish, soap, washbowl, brushes, and towel fell on top of him, and they all rolled over into the lee scuppers. His "forehead was bruised slightly," his "chin considerably," and his "nose bled profusely, knees, elbows, and wrists bruised variously" and two fingers on his left hand "were badly swelled and sprained." He added that "It was the beginning of a most miserable days work for some others as well as myself." Another passenger, whom he called Captain Snow, "was insensible for a length of time, lip cut through, head and body considerable bruised."[4]

Several passengers mentioned changes in weather—rapid, temporary as well as long-term seasonal—as problems. A passenger in the bark *Belgrade* reported that when they were in the area of Rio de la Plata the temperature was so hot early in the day that they had to put up an awning to shield them from the scorching rays of the sun. About 3:00 P.M. clouds appeared to shield them from the rays of the sun, and the wind began to blow. As the wind increased in velocity, they began to take in sails. Increasing winds caused colder temperatures. They shipped several seas. Before night they had to wrap themselves "in thick clothing to keep from freezing." When the bark *Gold Hunter* had been out from Bangor, Maine, about two months, a passenger reported mild, shirtsleeve weather in the morning but noted that within two hours after a wind began to blow, they had to put on overcoats to keep warm. They were then in latitude 46.43 south. Three days later he reported, "Mittens and great coats were worn from morning til night. A great many take to their beds to keep warm." Dress was still the same a day later, when they were in latitude 51 south. S. Mortimer Collins wrote when the ship *Magnolia* was two months out from New Bedford, Massachusetts, that a shower caused him to don his flannels again and indicated he would "keep then on now as long as I remain at sea, I think." The next day he reported the sun "was very scorching" and the tops of his feet were burned "nearly to a blister." He found it "uncomfortable to sleep" in his cabin below deck although those on deck were "very comfortable." John McCrackan indicated they left New Haven at the end of a severe winter, only to discover three weeks later that they were in summer; four or five weeks later they were back in winter; and a month later they were in summer again. He speculated autumn would have arrived by the time they reached San Francisco, and winter would have set in by the time they had established a place to live. A week after crossing the equator, Griffith Meredith wrote that the weather was becoming cooler as they sailed southward. He felt that within that week they had changed from summer to fall although by the calendar it was only late March. According to John Henry Corneilson, the doctor on board the bark *Hannah Sprague* told the passengers the frequent seasonal changes during their long voyage would "be the hardest trial we have yet experienced." He noted they experienced five changes in fewer than five months and added, "This weather is very trying." Harry G. Brown felt the passengers in the bark *Selma* had "passed through seven seasons in five months." After nearly four months at sea in the bark *Sarah Warren*, A. Bailey reflected that he had "been where the tropical sun poured his torrid rays upon my head in all the intensity of Equatorial heat," in a "latitude where Spicy gales are wafted from Isle to Isle—Where the fine sand dust from the great African desert fell upon my clothes," in the "cold, gloomy, sterile, and uninviting regions of Cape Horn," along the "inhospitable shore of Patagonia," and in the "most beautiful and delightful Sunny Clime of Chili and Peru where the Mighty Andes rear their lofty heads, covered with everlasting snows, and throw out fire & Smoke." He added that while in the last area he constantly feared he would make his eternal "bed in that great receptical of Oceans Sons, uncoffined unshrowded, save by the ever restless wave, with all its wild sublimity." Bailey concluded it was no wonder that he often felt lonesome and thought of home and family thousands of miles away.

A record of regular temperature recordings provides some indication of the various temperatures experienced by Argonauts in 1849. During their voyage from New York to San Francisco between January 28 and July 4, 1849, the passengers in the brig *Mary Stuart* experienced temperatures ranging from a low of thirty-six off Cape Horn to a high of eighty-seven fourteen degrees north of the equator in the Pacific Ocean. The first temperature reading recorded was sixty-eight at latitude 33 north two weeks out of New York. Temperatures ranged between sixty-six and seventy-one for the next six days. During the next week, while sailing south between latitudes 20 and 7 north, the temperature ranged between seventy-two and seventy-nine. Between February 27 and March 20 they ranged between eighty and eighty-four as they sailed from latitude 7 north to latitude 27 south. For the next six days there was a decline from seventy-nine to seventy between latitudes 27 and 37 south. Between latitudes 27 and 50 south, temperatures ranged between fifty-two and sixty-two. Temperature ranges between latitude 50 south in the Atlantic and latitude 50 south in the Pacific were from a low of thirty-six to a high of sixty with a gradual decline to thirty-six and a gradual rise from that low. From latitude 50 south to around latitude 25 south in the Pacific, there was a general increase from fifty-six to sixty-six with some minor fluctuations. The increased temperatures continued from seventy to eighty between latitude 25 south and the equator in the Pacific Ocean. Temperatures remained in the eighties regularly between the equator and latitude 16 north. Then they continued a gradual decline with minor fluctuations until July 4, when they arrived in San Francisco where the temperature was fifty-eight. The temperature was eighty-two on the equator in both the Atlantic and the Pacific Oceans. Keep in mind that these are temperatures only and do not take into account such factors as moisture and wind, both of which could make the temperature feel colder, or bright sunshine, which could make the actual temperature feel warmer.[5]

The two weather conditions that seem to have bothered passengers most were heat, especially when combined with bright sunshine and the absence of wind, and cold, especially when combined with cloudy skies and wind, rain, snow, or hail. The highest temperature noted by any passenger was 124 degrees in the sun on March 29, 1849, by John W. Bell in the schooner *Gager* of New York. He added it was 96 in the shade. Earlier in March he reported several days with highs over 100 in the sun and over 90 in the shade as far north as latitude 23 north. He thought they should have taken the southeast trade winds five degrees farther north but still had not taken them. Without better winds he knew they would have a long voyage, but he admitted they were never satisfied, as it "blows too hard too light, too Hot or too Cold. We have a touch of all kinds & do not feel satisfied with either." Moses Cogswell reported only eighty-seven in the shade and calm winds late in March, although the ship *Sweden* was much closer to the equator than was the schooner *Gager* when Bell reported ninety-six in the shade and noted, "we are all suffering with the heat and Langour." A few days later he wrote they "all felt Blue to think we are not gaining ground. Today is a complete repetition of yesterday. Cloudy rainy, and calm, The air hot and stifling." Near mid May a passenger in the bark *Emma Isadora* reported "110 in the sun, and as we are obliged to stay in the sun or be suffocated in the cabins, we felt the heat some" in latitude 29 south. On New Year's Day 1850 the passengers from Maine in the bark *Belgrade* experienced 112 degrees with "the sun pouring down hot enough to melt us" in latitude 3 north. Ten days later it was only 88, but the heat was "so powerful as to almost blister the feet walking the deck barefooted as the most of us have done for a fortnight past." A passenger in the bark *Canton* reported a temperature of 103 in the shade on May 4, 1849, and lamented the next day, "Oh, what oppressive weather and a perfect calm!" A month into the voyage of the bark *Hannah Sprague,* Alfred Wheeler reported that bad-tasting water, careless and filthy servants, passengers growing piggish at the table "combined with the oppressive heat keep one in a perpetual bad humor." He said the cabin was "as close as an oven" and on deck it was "sunny and hot." Samuel Curtis Upham saw "Shades of Lucifer!" in their high temperatures in February 1849 and wished he could "divest myself of flesh and sit in my bones for an hour or so" to cool off. Pierce W. Barker noted that they were becalmed on eighteen of the first forty-two days at sea in ship *Nestor* and added they had been within a hundred miles of the equator for nearly a week, "knocking about, with evry kind of a breeze but the right." They had expected to strike the southeast trades well north of the line, but finally the trades struck them one degree south of it. Passengers in the bark *Maria* had extra problems near the equator. They had headwinds in addition to heat and calms. Many of them slept on deck at night to escape "the hot and stiffling atmosphere below in the state rooms." Walter Balfour Gould wrote that he tried sleeping on deck two nights but got rained on. He concluded he would rather "take a baking instead of a shower bath while asleep," but he did move his mattress from his berth in the stateroom to the rows of chests in the center of the vessel, where he could get some air.

All the above wrote about the heat only in the Atlantic Ocean portion of their voyage. Perhaps by the time they reached the tropical region of the Pacific Ocean, heat was too trifling a matter to discuss. A couple of passengers mentioned heat problems in both oceans, however. Charles Henry Harvey noted it was stifling and uncomfortable just south of the equator in the Atlantic, but in the Pacific he and others "washed in salt water" almost every night when it was "almost to warm to sleep." By washing in salt water he appears to mean that they threw water on each other more in the vein of water fights. The highest temperature he noted on the equator in the Pacific was eighty-one in April 1850. John Taylor, a passenger in the ship *Orpheus*, reported passengers sleeping on deck in both oceans because it was too hot to sleep in the cabins below deck. They were particularly hot when the hatches had to be closed because of rain.[6]

Passengers wrote about the cold somewhat less frequently than they did about the heat and seem not to have complained about cold quite as much as they did about the scorching temperatures in the tropics. Nevertheless, cold temperatures presented problems. About four months into the voyage a passenger in the ship *Orpheus* reported there was little variation from thirty-nine degrees and that the cold greatly diminished their comfort. When they were on deck, they soon became "chilled through although wrapped up in our overcoats." Many of the passengers had badly swollen feet on top of the cold, probably "from want of exercise" but

"Maybe 'high living.'" By late June the passengers in the ship *America* had experienced "gales, winds, rain, and other bad weather for about three weeks," and the weather was "cold and tedious." The passengers tried to keep warm by "stamping and thrashing" as there was "no fire in the Cabin." Harry G. Brown wrote of shoveling snow off the deck of the bark *Selma* in late July, something he had never expected to do at that time of the year. He added the past week had been very unpleasant "being shut up in the Cabbin of a vessel and rolling and tumbling about." The weather was "so cold that one can not stay on deck." The rigging was covered with ice and the decks with snow. Two passengers wrote about conditions in the bark *Hannah Sprague*. One reported they hardly ever left their berths other than to eat and then only when they had "something extra to eat." He also stated that the cold caused him to have so severe a toothache that the doctor pulled the tooth. He concluded after having heard stories about rounding Cape Horn and experiencing it once, "it is more interesting to hear stories about it, than to enjoy the realities." The other passenger reported it was so cold that spray blowing over the bow froze on the masts, rigging, and sails as soon as it hit. It was so thick on the head sails that they could not have shortened sail had they needed to do so. They calculated fifty tons of ice coated the sails, masts, rigging, and deck. Passengers in the bark *Isabel* also suffered through the rigors of Cape Horn without any "fire to keep any degree of comfort." Several of them had badly swollen feet and legs that "itched just like chilblains." In some cases their skin broke open and "produced running sores, exciting fears of scurvy." One passenger noted that the whole time "was so disagreeable and so cold, that there is no pleasure in recalling . . . any thing that transpired during the time" they were rounding Cape Horn. A passenger in the bark *Emma Isadora* recorded temperatures at sunrise, noon, and sunset during much of the voyage. Between latitude 50 south in the Atlantic and latitude 50 south in the Pacific, the highest temperature was forty-three, and that was as they entered the region in the Atlantic. In the immediate vicinity of Cape Horn the temperatures ranged in the low to mid thirties, but there were almost constant gale winds with hail or snowstorms. On June 21, when they were south of Cape Horn, he wrote, "Here we are knocking about of Cape Horn among the snow and hail and cold weather in the middle of June with the Thermometer down to freezing and no fire to dry our feet or warm our fingers . . . who would not sell a farm and go to sea." William H. Dougal, a passenger in the bark *Galindo*, recorded the daily temperatures between July 25 and September 5, 1894 as they were in the vicinity of Cape Horn. The lowest was between twenty and twenty-two on August 6, when he reported their decks were a mass of ice and the rigging was covered with ice ten inches thick in some places. The highest temperature he reported was forty. On several days he mentioned gales, snow squalls, and heavy seas.[7] Some fortunate passengers experienced the cold and struggles at Cape Horn only a few days, but others experienced them for as much as six weeks.

Although few of the passengers sailing to California in 1849 had ever rounded Cape Horn, they certainly had heard enough about it to know that rounding it would be a severe challenge to them and their vessels. After having rounded it once, several vowed in their journals that they would never do it again, as reading or hearing about it was much preferable to experiencing it firsthand. As they approached the colder regions of the Southern Hemisphere, captains and mates began to make preparations for the storms of Cape Horn. They frequently took down upper yards and sails, inspected standing and running rigging and made necessary repairs, replaced the sails currently in use with older ones, and battened the hatches in hopes of preventing water from getting below deck. As he witnessed all this, a passenger in the ship *Sweden* noted, "We are soon to see the 'Elephant' of our voyage, Cape Horn." He anticipated they would be in the "smooth water of the Pacific . . . in three or four weeks" but recognized that the length of their overall voyage depended in large part upon "our success in doubling" Cape Horn quickly. Exactly four weeks later he noted with apparent glee, "I have now seen the <u>Elephant</u>" and added they went around Cape Horn "with all sail set, at ten knots an hour and continued on our course rejoicing." He admitted that they were "not at all sorry to get out of a bad <u>scrape</u> so easily as we did."[8] Some groups were equally fortunate in that they rounded Cape Horn even more quickly than did the *Sweden* while others were unfortunate enough to suffer the furies of the cape substantially longer.

The time it took a vessel to sail from latitude 50 south in the Atlantic to latitude 50 south in the Pacific has often been used as a measure of success in a quick passage around Cape Horn. The brig *Oriental* made it in fourteen days, the bark *Emma Isadora* in sixteen, the brig *Mary Stuart* in twenty-one, and the ship *Pacific* in twenty-two. All can be considered good times. The bark *Gold Hunter* passed the entrance to and exit from the Straits of Magellan in just under eight days whereas the brig *Sea Eagle* took five weeks to sail through the straits. The schooner *Gager* was at the entrance to the straits in late April but encountered a gale the next day and suffered sufficient damage for the captain to go back to Montevideo for repairs. It was not until June 16 that she reached the Straits of Magellan again. She passed through in nine days. The ship *Daniel Webster* passed the cape in between seven and eight days. A passenger in the bark *Strafford* reported they were "in fact farely around the Horn, that dreaded Cape Horn!!! where we have been dreading for three or four months. Got around in 8 days too when some vessels has been known to of been from 30 to 60 days in getting around." The brig *Sterling* of Beverly, Massachusetts, spent fifty days getting around Cape Horn. The schooner *St. Mary* reached longitude 78 west by September 16, 1849, but she then endured a series of gales that pushed her backward 360 miles. By October 7 she had reached only as far as longitude 67 west. She eventually rounded the cape by October 28. Thus she took about six weeks passing the horn. A passenger who reported on the slow progress of the ship *Charlotte* did not provide the number of days spent rounding the horn, but he did note it took forty-two days after sailing from Rio de Janeiro to reach a point four or five degrees east of the cape and added that they had expected to be in Valparaiso in that amount of time.[9]

Typical comments made by journalists while sailing around Cape Horn include "Strong West Winds. Heading South. Weather Cold"; "Frequent hail storms"; "Spent the day in bed to keep warm"; "The storm unabating, rain and snow, wind and water mingle together in wild confusion"; "Oh! June, June, sweet month of roses, never did I expect to see thee appear in such a strange character, or to witness such violence done by thy gentle nature!"; "Cold and dreary with head winds"; "The rolling & pitching of the vessel made it impossible to stand, sit, or lie still. . . . And so it went night & day, pitch, tumble, roll, roll, tumble, pitch, until one was pounded to a perfect jelly"; "Oh sea voyage, where are thy Charms?"; "A life on the ocean wave may be a very pretty thing to read about, but the reality is quite another thing"; "Wind dead ahead. Frequent squalls of snow"; "Hard winds, now truly is the winter of our discontent"; "Cold enough to freeze our winters to death at home"; and "Head winds, head winds, & nothing else. Cold, snowy, unpleasant weather." Occasionally there were encouraging comments including "Fair wind and weather" and "News of fair wind brought all hands on deck early and every one wore a happy face." The real encouraging comments came when the cape was passed: "We now began to congratulate ourselves that we had doubled Cape Horn. . . . This caused quite a change in the feelings of all on board & every face looked smiling & Happy"; "Happy men are we for we are now well around the Horn"; and "The winter of our discontent is fast being made glorious spring."[10]

The members of the California Mutual Benefit and Joint Stock Association and other passengers in the ship *Arkansas* experienced a five-day gale in the region of Cape Horn. A passenger reported that five experienced captains on board said it was the heaviest storm they had ever seen. Some sailors who had been to sea for thirty years said the same. Three officers who had rounded Cape Horn between eleven and sixteen times had "never Experienest such a gale." They lay to under a close-reefed topsail for five days. Many of the passengers, most of whom were Methodists, seemingly spent a great deal of time praying for their safety and were rewarded by having the vessel survive the storm without ever shipping a sea. Somewhat later that passenger reported they had been "trying to bete round the horn against wind and curent repeted snow squalls and gales of wind" for thirty-eight days. They finally rounded the cape on October 21.[11]

In spite of all the weather-related and other problems in rounding Cape Horn, once in a while passengers could find some humor in their adversity as noted by one in the ship *Plymouth* who had seen some "ludicrous scenes occasioned by the rolling of the vessel." Among them were "showers of cranberries, pigs feet moving with wonderful alacrity, but the prettiest sight was at the tea-table." He reported that "the ball was opened by the [illegible word that resembles "leg"] . . . of bacon taking a 'Chasser' to the leeward, followed simultaneously by the potatoes, butter, bread, tea, etc., which forced us poor unfortunates to the lee side, to display our agility, first in endeavouring to escape the stream of hot tea, and then to save the residue." He found himself "hard up against the partition, one hand holding my tea-mug in which there remained one third of its original contents, the other held what might be called a handfull, consisting of part potatoes, bread & sugar-bowl, whilst my lap was covered with part of the contents of the latter, whilst the deck looked as if there had been a minature hail storm."[12]

Occasionally passengers wrote instructions to others following them or recorded their thoughts about having rounded Cape Horn. In a letter to his mother, Robert La Motte advised other members of his family that they should "By no means . . . come by Cape Horn" and added that he would "rather go to the Penitentiary for 4 months." After describing a severe storm in the vicinity of Cape Horn, Alfred Doten, a passenger in the bark *Yoeman*, cautioned his readers, "this is no fancy sketch, but one of real life; this is Cape Horn now in the dead of winter. Don't talk of the times that tried men's souls after this, for such a time as this tries men's souls, and bodies too, and lays hold of his fingers, ears, nose, and toes, in a very peculiar manner."[13]

Storms were experienced in many places during the long voyages to California, and the passengers lived in both fear and awe of them. Numerous vessels were delayed several days during January 1849, as the Middle Atlantic and New England coasts suffered severe cold weather and a northwest storm. The ship *Morrison* encountered a severe and damaging storm on her second day out of New York. One passenger called it a hurricane that blew "with unabated fury." Early in the four-day gale the *Morrison* suffered severe damage to her masts and rigging, as the "lee main and maintopsail braces parted" and "the yards went swinging fore and aft." Then the "foretopsail was carried away . . . and in a few seconds the fore and main top gallant mast and the mizzen topmast" fell and carried with them the spanker gaff. They had to lay to throughout the storm while listening to the "howling of the winds and the crashing of the spars," which were still hanging by the rigging, "threatening the destruction of the crew who were trying to clear the wreck." The crew threw overboard a considerable amount of freight that had been stored on deck. After the four-day gale blew itself out on February 15, the crew spent several weeks repairing the rigging and masts and yards of the vessel while they sailed onward to California.[14]

At 10:00 P.M. on the fifth day out of New Bedford, the ship *America* was struck by a gale that carried her on at a rate of ten knots. The gale increased during the next two hours as the ship was pushed forward by the wind. There was still no abatement by midnight. Some of the passengers retired for the night, but many remained on deck to witness the "magnificent and sublime gale." Winds swept waves washing over the ship, and waters rushing into the cabin below deck awakened those who had gone to bed. The ship "rolled and plunged . . . violently," causing "chests and trunks, chairs, tables and other furniture" to be in "continual and rapid motion from one side of the cabin to the other." Passengers, furniture, pitchers, tumblers, crockery, and everything else not securely fastened were sent crashing by the violent motion of the vessel. One passenger concluded, "surely, they who go down to the sea in ships and are there overtaken by a violent storm are very near death!"[15]

A storm that one passenger described as "the most severe and terrible gale what ever swept the Atlantic" struck the schooner *Gager* about midnight on her ninth day out of New York. The passenger wrote, "words cannot begin to portray nor imagination picture the scene" of winds "Howling like a pack of Wolves & the Sea" was so tremendous that even a "hundred Niagaras could not begin with it boiling foaming hissing like a thousand engines." It was a horrible night, and although the storm seemed to have reached its peak the next day at noon, "it increased in fury and rages as if all the winds of the world were concentrated & let off in one Storm." The passenger saw visions of his entire family and scenes of his life, and he recalled the day exactly two years earlier that his wife died, leaving a young son. He feared for his own life as the storm raged and was sure his son would be left without parents. He worried that should he die at sea in this storm, his family would never learn of his passing and would be left in doubt of his fate. "A kind and Good God willed it other wise," and the gale broke, so they were all spared. He vowed that if he lived "a thousand years, that day & that night I never can forget."[16]

A. Bailey, a passenger in the bark *Sarah Warren*, described a gale that struck them two months out of Portland, Maine, after they had experienced several days of rough weather. It was quite a scary time for Bailey and the other passengers. The gale struck about 4:00 in the morning with "terrific . . . thunder & lighten." The wind was off the land from the west as they were sailing south. Bailey reported "having fearfull apprehension that we would not ride out the gale in Safety." He added that someone who had not been to sea could in no way imagine "how awful & dismal" a gale at sea can be with its "vivid flashes of lightening!" He shuddered even to "think of it after it" was over. He concluded that he had suffered enough in this and other storms to pay "for all that I may have done amiss," and should he ever see his home again, he "could be content with whatever my future lot might chance to be, without a single murmur." Even at the end of the day, the sea was "running mountains high," and the waves were "lashed by the wind into a feather white."[17]

The ship *America* encountered another storm of more than four days' duration about two and a half months after sailing from New Bedford. A passenger noted on June 18, 1849, that the morning opened with a continuation of the gale that struck them the previous morning. There had been "thunder and lightning and violent hail squalls" as the storm grew more intense. The barometer was still down, so there was no indication the storm would let up soon. At the start of the day he described the situation: "Sea awful to look upon and running high! Weather cold, cabin windows closed . . . lamps burning, passengers sitting about . . . in thick winter clothes, such as overcoats, cloaks, comforts, overshoes &c &c. It is too rough to write, and too dark to read, too cold and wet on deck as well as dangerous to be there, so here we sit like so many culprits awaiting sentence for our misdeeds." In the afternoon the storm was "worse if possible." On the morning of June 19 he reported they had drifted north and east a hundred miles during the past two days. Their captain, Charles P. Seabury, had been on seven long whaling voyages of two or more years and "says he never saw such severe times before." The passenger then wrote somewhat disparagingly of some other experienced sailors and officers whose demonstrated fear "was anything but crediable to their boasted experience or honourable to act as they did in the presence of so many inexperienced, frightened passengers." The winds increased further on June 20, and the passenger noted they were "in the midst of a perfect hurricane. . . . The worst since we left home." He added that "The worst I could wish an enemy would be that he should be near Cape Horn, Atlantic side, in the winter season with winds a head, and every day or two a gale . . . without a fire in cabin, and in a ship pitching and rolling to such a degree that to stand he would not only have to brace himself, but to hold on too, watching for a favourable opportunity to move." The winds abated considerably during the night of June 20, but there was still a heavy, irregular swell on the morning of the twenty-first. Some of the old veterans had resumed their card playing, much to the distress of "the canting pharasaic nincompoops . . . who have presumed to assert they held daily conversations with the Almighty that their prayers have favourably affected the winds and the weather." He indicated he felt the contention of those "self-rightous remnant of days long past" who claimed that if God allowed the ship to sink and destroy the lives of the passengers, it would be because of the "abominable amount of sin committed on board in playing cards and sundry other anti-christian peccadilloes." He felt these old veterans were types of men who should have long ago been forgotten. This was one of several condemnations of some of his fellow passengers concerning their attitudes that did not always fit their words.[18]

A passenger in the bark *Belvidera* noted on May 19, 1849, that in the past week they had made about one degree of latitude south and three degrees of longitude west in spite of the "constant succession of gales from the South West." He had not written in his journal during the entire week, as these gales "surpassed in violence anything we had yet experienced." They were fortunate to have a stove in the cabin so they could eat their meals in relative warmth, but it was not actually comfortable because of the constant rolling and pitching of the vessel. He added that "The howl-

ing of the wind which piped everything from a hoarse bass to a shrill tre-
ble, the dashing of waves over the deck, the thumping of loose boxes &
barrels & the creaking of timbers did not make a kind of music calculated
to lull one into gentle slumbers." It was truly the most "gloomy discouraging time" that could "be imagined." Nevertheless, they frequently enjoyed
"a hearty laugh" at the adversity of a fellow passenger who had a pitcher
of hot water, a bowl of molasses, or some other thing emptied in his lap.[19]

All of the above storms have been in the Atlantic. Storms seem to have
been encountered much less frequently in the Pacific, indicating perhaps
that the Pacific Ocean lived up to its name. Another possibility is that having described so many storms in the Atlantic and around Cape Horn, the
passengers simply did not bother to discuss some in the Pacific. The bark
Keoka experienced three days of storms in the Pacific. One passenger
thought they had "caught a Tartan in the gentle Pacific . . . when our
friend Boreas commenced sending his favors so fast . . . and the clouds
joined in the sport" and sent "down their water stores most copiously." He
added that "the Pacific is 'some pumpkins' and no mistake." The passengers had thought the Pacific was not a "blower," but the specimen they
had experienced "undeceived us." They concluded that the "Atlantic
couldn't begin to blow so hard." On the third day the clouds cleared away,
but then "old Boreas came thundering after us and soon forced us to lie
to." There was some damage to the rigging, and "the storm raged all the
afternoon with unabated fury." They were then only thirty miles from land
and feared they might drift ashore, as they were drifting at two and a half
knots per hour. Fortunately the winds lulled enough that they could set
some sail and halt the drift toward shore.[20]

As the bark *Croton* of New York sailed near latitude 15 north and longitude 114 west, she encountered some heavy winds, and the captain
ordered that the skysail yard and skysail pole be brought down, double
reefs be put in some sails, other sails be furled, and the ship be put as close
to the wind as possible. By the next day the wind "had increased to a perfect hurricane the like we had not before seen upon our voyage." The captain ordered more sails furled. Some other sails were split by the fierce
wind. They lost some casks, their sheep and chickens, and some provisions
stored on deck, as the main deck "was several times waist deep with
water." Their "hardened & weather beaten skipper" acknowledged "that he
vary rarely experienced a storm of such severity." For twenty-four hours
the storm blew from the north, but then it suddenly "shifted to the west &
south west & blew with increased severity." The gale was so strong that the

ship could not be controlled for eight hours. It was at its worst around 2:30 in the morning of June 22 and continued with less fierceness throughout the day. On the twenty-third there was still "a heavy rolling sea," but they "spent a happy day over the safe deliverance . . . from a most terriffick gale" and hoped they would not soon "experience the like again."[21]

After a particularly stormy day a passenger in the schooner *Damariscove* repeated the frequently quoted adage, "who would not sell a farm & go to California [usually given as to sea]" but added a new wrinkle when he wrote, "who would not leave a wife family & friends & home to encounter the storms and gales of the North and South Atlantic Ocean."[22]

As indicated, the passengers frequently were able to find humor in the adversity of either themselves or their fellow passengers during adverse weather. One passenger in the ship *Pacific* described such a situation following a storm shortly after they left Rio de Janeiro. He noted that "sometimes, even in scenes of danger, occurrances so ludicrous and rare, that it is almost impossible to suppress a smile though fully aware of its unfitness" and indicated that the "most amusing was between the forward cabin passengers and the hogs." He was not sure whether "the latter desired the comfortable apartments of the former, or whether the performance was accidental does not appear, but be that as it may, the hogs took occasion of one of the sudden lurches of the ship to make an unceremonious visit among the passengers below," where they "proceded to one of the berths and attempted to effect an entrance though much against the wishes and decided remonstrances of the occupant. A fearful strife ensued, and for some time it was doubtful on which side victory would rest." Finally the "passenger seized a board that came near his reach and placing it lengthwise in front of his berth decided the contest in his favor." He added that this was "only one of the many comical scenes producd by the storm" and that he could fill pages "with a recital of them, which would afford some amusement if the circumstances that attended their occurrence could also be given."[23]

Weather seems to have had a great effect upon the morale of passengers eager to get to California to harvest the abundant gold about which they had heard so much prior to leaving their homes and families on the Atlantic shores. Relatively minor delays during any part of the voyage could cause some grumbling and discontent among many passengers, but a sudden or even a gradual change to a favorable wind brought an almost immediate change in the attitude of those same passengers. On October

17, 1849, a passenger in the ship *Arkansas* noted that the wind was dead ahead, causing the California stock to decline and "long faces among the passengers" to be "in the ascendency." Even the captain and other officers were "cross as blazes." The next day they had a fair wind, "which makes smiling faces and light hearts." A. Bailey complained for several days about the terrible weather they were experiencing in the bark *Sarah Warren,* but suddenly on November 17, 1849, they reached the northeast trades, and Bailey reported jubilantly, "I am enabled this morning to take a <u>new text</u> and preach a different doctrine" because they had reached the long-expected northeast trade winds. He concluded that "Every one on board was a different man in his looks—and all shew in their countenances gratitude to heaven for the change." Pierce W. Barker commented upon how the passengers tended to criticize the sailing qualities of their vessel as "the d———t tub that ever went to sea" when they beat against head winds or were in a calm, but as soon as they get a favorable wind, they would praise the vessel and feel sure they will have "a shorter passage than . . . those that have gone to California before us." Early in the voyage of the ship *Orpheus,* one passenger commented that the weather was getting warmer and noted that their "feelings are much affected by it, relaxing our energies." Somewhat later in the voyage he reported they had a clear and pleasant day with a favorable wind and remarked those were "Two changes that much enlivens the dull spirited ones aboard." When the brig *Sea Eagle* had a favorable wind, one passenger noted, "Old Neptune give us prosperous gales . . . we are inspired with cheerfullness. Gladness is depicted on every countenance. . . . It would be unnatural to repine under our prosperity." Moses Cogswell, a passenger in the ship *Sweden,* provided a good capsule of feelings on board after 130 days at sea: "Thermometer on Deck 103, in the Galley 152, Between Decks 87, in the water 89. A dead Calm Sun, exactly overhead. Prospect dark and dreary. Temper cross, unaccommodating. Appetite completely satisfied. Body in a perspiration. Mind neither one thing or another. . . . Drink, Lime juice and Rain Water. Novelty, a large Shark. News, 'Old tiger' is dead. Signs, of an Easterly wind. Ideas, none in the market. Friends, few and far between. Wishes, to once more get on Land. Determination, to get Gold. Hopes, again to see home. Fortune, no account given. Love, all for myself. Faith, in a just 'Providence.' Consciousness, of <u>many</u> errors. Plenty of 'Life on the Ocean wave.'"[24]

It was during the last few weeks of the voyage as they neared San Francisco and faced head winds, fog, and other problems that prevented them from getting into the port so they could start their gold-hunting expeditions that the passengers really became disgruntled and frustrated with the weather. After the ship *Pacific* had been at sea fully six months, one of her passengers expressed his frustrations and impatience: "We are a company of tired voyagers. . . . No one sings 'Life on the Ocean wave' now. We are satisfied that that song is a humbug. The most popular of our songs have given out, even the virtues of 'good old ned' are no longer warbled upon the quarter rail, & as 'I strayed from my cot' has lost its music & its novelty. 'Life in the woods for me' so I get on land."[25] They arrived in San Francisco 16 days later, 194 days after sailing from New York.

Passengers in the bark *Croton* had also been at sea for six months when one of her passengers described how even the patience of Job would be tried during the last weeks of a long sea voyage around Cape Horn such as the one they had experienced. H. W. Chittenden noted that "Together with the contrary winds it has been our lot to meet . . . a dose which would be a pose to the renowned patience of old Job." He doubted Job "ever went to sea Although some men of modern science appear to think that the ships of Tarshish which Sollomon sent after the gold of Ophor, were sent around cape horn to California That the precious mettals which decorated Sollomons temple were the first tappings of the golden streams & tributaries of the Sacramento." He felt that "however the wise man might in his wisdom have planned and exicuted in olden time a voyage to San francisco Yet it would tax his or even old Jobs patience in this age of improvements in steam navigation To double cape horn & beat against head winds & head seas for 24 consecutive days & nights in a flatbotomed cotton ship."[26] Their frustrating voyage finally ended 19 days later, 189 days after sailing from New York.

After having been at sea for nearly six months, the passengers in the ship *Tahmaroo* knew they were nearing their destination, but they became frustrated by their inability to make headway toward San Francisco. One of the passengers had been commenting upon this regularly when he wrote, "Only made 66 miles since yesterday . . . rather discouraging floating so near our long looked for port . . . not able to get in on account of unfavorable winds." They were especially anxious to get the letters from family and friends they expected to find awaiting them in San Francisco. He then wrote in a pleading vein, "All we want is stiff breeze 48 hours." Frustrations continued as they made no "more than 10 miles the last 24 hours." Other comments he made in the following days were: "nearly a dead calm"; "still in nearly a calm"; "Not very pleasant, not much sail";

"Good breeze. Making 8 nots. . . . Skipper assertains his chronometer was out of order. . . . We are some 200 miles farther from shore than Skipper calculated"; and "Dull and foggy this morning. . . . Land is said to be seen to the North East of us." Finally on July 1 he wrote with glee and relief, "We now are to bid farewell to our galant old ship that has carried us away from our friends and around the dangerous point of Cape Horn and delivered us to the shores of San Francisco."[27]

Fog was reported as a regular problem by passengers in the bark *Belvidera* for several days before October 2, 1849, when they were 250 miles from San Francisco, and continued to be a problem after that. Four days later land was sighted, but the captain ordered the ship about as "Fog! Fog! Fog! a thick impenetrable fog!" made sailing toward land risky and kept them from obtaining accurate readings to calculate their exact latitude and longitude. The sun broke through, and they discovered they were "12 miles north of S. F." One passenger compared their position with that of the Israelites in the desert during their forty-year wanderings, as he said, "we are unable to go in and possess the promised land, although we are but a few degrees from it's much desired and long wished for port." On the night of October 8 the fog cleared, and the moon and stars were visible to all. One passenger reported, "There was a great rejoicing at our deliverance. We felt like prisoners suddenly released from captivity." Two days later they were hit by a storm, which one passenger referred to as "Cape Horn in the full sense of the syllable." The strong winds were dead ahead, preventing any progress toward their destination. Finally the fog lifted on October 12, and they made their way into the harbor of San Francisco around 3:00 P.M. One passenger commented, "Hurra, Hurra! Hurra!" They got their first introduction to San Francisco prices when a small boat came alongside and offered to take them ashore for the "moderate charge of $2.50 off and $5 back."[28]

On July 26, 1849, after the ship *Pacific* had been at sea six months, a passenger gleefully wrote, "About 3 oclock quite a fine breeze sprung up from the westard and we squared the yards and set our stunsails fore and main. This put us all in fine spirits. . . . We are thankful indeed and only want it to last for 3 or 4 days." During the succeeding days they encountered storms and headwinds, causing the passenger to comment that the "sailing for the last fortnight belies most decidedly the much lauded beauty of the Pacific. . . . Sea running like old Cape Horn on a fair day." He added that the blues were "very prevalent indeed and we have become tired of foretelling when we shal arrive." The next day they made a "very fair headway . . . and that covers a multitude of evils," noted the passenger. The next day was different, however, as he lamented, "Oh for a fair sunny day to give us our usual spirits." For the next three or four days the fog was thick, and the winds were either nonexistent or from the wrong direction. Finally on August 4 they were able to enter the harbor of San Francisco, and that passenger noted, "This has been a day of excitement."[29]

A. Henry Stevens was "almost discouraged in writing a journal, as it is the same thing to record about wind & weather, at least so it has been for the last fortnight." The winds had been from "the same old quarter . . . N. N. E.," the direction they were attempting to sail. The passengers in the bark *Emma Isadora* were also on a water ration of two pints of water for drinking and were eating only salty food to further complicate matters. He added, however, "But all this could be borne if we could onley have a fair wind for a few days." Everyone was "discouraged and complaining." The next day, September 3, 1849, he noted that it had been twenty days "since we had a day of sunshine" but added the prospects looked better than they had for many days. They had three more days of headwinds, but then he noted that a little favorable breeze sprang up and added, "it can hardly be immagined what a thrill of joy ran through the ship when we found we had a <u>fair wind</u>." He went on to argue that those who talked about the "smooth & plesent Pacific" were "all humbug!" They had not seen the sun since they crossed the equator and had experienced "high seas and blowey weather the old Atlantic cannot hold a candle to." The breeze lasted only a day, and he noted he was "about sick of this passage." The next day they moved "slowly towards our destination" with a light breeze, and the passengers grew "more and more anxious to reach" their destination. On September 9 Stevens noted that if their wind held and "if our reckoning proves right we shall be at anchor to night in San Francisco." Early that evening he was discouraged that they had not yet "seen land or anything that looks like it except a change of the collor of the water." Because of fog and uncertain position calculations, the captain ordered the ship to stand off until daylight. On the morning of September 11 they saw land to the northwest about five miles distant but did not make the harbor before evening. The captain did not want to risk entering the harbor at night, so he ordered the ship put about to stand off until morning. The next day was damp and foggy, but they were eventually able to enter the harbor of San Francisco and dropped anchor at 3:00 in the afternoon and were greatly surprised at the number of vessels there. They were also surprised to learn that many of the vessels had much longer passages than theirs.[30]

Many other passengers in other vessels had experiences similar to those described above. Some had better luck in getting into port while others had worse. Eventually they all arrived at their destination and had their chances at harvesting their fortunes in either the goldfields or whatever other occupations they chose to pursue. Only a small percentage of those who went to the goldfields became wealthy from collecting gold along the rivers and streams of California. Instead it was those who became involved in real estate investments or went into the business of providing the tools, equipment, supplies, and services to the miners who became wealthy. It is commonly believed that those who successfully pursued the gambling profession also became wealthy. If any of them did, it likely happened because they used whatever winnings they accumulated from gambling to start a highly successful business such as speculation in real estate.

7

People Problems

Argonauts of 1849 experienced a variety of problems with people on their long voyages to California. They sometimes had disagreements, arguments, and even fights among themselves. At other times some of them had conflicts with the officers of their joint stock company or association. On occasion they had conflicts with officers, especially the captain, of the vessel in which they sailed. In a few instances they had quarrels with owners of, or shipping agents for, the vessel. Questions, disputes, or disagreements arose over the quality and quantity of their food, the way they were treated by those with at least some authority over them, how well or poorly the captain commanded the vessel, how well or poorly the elected officers managed the affairs of the company, or how they treated each other and respected the rights of others. Any or all of these types of problems affected the level of satisfaction the passengers experienced during their great adventure to the new El Dorado.

People problems developed from a variety of factors. First, few of the captains, officers, and sailors responsible for carrying passengers to California had ever had that responsibility. Also, few of the passengers had ever been to sea. Hence, neither group knew what to expect from, or how to react to, the other. Some captains attempted to treat passengers the way they normally handled sailors. That was a serious mistake in most instances, as the passengers expected, usually with good reason, to be treated much as they were accustomed to at home. The passengers paid good money, some of it borrowed, for the right to go in a particular vessel and had either written or verbal commitments from owners and/or agents of the vessel about what to expect. It appears that sometimes the commitments to passengers were different from the instructions to the captain.

In those situations in which passengers were members of joint stock companies, there were ample possibilities for conflicts between officers of the company and other members, especially if some of the members felt they had been mistreated or discriminated against. Factors such as weather, temperature, delays, shortages of food and water, and a host of other matters led to increased agitation and short tempers that often led to confrontations between individuals and groups.

When one considers all the factors that could cause problems between people, it is not surprising that few passengers in sailing vessels bound for California in 1849 could write, as one passenger in the ship *Magnolia* did after only a month at sea, "All hands well and happy, have good usage and good food." He went on to mention that the passengers and the crew mingled in sports and amusements and that he thought they had as good a company as could be "scared up" to go "out with golden expectations." Even fewer could write as did one in the bark *Strafford* after nearly five months of the seven months voyage, "Our company agrees first rate and we have but very little difficulty with each other or disputes of any kind." He went on to write that he thought it would be hard to "pick one hundred men that could agree better than our company does" and added they were "most all strangers when we came together." He concluded by noting they all seemed to "remember in unity there is strength and that united we stand and divided we fall."

An anonymous passenger in the ship *Pharsalia* seems to be much more representative when he assessed the situation of a large group of men confined in a vessel after nearly three months of a voyage that lasted nearly six months. He noted, "I have frequently heard it said of the other sex that they were <u>more</u> inclined to talk, make mischief, have the last word, &c, Than the lords of creation" and added that he could "now fully comprehend the reason, (if such is really the case)." He had come to believe that if "a number of <u>men</u>" were "confined together for any length of time on board ship, or (in the house as the Ladies are) and the same number of <u>old maids</u> could not have more small talk and petty quarrels. This I could wish to remember for <u>I know it to be true</u> otherwise it never would have suggested itself to me."[1]

Some hints of problems between or among passengers have been given in the discussions of the problems of drunkenness and the infringing upon the comfort of others by keeping them awake at night through loud carousing. Passengers in these vessels argued and fought over a variety of matters, in some cases virtually from the time they sailed to the time they arrived. They gossiped about each other, became insulted when no insult was intended, felt they were being mistreated when they compared themselves with other individuals or compared their group with other groups, became upset over trifling matters or acts of others, and sometimes bullied and abused each other, both verbally and physically, as is evident in the examples below.

The members of the Bunker Hill Trading and Mining Association in the ship *Regulus* of Boston seem to have had the greatest disagreement of any group. Everyone on board the *Regulus,* including the captain and all mariners, were members of the company, and Capt. Daniel Bradford was also president as well as chaplain of the company. They had a written constitution and bylaws in which it was noted that all would share and share alike, that everyone would work and share in the profits and proceeds of everyone else. The first hint of real trouble arose nearly six months into the voyage when Thomas Williams described a meeting of the company to elect officers and noted that "the whole Company seemed Jealous of one another, and easpeacialy the officers." Then he added that the "spirit of dissatisfaction, uneasiness and Jealousy commenced very soon after we Left Boston." The major complaint the members had was that they had not been allowed to examine the books and other records of the company as they had expected. Pres. Daniel Bradford "flatly refused" to permit the members to examine the records. This confirmed the suspicion in the minds of many that some shady deals had been made. Williams noted that according to the constitution and bylaws, every member was supposed to be capable of doing hard work of all kinds, but when they departed from Boston he had noted that "nearly a third of this company, composed of Boys and drinking Characters and some slim counter jumpers and clerks that are good for nothing, nor never did any hard work in their lives." He reported that there was a movement by the leadership to break up the company before they arrived at Callao. A meeting was held "for the express purpose of altering the Constitution," which was approved, but they also decided to select a committee to look over the accounts. Later, Williams noted he had never before seen "such antipathy in any community" or "so much deception" or "a more hypocritical set of men" than he had witnessed in the company. Although the Bunker Hill Trading and Mining Association apparently was supposed to be a temperance group, Williams reported that some of the men "never saw a sober day from Boston to Rio Janeiro," and some were "never sober from the time they left home, untill we rounded Cape Horn." He believed that "if the Liquer had held out, they would not have known what a sober day was the whole voiage." He listed a few examples of how unequally some of the members were treated. They had purchased twelve dozen cans of milk for their coffee and between four and five hundred dollars of canned meats that were to be used by all, but most members never tasted any of those things. Rather the company leaders and some others who resided in the cabin consumed all of the canned milk and meat. At a later meeting the committee appointed to examine the books reported such things as the purchase of $10,000 of ship stores from one business without obtaining the customary six-percent discount, an advance of $450 to Capt. and Pres. Daniel Bradford to pay his personal debts, the expenditure of $40,000 for supplies with no record in an account book and documented only by receipts, and payment by the company for detaining the pilot in Boston for two or three days while certain members satisfied their personal debts. Williams then noted he considered the "company virtually smashed up" and called it "the most disgracefull company that ever existed." In ensuing days and weeks there was constant talk among the members about forming new companies and what to do with the ship, which the company seems to have owned, and the large quantity of freight. The final decision was that all who wanted to leave the company when they arrived in San Francisco could do so and could "take his share of what was left with him."[2]

There seems to have been some religious overtones in one incident described in the ship *Arkansas*. The ship was owned by the California Mutual Benefit and Joint Stock Association, a group composed of members of the Methodist Church or others who agreed with them in sentiment. There were also some passengers who were not members of the association. Three nonmembers provoked a man named Marker, who threatened to "get a stick and bete the D[evil?] out of them." Marker then went below and got a fender off the cabin table and "went at them with a good will," but he was eventually overtaken when one of the others kicked him in the head. One passenger noted, "There was a grate excitement between the two partys methodist and anti methodists" but added, "it was quelld and pece restored."[3]

Sometimes the disagreements were between passengers in different portions of the vessel. This was the case in a squabble on board the brig *Osceola*, where one of the after-cabin passengers told those in steerage they had no right to promenade on the quarterdeck. The lengthy quarrel was eventually settled by Captain Fairfowl, who declared that the steerage passengers had equal rights on the quarterdeck with "their aristocratic neighbors" in the cabin.[4]

A brief fight occurred between a Mr. Hazard and a Dr. Hazlett in the bark *Hannah Sprague* about six weeks into the voyage. It seems that Dr.

Hazlett booked passage to sleep in the midship house on deck but to eat below deck with passengers who resided there. He apparently had been eating with the midship house men, but they refused to allow him to continue to eat with them. The between-decks passengers did not welcome him there either. Apparently, Dr. Hazlett made it to the table between decks one morning and occupied the seat normally occupied by Mr. Hazard. When Hazard discovered the doctor in his seat, he attempted to remove him by force. Dr. Hazlett grabbed a knife from the table and cut Hazard's nose and face badly. A number of passengers were upset by the incident and saw fault on both sides. Hazard should not have used force, but Hazlett definitely set a bad precedent by using a knife, as almost everyone on board had a knife. The passengers decided to have a trial with Alfred Wheeler, a lawyer by profession, as the judge and six of the "oldest & most dignified of the passengers" as jurors. Witnesses testified to what they saw and were examined by both sides of the dispute. The jury found Hazard guilty of a misdemeanor for using force and Dr. Hazlett guilty of a high crime in using a knife and ordered him to apologize and pay whatever expenses Hazard had in having his face treated by Dr. Webster. Dr. Hazlett was also ordered to "pledge his honor hereafter to conduct peaceably & abide by the rules adopted between decks for their comfort & convenience."[5]

Fights between passengers were a fairly common occurrence. They sometimes happened as a result of trivial matters. Most fights resulted in a few bruises and perhaps a black eye or two, but none seem to have resulted in injuries such as occurred during one in the ship *Reindeer*. Passengers named Raymond and Wardwell, who previously had not been on good terms, had a fight when Raymond stepped on Wardwell's toes. Passengers named Bonney of Pawtucket, Rhode Island, and Reynolds of Providence, Rhode Island, fought over who would sleep in a particular location. Bonney had chosen a place to sleep on the poop deck and mentioned it to Reynolds, who apparently decided it would be a great place to sleep and got his bedding and arrived there before Bonney. When Bonney arrived and found Reynolds in his chosen spot, he attempted to evict Reynolds. They struggled and quarreled and finally determined to select two referees to decide the issue. Both men testified, as did other witnesses. The referees decided Bonney had the right to sleep there for that night but felt there was ample room for Reynolds there too. Bonney declined to sleep "with his enemy and he said that his rival might have the whole place to himself." One passenger commented it "was rather a trifling thing for two men to fight about" but added that it "caused a great deal of sport amongst the members" of the Narragansett Association who sailed in the bark *Velasco*.[6]

There appears to have been some regional rivalry between passengers from New York and those from Boston in the ship *Daniel Webster* out of New York. The New Yorkers seemed to be jealous because those from Boston had all the berths in the after cabin, but the Bostonians felt that since they were the first to sign on, they should have the best spaces. The Bostonians felt that the New Yorkers were rowdy, inconsiderate drunks, and not true Yankees. One passenger from Boston noted there was a "distinct difference" between the two groups and added, "We cannot associate togather, we cannot like one another, we are too sober, too quiet for the noisy devils." He was especially disturbed when the New Yorkers "stole papers from the reading room [in Valparaiso] regardless of the wants of the future arrivals." The New Yorkers apparently did not like Capt. I. G. Pierce, but the Bostonians did like him, as they understood him and enjoyed playing cards with him occasionally. The two groups and Captain Pierce seem to have buried the hatchet during the Fourth of July celebration, however.[7]

From time to time certain groups of passengers incurred the wrath of other passengers by staying up late and making noise, which disturbed the sleep of those who had gone to bed early. Those whose sleep was disturbed occasionally retaliated in the same way those in the bark *Daniel Webster* did on two occasions. A little over three months into their voyage one passenger reported that many of the passengers had their sleep interrupted by a few who were partying, singing, and making "all the noise they could to disturb the rest of the passengers" even though the rule on board was that there should be "no unnecessary noise" after ten o'clock. When the noisy ones finally turned out the light and went to bed, those whose sleep had already been disturbed started making noise of their own and kept it up until morning to prevent the others from sleeping. About a month later a similar episode occurred. When one of the cabin passengers complained about being awakened by the noise, another passenger apologized and indicated they were retaliating against another group and were also trying to force the captain "to look a little more after the comfort of his passengers." Capt. Joseph Higgins finally appeared and warned that "he would either have less noise or more." This was taken as a clue that he would assume more control over the first offenders.[8]

Other than the problems in the ship *Regulus*, few of the disagreements and conflicts between and among passengers were serious. They were mostly the result of too many young men with little or nothing to do for long periods of time confined to the space of a single sailing ship, few of which were larger than about 35 feet in width and 175 feet in length. Small, aggravating incidents were magnified in significance, but most of them were forgotten within a short time.

There were occasionally problems between the captain and other officers and between one or more of the officers and one or more of the crew on California-bound sailing ships just as there were on other sailing vessels. In many instances the conflicts were short-lived and were soon settled by the captain or another officer. While at sea, captains had all the powers of judge, prosecuting attorney, and the deliverer of justice, and some captains seem to have enjoyed those roles while others appear to have conducted themselves and the ship's business in a manner that made judging, prosecuting, and delivering justice unnecessary. The most frequently imposed punishments were flogging, putting in irons, and locking offenders away. Sometimes all of them were combined in a single punishment for serious offenses. Probably the most feared conflict involving captains and their crews in the minds of the general public was mutiny, which one normally thinks of as forcefully taking control of the vessel. Maritime law defines mutiny as any refusal to execute an order of a superior, so a sailor refusing to go aloft when ordered to do so was guilty of mutiny, especially if he verbally refused. If a sailor was told to do something and walked off as if to do it but did not perform the duty, he was unlikely to be charged with mutiny. Conflicts between captains and crews in sailing vessels bound for California ranged the gamut from simply being derelict in duty to extreme mutiny.

Captain Fairfowl of the brig *Osceola* seems to have been one of those captains who enjoyed jousting with his other officers and sailors. Less than two weeks into their voyage from Philadelphia, he and his first mate "had an altercation this morning," and the captain dismissed the mate from duty. Within two weeks the captain had an altercation with the new mate regarding the pumps and put him off duty. Two weeks after that altercation more than fifty of the passengers sent a petition to the captain, protesting that the first mate's watch was kept by incompetent persons and requesting that Mr. Howell be restored to his former position. The captain refused and stated that Mr. Howell would not be restored to duty as long as the captain "breathed the breath of life." While they were in Rio de Janeiro the U.S. consul heard charges brought by Captain Fairfowl against mate Howell and discharged Howell from the brig. The second mate was also discharged in this port. About a month after they left Rio de Janeiro, the captain and the new second mate argued over the latter's duties, and the captain broke him and ordered him to the forecastle. A few days later Captain Fairfowl argued with the new mate, but nothing further happened. The second mate was later restored to his duties, but almost immediately the captain and the first mate had another confrontation about the mate's duties, and the captain said he would discharge the mate in Talcahuano. The second mate indicated he would discharge himself in that port if the captain did not discharge him. Captain Fairfowl shipped a new first mate in Talcahuano, but the mate became dissatisfied almost immediately and deserted the vessel and was immediately replaced. Within three weeks the captain discharged this new officer. A bit later in the voyage the captain had an altercation with the steerage cook who objected to having to stand watch as well as cook. The captain beat the cook on his back and shoulders with a rope. The cook knocked the captain down, and the captain ordered him placed in irons but released him a few hours later. Near the end of June, Captain Fairfowl got into a fight with a sailor named York that resulted in York being put in irons for several days. At this point one passenger noted that the "Cap'n sick from over excitement and rum." The captain later admitted he had drunk some brandy but asked the passengers not to charge him with being drunk.[9]

Several men in the ship *Sheffield* refused to perform a command given by the first mate as they were preparing to depart from Valparaiso. He put twelve of them in irons and sent them below. The next morning Capt. Thomas W. Royes punished seven of the twelve by giving one twenty-six lashes, one nineteen lashes, three seventeen lashes, and one ten lashes and sent them all to the forecastle. The other five returned to their duties. The seven who were flogged apparently continued to cause problems, as they were later put in irons again and locked up below about six weeks after they departed. One was released the following day, but the other six remained in irons in confinement until they arrived in San Francisco. During that portion of the voyage, some crew members learned of a plot by those confined in irons to kill all of the others and take over the vessel. The six were turned over to the commander of the U.S. sloop of war *Warren* in San Francisco.[10]

An even more serious but equally unsuccessful mutiny occurred on board the ship *Memnon*, the largest vessel to carry passengers to California in 1849. Around May 20, 1849, when they were near Montevideo, mutiny broke out when first one and then several men refused to perform duties as ordered. The captain and first mate put two or three men in irons and in confinement to prevent others from attacking and injuring the captain and first mate. Both captain and the mate then got their guns and, with the assistance of some of the passengers, made an attack on the crew with orders to shoot any man who refused to go aft to perform his duties. Eight additional sailors were put in irons and placed in confinement. The captain then decided to enter Montevideo, where the mutineers were turned over to the commander of the U.S.S. *St. Louis.* When some of the sailors refused to perform duties the next morning, the captain of the warship ordered them all flogged. The voyage to San Francisco was then continued.[11]

The second mate of the ship *Susan G. Owens* attempted to lead a mutiny in Rio de Janeiro. He seems to have wanted to be first mate and persuaded the sailors to refuse the order of the first mate as they prepared to depart. The captain sought assistance from the U.S. consul, who dispatched some marines from the U.S.S. *Brandywine* to suppress the mutiny. They put the second mate and crew in confinement without food or water for twenty-four hours. When the mutineers were asked if they would thenceforth obey the first mate, the second mate refused to answer and was immediately triced in the rigging. It took only five blows on his bare back for him to agree to submit to the orders of the first mate. The crew all agreed to submit without being whipped.[12]

Capt. I. Spaulding had problems with a sailor and a cook during the voyage of the ship *Morrison.* The sailor threatened to harm the officers and some of the passengers. He was put in irons and confined until they arrived in Rio de Janeiro, where he was taken before the U.S. consul. The consul first decided to free him, but then he made more threats against the captain and some of the passengers. He was then put in irons and confined until he could be sent to the United States for trial. The cook seemingly disobeyed and lied to the captain, who ordered that he be given thirty lashes with a seven-strand rope by the mates. He presumably returned to duty after being punished.[13]

Being an officer must at times have been a frustrating experience when sailors argued with the officers and when passengers sometimes questioned their actions as well. This seems to have been the case in the bark *Sarah Warren.* When Edwin Rogers was ordered by the mate to furl the topgallant sails, Rogers answered they should be left as they were because the mate would soon want them set again. Rogers eventually furled the sails. Later, when Rogers was at the wheel, the mate cursed Rogers for questioning him about furling the sails. Rogers told the mate he lacked the one essential ingredient to be a good sailor—judgment. After all this bickering the captain told some passengers they would have to fend for themselves, as he would no longer attempt to manage the vessel. Next morning one of the passengers questioned the advisability of continuing to sail southwest. When the mate indicated the captain had ordered them to sail southwest, the passenger informed him they would run upon the rocks if they continued that course and suggested he awaken the captain. The captain came on deck and immediately ordered that the course be altered. The mate told the passenger he did not care if the "damned Vessel went to hell!" A couple of days later the passenger noted that the "officers of this ship do not try to get along." Rather, he wrote, "They appear to be contrary in order to gratify a sort of revenge or tyrany over the Passengers and crew."[14]

On occasion the antics of some of the passengers may well have contributed to the problems of maintaining discipline in the sailing vessels. One passenger in the ship *Orpheus* noted that he charged upon deck after hearing the cry of "Oh! g—d, murder." There he found the officers hoisting the drunken steward, who had once before been flogged, into the long boat while the captain was whipping him with a ropes end. The steward had been insulting the officers. While this was going on, other passengers were throwing flour on the cook, who ran screaming from the galley, "causing a roar of laughter." These actions by passengers must certainly have had an adverse effect upon the officer's ability to enforce discipline. The next day the captain flogged the steward again and told him to apologize for his insulting remarks to the officers and promised not punish him more if he made a full confession. The captain asked him if he had stolen any liquor. He denied having done so. The captain then asked where he had gotten the rum he drank the day before. He replied he had not had any rum. The captain ordered him triced in the rigging and gave him a dozen lashes and then asked him if he would confess and behave himself. When he sullenly refused to do that, the captain ordered that the steward's shirt be removed and gave him a dozen more lashes on his bare back and sent him to be confined in the long boat again. It was anticipated he would remain in confinement until they reached San Francisco.[15]

Decisions to punish were regularly made quickly, and the punishment was executed with equal speed. The first mate and the captain in the brig *Mary Stuart* had a "little difficulty" one morning that resulted in the mate receiving "a good shaking" and being demoted to the forecastle and the second mate being elevated to first mate. The mate in the ship *Pacific* ordered a sailor into the maintop "to remain during his watch," but the sailor "came down the lee rigging. A ropes end was the consequence." When the first mate and a sailor got into a scuffle in the ship *Pacific,* the captain "inflicted a wound on the head of the sailor," causing one passenger to note that "an iron belaying pin . . . settled the matter immediately."[16]

Problems between the captain and his other officers and between the officers and sailors seem to have been common on sailing vessels bound for California in 1849. Punishment for offenses was usually swift and harsh. All this seems to confirm that the captain of a sailing ship truly had all power in his hands and exercised that power with great regularity. Some seemed to enjoy it while others did so out of necessity in order to prevent more serious problems from arising.

Although passengers could not have direct conflicts with shipping agents who stayed at home to entice other potential passengers to sail in other vessels, the passengers often recorded grievances and complaints about shipping agents. Sometimes owners of vessels acted as their own shipping agents. The shipping agents commonly sold tickets to passengers and gave them information, frequently in writing, of what they could expect in the form of food, services, and living conditions. Basically they told passengers what they would get for their passage money. Many passengers complained in their journals about being misled, if not actually lied to, by shipping agents while others simply noted they had been taken advantage of by agents or owners or both. A number of them submitted petitions to their captains, as was noted in chapter 3. They normally recognized that the captain was not really at fault, but they asked him to do whatever was in his power to provide them what they were promised. A few examples of situations encountered by passengers illustrate the nature of the problem.

Steerage passengers in the brig *Osceola* felt that they had been greatly imposed upon by the owners Burling & Dixon, as a large portion of the space in steerage was filled with freight and luggage belonging to the cabin passengers. They felt that the freight belonging to the cabin passengers should have been stored in the hold rather than in the area in which the steerage passengers resided. Charles Shewell McHenry felt that the passengers in the ship *Grey Eagle,* which sailed form Philadelphia, had been greatly imposed upon by the agents Potter McKeever & Company. McHenry said they had paid three hundred dollars, or fifty dollars above the usual fare "to have extra living." Warm weather spoiled all their vegetables, leaving them only salt beef, pork, tongue, and mackerel to eat, which was soaked in salt water until the company representatives felt the passengers ate too much. Then it was no longer soaked at all. Much of their bread was stored in old whiskey barrels and became musty. Several of the passengers were veterans of the Mexican War and of the war against the Indians in Florida and said that even in those wars they had fared better than they did in the ship *Grey Eagle*. McHenry noted he had gone hungry for two days in order to be able to eat some of the bad food they were served. A passenger in the ship *Crescent* described some pork that had been provided by the shipping agent Bowker. All the pork in the barrel was rusty, as was virtually all of the pork provided them. One piece was half of a hog's head with nearly all of the bristles remaining.[17]

Both first- and second-cabin passengers in the ship *Elizabeth Ellen* delivered letters to Capt. Daniel H. Truman complaining about how the agreement shown them by shipping agent E. Richardson & Co. of New York had been violated. First-cabin passengers did not report what they paid for the passage and found, but the second-cabin passengers paid $150. The first-cabin passengers stated they had been promised food equal to that provided on the packet ships sailing between New York and Europe or any well-regulated hotel, but what they received was far below that. They also complained that some of the second-cabin passengers had been assigned to eat at their table and ate more than their share. The second-cabin passengers reported they understood they were to provide their own dishes and eating utensils, which were supposed to be washed and cared for by the stewards. They reported that this was not done. They also complained that the cabin was filthy although they had been promised it would be kept clean, and said they had been told there would be plenty of cooks to prepare and stewards to serve their meals, but complained that they had to cook many of their meals and serve themselves. These passengers wanted the U.S. consul at Valparaiso to force the captain to purchase the supplies in Valparaiso that would enable them to receive what they claimed they were promised by E. Richardson & Co. Passengers in both cabins delivered a petition to the U.S. consul in Valparaiso on these matters. When he refused to listen to their complaints and to answer their questions, they wrote a letter of protest to the U.S. secretary of state. Some of the passengers seemingly wanted to leave the ship in Valparaiso and sell their passage to San Francisco to others. They asked the U.S. consul, Mr. Morehead, if a passenger might dispose of his berth in a foreign port. The consul refused to answer their question, and shortly before the *Elizabeth Ellen* was to sail from Valparaiso, he notified the passengers he would "call into requisition all the armed ships then in the harbour . . . and bring us into obedience."[18] Apparently the U.S. consul was prepared to use the power of the U.S. Navy to force the passengers to continue in the vessel.

Problems between passengers and captains were likely the most serious people problems. Part of this resulted from the lack of experience most captains had in dealing with large numbers of passengers and the total inexperience of most passengers with all the problems and frustrations associated with long sea voyages. As the captain of any sailing vessel was the absolute ruler during the voyage, he was the person to whom the passengers complained whenever anything happened to their disliking. By the same token, captains had a tendency to place blame for many problems squarely on the passengers who disrupted his usual routine.

The most serious conflict between passengers and a captain was that between the first-cabin passengers and Capt. Hall J. Tibbits of the ship *Pacific*. They constantly fought verbally between New York and Rio de Janeiro. When the passengers sent a delegation to Captain Tibbits to seek redress for their grievances about food, the captain threatened to blow up the ship or to lay back the sails and hold the ship on the equator. The conflict escalated to such an extent that the passengers took their grievances to the U.S. consul in Rio de Janeiro, Gorham Parks. They filed charges against Captain Tibbits, who filed countercharges against the passengers. Mr. Parks took testimony from several passengers and received documents signed by many. He also consulted with Ambassador David Tod. The two agreed that Tibbits should be removed and a new captain appointed even though Tibbits was half owner of the *Pacific*. Consul Parks also removed John A. Brown from command of the ship *Xylon* of Baltimore and William Long from command of the schooner *Sacramento* of New Orleans. Passengers in the *Xylon* charged Brown with brutal treatment by furnishing spoiled and unwholesome food poorly cooked, almost suffocating them by keeping the hatches closed whenever it rained, and failing to provide chloride of lime to purify the living quarters. They also said he sold liquor to some of the passengers. No reasons were identified for the dismissal of William Lord. These actions caused an uproar among the shipping houses and insurance companies in New York, especially after Captain Tibbits returned to New York and met with them, and quickly led to the removal of Gorham Parks as U.S. consul in Rio de Janeiro.[19] Other conflicts between passengers and captains were less severe and had much less dramatic effects. Some conflicts seem to have been over rather trivial matters, at least from the perspective of history, while others were of a more serious nature.

Capt. Jesse G. Cotting of the ship *Sweden* and a passenger named Dr. Elliot had a falling out. After the doctor had a scuffle with a passenger named Carter, the captain had Elliot put in irons. Then he released him after an hour or two. One passenger noted that the two had been at odds for some time. He thought it was because Elliot defended his own rights and those of other passengers. Captains routinely put sailors in irons and occasionally did the same to subordinate officers, but they rarely did that to passengers. A passenger in the schooner *Gager* wrote that he and the captain, whom he described as "the meanest of all mankind," had previously had a fracas during which he gave the captain an "old fashioned tongue lashing" and told him what he must do to keep his job as captain and promised to "whip him as soon as we reach our journeys end." He added that they later talked at length and promised to attempt "to make the remainder of our trip as comfortable as possible for his own sake." Perhaps this passenger was more deserving of being put in irons than was Dr. Elliot.[20]

Two passengers in the ship *Magnolia* described how some of them had incurred the wrath of their captain and how they retaliated. A number of them were congregated around the forecastle singing songs, laughing, joking, "and making a considerable noise" during the dog watch. When the watches were changed at 8:00, they gave the larboard watch three cheers. Capt. Benjamin Frank Simmons then "came forward and in a haughty, ungentlemanly manner commanded them to stop that devilish noise." When he started to leave, the passengers groaned, which further angered the captain. He returned and asked if they were groaning at him. When he turned to leave again, one of the passengers gave a loud whistle. The captain wanted to know who had done it and promised to "whistle him" and declared, "I will not be whistled at, and groaned at." One of the passengers added that he doubted Captain Simmons had a single friend among the passengers "owing to his overbearing manner."[21]

The passengers in the ship *Glenmore* of Hampton Roads, Virginia, "hated" their captain Poythries, but they all "loved" the first mate Cope. One passenger reported that the captain drank excessively and became "very abusive to the crew." Before they reached Callao the owners decided to remove Poythries and leave him in that port and replace him with Cope, but the latter advised them against doing that, as it would cause a long delay in Callao. The captain promised that "no more liquor should go down his throat," but he quickly broke that promise. As they neared San Francisco some of the passengers sought permission to take a boat and row into the port to report their arrival. Captain Poythries refused, but the passengers took the boat anyway. The tide was running out and caused the boat to drift seaward. The captain was going to allow them to be carried away, but mate Cope intervened and reminded the captain he had stood by him all during the voyage, but he would "knock every tooth down" his throat if he did not pick up the passengers. Thus it appears both the mate and the passengers had conflicts with Captain Poythries.[22]

Thomas Whaley noted that Capt. James H. Wardle of the ship *Sutton* was disliked by all the passengers, but the feeling seems to have been mutual, as Wardle apparently disliked the passengers. Whaley wrote that Wardle "Sometimes . . . wished them to the four corners of Hell, and says he shall be Damn glad" when they arrived in San Francisco. Whaley added that the captain "need not bother himself" about providing breakfast for them after they arrive, as they "will be as glad to leave him, as he will be to get rid of them." Perhaps the captain's worst attribute was his inconsistency. For example, wrote Whaley, Wardle banned smoking in the cabin, but a few days later he was playing whist with some passengers there and decided "it would add to his comfort to Smoke" while playing cards and promptly lit up. Afterward everyone began to smoke in the cabin again. When a loaf of bread was stolen from the galley, the captain ordered that there would be "no more Soft tack . . . for the cabin!" The next evening he had a loaf of soft bread flavored with raisins and coriander seeds, which he shared with those playing cards with him. He later picked all the raisins out of the remaining portion of the loaf and discarded the bread from which he had picked the raisins. On another occasion Whaley described a fierce confrontation between Wardle and a passenger named Elijah Johnson. That verbal exchange included some of "the most horrid volley of oaths" Whaley had ever heard. The captain threatened to "break Johnson's head if he dared utter another word" and accused Johnson of fomenting discord against him among the other passengers. The next day the captain and Johnson appeared to be bosom friends. A captain who was consistent in his enforcement of orders and who obeyed them himself, no matter how harsh they might be, seemingly was better than one who constantly changed as did Wardle.[23]

Augustus FitzRandolph Taylor, a passenger and president of the New Brunswick and California Mining and Trading Company, and Capt. Nicolas R. Brewer of the bark *Isabel* demonstrated that disagreements could be overcome and good feelings restored if both sides aired the issues and endeavored to understand each other better. Captain Brewer noticed Taylor using fresh water to brush his teeth on deck and severely cursed him and said he was setting a bad example for the other passengers. Taylor defied the captain to prevent him and told the captain he "had made a fool of himself" in his relationship with the passengers throughout the voyage. Captain Brewer said he would call a meeting of the company and report Taylor for wasting water that supposedly was in short supply, as several of the water casks had leaked. Taylor eventually called a meeting to decide whether the captain or the company was in control of the use of water. There was an effort for some others to take control of the meeting, first by suggesting that Taylor name someone other than himself to preside, but he insisted the constitution required the president to preside. Captain Brewer then charged Taylor with wasting water. Taylor said he would stop using fresh water to brush his teeth whenever the captain stopped using it to shave. He also said that Brewer "had played the 'petty Tyrant' to perfection" and repeated complaints made to him about Brewer. Taylor accused Brewer, who was also the chaplain of the company, of setting a bad example in swearing at him about the use of fresh water. The company voted that the captain had no control of the water. Brewer acknowledged that to be true but added he had attempted to take control of the water for the safety of the vessel. He also offered to resign as chaplain, but the offer was refused, although an assistant chaplain was named. On the following Sunday, Brewer appeared in his role as chaplain freshly shaved in a clean white shirt. He made an "abject and ample apology for the position which he had assumed" regarding water and also "acknowledged his faults in taking the name of the Almighty in vain." Near the end of the worship service, Taylor went forward and said that as Brewer had apologized for his words and actions, he too would apologize for his harsh words about Brewer. Brewer began to cry, as did many of the other members. Taylor noted the day would be long remembered and expected that Captain Brewer had "marked it among the things not to be easily disremembered." Although the relationship between Brewer and Taylor improved somewhat, it was not totally amicable, and Taylor recorded other conflicts before the end of the voyage.[24]

Although it seems as though there were conflicts between the passengers and the captain in every vessel, not all of them were as fierce as some of those described above. In some instances the passengers actually passed resolutions thanking their captains for being so kind and thoughtful.

About three months into the voyage of the ship *Arkansas*, the passengers in the main cabin held a meeting "to express their feelings in relation to the treatment they receive from the Captain and the members of the Association and their privalidges on the Poop Deck." One of the passengers described the meeting as being "characteristic of that harmony that has ever actuated the passengers of the cabin." The chair appointed a committee to "draft Resolutions expressing the sense of the meeting." At the end of the voyage of the bark *Hannah Sprague*, the passengers adopted resolutions about Capt. David F. Lansing, first mate William D. Folger, and second mate E. D. Bills in which they offered their "earnest thanks as an expression of our full satisfaction." They indicated that in Captain Lansing they had "found combined the courtesy & generous impulses of a manly heart, and the skill and sagacity of a seaman perfect in his profession" and they extended their "best wishes for his future welfare and prosperity." They found the two mates to be "courteous and skillful men, well qualified for the duties devolving upon them" and wished "them such fortune as the brave and ambitious merit." Each man was to be given a copy of the resolutions, and a copy was to be sent to a newspaper in San Francisco for publication. The passengers in the ship *Andalusia* also chose a committee to draft resolutions of appreciation for Capt. F. W. Willson. They expressed "gratitude" for his "kindness and attention." Although the shipping agent apparently had "grossly deceived" the second-cabin passengers "about the fare" they were to receive, Captain Willson gave them food not mentioned in the bill of fare that mitigated the trying situation and greatly reduced the "privations." The captain was especially thanked for his contributions of foods for the Fourth of July celebration.[25]

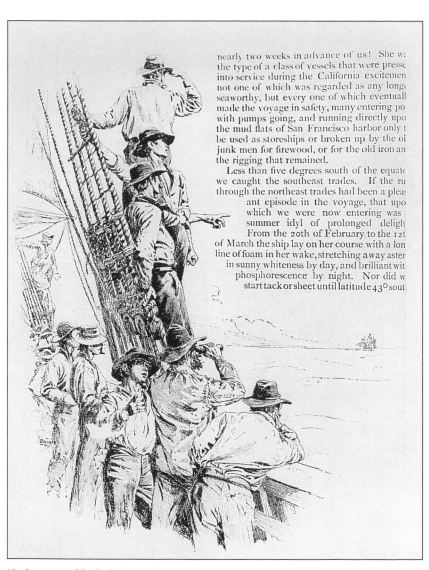

nearly two weeks in advance of us! She w: the type of a class of vessels that were presse into service during the California excitemen not one of which was regarded as any long seaworthy, but every one of which eventuall made the voyage in safety, many entering po with pumps going, and running directly upo the mud flats of San Francisco harbor only t be used as storeships or broken up by the ol junk men for firewood, or for the old iron an the rigging that remained.

Less than five degrees south of the equato we caught the southeast trades. If the ru through the northeast trades had been a pleas ant episode in the voyage, that upo which we were now entering was summer idyl of prolonged deligh From the 20th of February to the 12t of March the ship lay on her course with a lon line of foam in her wake, stretching away aster in sunny whiteness by day, and brilliant wit phosphorescence by night. Nor did w start tack or sheet until latitude 43° south

"Sighting an old whaler." When word was given that a vessel had been sighted, passengers dashed to the rigging and other high places to get a better view of the event. Many also rushed to finish letters in hopes that they could be put on board the other vessel and eventually be delivered to their loved ones at home. From *Century Magazine,* July 1891.

"Fair weather." Some 1849 California-bound vessels might have actually been this crowded during days when the weather was pleasant. The vessel involved in this late-nineteenth-century account of an 1849 voyage had about 150 individuals on board. The number of sails in sight is undoubtedly an exaggeration, as most passengers recorded few sightings of vessels, and only on rare occasions did they sight more than one vessel at a time. From *Century Magazine,* July 1891.

Rev. William Taylor. This famous Methodist missionary to California sailed in the ship *Andalusia* out of Baltimore in 1849 and ministered to immigrants for many years. From *Seven Years' Preaching in San Francisco*.

"A Fourth of July oration." Passengers who celebrated the Fourth of July at sea in 1849 usually chose an orator for the day and listened attentively to what he had to say. Such orations and all of the other things the forty-niners did to celebrate Independence Day at sea were typical of what they were accustomed to doing ashore at home. From *Century Magazine,* July 1891.

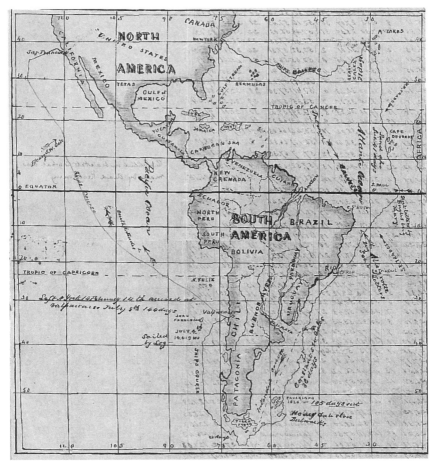

Track chart, ship *Sarah & Eliza*. The route as recorded on this hand-drawn chart indicates how far eastward sailing vessels sometimes sailed at the outset in order to get around South America. Note that on the legs between New York and Rio de Janeiro and between Rio de Janeiro and Cape Horn both the intended and the actual courses are indicated. This illustrates quite well how adverse weather could lengthen a voyage. From the Floyd-Jones Family Correspondence. Courtesy of the Bancroft Library, University of California, Berkeley.

Track chart, ship *Andalusia*. This is the center part of a hand-drawn chart of the world showing the track of the ship *Andalusia* from Baltimore to San Francisco, April 18 to September 21, 1849. It was drawn by Douglas S. Hubbard of Pittsfield, Massachusetts. Hubbard notes via the solid line that the vessel reached the Azores in May, Cape Horn in July, Valparaiso in August, and San Francisco in September. The return voyage to Valparaiso in November and December appears in much greater detail with each day's location marked off clearly. Several portions of the chart reveal how far off of a straight line sailing vessels often traveled in order to follow or seek favorable winds. Courtesy G. W. Blunt White Library, Mystic Seaport Museum, Inc., Mystic, Connecticut.

"The [brig] *Osceola* in a gale off Cape Horn." Few passengers bound for California in 1849 had ever been away from home before much less around Cape Horn, but they had all heard about that dreaded place long before they arrived there. For a great many of them one passage around Cape Horn was enough for a lifetime. Hence many returned home via Panama. From Upham, *Notes of a Voyage.*

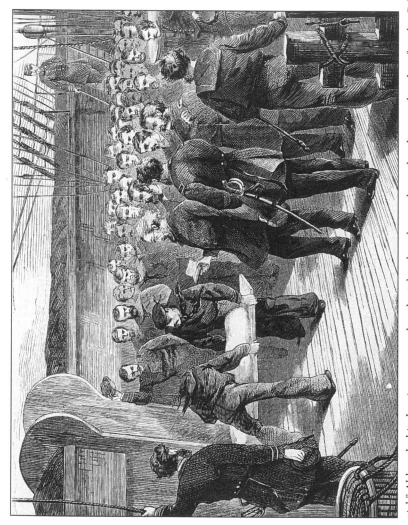

"The seaman's burial." Although this drawing seems to be a burial on board a naval vessel and is two decades after the California gold rush, it does represent the solemnity of the burials that took place on board several California-bound vessels in 1849.

"Beach of Yerba Buena Cove, 1849." This drawing gives a good indication of the "forest of masts" in the harbor as many forty-niners described them. From Upham, *Notes of a Voyage.*

"View of 'Prospect Hill' San Francisco," in January 1850. This drawing from the journal of Isaac W. Baker in the bark *San Francisco* includes several of the elements frequently described in passengers' journals—an abundance of waterfowl, lots of tents, few permanent structures, hilly terrain, vessels at anchor, and passengers being rowed either ashore or back to their vessels—but mysteriously omits what some described as a forest of masts. The artist added a note in which he indicated this hill was later called Telegraph Hill, undoubtedly for the telegraph station established there to signal the types of vessels entering San Francisco. Courtesy of the Bancroft Library, University of California, Berkeley.

San Francisco in 1849. This primitive painting of Telegraph Hill presents a vivid impression of the number of tents that existed in San Francisco at the time. It also includes the signal station at the top of the hill by which merchants and others in the city were informed when a vessel was arriving and what type vessel it was. Courtesy of the Wells Fargo Archives, San Francisco.

"Post office, 1849." Several passengers described their trips to the post office and the numbers of people in line to obtain mail they hoped would be waiting for them or that would come with each steamer. From Upham, *Notes of a Voyage*.

"Muddy streets, winter of 1849–'50." Several passengers described the difficulties of crossing the streets of San Francisco during the wet season. This illustration accurately depicts the extreme difficulties people, animals, and vehicles experienced in traversing those streets. From Upham, *Notes of a Voyage*.

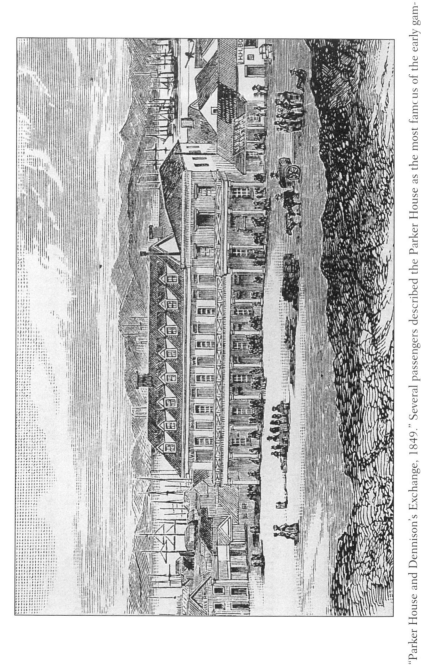

"Parker House and Dennison's Exchange, 1849." Several passengers described the Parker House as the most famous of the early gambling establishments in San Francisco. From Upham, *Notes of a Voyage.*

8

Miscellaneous Problems

Passengers in sailing vessels bound for California in 1849 experienced numerous vexing problems of a miscellaneous nature. Some, such as delayed departures, food and drink, methods of keeping themselves occupied during the many months at sea, and the weather as well as those with other people have already been discussed in previous chapters. There were additional problems involving their health, encounters with a variety of insect and animal pests, occasional overconsumption of alcohol, theft and other forms of dishonesty among passengers and sailors, occasional fires and leaking vessels, and rare stowaways. The presence of females sometimes created problems and other times created a degree of civility that might not have existed without them. The number of African Americans identified in sailing vessels was very small. Most seem to have served as cooks or stewards, but a few vessels carried them as regular passengers. For some passengers, their presence was a problem.

Since such a large percentage of the passengers were young men in the prime of their lives, there was not a great deal of sickness among them in spite of the frequent drastic changes of weather. Yet there were some serious illnesses as well as a number of accidents. There were several deaths and a few births recorded by those keeping journals during their great adventures. Considering the complaints that were made about the food and water in some of the vessels and the monotonous diets in a large percentage of them, it is not surprising that there were a variety of food-related illnesses. Passengers in the ships *Arkansas, Mount Vernon,* and *Sheffield* and the barks *Gold Hunter, Hannah Sprague, San Francisco,* and *Sarah Warren* noted their own or other passengers' problems with diarrhea, dysentery, and constipation. Some attributed their problems to poor drinking water that was so bad they consumed very little liquid. Only John Henry Corneilson in the *Hannah Sprague* recorded what medicines he took for his problems. He was unable to get at his own medicines, as they were stored below, so he had to depend upon what others gave him. One person suggested he try homeopathy, but he declined. Another gave him "1/4 tumbler of what he called cholera medicine," but he found the red pepper and alcohol in it too spicy. The captain give him some rhubarb, but since he had no magnesia to take with it, "it did not have the effect I had hoped for." Later he took some "Diarhoea syrup" and thought it helped him. At the end of three weeks he noted his diarrhea was "still better" and that he was "once a day and regular now but still not perfectly well." One passenger in the brig *Perfect* suffered a few days from an intestinal disease, but it is uncertain if it was nausea or diarrhea. He complained he "had to keep running all night and could not sleep any" and said most of the rest of the company were "as bad of as I am." He thought it was caused by the fresh meat.[1]

Incidents or outbreaks of scurvy were mentioned by passengers in the ships *Brooklyn, Daniel Webster, Europe,* and *Pharsalia,* the barks *Sarah Warren,* and *Velasco,* and the brig *Osceola* although in a couple of cases they were uncertain of the exact disease from which they suffered. A passenger in the brig *Osceola* noted that fully a third had badly swollen feet and legs, which normally indicated chilblains. He admitted some uncertainty but believed that it was "the incipient symptoms" of scurvy. The captain of the ship *Daniel Webster* thought the swelling in the arms and legs of one passenger was the result of scurvy, but Dr. Gunn said it was chilblains. The doctor contended that eating grease was the best antidote for scurvy and that the steerage passengers in the vessel had no scurvy because they ate lots of it. The passenger with the swollen limbs argued the cabin passengers ate lots of foods cooked in lard and butter while the steerage passengers had neither lard nor butter, so they could not be eating the most grease. Still he admitted that it could be chilblains and indicated it itched considerably in the evening. A passenger in the bark *Velasco* reported there was a hint that one of the sailors had scurvy and added that, if it really turned out to be so, they would make an unscheduled stop in a port in Chile for fresh provisions and vegetables. Two of the sailors in the ship *Europe* reportedly suffered from scurvy. The swollen hands and feet of passengers in the ship *Pharsalia* were thought to be caused by scurvy, but they were not sure. There was a hint they would stop and get fresh provisions. Passenger A. Bailey reported he suffered from swollen hands with "little red spots on them." Other passengers also had the same problem, but no one knew for certain it was scurvy. Bailey did offer the opinion that no vessel bound for California should pass by Rio de Janeiro without obtaining fresh provisions and vegetables and fruits. The worst incident of scurvy was apparently in the ship *Brooklyn*, where between forty and fifty people suffered from the disease. Their legs and arms were swollen to nearly twice the normal size. Some of the afflicted also had sore mouths with swollen gums. One passenger blamed their diet that was limited to salt beef and pork, hard bread, and molasses for the onset of the disease.[2]

Considering the amount of complaining passengers did about the heat and the cold, one would have thought there would be a large number of heat- and cold-related diseases and other physical problems, but the opposite is true. Passengers in only the ship *York* and the bark *Anna Reynolds* wrote about suffering from chilblains, a painful swelling primarily of the feet and lower legs that sometimes also appears in the hands and fingers. A passenger in the *Anna Reynolds* wrote that nearly everyone in that vessel suffered from chilblains, but the passenger in the *York* who wrote about that problem indicated only that some passengers had the affliction. He indicated the cause was cold weather, lack of exercise, and "want of vegetables & change of linen." He gave "warm baths, acid [illegible word] & spare diet" as the remedies. One passenger in the bark *Keoka* wrote that several passengers had "their feet severely burnt by exposure to the sun, so much so, that they can hardly walk," and a passenger in the ship *Pacific* wrote that his badly sunburned feet bothered him for about ten days and that Dr. Hall gave him "a wash which did me much good." As much as the passengers in all vessels were exposed to that scorching sun and as commonly as they went without shoes on deck, it is surprising there were not lots of incidents of this problem. One passenger in the brig *Perfect* complained of suffering and inability to sleep because of prickly heat. He took sulphur for the problem. A passenger in the brig *Mary Stuart* complained of a body rash that looked like measles in the tropical climate but attributed it to a combination of the warm weather and the red flannel shirt he had worn constantly since leaving home. Changing into a white cotton shirt brought immediate relief.[3]

With the cold and damp weather that many passengers encountered, it is not surprising that some passengers experienced colds and flu. Anne (Willson) Booth reported both she and her husband, whom she referred to only as Mr. Booth, suffered colds. Her cold was so bad that it kept her from writing in her journal for a week. She called what she had a cold, but she had considerable pains. The doctor in the ship *Andalusia* diagnosed her malady as pleurisy, gave her medication, and recommended she apply mustard plasters. The two treatments seem to have cured her ailment. It was more than two months later that her husband became ill. She could do little for him, as she was in the cabin on deck while he occupied a room below deck, but the men living in the same area seem to have taken good care of him. The doctor also gave him medicine and washed his feet in warm mustard water. He recovered in about three days. One passenger in the ship *George Washington* reported on May 8, 1849, he took some of "Perry Davis' pain killer" for his cold and added that "on going to bed and found on . . ." The entry ends there, but the journal continues through May 18, so presumably he recovered. A passenger in the bark *San Francisco* reportedly contracted a cold and cough before they sailed from Beverly, Massachusetts, that developed into "a sort of Catarrh . . . accompanied by loss of appetite" and was "the source of much trouble." There is no record of any treatment or how soon he might have recovered. James F. Caine reported that he and his brother Edwin, both passengers in the bark *Belvidera,* suffered from severe fever and ague for two and a half months. On one occasion he described "the horrors of sickness at sea. Wracked and tossed by pain and to add to the misery of the afflicted is the continued rocking of the vessel not allowing one moment in which he may rest his weary bones." William M. Hatch, a fifty-year-old passenger in the schooner *Damariscove,* suffered from a cough and cold for about four months during which time he treated his condition with various cough syrups made from onions and motherwort. The captain gave him a bottle of syrup made from thoroughwort, sometimes called aguewort or feverwort. He also took a bottle of "Friars Balsom," but none of them seem to have given much relief. Hatch also smoked his pipe frequently and occasionally mentioned it as a contributing factor. He reported that he had stopped smoking on two occasions and "found the result to bee good for I do think that useing tobacco freely is injurious to any ones health." His age may also have been a factor in his health problems just as were the ages of other passengers whose ailments he documented. The percentage of men over thirty was considerably larger in the *Damariscove* than it was in other vessels.[4]

Some instances of the highly contagious diseases, including measles, mumps, and smallpox and one or two instances of cholera, were reported on board the California-bound sailing vessels. The ship *Sweden* may have had the most serious outbreaks of measles and mumps. Measles appeared a week after they departed from Boston but were first thought to be smallpox. They appear to have run their course in about a month, as they were not mentioned by passengers after early April. Near the end the voyage

210

one passenger estimated that fully a fourth of the "whole ships company" of approximately 180 passengers had experienced either the measles or mumps while at sea. The mumps first showed up in passenger journals early in June. They too seem to have run their course in about a month. In late June one passenger indicated about twenty of the men had the mumps. There was also an outbreak of both measles and mumps in the ship *Pharsalia* that lasted about three weeks. A passenger in the ship *Tahmaroo* reported that he and several other passengers had the mumps all within a week of each other about a month after they sailed from New York. The mumps was reported in the bark *Croton* for a month about six weeks after they sailed from New York. A passenger in the *Croton* wrote that his face "feels vary like an Englishmans belly looks who had guzzled his ale until life has become a burthen & his brains & bowels have swelled there casements to burstigication." He estimated that the epidemic would "go through the entire ship company" but did not provide any indication of that in later entries. About ten days after they departed from New York, a passenger reported a case of smallpox on board the bark *Croton* and noted there was "considerable fear" because of it. Two weeks later there had been no new cases reported. This actually may have been the first case of mumps, as in writing about that epidemic he referred to an earlier scare of smallpox. There was a disagreement between the passengers and the physicians on board the ship *South Carolina* about whether it was smallpox or some other disease several patients had. The passengers were positive they were right and convinced the captain to set up a tent on deck for those with the disease and to throw all their beds and clothing overboard. Whatever the epidemic was, it was discussed by Albert Wilson Bee in his journal for nearly three weeks. Capt. J. A. Gray of the ship *Architect* threw a letter on board the bark *Delawarian* at sea on February 1, 1849, reporting that six of the passengers in the ship had died of cholera. All the remaining passengers were in good health. Of all these diseases, cholera was probably the most feared and smallpox the second most feared.[5]

In an era during which there was not the type of preventive dental care available in the late twentieth century, one might have expected several problems with passengers' teeth, but that was not the case. Few toothaches were reported. People in 1849 probably consumed much less sugar than people in the late twentieth century. This was possibly a factor in the small number of passengers having problems with their teeth. Only a single passenger in each of the ships *Crescent, Magnolia,* and *Sheffield* and the brigs *Perfect* and *Mary Stuart* complained of toothaches. The man in the *Mary*

Stuart seems to have had the greatest pain. His tooth had been filled by his dentist at home shortly before he sailed. The captain of the *Sheffield* pulled the tooth for his passenger and "performed the operation well."[6]

Two passengers in the ship *Magnolia* chronicled a long illness of a Mrs. Hoxie, who was the servant of Mrs. Benjamin Frank Simmons, wife of the captain of the ship, but they never identified the nature of her illness. On March 10, 1849, one of them reported that she fainted and "remained so for one half hour." Both passengers regularly reported on her condition. On July 8 or 9 both reported she was not expected to live through the day, and if she died Captain Simmons would stop at the Galapagos Islands and bury her. She recovered from that serious state, and by July 17 it was reported she "has got quite well again." By July 21 she was reported as "getting quite smart."[7] It seems to be a tribute to the concern of those two men to continue to report on the condition of the servant of the captain's wife.

Several passengers in other vessels reported a variety of illnesses and accidents that resulted in the death of passengers. One or more deaths and burials were reported in the ships *Alhambra, Arkansas, Brooklyn, Europe, Hampton, Magnolia, Mason, Mary Adelaide, Sutton, Sweden,* and *Tahmaroo*; the barks *Belgrade, Belvidera, Croton, John Walls, Norwich, Orion,* and *Velasco*; and the brigs *Forrest* and *Sea Eagle*. One of the passengers in the *Arkansas* drowned while a group of passengers were overboard swimming; a passenger in the *Sutton* committed suicide; and an infant in the ship *Europe* died as the result of an accident. All the others resulted from illnesses.

A man listed only as "Old Mr. Johnson" died in the ship *Alhambra* around midnight July 6 and was buried at 11:00 A.M. with Captain Coffin presiding, using the service in the Episcopal Book of Common Prayer. A black cook hired at Rio de Janeiro died during the night of September 22 or 23, 1849, in the ship *Arkansas* from injuries suffered in a fall down the forward gangway after becoming intoxicated on alcohol given him by two members of the California Mutual Benefit and Joint Stock Association, who were not supposed to have any alcohol because of their association with the Methodist Church. He was buried at sea the next morning. The following day Dr. M. Flagg, a fifty-year-old passenger from Martinburg, Virginia, died after a brief bout with diarrhea. Although he had been a Universalist and had refused to allow other passengers to pray for him, he was buried at sea using the Episcopal service. On July 5 a young man from New York named Charles M. Griffith drowned while he and several others were swimming alongside the *Arkansas*. Capt. Philip W. Shepeard dove from the deck and made a heroic but fruitless effort to save the swimmer and nearly lost his life in the effort. Committees were appointed to take charge of his effects and to prepare resolutions expressing the feelings of the company to be sent to his family. His effects were auctioned the next day by the captain with the proceeds to go to his family. Items sold for much more than their value in New York.[8]

Seven passengers in the ship *Brooklyn* died, most of them from scurvy. Five of the deaths occurred after they arrived in San Francisco. One passenger's brother was with him and had a coffin built to carry the body to San Francisco for burial. A coroner's inquest was held in San Francisco in which Capt. Joseph W. Richardson was found guilty of having caused the deaths and was fined two thousand dollars. Jerome Sterling, a nine-month-old infant, died on board the ship *Europe* from injuries he received when his mother fell while carrying him. Ezra Witman of Waterville, Maine, died on September 29, 1849, only three weeks after the ship *Hampton* sailed from Bangor. He had been ill from the time they sailed. The Church of England service was used in the burial. A. Delano of Fairhaven, Massachusetts, suffered with dysentery for two weeks before he died on the morning of June 20, 1849, on board the ship *Magnolia*. He was buried two hours later during a raging storm because the nature of his disease made keeping the body longer a risk to other passengers. Capt. William Bell, commander of the ship *Mason,* died on September 3, 1849. No cause of his death was reported. His body was put in a barrel of whiskey and taken to San Francisco for burial.[9]

A passenger in the ship *Orpheus* reported speaking with the ship *Mary Adelaide* on June 14, 1849, and learning that there had been six deaths between New York and Valparaiso and three more since sailing from that port. Theophilius Valentine, a thirty-five-year-old native of Switzerland, "blew out his brains" on board the ship *Sutton* while they were in Rio de Janeiro. He was buried in the English burial ground following an inquest. There was a death and burial on board the ship *Sweden,* but some uncertainty about the name of the passenger and date of death and burial in the minds of passengers. Two passengers noted the name as Clinch with one giving an age of 28 and a first name of Benjamin. One recorded it as happening on April 30 and the other as May 6. Another passenger gave the date as April 30 but reported his name as Barry McLinch of Calais, Maine. All three passengers indicate the deceased had been ill ever since they sailed from Boston. The ceremony in the *Sweden* was possibly more elaborate than those on any other vessel in that James L. L. F. Warren composed two hymns for it. Edwin Hally of Avon, Connecticut, died in the ship *Tahmaroo* on January 30, 1849, and was buried at sea the next morning. His body was sewn in a hammock.[10]

Three passengers died on board the bark *Belgrade* between March 2 and April 14, 1850. Several passengers became ill soon after they encountered a severe storm about two weeks after sailing from Rio de Janeiro. Edward F. Jacobs of Cherryfield, Maine, was the first to die after having been ill for more than two weeks. Another passenger described the traditional burial at sea and then commented upon the difference between a burial on land and one at sea. When a person is buried on land, family and friends can always return to the burial place and remember the departed loved one; but when someone is buried at sea, family and friends can never return to that site, for it is far away and locating the exact site is virtually impossible. No memorial can be placed at sea as can be done on land. Hiram D. Tibbits of Columbia, Maine, died around 7:00 A.M. on March 29 after an illness of three weeks and was buried in the early afternoon. David A. Cates died early in the morning of April 15 and was buried that afternoon. William W. Tuttle, a passenger in the bark *Belvidera,* developed dysentery shortly after they sailed from Callao, possibly from eating too much fresh fruit. He apparently did not consider his problem a serious one and refused medical treatment until it was too late. Most of the treatment he received was from a passenger named Nelson, who used hydropathic treatment although he also gave him some "Forgate's Cordial." Tuttle died around 1:00 A.M. on August 29, 1849, and was buried at sea a few hours later because of the extreme heat.[11]

Because the bark *Croton* was so near San Francisco when a passenger named either A. D. Johnson or Joseph Johnson from Seneca Falls, New York, died about midnight on July 27, 1849, another passenger built a coffin to hold the body and bury it in port at San Francisco. Johnson had been in the last stages of consumption for three weeks at the time of his death. A passenger in the bark *John Walls,* identified only as Mr. Carrington, died and was buried at sea on July 21, 1849. No cause of death was given. The African American second cook in the bark *Norwich* died and was buried at sea on June 22, 1849. Oliver B. McIntire of York, Maine, became ill with "bilious inflammatory fever" in late January 1849 and died from that illess in 7 days. Because of the nature of the illness, he was buried at sea almost immediately; his clothing and bedding were thrown overboard; and tar was burned in the cabin to prevent the fever from spreading. James Smith of Pawtucket, Rhode Island, apparently suffered from consumption when he sailed in the bark *Velasco*. Fellow passengers urged him to return home when they stopped at the island of Fayal, but he refused. He died around 10:00 P.M. on June 16 and was buried at sea at 1:00 p.m. on June 17, 1849. A committee of three members of the Narragansett Association was appointed to look after his possessions, which were sold at auction by the captain on September 11, 1849. The nearly two hundred dollars realized from the sale were sent to his wife. Hiram Doter or Doten died of consumption on board the brig *Sea Eagle* early on the morning of October 7, 1849, and was buried that morning at 10:00.[12]

In each instance of death from illness or accident (except when a drowning victim's body was not recovered), a funeral was conducted that included prayers, reading from the Bible, songs, and reading of a burial service from a church book, frequently the Episcopal Book of Common Prayer. Services were normally held within a matter of hours after the death. As a general practice the vessel was slowed as much as possible by taking in some sails and laying back the main or main topsail; the flag was flown at half mast; and the bell was rung to call everyone on deck for the service. The body was clothed and sewn in a canvas bag with weights attached, placed on a board or a cabin door, covered with a flag, and dropped over the lee side at the end of the service. The vessel was ordered underway as soon as the service ended. The effects of the deceased were sold at auction to the other passengers in the ship *Arkansas* and the bark *Velasco*, but auctions were not mentioned in other vessels.

Given the fact that few California-bound passengers had ever been on board a sailing vessel and therefore unaccustomed to getting about in rough weather, it is understandable that some of them would have accidents such as falling down stairs, slipping on deck, falling from the rigging, being tossed against bulkheads or other stationary objects, or being knocked overboard by booms. Participating in skylarking either on deck or in the rigging also created opportunities for accidents. Probably the scariest and most dangerous accident possible was falling or being knocked overboard, especially in shark-infested waters or in the cold regions of the southern latitudes. Both passengers and crew members had accidents of various types during the hundreds of voyages to California in 1849. The cabin boy Charley in the brig *Mary Stuart* was badly scalded when a container of boiling water was turned over in the galley during a storm. His arms and one side of his body were badly burned. A space was apparently later made for his recovery in the forward cabin. A passenger identified only as Mr. Bailey, also in the *Mary Stuart*, injured his legs and back when he fell down into the middle hatch while carrying a box on the promenade deck. Benjamin Fuller, a passenger in the ship *Nestor,* received a bad cut on his hand while playing with another passenger who had his knife open. The doctor on board sewed up the cut. Isaac M. Jessup fell to the deck and injured his head and knee while assisting in moving the fore spencer from the lee to the weather side of the ship *Sheffield.* As two passengers in the bark *Orion* raced to the dinner table, one tried to jump over a chest and was knocked senseless when he hit his head on one of the beams. James Monroe, a passenger in the ship *Europe,* fell down some steps while carrying a pot of coffee that spilled on him and burned his right arm and hand. Sweet oil and turpentine were applied to the burned areas, and he recovered quickly. John Parnell, a sailor in the ship *York,* injured his head and shoulder when he fell from aloft while reefing topsails. A couple of days later a passenger received a broken leg when a washtub broke loose from its lashings and pinned him against the bulkhead. A sailor named George Blasedell in the bark *Sarah Warren* received a severe cut when he sat down on a sheath knife. He required stitches to stop the bleeding. A passenger named D. Hunt from New York in the ship *Tahmaroo* was knocked senseless when he fell from the main yard while helping take in sails. One passenger in the brig *Perfect* shot himself in the finger; another jammed his finger while moving the longboat; a third injured his arms while steering for four hours in heavy weather; and still another stuck a nail in his foot. In addition one man fainted while at the wheel. The man with injured arms used horse liniment, hunter liniment, painkiller, pain extractor, and a Mexican cold preparation to solve his problem. James H. Gager, a passenger in the ship *Pacific,* fell on deck and broke his nose and his glasses. Capt. James McGuire of the bark *Keoka* broke his ankle the day after they sailed from New York and was partially disabled for a period of time.[13]

Other than a shipwreck, falling or being knocked or washed overboard was probably the most serious accident to occur on board a sailing vessel. A fourteen-year-old cabin boy named Johnson lost his hold while stepping from the top of the house into the main rigging on the weather side of the bark *Elvira* and fell into the sea. He was noticed immediately, and a boat was launched. He was rescued in twelve minutes. A sailor named Tobey, who had only recently changed from passenger to sailor, fell from the martingale of the ship *Magnolia* while trying to harpoon a porpoise. He too was noticed immediately. The second mate, G. Parlow, heard the cry "man overboard" while in his cabin and rushed on deck clad in only his drawers and ordered a boat lowered to rescue Tobey. That was accomplished in ten minutes. Tobey was described as an excellent swimmer who was able to remove his coat and one of his boots and keep his head above water all the time he was in the frigid waters off Cape Horn. One passenger noted that this was the most exciting event during the entire voyage. Ab. W. Pitts from Smithfield, Rhode Island, fell from the bark *Strafford* while attempting to draw a bucket of water from over the bow. He had one foot on the rail and the other on a brace but slipped and tumbled into the water. He was fortunate to catch hold of the rope he had been using to fetch water, as he could not swim. Others were able to haul him safely on deck.[14]

Not all of those who fell or were swept overboard were so fortunate. The ship *Sutton* was lying to while riding out a gale and making considerable leeway. Several men were seated in the stern boat, which was suspended from davits, when the fastening at one end gave way due to the excessive weight. Four saved themselves by grabbing hold of some part of the boat and climbing up to the deck. A fifth held on to the gunwale of the boat while he was partially submerged. Another, who was unable to swim, held fast to a rope and called for aid until he was heard and rescued. Two who were expert swimmers drifted some distance from the *Sutton*. Various things that would float including benches and stools were thrown overboard toward them, and both quarter boats were launched to attempt to rescue the men. As the captain shouted encouragement to those stranded in the water, the boats pulled toward them. The starboard boat picked up one of the men. The last man grabbed hold of a large albatross in an effort to remain afloat until the other boat could reach him, but the bird escaped and the passenger named Angelo Schoonmaker sank into the ocean and never came up again. Soon after the boats were back on deck and properly stored, the passengers saw a large shark prowling around the ship. Sailors said that sharks are always seen immediately before or after the death of a person on board. Hervy Harrington, a passenger in the ship *George Washington,* appeared on deck eating a piece of cake during heavy weather. Another passenger fell against him when the ship lurched and knocked Harrington down, causing him to slide across the deck and into the sea. A rope was thrown to him, but he never took hold of it. Passengers assumed that he had hit his head, or he certainly would have grabbed the rope within his reach. He was a hundred yards behind the vessel when he rose to the top and seemed to wave his arm to those on board. He sank again and never rose to the surface again. It was assumed that a shark pulled him under. The mate offered to take a boat out to attempt a rescue, and a crew volunteered to go with him, but the captain would not permit it, as no boat could survive in the tempestuous sea. Capt. N. Varina, who was then at the wheel, and three others were washed overboard from the brig *Forrest* in the vicinity of the Falkland Islands. The captain managed to cry "man over-board" as he was being swept away. Ropes were thrown to all four, and they were all brought back on deck. One of them named Carpenter apparently got the rope around his neck in wrapping it around his body and choked to death as he was being pulled back to the brig. He was buried at sea almost immediately. A passenger in the schooner *Rialto* reported speaking with the brig *Forrest* of Newburyport, Massachusetts, and learning that nine men from the brig were washed overboard by the spanker boom during a gale off Cape Horn. Two of the men were never recovered.[15]

Lives and comfort of passengers in a number of vessels were made uncomfortable, if not indeed miserable, by a number of pests including bedbugs, fleas, lice, mice, rats, and roaches. Bedbugs were most prevalent in the warm climates. Fleas were most often mentioned after vessels sailed from Valparaiso, Talcahuano, or Callao. The other pests appeared at various stages of the voyage. Bedbugs caused loss of sleep in the ships *Arkansas, Edward Everett, Europe, Florida, Magnolia, Orpheus, Regulus,* and *Sutton;* the barks *Belvidera, Canton, Keoka,* and *Yoeman;* and the brig *Osceola.* Passengers reported having to sleep on deck and on chests to avoid the infestations of bedbugs in several vessels. Some passengers tried oil, and others tried burning but had little success in getting rid of these pests. A passenger in the ship *Edward Everett* included a drawing of a bedbug in his journal. H. F. W. Swain noted that three thousand bedbugs were killed in one berth of the bark *Belvidera* and reported he had preserved a few dead ones in his journal. The suffering caused by bedbugs was "intolerable" according to one passenger. Fleas were mentioned as being serious problems in the ships *Daniel Webster, Europe, Hopewell, Magnolia,* and *Regulus;* the barks *Keoka, Midas,* and *Velasco;* and the brigs *Osceola* and *Perfect.* Fleas are mentioned shortly after the ships *Magnolia* and *Regulus* sailed form Callao. The other vessels stopped at Valparaiso or Talcahuano. A passenger in the *Regulus* wrote that the fleas were more of a problem than the bedbugs. Another in the ship *Europe* noted they were "almost devoured by fleas" in Valparaiso, but they were rid of them shortly after they left. A third passenger in the ship *Hopewell* felt they would be "lucky" if the fleas did not "eat us up before we compleat our voiage." The presence of lice is specifically mentioned on board the barks *Keoka, Maria,* and *Velasco* and strongly hinted at in the ships *Magnolia* and *Reindeer.* A passenger in the *Keoka* hinted that lice came on board in Valparaiso; one in the *Maria* found them on another person who then found several more on himself; and a third in the *Velasco* noted, "There has been considerable washing since the lice was found." William F. Reed of the *Magnolia* mentioned the presence of vermin, "which does not indicate a verry strict regard to cleanliness" and which caused everyone to examine their own clothes. A passenger in the *Reindeer* wrote that some passengers had "found some live stock on their clothing" and that he doubted they were natives of Valparaiso as was claimed by others. Rats were found in abundance on board the ships *Andalusia, Apollo, Arkansas, Florida, Pacific, Plymouth, Regulus,* and *York* and the barks *Anna Reynolds, Midas,* and *Velasco.* Anne (Willson) Booth reported several sleeping passengers had been bitten by rats in the ship *Andalusia.* The same was reported in the ship *Pacific,* where rats also destroyed one passenger's flag, and dead ones were found in casks of drinking water. Passengers in the ship *Florida* and bark *Midas* made traps to catch rats. Any caught were made to "walk the plank" or were assigned "to the mercy of old N[eptune]." Passengers who caught a rat during daylight in the ship *Plymouth* gave it to the cat "for dissection." Based upon the frequent complaints of Thomas Williams, the ship *Regulus* seems to have had the worst infestation of rats. Some of her sailors said they had never seen so many rats in a single vessel. Passengers in the bark *Anna Reynolds* put their tents and canvas in casks to keep rats from ruining them. Rats in the bark *Velasco* were thought to have killed the two guinea pigs purchased in Talcahuano, where they had smoked the vessel but did not completely rid it of rats. The extent of the rat population in the ship *Apollo* can best be imagined by considering the quantity of them killed by smoking the vessel in San Francisco by burning sulphur in iron kettles in the lower hold. After the vessel was aired out so as to be safe for humans, four flour barrels were filled with dead rats in the lower deck and two more barrels were filled from the dunnage and the bilge areas. The bark *San Francisco* was the only vessel in which mice seem to have been a problem. Isaac W. Baker built a trap and caught several on each of six nights. His journal contains a drawing of a passenger chasing mice. Roaches were mentioned only in the ship *Daniel Webster* and the brig *Perfect.* Passengers in the brig *Perfect* spent some time picking over turnips and onions to kill the roaches that chewed on those food items. One man reported finding a quart's worth of roaches in a barrel of vegetables.[16]

Excessive drinking of alcohol or drunkenness among passengers, sailors, or officers on board sailing vessels bound for California in 1849 seems to have been limited. On the other hand, it simply may not have been recorded by those who kept journals of their voyages, as some intended to send or take those volumes home and may not have wanted their families to know that there was excessive use of alcohol in their vessel. Even though most of the joint stock companies seem to have prohibited the taking and consumption of alcohol, little temperance activity was reported in passengers' journals. Other than major celebrations such as the Fourth of July and George Washington's birthday, drinking to excess seems to have been limited to a few isolated instances in a handful of vessels at sea. There were some indications that there may have been considerably more drinking by passengers when they were in some foreign ports. Only one instance of excessive drinking at sea was reported by one of the four or five passengers who kept journals in the ship *Pacific*. This seems odd in lieu of the claims of habitual drunkenness passengers made against Capt. Hall J. Tibbits between New York and Rio de Janeiro. A passenger in the bark *Strafford* made mention of "a drunken rowe" in the captain's cabin by about ten members of the New York Mining Company approximately six weeks into the voyage. He also noted excessive drinking while they were at St. Catherines Island. On two occasions four or five passengers in the bark *Croton* drank to excess. The excuse for the second occasion was that "they were off the horn & must take a horn." On one occasion when the middle hatch was opened to get coal on board the brig *Mary Stuart*, they brought up ten gallons of wine and had an all-day spree in which every member of their unnamed company participated. Anne (Willson) Booth reported only one instance of drinking and fighting in the ship *Andalusia*, which Captain Willson quickly quelled by locking up the participants. Two passengers in the ship *Sweden* reported widely separated instances of excessive drinking. In one of the incidents, officers of one the companies on board claimed the liquor was smuggled on board and stolen by some of the passengers. Enos Christman reported four fairly widely separated instances of intoxication in the ship *Europe*. In one instance the captain threatened to put one of the revelers in handcuffs. A passenger in the brig *Osceola* reported that on one occasion the man at the wheel was found to be slightly inebriated. A jug of whiskey was found in his sea chest and was thrown overboard. On another occasion four first-cabin passengers had a lengthy "jollification." There is some indication in three sources that the captain of the bark *Selma* may well have had a drinking problem. Such was hinted at by one passenger who described a problem with lowering sails in a storm when they were close to the shore. Another passenger stated the captain was drunk on that occasion. The second mate, who was keeping the logbook, a duty normally assigned to the first mate, implied on that occasion that the first mate was in no better shape than the captain. That same second mate noted that the captain announced in Valparaiso that the first mate had resigned and offered his own resignation if the members of the Fremont Mining and Trading Company wanted him to do so. They voted unanimously to retain the captain. Two passengers in the ship *Jane Parker* noted instances of drunkenness by one passenger and one cook and among some of the sailors. Six of the nine sailors being intoxicated nearly caused a serious problem when a squall came up, but passengers assisted in taking in sails. The captain beat the cook and locked him in the "Round House." A drunken cook was also noted very early in the voyage of the bark *Orion*. His jug was found by the captain and thrown away.[17]

Temperance activities were found in only five vessels. There seems to have been a more active group on board the ship *Euphrasia* than any other vessel although there was also active drinking in her. About seventy passengers reportedly signed the temperance pledge about three months into the voyage. One passenger, said to have "taken more liquor than any other person on board" the bark *Orion*, signed a temperance pledge and then recruited others to do the same. One passenger noted that those who had witnessed activities of other passengers in foreign ports should have seen enough of the evils of intemperance to abstain from intoxicants. A temperance society was formed in the bark *Gold Hunter*, and fifteen members joined that day. There was a noisy temperance debate on board the ship *Argonaut* one evening, and two days later they held a temperance meeting. Thomas Whaley seems to have vacillated on the matter of temperance. On one occasion he wrote his mother that he was secretary of the temperance society in the ship *Sutton*, but he later noted that he had not joined the flourishing temperance society and thought he would never do so.[18]

Theft of food, money, alcohol, and other commodities was a relatively minor problem in California-bound sailing vessels. The most significant theft seems to have occurred in the ship *Balance*, where one passenger estimated that two thousand dollars' worth of food had been stolen or wasted. He felt sure that the food that was stolen was all eaten by the thieves. Among the items he specifically mentioned were hams, tongue, raisins, almonds, dried fruit, and wine. This was all taken from the supply put on board by the charterers of the *Balance*. Sweetmeats, jellies, and other private provisions were stolen from passengers. The passenger who reported this indicated that if the inexperienced charterers had hired professional

221

cooks and stewards rather than allowing untrained and inexperienced persons to work their passage to California, the thefts from the ship's supply would have been prevented. A passenger in the ship *Andalusia* reported to Captain Willson that eight hundred dollars had been stolen from his trunk. The captain ordered a search of the vessel, but five hours of searching proved fruitless. Suspicion was centered around one person, but no proof was found. "A good deal of thieving" happened during the early part of the voyage of the ship *York* with most of the suspicion centered on the first mate, but the theft problem was reduced during the latter portion of the voyage. A passenger in ship *Nestor* noted that a keg of barberries was reported stolen but stated he did not "know as it can be cawled stealing" because "allmost evry one practices" snitching food "with impunity." A cabin boy in the ship *America* had his liberty on shore taken away at St. Catherines Island as punishment for stealing money and jewelry from a passenger. A passenger in the ship *Tahmaroo* had two hundred dollars' worth of jewelry stolen. Two individuals were suspected of pilfering of various items in the bark *Helen Augusta,* and a meeting of the company was called to "lay the subject on the table for future consideration," but nothing more was reported on the issue. When some people broke open a cask of raisins on board the ship *Reindeer,* the captain ordered a search by the mates, but they found nothing. About the same time someone stole a case of eleven bottles of gin the minister named Evans bought in Valparaiso for medicine. Over a period of a week James H. Gager reported that his towel, overshoes, and sheet were stolen and noted at that rate he would not have any bedding left when he arrived in California. The theft of butter and raisins put on board the ship *Orpheus* for the second cabin created quite a controversy, as those passengers wanted the captain to purchase replacements for what was stolen, and the captain refused to do so. The passengers threatened to get into the ship's supplies and take what they felt was rightly theirs. The captain replied he would lock them up and take them into a port for prosecution if they took food as they threatened. The controversy was ended when the captain offered to double the ration of flour rather than purchase more butter. One passenger was greatly disappointed in his fellow passengers, "more than one half" of whom he said fell "far short" of the "excellence I expected to see at the time of our sailing." He added he would receive "much pleasure at the close of our voyage to be rid of their presence." Several boxes of vinegar "or whatever it was . . . wine or some other liquor" were pilfered on board the ship *Argonaut,* but a number of passengers paid fifty dollars to cover the cost to settle the matter. Two members of the company in the ship *Edward Everett* were suspected of theft. They had a rather stormy business meeting in which the members voted that both were guilty, but they decided to expel only one from the company. Three different incidents of theft were reported in the ship *Sweden*. When two or three dozen bottles of brandy stored in boxes labeled codfish were stolen from under the table, Capt. Jesse G. Cotting ordered everyone on deck and instructed the mates to search every stateroom and chest. Many passengers refused to permit their things to be searched. Some harsh words were exchanged between some passengers and the first mate. One passenger was sure the liquor had already been consumed by the time the theft was discovered. On another occasion some gin, cigars, dried fruit, and almonds were reported stolen from the captain's stateroom. During a search of the ship, a part of the almonds and a bucket of almond shells were found leading to one passenger suspected of the theft. On another occasion money was stolen from one passenger and found in the chest of another. None of the journalists reported any punishment being administered to either person. A passenger in the brig *Sea Eagle* had some of his drinkable medicine stolen, and another in the ship *Europe* had a cup and some cheese taken.[19]

These incidents illustrate theft in only a small number of vessels and by a small fraction of the passengers included in this study. Thus it would seem that although there were a few dishonest individuals in sailing vessels bound for California in 1849, the vast majority were among the most upstanding and honest members of their communities. Considering the large numbers of people who sailed to California, it would have been unusual to have found no instances of theft.

Leaking vessels and small fires were minor problems in a few of the California-bound vessels. The ships *Sabina* and *Nestor* had leaky hulls that required the vessels to be pumped with some regularity. Passengers and crew in the *Sabina* had to repair both pumps and then stop at St. Catherines Island to try to stop the leak. One passenger reported she leaked about one thousand strokes per hour. The *Nestor* apparently leaked only in heavy weather, but at those times the pumps had to be kept going about two-thirds of the time. The schooner *Osceola* and the ship *Orpheus* had leaky decks, which allowed water to drain into the passengers' quarters whenever they encountered heavy seas or a rainstorm. In many other vessels water sometimes rushed down the hatches when seas washed over the deck.[20]

Fires in the galley were reported in the ships *Europe* and the bark *Hannah Sprague,* and a fire in the sails was noted in the ship *Nestor.* The upsetting of a pot of pork fat on the galley stove caused the fire in the *Europe,* but it was quickly put out with a few buckets of water. The cook in the *Hannah Sprague* had too hot a fire in his galley, causing the stovepipe to become red hot and start a fire that was quickly doused. This happened on more than one occasion. A careless smoker in the ship *Nestor* threw his still-burning cigar overboard only to have it blown onto the water sail that was hanging from the swinging boom. Quick work put the fire out before it spread to any other sails or into the grease- and tar-covered standing rigging. Passengers on board the *Nestor* later signed an agreement to limit smoking to the area forward the foremast, to refrain from taking coals from the galley stove to light their pipes, and to avoid throwing any piece of a cigar, whether lighted or not, over the rail.[21]

One might logically conclude that with so many people wanting to go to California in 1849, some of whom likely did not have the funds to purchase passage and the necessary tools, supplies, and clothing, that stowaways would be a major problem on vessels sailing to California. That logical assumption was incorrect, however. In all the vessels included in this study only two stowaways were found in vessels departing from the east coast. A young man about eighteen years old suddenly appeared on deck of the bark *Strafford* three days after she left New York. The captain assigned him to be steward in the cabin. He seems to have worked out to the satisfaction of the passengers. Nearly a week after the ship *Tahmaroo* sailed form New York, they discovered a new man on board. The captain assigned him to work as a steward in the second cabin. He seems not to have taken to his work very well, as about a week later he "was rope ended by the first mate for neglecting his duties." This action by the mate disturbed the captain, and the two exchanged heated words. People gaining unauthorized access to sailing vessels in South American ports was a bit more of a problem. Stowaways were found in the bark *Gold Hunter* and the ships *Reindeer* and *Euphrasia* one or two days after they sailed from Valparaiso. The one in the *Gold Hunter* had run away from an English frigate. The sailors in the *Reindeer* assisted three sailors from other vessels in stowing away. When the mate took them to the captain, he ordered them to be put in irons and locked in the sail room until he could put them ashore, but "in about 13 minutes" they were all put to work in the ship. The one in the *Euphrasia* had been in California and had gone from there to Valparaiso, where he spent all his money. He wanted to return to California to replenish his money supply. He was put to work immediately to replace a sailor who had been unfit for work for most of the voyage. A single stowaway was discovered in the bark *Oxford* two days after she sailed form Talcahuano. He was named Joseph Taggard, about twenty years old, and had run away from the ship *Daniel Webster* in Talcahuano because of mistreatment. He was immediately put to work as a sailor. One of the sailors in the ship *Jane Parker* was surprised to see a new face in the vessel the second day out from Callao. The first mate was called and met the man and put him to work as a sailor.[22] Undoubtedly owners of vessels, shipping agents, and officers of joint stock companies were well aware of the numbers of people who wanted to get to California and took measures to prevent stowaways from getting on board in both United States and foreign ports.

Women on board the sailing vessels bound for California cannot really be called a problem although having women in what was traditionally an all-male society and having to make accommodations for females in situations where privacy normally did not exist created some problems for owners and officers of companies. The presence of women has been considered to have had a positive influence on the behavior of males in a vessel. Many sailors considered a woman a jinx on board a sailing vessel. At times, however, they were a temptation to certain of the males. A few single passengers met, fell in love, and were married during the voyage. In a number of cases married women gave birth to children during their expedition to California. Occasionally having a husband and wife on board together resulted in some domestic squabbling.

In his fictionalized account of the voyage of the ship *Magnolia*, [George Payson] reported there was a library, a piano, and some ladies on board to provide learning, song, and beauty. The women were to provide the beauty and shed a benign and humanizing influence over the men. He went on to say the library consisted of books they had already read or ones that no one ever read; the piano was out of tune; and there were far too few women to prevent the men "from sinking back into worse than heathen darkness and barbarism." That women did not always succeed in providing that humanism is demonstrated by an incident on board the ship *Nestor*. Someone wrote an abusive and insulting message on the wall of the deckhouse, where everyone, including the ladies, could read it. It was directed toward one of the ladies. The captain indicated it was an insult to him and to the lady and asked all hands if they had anything to do with the message. He also promised to severely punish the culprit if he was ever discovered. Everyone denied having written the message. The ship *Trescott* took in three passengers at Talcahuano, two of whom were female. All three had paid for accommodations below deck, but there was no place for the women there. Capt. J. Mallory allowed the two women to share the top bunk in his cabin while he occupied the narrower lower bunk. The captain also kept a demijohn of brandy on the floor near his door from which the third mate was in the habit of sneaking drinks at night. One night after he had drunk his fill, the mate decided to get into the bunk with the two women. The women told him to go away lest he wake the captain. Eventually he drank some more brandy and went away to sleep off the liquor. The next morning the women told the captain what had happened the previous night. Captain Mallory called the mate to his cabin. Upon being confronted with the accusations, the third mate replied that another man had told him the women had invited him to join them, but he went instead. When that man was called down, he admitted that he had lied. The captain told both men if they ever came to his cabin again he would "thrash them as he would a dog And put it down in the Ships log." There was slight indication of some domestic difficulties among one or two married couples in the ship *Arkansas*. One passenger reported harsh words between Mr. Stone and his wife because of her passion for strong drink. Another passenger reported somewhat later that one man's wife had fallen in love with another man.[23]

Sophia A. Eastman, a young single woman from Massachusetts, was sailing to California to seek work as a teacher. She made the trip in the brig *Colorado* on board of which there were several women, some married and some single. Miss Mary Jane Stenchfield seems to have been a servant to Mrs. Brocket, but they had a dispute of some sort, possibly over Miss Stenchfield's relationship with one of the male passengers named Henry [Grush?]. Miss Stenchfield and Mr. [Grush?] were married on February 26, 1849, by Capt. William P. Baker in a happy ceremony attended by everyone on board. A special dinner was prepared for the occasion. At midnight the Owl Club serenaded the happy couple. Capt. George Coffin wrote about a Mrs. Lathrop, a widow woman looking for a second husband, in the ship *Alhambra*. She came close to getting the first mate William Higgins to marry her. Actually Higgins asked permission of the captain to marry her in Valparaiso, but the captain persuaded him to wait until they arrived in San Francisco. If he still wanted to marry her then he would give his blessings. During the interval Mr. Higgins had a change of heart. By doing so he incurred the wrath of Mrs. Lathrop. The two were married after arriving in San Francisco, but the marriage was soon terminated after she became involved with another man. A passenger in the bark *Hannah Sprague* noted the marriage of a Mr. Huyck to an unnamed women he referred to as "the venomous old maid of whom I have spoken." He obviously did not approve of the wedding and could not see why Mr. Huyck would marry her, as she only "winds her spell about him like some keen-eyed snake."[24]

The birth of children on vessels bound for California was always a happy occasion. Typical of the times, however, nothing was said about the condition of the mother prior to the birth of the child. A son was born to Mr. and Mrs. M. Mahand on April 2, 1850, on board the ship *Hannibal*. He was named George Hannibal Mahand and weighed ten pounds and was said by one passenger to be "as smart and bright as a dollar." His birth created "a good feeling in the after house and finally through the whole ship." Anne (Willson) Booth reported the birth of a daughter to Rev. and Mrs. William Taylor in the ship *Andalusia* on June 21, 1849. A month later she reported she believed Mrs. Taylor had decided to name her Corriente, which is Spanish for current, because that was the name of the cape near the River de La Platta where the girl was born. In his book *California Life Illustrated* William Taylor referred to his daughter as "my little Oceana." A son was born to Capt. and Mrs. Benjamin Frank Simmons on board the ship *Magnolia* on August 17, 1849, just one day before they arrived in San Francisco. He was named Charles Henry Simmons and was the couple's first child. The wife of Capt. Philip W. Shepeard of the ship *Arkansas* gave birth to a daughter in the vicinity of Cape Horn on October 3, 1849. She was baptized Teresea Cornelia Randal Shepheard while they were in Talcahuano a month later. Capt. David F. Lansing ignored the doctors on board the bark *Hannah Sprague* and assisted his wife in the delivery of their daughter on October 28, 1849. One passenger wrote they considered the birth a happy omen, as Neptune sent them a calm during the night to keep the ship "as quiet as a conch for the happy mother." A Mrs. Frye, the wife of one of the owners or charterers of the ship *Balance,* gave birth to a daughter on July 10, 1849, off Cape Horn. The professional midwife was below deck at the time and was unable to assist, but a Dr. Brooks assisted in the delivery. A nurse named Bridget also seems to have been present during the birth or immediately afterward. This birth also was seen as a good omen for the ship, as immediately after the birth the wind changed and became favorable. Mrs. Frye decided to name her daughter Mary Seaborn. The wife of Capt. Jesse G. Cotting of the ship *Sweden* gave birth to a son on July 13, 1849.[25]

Listing African Americans as a problem in sailing vessels bound for California might be a bit misleading, but their presence in some instances resulted in problems. There are no statistics to indicate how many African Americans went to California for the gold rush, but there certainly were some. A small number went as members of joint stock companies; some went as employees of those companies; a number went as cooks and stewards paid either by the owners or charterers of vessels or by organized companies; some went as the property of southern slaveholders; and some undoubtedly went as free and independent individuals. Most often when African Americans were referred to, the journalists used terms deemed unacceptable in the late twentieth century. A few references have already been made in previous sections of this work to African American cooks and stewards.

A group of merchants in New York organized a company of ten African Americans who sailed for Panama in the ship *Hampton*. In November 1849 they traveled overland to the Pacific and caught another vessel for San Francisco. Another group of African Americans, headed by a minister named Ward, sailed from New Bedford, Massachusetts, in the ship *America* according to one passenger, who seems to have also had an African American as his personal servant. One of the cooks in the ship *Edward Everett* was an African American whose name was not given. An African American steward in the ship *Orpheus* was flogged for allegedly refusing to give some cheese to a little girl and for cursing her when she did not leave the galley. He was flogged again later for allegedly being intoxicated and was then confined below until they arrived in San Francisco. A passenger in the bark *John Walls* reported that some passengers stole an African American slave in Rio de Janeiro and smuggled him on their vessel along with a "White Chap" who had run away from an English ship. An unidentified person offered eight hundred milreis (somewhat over four hundred dollars) for the African American, but the passenger refused to give him up. There were two African Americans in the ship *Pacific*; one was named Charles and the other Primus. Primus seems to have been attached to a company from Hartford, Connecticut, whereas Charles was attached to a company from New York. They both shipped as waiters or stewards to work their way to California. Soon after they sailed from New York, Capt. Hall J. Tibbits saw the two men relaxing in the sun and flogged both of them. Some of the passengers who wrote about this incident in their journals had different opinions. One indicated that friends of the two African Americans took great offence and said the captain had no right to punish them, as they were not employees of the ship but were rather employees of the two companies. Another passenger speculated that the fact the two men were African Americans made flogging them justifiable. John Ross Browne, who had been on a whaling voyage a few years earlier and was accustomed to harsh treatment of sailors and others employed in sailing ships, felt that Captain Tibbits was entirely justified in flogging the two men. As the result of objections from some of the passengers to his actions, Captain Tibbits posted a notice that anyone who interfered with his authority in the ship would be put in irons and kept there during the captain's pleasure. This further infuriated the passengers, whose anger became so strong that they were able to have Captain Tibbits removed from command when they arrived in Rio de Janeiro.[26]

Some of the issues handled here were serious or at least semiserious problems for the passengers involved. Others may well not have been problems at all, but nevertheless they were circumstances that were of concern or interest to some of the passengers. These incidents or happenings gave the passengers something to discuss, to write about in their journals, or to argue about so they could momentarily forget about the tediousness of the long ocean voyage. For that reason, if for no other, they were important at the time and remain so today.

9

Duties and Responsibilities

Whether they were members of organized joint stock companies or were traveling as independent individuals, passengers sailing to California in 1849 had personal duties to perform. Most often these were limited to washing and mending their own clothes. Sometimes they made articles of clothing such as foul-weather gear and hats. Occasionally all the passengers in vessels with only independent passengers were organized into messes to assist with the preparation and serving of the food. In a few instances passengers assisted in operating the vessel, but this occurred most frequently in emergency situations. Those passengers who were members of organized joint stock companies often were divided into messes to assist with the preparation and serving of the food. They also attended regular and sometimes frequent meetings of the company. In addition they participated in making preparations for going to the mining fields when they arrived. This included a great variety of activities from making tents and other articles to building small boats and even steam engines to power them.

Because of the nature of society in mid nineteenth century, few men ever washed clothes, and clothes were washed much less often than they are today. People also bathed much less often than they do today. Washing clothes was all done by hand, and the drying was done by the wind and sunshine. Washing clothes on board a sailing vessel was quite different from washing them at home on land. The principle difference was that at sea the washing was most often done with cold salt water. This required a different kind of soap than was used with hot or warm fresh water on land. Sometimes passengers were able to catch fresh rain water for washing their clothes and themselves. A number of the men wrote about their efforts at washing their clothes.

Charles Williams, a passenger in the ship *Pacific*, first mentioned washing clothes on February 15, 1849, three and a half weeks after they sailed from New York. He noted that they were successful in catching rain water and "afterwards all dirty clothes for washing were brought out. It was an amusing sight to see us stripped of shoes & socks, pants rolled up and shirt sleeves, over our miniature wash tubs, in the broiling sun." He added that he washed two shirts, four pairs of socks, and two handkerchiefs. It is quite revealing that he washed only that small quantity of items after that length of time. He did not mention washing clothes again until late June 1849, but it appears from his writing that he had washed clothes occasionally in the interval. They caught more rain water on June 25 and washed clothes the next day. Williams wrote that he "went into the mysteries of a washing with which I am getting quite familiar" and added that he had completed his chores by breakfast time. Surely he had not washed four months of clothes in so short a time even if he was by then "quite familiar" with "the mysteries of a washing."[1] Enos Christman, a member of the California Gold Mining Association of Philadelphia in the ship *Europe,* noted early in his voyage that "It would be amusing to some of our old washer-women to witness us washing our clothes" and added that he "used to deem it play," but his recent experiences in washing in salt water without soap "taught me to appreciate the feelings for which the ladies are proverbial on washing day." He expected to be an expert at washing by the time he reached San Francisco. Near the end of his voyage he reported he "did an extensive washing to conclude the old year." It was done "most beautifully and with little trouble by hanging the clothes into the water and towing them a little while." He added that "woolen or cloth can be washed in as good if not superior manner" using this method but cautioned that "much care must be taken not to drag them until they ravel and go to pieces."[2]

Pierce W. Barker reported on the various methods of washing employed by the passengers in the ship *Nestor* about five weeks into the voyage. He wrote that he would describe "the different manuvers" as he found them after he finished washing his own things and admitted that he might "fail to give a true picture, considering the variety of ways it was done." He noted that "One was sitting down flat on the deck with a tin wash pan between his legs. He had partially scrubbed the dirt out of one thing, when he wrung it out (as the women say) and threw the water over the rail." At that point another passenger informed him he had thrown the "soap and all overboard." Barker went on to note that the "scuppers on the lee side of the Ship were stopped up so it held the water on deck" and that there were "perhaps half a dozen" who had their "cloths down on the deck treading out the dirt with their feet the same as a horse would tread out grain. Another had a heap of shirts layed down on the deck pounding out the dirt with a stick; but I guess he pounded out more threads than dirt."[3]

Both Richard Hunt Hale, who seems to have been an independent passenger in the brig *General Worth,* and Griffith Meredith, a member of the New York Mining Company in the bark *Strafford,* thought it would amuse the young ladies at home to see the men washing their clothes. Hale noted they had no tubs or washboards but instead used clubs to maul the "wet Sopping clothes on the deck after they have been well towed on the trail line." Then they were towed again until they were clean. Once the clothes were clean, they were hung in the rigging until they were dry. Hale felt the "girls would think" they looked "more like a laundry than a California droger." He added that washing was not done "every Monday as on shore" but rather was done "when the clothing is too dirty to wear" or "when the spell comes on, and above all, when the weather is fitting." Meredith decided to wash his soiled clothing when they were nearly five weeks at sea. He was reminded of the times in the country when he saw his mother and sisters do the washing, and he "helped them use the pounder" and thought that "without doubt" some of his young female acquaintances in New York as well as those in the country would "laugh to see me over a <u>wash tub</u>, wringing and twisting the shirts . . . and perhaps some of them <u>blush</u> to see how much more handy I can use the wash board than they can. Probably some of them never used one in their lives." Some of the other passengers who watched him thought Meredith "worked very handy" but did not think he "understood it well enough to teach it." J. L. Akerman, a passenger in the bark *Daniel Webster,* thought his wife "would Laugh or scold if she were to see some of my shirts at this time." He added that he could "get the dirt out but they look very dingy and yellow."[4]

Chester Joseph Snow, an independent passenger in the ship *Euphrasia,* confirmed the inexperience of the men at washing when he wrote about trying their luck at washing and concluded that "Some of us however are rather green. One man said he had washed a pocket handkerchief before." John T. Howard noted that Monday, November 26, 1849, was "Washing day" on board the bark *Midas* and added, "it makes about the same trouble as it does on shore, bitter complaints, water used up, clothes line gone, wind blows, can't find the soap, the bucket misplaced, and several other smaller troubles, but no trouble about smoky fires or poor wood, as we use cold water altogether." A few days later he reported he "washed a shirt for the first time but made a bad job of it," thereby confirming his lack of experience. Some time later he noted that there were "but few who can make clothes look white and clean by washing in cold water. It requires much time, patience, soap, and a lot of hard rubbing." An anonymous passenger in the ship *Plymouth* referred to Monday, February 25, 1850, as "Washing day!!!" He added that after this experience he would "never trouble a woman on washing day," as he could now "appreciate her troubles." He had washed seven "pieces & <u>dirty</u> at that" by scrubbing until he had "peeled the skin from off my knuckles." J. Haskell Stearns decided to make Monday, April 9, 1849, his "washing day," as he had collected "a fine lot of rain water during the last two days." He had on hand "what the ladies in the country call 'a large washing' . . . and found the operation rather a laboarious one." By the time he had finished his washing, he "was pretty much tired out" in part because of the "scorching heat of the sun" that "completely blistered" his arms and feet. He concluded that he "would never wash again while so near the equator." He had earlier noted that washing was "rather hard work."[5]

John Taylor, one of 198 passengers in the ship *Orpheus*, also wrote about washing on a Monday even though he did not wash on that day. He described the way others had washed their clothes on previous days and referred to the length of time some passengers used their bedding before washing it. He thought "the appearances of men and shirts during some of the washing scenes" would "cause a smile on the countenances of our mothers could they witness them." He thought their "modes of operations" and the motions they went through "to remove the thick covering of dirt would be sufficient." While he was doing his own washing, Taylor witnessed "one fellow passenger" who "spread his hicory on the deck and commenced scouring it with a scrubbing brush. He was told he would get it more covered with dirt than before, as the deck was very dirty, and at every roll of the ship the muddy greasy water would wash completely over the article he was cleansing. Ah! I care little for the loose grease he said if I can stir up the foundation of the old." Taylor thought "a washwoman would faint at the sight . . . of white pieces." He also wrote of "a young Doctor from Pittsburgh" who was gathering his washing and "said he <u>believed</u> he must wash his sheets. I declare, he exclaimed, they are getting quite dirty, and I have worn them but <u>three months and a half</u>. As for pillow cases I find it difficult to use them more than two months before they require washing too."[6] One wonders how long that young man would use his sheets and pillowcases at home without having them washed.

J. T. Woodbury, a passenger in the ship *Argonaut*, wrote the most detailed description of washing clothes of any passenger and also mentioned some of the methods of washing clothes by other passengers. He noted that he and a man named Augustus washed together in a single bucket filled with rain water. Augustus had washed clothes before, but Woodbury had not. He noted they were "dressed in oil clothes & 'Southwesters'" and had their bucket "under the lee rail against some spare spars." Augustus sat on the spars and Woodbury on a piece of plank on deck. Augustus laughed at Woodbury, who threatened to throw Augustus overboard but decided not to do so. Woodbury had no soap, so was using a bar belonging to Augustus, but he placed the bar on one of the spars. It fell off and slipped away where Woodbury could not find it. This brought some wrath from Augustus. Woodbury wrote that in washing his shirt, "I began on the wristbands. . . . I suppose the ladies will know, of course, whether this is the systematic point of beginning. . . . I soaped them and rubbed them, and rubbed them & soaped them till I was tired; & even then it did not look like one just out of the upper drawer." His "next point of attack was the neck & bosom, the last of which had a monstrous great spatter of ink on it." Here he "adopted the same method with those as with the wrist bands & thought the more I washed the ink the brighter it looked." After exhausting most of his "patience on the parts above named," he "engaged the whole body at large." Here he "pursued a different mode of operations. I soaped it in spots, doused it into the water & out, then gave it a tremendous jamming with my hands & repeated it till it drew as hard on my strength as the other parts on my patience." When he and Augustus were finished washing, they put their "clothes in soak where they now remain." He concluded his discussion of washing with a description of how others washed their clothes. He noted that he had "seen some wash their clothes by tying a rope to them & throwing them over the ship's bows; the dashing through the water done the washing" while "others put their clothes into a barrel & then get in themselves & tread & stamp on them as though they would jam them down to the bottomless pit." Still "others have regular wash boards which they seem to use to good advantage." He ended with this brief poem.

> I thought of home on washing day—
> Cooking & that together,
> And in the future I can say
> Deliver me from either.[7]

Charles Herbert Fuller, a passenger in the ship *Sweden*, wrote about washing clothes by himself as well as others more than any other passenger, as he did so on nine different occasions between March 9 and July 3,

1849. Like others, he found it to be difficult work that took a long time to complete. He reported on one occasion having spent the entire morning washing two shirts, two pairs of drawers, and a handkerchief and still indicated they would not pass inspection. Later he managed to wash two shirts and a pair of stockings in only two hours. On another occasion he said washing clothes was the hardest work he had ever done. Toward the end of the voyage, he was able to report that he got his clothes "very clean."[8]

Anne (Willson) Booth provided some female perspective on the matter of washing clothes by the men on board the ship *Andalusia* while they were sailing between Valparaiso and San Francisco. She noted the women were amused by the fuss and awkwardness the men displayed in washing and ironing their clothes but added they did it "so good humoredly." As the men expected to do their own washing in California, Booth presumed the practice would help them after they arrived. Booth noted that they learned in Valparaiso it cost eight dollars per dozen items to have them washed in San Francisco and that their stay in Valparaiso had been too short for the men to have their clothes washed there.[9]

At home males could always depend upon wives and mothers or perhaps tailors to repair and make clothes for them, but at sea they had to do the mending and the making of clothes themselves, or they did not get done. A few passengers wrote about making and repairing garments. J. L. Akerman, a passenger in the bark *Daniel Webster,* reported he needed gear for protection in the rainy weather and purchased oilcloth pants and a hat, but he was making an oilcloth jacket. Joseph Augustine Benton, a passenger in the ship *Edward Everett,* mentioned on one occasion he was "preparing for small jobs of sewing." John Brannan, a passenger in the bark *Norwich,* wrote his wife that he had made a blunder in cutting out cotton drill for a pair of drawers. He discovered when he began to sew that he had cut both of the legs for one of his legs. Since he was a novice at the sewing business, he was not worried, but if his wife had made the blunder he would have been concerned. William M. Hatch made frequent mention of individuals on board the schooner *Damariscove* making trousers of the duck they had purchased for making tents. He also noted that two people were making "a pair of indispensibles." Enos Christman in the ship *Euphrasia* wrote that he "did considerable mending this forenoon and have much more to do."[10] Several passengers made passing references to darning socks and mending clothes by either themselves or others as they approached San Francisco. Seemingly they put off to the last minute these necessary chores.

235

Passengers who were members of organized companies and who were independent individuals were sometimes organized into groups or messes for convenience in eating and performing occasional chores. Jonathan Frost Locke, a passenger in the brig *Sea Eagle* in which all passengers seem to have been independent individuals, reported they were divided into messes of ten members each for convenience in eating. Their cook failed "through ignorance" and the steward "almost through laziness." Therefore the passengers had to assume the responsibilities of cooking and serving the food. The messes took turns supplying two persons, one to cook and one to serve. He reported his mess had the duty for a fortnight early in the voyage, but he was not asked to do any of the work. Near the end of the voyage, however, he served for a week in the galley and added it was quite a challenge due to the poor quality and limited quantities of the molasses, flour, beans, and pork from which he had to prepare meals for 83 men. Locke also noted that the passengers frequently had to break out the hold to bring up various items of food to be cooked. He indicated it was a difficult job, as they had to remove all their chests and take up the temporary deck before they could get access to the supplies stored below their living quarters. Although it was heavy work, the passengers did not mind it because they thought the work would help "keep off the scurvy." Jared C. Nash, a passenger in the bark *Belgrade,* reported that each week three different passengers from a mess took their turn to wait on the table, carry the food from the galley to the cabin, and wash dishes. They also had to clean the cabin three times during that week. Two other passengers pumped the ship regularly. John Van Dyke, a passenger in the ship *Tahmaroo,* reported early in the voyage from New York that "a committee was appointed to organize a night watch to guard against fire." He made no further mention of this activity.[11]

Soon after the schooner *General Morgan* sailed from New York, the members of the Connecticut Mining and Trading Company were divided into the starboard, larboard, and middle watches, who then served two watches of four hours each day. Somewhat later a passenger noted that each "watch furnishes a man at the wheel during the day, and we all occasionally lend a hand, but in general we have nothing to do." Moses Cogswell, a member of the Roxbury Sagamore Company in the ship *Sweden,* reported that his week as steward in the vessel was not a "pleasurable job for there is always some fault or other to be found" in the quality or the quantity served to passengers. The Roxbury Sagamore Company was only one of several companies in the *Sweden.* It is uncertain if he served everyone on board or only members of his company. Joseph Augustine Benton, a member of the Boston and California Mining and Trading Joint Stock Company sailing from Boston in the ship *Edward Everett,* mentioned a variety of duties to which he was assigned. Early in the voyage he spent several days helping organize the company's library. Later he picked over beans in the galley, peeled potatoes for breakfast, picked over raw potatoes, and served as captain of his mess of ten individuals. In that capacity he served as the "maid of all work" and noted it was a "rather weighty" responsibility. Presumably he served as captain of the company once every ten weeks. The members of the New York Mining Company in the bark *Strafford* appear not to have had regular duties but were occasionally assigned specific tasks. Company member Griffith Meredith reported early in the voyage that he and two other men opened the hatches and took out the lime that the captain and some members feared would ignite if it got wet because of the heavy seas they had experienced since sailing. He noted it was hard work, for they knew only that it was stored "somewhere in the hold." They found it all dry but still threw overboard all but two barrels, "which was saved for the assayers business." Somewhat later he was assigned to assist in taking up the oilcloth on the cabin floor, as it made the floor so slippery "we could hardly walk." The members of the Salem Mechanics Trading and Mining Association in the ship *Crescent* also seem not to have had any regular duties, but they did assist in making repairs to the vessel after she collided with the ship *Charles* while some of the passengers in the two vessels were attempting to visit each other when they were in a heavy sea. There were several organized companies on board the ship *Andalusia,* and they too did not have regular duties, but they also assisted in repairing the masts, spars, and rigging damaged during a storm in the Pacific Ocean.[12]

Those passengers who were members of organized companies had to attend meetings that were held with varying frequencies. Some groups met at the call of the officers while others met at regularly scheduled intervals such as monthly, quarterly, or semiannually. Some of the meetings were quiet with little business, and others were stormy when attempts were made to amend constitutions or bylaws or to dissolve the company. Many passengers made occasional passing references to meetings of the company and sometimes described what actions were taken. Other passengers regularly made note of meetings and of any actions taken.

Thomas Reid kept a diligent record of the actions of the eighty-five members of the Narragansett Mining and Trading Company as they sailed from Boston to San Francisco. He wrote of the actions taken in many meetings and about many rumors of possible actions circulating among the members between March 24 and September 15, 1849. Some of Reid's comments shed light on the frenzied activities of the time in forming companies and getting underway; others reveal the trivial nature of some meetings; and still others relate to the serious nature of some meetings. His first reference to a meeting was more than a month after they sailed from Boston and just after they departed from Fayal. The purpose of the meeting was to have the company members sign the constitution and bylaws and to appoint a committee to examine the books. Probably under more normal circumstances each member of the company would have signed the constitution and bylaws at the time they joined. Five or six members refused to sign until they had seen the committee report. The committee reported on March 28 that a few dollars could not be accounted for. A few days later every member who wanted a certificate of membership was given one. In late May, Reid noted some talk of some members forming a separate company and surmised that they would divide into three or four smaller companies before they arrived in California. The company held its regular monthly meeting on June 8 at which some concern was expressed over the amount of beef consumed. The next day they had a called meeting and decided to ask the captain if he would allow them to appoint two men of the company to weigh out the provisions daily and keep a regular account of provisions consumed each week. Capt. E. B. Morgan was not in favor of such action but said he would not object if the company really wanted to do so. They decided not to take the action. Captain Morgan later told some members that in the future the company could hold only its regular monthly meetings. This informal ruling was soon ignored, as on June 26 they had a meeting to investigate the theft of a keg of wine from the room of a board of directors member named Chase. A committee appointed to search the ship failed to find the wine. As they approached Talcahuano in early July, Reid noted much discussion and argument about dissolving the company but added he was unsure of what would actually happen. While in Talcahuano they had an offer of seven thousand dollars for the *Velasco,* and the board of directors voted four to three to sell her. The members also voted forty-three to thirty-one in favor of selling. Part of the deal required them to transport eight men to California. The members could take as much freight as they wanted at $27.50 per ton. Reid voted against the sale, as the original bylaws of the company allowed the members thirty days to remove their belongings and freight from the vessel whereas the new owners would give them only five days to do so. Reid thought it would cost a great deal to store their things on shore. He reported that some of the members who opposed the sale called on the U.S. consul in Talcahuano to see if he would stop the sale of the *Velasco,* but he "laughed at them and said that the ship was not worth three thousand dollars and they ought to be glad they could get so much for her." After they left Talcahuano, Reid noted that some members consumed "freely of ardent spirits" in Talcahuano in violation of the company bylaws but nothing was done, as a majority of the members were involved in drinking alcohol. Someone attempted unsuccessfully to initiate a temperance movement on board the vessel. Talk of dissolving the company continued on board. More excitement was created on August 8, when the treasurer Elisha Bucklin expressed the opinion that if the company dissolved, those men who were on board as substitutes of members could not receive the members' portions of provisions and other things. The substitutes signed papers to that effect in Pawtucket, and the treasurer had those papers. Only members were entitled to the value of the provisions and other things owned by the company. The excitement over substitutes subsided as did the talk of dividing the company for a few days. On August 16 they held a meeting and decided to build an additional six gold washers while sailing to California. The next day one of the directors posted a proposal on the mainmast to alter the constitution regarding the division of profits of the company by changing from an annual to a monthly schedule and by deducting from the share of any member who was absent during working hours an amount proportionate to the time he was absent. They held a meeting the next day and rejected all motions to amend the constitution. A few days later Reid noted that members were no longer making things for the company but instead were making tools and equipment for themselves. By the end of August he was of the opinion that dissolving the company was the best thing that could happen because of the great dissatisfaction that prevailed throughout the membership. He noted that already seven or eight new companies had been formed and that he had joined one that would have twelve or fourteen members. On September 3 the company had its monthly meeting at which thirty-one members petitioned to be released and given their shares of the provisions and other things when they arrived. There was strong opposition to the resolution, and a heated debate ensued. A substitute resolution was introduced to dissolve the company as soon as they arrived in California and received their provisions and cargo. After all the business of the company was settled, every member could take his share and go wherever he desired. A vote on that resolution was not taken until September 7 at which time fifty-four voted in favor, twenty-one against, and ten members did not vote. Reid later noted there was more peace on board now that the company had decided to dissolve. On September 10 the directors decided to divide some tent cloth among the various new companies. The cloth had originally been purchased for making tents for all the members of the Narragansett Mining and Trading Company. During that meeting the secretary resigned in a huff over some criticism, but the directors smoothed out the difficulty, and the secretary agreed to continue in that capacity. They also voted to divide all tools and equipment before they arrived in California, and that division was carried out over the next five days. That ends Reid's description of the turbulent experiences of the members of the Narragansett Mining and Trading Company on board the ship *Velasco* although they did not arrive in San Francisco until October 17, 1849.[13]

Three passengers in the ship *Crescent* mentioned meetings. Charles Henry Harvey noted at least seventeen meetings between December 13, 1849, and May 6, 1850; William Graves noted a meeting about entering St. Catherines Island and the Island of Juan Fernandez, a meeting about instructing the head steward and allocating molasses to be made into candy to celebrate George Washington's birthday, the semiannual meeting to elect officers, a meeting to hear a report on the books of the company, and one monthly meeting scheduled for the first Monday of every month; and William Berry Cross mentioned only the semiannual business meeting to elect officers, but he also recorded actions in San Francisco that resulted in the dissolution of the Salem Mechanics Trading and Mining Association. Harvey reported on December 13, 1849, they chose four stewards to "see to the tables and give better liveing than we have yet had" and agreed to pay them fifty dollars for the voyage. On December 26 they appointed three men to take care of the hogs and agreed to fine anyone who smoked abaft the mainmast a dollar. Two days later they decided to fine anyone who smoked between decks a dollar and appointed a head steward at $150 for the voyage. On January 7, 1850 they voted thirty-seven to twenty-two to sell raisins at cost. On January 26 they voted to go to St. Catherines Island. On February 7 they voted to give the head steward "the whole control of galley and provisions." The next day they voted to adopt a bill of fare that listed all the food to be served each meal every day of the week. On February 22 they voted to use five gallons of molasses to make candy to be divided equally among the members. A motion to give each member three pounds of raisins was defeated. One member moved that the proceedings of the meeting not be recorded, as he was ashamed of them, but his motion was ruled unconstitutional. The regularly monthly meeting of Monday, March 4 was adjourned "to the first fare [fair] day." On March 12 they met all morning and two hours in the afternoon while they argued about stopping at Juan Fernandez Island or Valparaiso. They met on this topic again the next day but adjourned until the sixteenth. There was some disagreement among the members over whether they had enough water to reach San Francisco without stopping. Their semiannual business meeting was held on April 1, 1850, at which time they decided to reduce the number of directors from seven to three and elected new officers and directors. A week later they voted to divide the figs equally among the company and learned that their books "show a complicated mess and we cannot tell the right from the wrong" other than that they were "over 1350 dollars in debt" when they left Salem, Massachusetts. During the next two days they met again and ultimately decided not to alter their constitution. On May 6 they voted that "each member that did not fetch his two barrels shall have five dollars paid back to him." This apparently is a rebate for those members who did not bring the two barrels of freight each member was permitted to bring without charge. They arrived in San Francisco on May 26 and two days later voted "to give our board of managers the power to dispose of our cargo at their own discretion and to sell the steam boat for 20000 dollars or more." They had been offered $14,000 for it. Two days later they sold it for $15,400. On June 3 the directors sold the *Crescent* for $11,250. The directors also continued to sell the cargo, but Capt. John Madison stopped the sale until he was paid for his services in bringing the ship to California. On June 7 the directors declared a dividend of $225 for each member. The Salem Mechanics Trading and Mining Association held its last meeting on June 8, 1850, at which time they "Voted to desolve the company as soon as the business is settled."[14]

Members of the Boston and California Mining and Trading Joint Stock Company sailing in the ship *Edward Everett* apparently met less often than did those in the ship *Crescent* and the bark *Velasco*, but some of their meetings seem to have had greater meaning. The first meeting on board the *Edward Everett* was on January 27 at which time they elected a librarian and an assistant librarian and voted "on certain questions of membership." They also passed a few resolutions of thanks to individuals. On April 6 and 7 they held long meetings at which they discussed and voted on the guilt or innocence and punishment of two members who allegedly broke into the pantry. Both were found guilty of theft, one by a vote of 115 to 25 and the other by a vote of 90 to 49. They voted 98 to 10 to expel the first from the company but decided not to expel the second, as he was considered only an accomplice. The tenth section of the company bylaws provided that anyone guilty of theft would be expelled. On May 16 they met to consider a petition by thirty-three members to dissolve the company and divide the property upon arriving in San Francisco. Substitute motions were made, but no one spoke in favor of them. They voted by a large majority not to dissolve the company. A committee appointed to investigate charges against one of the directors met at some length during the next two days. The members voted sixty-nine to forty-one with thirty-nine not voting to acquit the director. Joseph Augustine Benton noted it was "Bad business, badly done!!"[15]

Griffith Meredith wrote about ten meetings of the one hundred members of the New York Mining Company in the bark *Strafford* between February 14 and July 2, 1849. On February 14, their twelfth day at sea, they elected a purveyor and two assistants to keep record of all provisions used and selected a court of referees consisting of one member from each squad, or mess, to settle disputes between members. At the regular first Monday of the month meeting on March 5 the members heard reports and discussed the ventilation of the cabin and berths and amendments to articles 26 and 27 of their constitution. Two weeks later they met again to discuss and vote upon the proposed amendments to the constitution. The amendments did not pass, as they received only sixty-three votes, and seventy-five were necessary to change the constitution. Meredith noted the "meeting adjourned with a good deal of warmth," but he never reported the content of articles 26 and 27 and the amendments. On March 27 they met to hear committee reports and a report of the treasurer and to elect replacements for company officers who had resigned "in consequence of some little difficulty of no great importance." Four days later the president called the members together to elect officers for the next three months. Meredith reported the results and indicated there had been a considerable amount of electioneering that reminded him of elections in New York although they did not have any fights on board the *Strafford*. Amendments to articles 26 and 27 of the constitution were considered again at the regular first Monday of the month meeting on April 2 but were initially defeated. Then two members "divided the amendments to cover the grounds sought for and they passed it almost unanimous." Amendments to articles 4 and 11 of the constitution were considered at the regular first Monday of the month meeting on June 4 and were defeated. On June 14 the company met to form a military company and choose officers from whom they could learn military tactics that might be necessary in California. They had military drills for several days thereafter. June 30 was the date for the next election of a president, vice president, treasurer, secretary, finance committee, eight directors, and a purveyor and two assistants for the next quarter. The electioneering started at least as early as June 29, when several of the aspirants gave speeches and received "cheer after cheer." The newly elected officers took office at the next first Monday of the month meeting on July 2. Several gave speeches, and various committees presented reports. After the conclusion of the meeting, they "got up a dance which all might enjoy themselves well."[16]

Henry H. Hyde Jr. mentioned eight meetings of the New England and California Trading and Mining Association on board the ship *Lenore* between February 12 and June 22, 1849, but only two were significant. On June 4 and 5 they had a lengthy discussions about amending the constitution. Apparently there was no provision in the original for amending it. They finally agreed that they could amend the constitution with a two-thirds vote. One of the directors seems to have taken a major role in getting the constitution amended, as there "had been dishonest proceedings in the board while at Boston," and "the corruption did not stop there." Some of the articles of the constitution appear to have been subject to double meanings. On June 11 they met to consider charges brought by one director against three other directors, one of whom was on board and two of whom remained in Boston. The complainant indicated the vice president had "intended to defraud the company out of $1500" and to sell the company an old vessel in which he held a share. He also indicated that three directors had run "roughshod over the Association."[17]

The two passengers in the bark *Hannah Sprague* whose journals exist seem to have been members of different joint stock companies. Alfred Wheeler, who was one of the twenty-nine members of the California Mining Association, did not mention any meetings of that company. John Henry Corneilson, who was one of thirty-one members of the New York Commercial and Mining Company, mentioned two meetings, one of which occurred before they arrived in San Francisco. On November 1 he wrote that they passed a resolution which provided that any member who left the company would forfeit all his interest. On December 22 they met for what must have been the final meeting of the company. They passed seven resolutions, all relating in some way to the dissolution of the New York Commercial and Mining Company. It appears that this company owned the bark *Hannah Sprague* and was in the process of selling her. Corneilson obtained from the secretary a record of the assets and liabilities of the company. After deducting the liabilities from the assets, they were left with $10,119.48 to be divided among the members. Each person was due to receive $337.31. Their original shares had cost $600.[18]

Many other passengers made references to meetings in their journals, but this sampling should be sufficient to illustrate that the companies considered important issues as well as trivial matters during their voyages. These examples also help to confirm that most, if not all, the joint stock companies experienced difficulties and disbanded before or almost immediately after they arrived in California. There is evidence that some individuals took advantage of their leadership roles as well as evidence that there was democratic government in some of the companies.

Company members had many other duties and responsibilities in preparing for their arrival in California and their mining activities. They often made many of their own tools and mining equipment as well as their cooking and eating utensils. A large number of members described these activities in their journals. Some of the joint stock companies recruited individuals with certain skills so that they could make the needed tools, equipment, and utensils. Among the craftsmen included in many companies were blacksmiths, tinsmiths, house and ship carpenters, painters, lathe operators, joiners, and engineers. Others such as sailors or mariners possessed a variety of skills that could be put to good use. It is likely that some of the farmers possessed a variety of necessary skills. Those who possessed the necessary and desired skills could likely teach others the basic rudiments needed by the clerks and others to help make needed items. From dozens of passengers' journals it is clear that they made tents, tent poles, tent pegs, mallets for driving tent pegs, and tent ropes. They also made rowboats, sailboats, steamboats, steam engines, oars, sails, spars, blocks, belaying pins, and ropes and lines for rigging. Items associated with cooking and eating included pots, pans, kettles, cups, wooden salt cellars, rolling pins, and fishing nets and seines. Items relating to protection included knives, sheathes for knives, dirks, shot, shot pouches, rifle balls, powder horns, powder flasks, and leather holsters. Items related to mining included picks, hoes, and handles for shovels as well as money belts, gold washers, wheelbarrows, carts, and mud scows for traveling shallow waters. Other miscellaneous items included hammocks, clothes bags, oil cans, buckets, boxes, and wagons. Passengers in the ship *Mount Vernon* made a small schooner and sails for use in California. Those in the ship *Crescent* and the barks *Anna Reynolds* and *Helen Augusta* made small steamships including the steam engines needed to propel them. Passengers in the ship *Edward Everett* built five boats and a scow as well as a steam engine, and the sailors built one boat.[19]

All this activity helped relieve the monotony of the long and tedious voyages, tended to keep the men's minds off the delays they experienced in getting into San Francisco, and provided them some exercise for their muscles that probably had become soft during the voyage. That exercise was needed to prepare them for the hard work of getting to the mines and working in the minefields digging up gravel and sand in which gold grains and nuggets were found, swirling rocks and sand around in pans, turning cranks of gold washers, hauling rocks and sand to sluices for washing gold, and other activities associated with getting the gold. Those who did not go to the goldfields immediately or at all also needed hardened muscles to do the building, lifting, hauling, and shoveling to unload their own vessels and to construct buildings and streets and roads in San Francisco and Sacramento. Even those who became shopkeepers needed strength to haul in the tools, provisions, clothing, alcohol, tobacco, and whatever else they sold in their stores.

10

First Impressions

The bark *San Francisco* arrived in San Francisco from Beverly, Massachusetts, on January 11, 1850, with the forty members of the Beverly Joint Stock San Francisco Company. Passenger Isaac W. Baker wrote that when he viewed the port after they anchored, he thought it was "A beautiful country, romantic scenery—excellent harbor, a fine climate and plenty of game.—This is the place for <u>me</u> in the winter season." Later the same day he recorded a different impression of the place "five minutes after being landed on shore." He then thought "It is the most degraded, immoral, uncivilized and dirty place that can be imagined, and the sooner we are away from here the better for us."[1] It was not at all unusual for passengers to be delighted with the scenery, the bird life, the hillsides and mountains, and the green grass but have a different impression of San Francisco after they had visited on land.

John Ross Browne, who traveled to California in the ship *Pacific* as an agent of the treasury department charged with preventing the desertion of American sailors from their vessels, spent a few days traveling around San Francisco before recording his first impressions. He provided a general summary of conditions and some thoughts and reservations about California in a letter to his wife. Browne first noted that the glowing accounts of the goldfields published in the newspapers at home "are, for the most part, utterly rediculous" and added that "thousands of people who have no other means of judging are grossly deceived by them." He felt that "A young man having no family ties may do well to come here" but it was "the greatest folly" for anyone with "a good business at home, or who has any prospect of doing well, to sacrifice his property and separate himself from his family on the uncertain contingency of making money in California." Although he admitted that occasionally someone discovered a fortune in gold, "hundreds barely make a living." The risk to their lives and health was not worth it even to those who could clear expenses and "return in one or two years with a competency." While the wages for common laborers and craftsmen were much higher in California than at home, the expenses of living there were so much higher that few of them could ever get ahead and save money. Browne noted he had "met hundreds who lament in doleful terms ever having left home." Other factors against coming to California included "sickness and suffering, the terrible hardship, the depraved society, the anxiety of mind, the constant wear and tear of body." Browne noted further that "the uncertainty of ever reaching home, the expense of getting here and back, the disappointments, are all lost sight of." Browne also wrote of the "cold, damp, foggy, and windy" weather, and this was in the dry season, as he also mentioned the great quantity of dust that filled the town. He added that gambling was "carried on to a horrible extent." He saw "Hells of all sorts . . . throughout the town" and thought it was "awful to witness the scenes that take place there daily and nightly." He had never seen "vice in a more disgusting form" and wondered "What pecuniary considerations would compensate a man of family for the trials he must necessarily endure at such a place?"[2]

One of the first things new arrivals wrote about was what they saw in and around San Francisco and the harbor. They noted the magnificence of the harbor, immense flocks of birds, the large number of seals in the harbor, the cattle and horses grazing on the hillsides, the number of vessels anchored there, the mix of peoples in the city, and the effects of seasonal weather changes. One of the first things the arriving Argonauts sought to learn was how much success earlier arrivals and those who had been there before the discovery of gold had experienced in finding gold. Passengers also frequently recorded the prices of wages, accommodations, and many other things they bought or sold, recorded their visits to the post office, commented on the care of the ill and injured, reported on a low crime rate and severe punishment for anyone caught stealing, expressed shock and amazement at the gambling they witnessed, and lamented the shortage of churches.

Benjamin Bailey in the ship *Sweden* noted he never wished to see "a more beautiful harbor" and added, "It would be impossible for me to undertake to pen down with pen & ink the scenery at the Entrance of the harbor." He was impressed with mountains that had "a Coppery appearance" and extended "as far as the Eye can reach." Jonathan Frost Locke, who arrived in the brig *Sea Eagle*, indicated he would "make an attempt" to describe what he saw but admitted he could not do it "very perfectly." He noted that the earth was "of volcanic origin" and was "piled up in rounded and steep peaks," some of which were barren, but most of which were "covered with stinted shrubbery and vegetation." Some of the region was "good grazing pasturage for sheep." He noted the valleys would "not produce much without irrigation" and that there were "but few patches cultivated near" San Francisco. A passenger in the bark *Anna Reynolds* seemed surprised that the "valleys look fertile altho it is November." Another in the bark *Gold Hunter* noted the harbor was "surrounded by hills and dales of great beauty" and added that the hills were "of gentle ascent" and "presented the appearance of a smooth mowing field in the spring of the year when it is completely clothed in green." Jacob D. B. Stillman, who arrived in the ship *Pacific,* was delighted with "the rich green" appearance of the hills and "the numerous cattle and horses grazing" on them. Alexander F. Spear in the brig *Perfect* also commented on the "very green" hills, noted the absence of trees and bushes, and indicated the "Mostly clear land that looks like fields of grain about six inches high." Anderson Hollingsworth in the ship *Daniel Webster* simply called it a "magnificent harbour." Occasionally, however, someone had a different opinion. A passenger in the brig *General Worth* presented his view of San Francisco. "There it lies! But with all the glamour our wildest enthusiasm can paint it, it is yet only an uninviting stretch of waste land, and sand-banks."[3]

Others wrote about what they saw in the water and the sky. One was "delighted at the innumerable number of birds large & small, immense flocks of the Pelican." Another noted the "immense quantities of Birds swiming with their young." Yet another mentioned not only the birds but also the seals that lined the harbor. He also referred to the guano several feet thick that was "heaped upon the tops of rocks & islands." William S. Hull in the ship *Jane Parker* mentioned being "surprised at the number of Ducks on the Water." A passenger in the bark *Hannah Sprague* reported seeing "flocks of Pelican and ducks" as well as "flocks of seal . . . upon the rocks" and added he could hear the seals barking.[4]

Numerous passengers wrote about the number of vessels in the harbor, and some gave estimates of the number that undoubtedly varied depending upon the time at which those passengers arrived since vessels were constantly arriving at San Francisco, and few of them left. A passenger in the ship *York* wrote, "What a forest of masts. O I wish there was less excitement" as they sailed into the harbor. He then added, "I would like to write it all out, but good bye for two years to writing," as he intended to head directly to the mines and would be too busy to do more than "merely put down heads of suggested thots." Other passengers gave widely different estimates of the number of vessels. One in the ship *Balance* estimated there were between three and five hundred in the harbor and as many more up the Sacramento River. Jonathan Frost Locke thought there were "three hundred sail anchored in the harbour" and they enlivened "the scenery beyond description." William S. Hull noted that "Every little cove had from one to Eight large vessels anchored in it" and they all appeared to be "totally deserted by their Crews" except one or two that were flying the American flag. When they had sailed "some four or five miles" into the harbor, they saw an "immense number of vessels laying at anchor, large and small, mostly the former." A passenger in the bark *Maria* noted some vessels had been "run ashore & converted into boarding houses." A. Bailey reported there were "over 400 large Square rigged vessels lying at anchor" in April 1850 and a large number of other vessels had been "hauled in to the Shore and roofed over like a house having their anchors buried in the ground on shore." John Henry Corneilson in the bark *Hanna Sprague* noted the "shipping was immense, a perfect forest of Masts, outdoing N.Y. almost double." A passenger in the ship *America* noted the number of vessels in San Francisco also reminded him of New York and that they came from all nations "from Oregon and Northwest, down through 'Spanish Main' S.A., United States to Pasamaquaddy; from all parts of Europe, and some from China." He added that the "styles of nautical architecture" ranged "from the 'gundaloe' to the 'long low rakish looking dark schooner,' up to the magnificent ocean steamer, and from the Chinese Junk to the almost perfect symetry and proportion of some of our men-of-war." Richard Hale, who arrived in May 1850, estimated there "must be close to a thousand vessels at anchor in the bay."[5]

Several passengers noted the great mix of people they encountered in San Francisco. Some noted running into or looking up acquaintances from home who had come out in earlier vessels. Charles Williams went on shore soon after the ship *Pacific* anchored in San Francisco and quickly met a friend whom he identified only as "young Mead," and soon thereafter he met Mead's father. He also noted what he saw was "a most ludicrous singular and grotesque scene" that included "groups of all nations" including "Yankees, English, Chilanos, Spaniards, Mexicans &c and Chinese." Thomas Reid also noted witnessing "all nations collected here" and listed Indians, South Americans, Spaniards, Mexicans, Yankees, English, French, and Chinese. When J. Haskell Stearns visited Portsmouth Square, he was "surrounded by a crowd composed of men from almost every nation & class under the heavens" and mentioned that "American,

English, French, Dutch, Mexicans, Indians, Chilanos, Sandwich Islanders, and Chinese in all varieties of dress were mingled together, bending over the tables and watching the turning of the cards with eager curiosity." John Henry Corneilson mentioned being "besieged with people of all kinds" and referred to Sandwich Islanders, Chinese, South Americans, Indians, Californians, Poles, Irish, Russians, Germans, French, Mexicans, Dutch, and Americans. William S. Hull concluded that San Francisco "beats all I have ever beheld. . . . Men of all ages, and all countries seem to be here assembled together, the most graffic pen that ever soiled paper could not portray it truly."[6]

Much has been written about criminal groups such as the Sydney Ducks and the vigilantes who tracked down and punished criminals in early San Francisco. Thus people commonly assume that there had always been lots of crime in the city. Argonauts who arrived in 1849 and early 1850 reported the opposite. They saw a virtual absence of crime and attributed that to the swift punishment of the few who engaged in crime. Jacob D. B. Stillman seemed pleased to note just after arriving in the ship *Pacific*, "instead of robbery and anarchy, as we expected, there is the best of order." He added that "millions of dollars worth of goods" were "lying about the hills . . . in the open air, without a guard, and the choisest goods are stored in tents; yet no one thinks of losing anything by theft" and that the "same state of things is said to exist throughout the country." After arriving in the ship *Daniel Webster*, Anderson Hollingsworth and some fellow passengers moved on land and lived in a tent. He reported their neighbors were "so honest that you can leave anything upon the beach or anywhere else without fear of their being stolen." He also emphasized that the laws were "very strict and punishment severe, if theft is detected." On his first day in San Francisco, Walter Balfour Gould wrote, "I never was so astonished as I have been today. Gold is thrown about in the loosest manner. Tents are left half the night and thousands of dollars in them. Nothing is disturbed and every thing seems orderly and quiet as in Boston." The next day he noted, "Lynch law is the only law here." John McCrackan also implied that "lynch law" was prevalent in the area when he noted that "If a man is detected stealing he is either shot or hanged immediately & the one who shoots him goes before the Alcalde & with his witness proves the act, & the judge dismisses the case." Because of this he felt there was no "anxiety" about leaving clothes, money, or anything else "unguarded." Then he asked, "strange is it not?" Charles Williams, another passenger in the ship *Pacific*, indicated that "the utmost order prevails" since the authorities had caught and "punished severely" and "put a stop to" the "troubles" caused by some "regulators who called themselves the hounds." Thomas Reid wrote on his first day in San Francisco that the laws were "very strict for theft," as they "cut the ears off for the first offense" and hang second offenders "with out ceremony." Moses Cogswell, a passenger in the ship *Sweden,* had a slightly different idea of the punishment. He reported the punishment for theft was "to be sent home in a 'Man of War,' which is the worst that can be inflicted except, perhaps, Death."[7]

The time of the year passengers arrived in San Francisco had a direct bearing upon what they thought of the place. During the hot summer season it was dry and dusty, but in the wet season there was lots of mud. Henry H. Hyde Jr. reported in early July 1849 that San Francisco was a rather "uncomfortable place when the dust blows from the hills and streets to fill your eyes." John Ross Browne noted in late August 1849 the city was "about the most miserable spot" he had seen, as it was "filled with dust during the greater part of the day." Moses Cogswell noted in August 1849 that "There cannot be a dirtier place than this." He felt it was "usless to attempt to wear good clothes," as the sand and dust filled the air and covered everything every afternoon. Thus, "in order to keep clean" people ventured "out only in the forenoon." At a different season of the year, Charles Goodall reported in January 1850 that there was "a continual scrabble of passing persons" moving about on business even though the mud was up to their knees. More than two months later George Osborne Wilson also wrote about trudging through knee-deep mud. In December 1849 Robert La Motte asked his father to send him some boots that would come "six inches above the knee," as he could not cross the street without getting knee deep in mud. A month later he reported that "nine tenths of all the streets in San Francisco" were in worse condition "than any hundred yards of road" at home in Delaware County, Pennsylvania. He added that he witnessed a man who "was about half drunk" attempt to cross Montgomery Street, "where there were no bushes laid down nor boards to walk on." He first "floundered in up to his waist; then up to his neck" and would have gone even deeper "had not some persons thrown him a rope." La Motte added he had frequently witnessed mules and horses "up to their bellies in mud, while their drivers were endeavoring to extricate them by putting pieces of scantling under them." He concluded, however, that the rains and mud were "not half so bad as the snows, sleets, and freezes" of Pennsylvania. C. W. Haskins described a unique "newly-constructed sidewalk" of about seventy-five yards. The first portion consisted of one-hundred-pound sacks of Chilean flour. The middle portion was made of a "row of large cooking stoves," but he noted one had to be careful walking on them, as some of the covers had been "accidentally torn off." The last portion was made of "a couple row of boxes of tobacco, of large size." He noted that "In any portion of the earth except California, this sidewalk would have been considered a very extravagant piece of work, hardly excelled by the golden pavements in the new Jerusalem." At that time in California, flour, cooking stoves, and tobacco were considerably cheaper than lumber, which was in "the greatest demand, selling in some instances at $600" per thousand feet.[8]

Since nearly everyone who sailed to California in 1849 did so in order to obtain as much gold as possible and return home to live in comfort, they wanted to learn as quickly as possible how much gold was available or at least how much they might reasonably expect to gather for themselves. Charles Henry Randall wrote his family three days after arriving in the ship *Samoset* that he had heard "every kind of story, good, bad, and indifferent" but added that "nearly all the miners that come down here return again in a few days." This presumably meant that they were finding gold. He did caution his family not to "believe any stories that say a man cannot make money and make it fast in this Territory" and added that from what he had seen he was "perfectly satisfied that I shall get what I come for." Although he noted in his first letter, "Very few have left California because they could not pick up the lumps off top the ground without labour," he reported in a second letter that some of those who came to California were "astonished to find no gold lying in plain sight upon the ground." Randall thought "such men . . . should stay at home and not expose their weakness" as had thousands who had come "hoping if not expecting that they might get rich with their hands in their pockets." He added that California was "the working mans country and very few others will make much money except heavy and wealthy speculators who have means enough to control their business." Charles S. Putnam wrote his sister that "the news . . . from the mines is about the same as you get at home." He added that some who had returned to San Francisco from the mines reported great success while others reported having trouble making ends meet. Putnam also reported that many miners quit working their holes too quickly and repeated a story he had heard of a group that quit on their hole and went elsewhere. While they were moving, one of they party became ill, and they stopped while he recovered. During the wait they commenced digging in someone else's abandoned hole and took out between five and six ounces per person per day. Henry H. Hyde Jr. seemed delighted to note that miners "continually bring" gold "from the mines. The news is that it is <u>plenty</u>." Christian Miller wrote his parents after arriving in the ship *Mason* in late October 1849 that the letters that had been published in the newspapers at home "were not exagerated. It is all truth." He had talked with miners who assured him that "every man that is industrious can get an ounce a day, without luck" and added that there was "a lump of gold weighing 5 lbs." in one of the hotels. Alexander F. Spear did not discuss the activities at the mines in his journal when he arrived, but he did note that "There is one lump in a hotel which weighs 32 lbs.," implying thereby that quite large nuggets were to be found in California.[9]

Most of the passengers who arrived from their East Coast homes of solid wood, brick, and stone were sometimes shocked at what passed for buildings in San Francisco. Other passengers sometimes saw things a bit differently depending in part upon when they arrived. Albert Lyman, who arrived in August 1849, noticed the "constant sound of the hammer" and was seemingly pleased that "Quite a number of smart looking Yankee frame buildings are seen, some in progress, and others already completed." He also noted a few old Spanish adobe houses. About two months later J. Haskell Stearns reported San Francisco had a population of twenty to thirty thousand souls and described it as "<u>such</u> a town probably was never seen before." He thought it looked like "a large army had stopped in its march at some little village & had formed an encampment for temporary occupation." There were houses of "wooden frames & covered with canvass, tin, iron, or copper. Shanties & cabins of all imaginable forms & sizes." There were also "tents of canvass & india-rubber cloth by thousands and "here & there a building of respectable appearance." In April 1850 A. Bailey reported San Francisco had a floating population of 175,000. He noted that "Every body is flocking here, and the <u>canvass</u> tents as thick as would be if an army of 200,000 men" had moved in "all over the shores and ajacent hills." Bailey felt that such inadequate housing and other conditions caused "a good deal of Suffering here" and concluded, "Indeed there is a <u>dark side to this</u> golden Picture!"[10]

One thing that the new arrivals quickly learned and commented on regularly was the price of everything including food, supplies, lodging, and services. William S. Hull reported that a pilot asked "<u>only</u> . . . ten dollars the foot" to take the ship *Jane Parker* to her anchorage. He noted this would take only two hours, and the cost would be $150. Thus the charge must have been per foot of draft rather than length. A severe windstorm blew the ship *Arkansas* into some rocks, causing some damage to the hull and major damage to the rigging the day she anchored in San Francisco Bay. The next morning Capt. Philip W. Shepeard sought a steamboat to tow the ship ashore. The cheapest steamboat was $5000. He finally found a man who had two or three small steamboats who would do the two-hour job for $1200. Passengers in the ships *Brooklyn* and *America* and the barks *Anna Reynolds* and *Maria* reported being quoted prices between one and three dollars to be rowed to shore and an equal amount to be rowed back.[11]

Many passengers who wrote in their diaries or in letters commented upon the prices of foods and other necessities, labor, and real estate. A few contrasted the California prices with those at home although that was hardly necessary, as those at home knew the prices there. Argonauts also wrote of the fluctuations in the prices depending in part upon the quantity of a given commodity that was available at the time. J. Haskell Stearns, who arrived in the bark *Belvidera,* provided prices for several items at three different times. John McCrackan, who arrived in the ship *Balance,* and Robert La Motte, who arrived in the bark *Maria,* gave prices for yet other times. These prices are presented in the table below.

Several passengers wrote about prices of other commodities, living accommodations, places for doing business, real estate, and other items. Robert La Motte noted a head of cabbage and a turnip were five dollars each, but brandy, cigars, and tobacco were "low." He added that silk handkerchiefs and cravats "of good quality" sold "almost every day" for twenty or thirty cents each. The cost of washing clothes was between six and seven dollars per dozen items. Consequently many people sent their clothes to the Sandwich Islands (now Hawaii or Hawaiian Islands). La Motte mentioned that a man took dirty clothes, made a bill of lading for them, insured them, sent them there and back for two to three dollars a dozen. He did not indicate how long this took, however. A passenger in the ship *America* quoted a price of six to eight dollars per dozen items in California and indicated many people simply wore their clothes "as long as they can with decency" or until the clothes "are as dirty as can be rendered." They then purchased new clothes, went down to the shore for a bath, donned their new clothes, and left the dirty ones behind. La Motte also noted that newspapers that sold for one to three cents in New York cost between fifty cents and a dollar in California. He reported that "Little frames, such as not the meanest hand or laborer about you would live in" were rented as stores for between $800 and $2,000 per month. A Mr.

Commodity	Stearns 10/14/1849	Stearns 11/17/1849	Stearns 11/17/1850	McCracken 11/24/1849	LaMotte 12/15/1849
Beef, fresh, lb.	.10–.20	.18–.20	.12–.18	.25	.25
Board, week	$10–35	$15–25	$10–25	$30–50	$40–60
Boots, pair		$15–25	$3–8	$25–100	$40–60
Bricks, 1,000		$70	$20–25		
Butter, lb.	.90		.25–.40		$1
Candles, lb.	.90–$1.25	$3.00	.55–.65		$4
Flour, bbl.	$12	$35	$18–20	$45–50	
Hay, ton	$150				
Labor, common	$6 day	$10 day	$4–6 day		
Labor, skilled	$12–15	$16	$10		
Lumber, Mft.	$225–300	$350–450	$300–500		$200–350
Pork, mess, bbl.	$28	$45–50	$23	$60	
Potatoes, lb.	.15	.25	.12		.50
Shingles, M		$35	$8		
Sugar, lb.					.45
Ham, lb.				$1	
Cheese, lb.				$1	$2
Bread, loaf				.50	.37½
Eggs, doz.					$7

Prices of Various Commodities, October 14, 1849–November 17, 1850[1]

[1]Stearns, Journal, bark *Belvidera,* loose sheet in volume; McCracken, Letter, November 23, 1849: and LaMotte, Letters, December 30, 1849, to his father and his mother.

Winston paid $200 per month for a six-by-ten-foot office and $51,000 annual rent on his store of undisclosed size. John McCrackan reported that the cheapest dinner was $1.50, and prices ranged up to $20 or $30. Board in hotels cost from $30 to $50 a week. Extremely small rooms cost $150 dollars a month. He had heard of one room that cost $6,000 per month. Building lots that cost $300 in August or September 1849 sold for $10,000 in November and December 1849. McCrackan mentioned an individual from New York who had allegedly "cheated the Banks in N.Y. out of 200,000 dolls. & absconded," became rich in real estate by purchasing land at $10 to $20 per acre and selling it for $10,000 to $20,000 per acre. He noted that they never saw silver less than a quarter, as everything cost at least that much. Both silver and gold were packaged in brown paper in amounts between $5 and $100 packages with the amount of money inside marked on the outside and circulated in that manner. McCrackan noted the packages were rarely opened, as the degree of honesty in California was high. A passenger who had recently arrived in the ship *America* wrote that "through the entire town miserable shanties that are scarcely large enough to 'sling a cat round in' command rents from 300 to $800 per month, and scarce to find at that." He added that one blacksmith paid "$20 per day . . . for the privilege of working [blacksmithing] in the shade of a small tree!" La Motte also mentioned that he had lent a friend, Hob Smith, "about $600 . . . at the rate of 4% pr month" and added that was two to six percent below "the market rate per month." The note was payable on demand and was secured by a lien on Smith's sloop valued at $3,000. A. Bailey, who arrived in the bark *Sarah Warren*, confirmed the accuracy of La Motte's figures when he noted four days after arriving that "money cannot be had here under 10 per cent per month!"[12]

One of the first things that most passengers did when they arrived in San Francisco was go to the post office to see if they had received any mail from their families and friends at home. For those who had mail it was a pleasant experience, but for those who did not have mail it was a great disappointment. For all of them, however, it was usually a long wait in line to get to the postal window to even ask about mail. Robert La Motte wrote his father that the urgency for mail was so great that it was not uncommon to see a person at or near the end of the line pay twenty to fifty dollars to someone near the head of the line for that person's place. Robert N. Ferrell wrote that men frequently offered between five and fifteen dollars to move to the head of the line at the post office and that it took half a day to reach that point. He also had some harsh criticism of the post office, calling it "a most miserable affair" and adding that it "ought to be amended at once." La Motte reported that the mail from the steamer that arrived "before daylight"on Saturday was not sorted until Tuesday, "the day the return steamer left." That meant those who received mail in the Saturday steamer would have to wait until the departure of the next steamer a month later to send replies to their letters. Albert Lyman wrote that their "first point of attraction" once they landed in San Francisco was the post office. He was "among the fortunate ones," as he received "three well filled letters from my far distant home" and noted that others were "bitterly disappointed." Two bags of mail had been lost when mail crossed Panama, and Lyman speculated that mail to the disappointed ones was in those bags. He wrote that he "sat down at once on the steps of the postoffice" to give those letters "a hasty perusal . . . regardless of every thing around me." After taking a walk around town and a climb up a hill behind the town, he sat down to "devour every word" of the "precious contents" of those three letters. As he did that his imagination faithfully brought "every familiar and loved face" to mind. He was obviously delighted with "visions of days past and scenes of home" that "flitted across" his memory as he read the letters. Ebenezer Sheppard went to the post office the day after he arrived. He received four letters and commented, "Ah these were as cool water to the thirsty soul—Joyous indeed." William Berry Cross was also fortunate to receive one letter when he arrived in the ship *Sweden.* Charles Herbert Fuller's visit to the post office the day after the *Sweden* arrived was a sad one, as no mail was there for him. He concluded they had so much mail to sort that not all of it had been sorted yet. He vowed to return the next day and "keep calling untill" he received a letter. Joseph Augustine Benton and a few other passengers in the ship *Edward Everett* went ashore almost immediately after they dropped anchor and headed directly to the post office. Benton received "a couple of letters from N.Y. City" but "None from Boston." He understood their mail from Rio de Janeiro had been mishandled, and that caused his not getting more mail on his arrival. Anderson Hollingsworth did not receive any letters upon his arrival in the ship *Daniel Webster* and believed "the business of the [post] office is sadly conducted." James F. Caine and some fellow passengers in the bark *Belvidera* made a "Grand rush to the postoffice," but to his "disappointment" he "found nothing."[13]

Proper and adequate medical care should probably have been of concern to many Argonauts, but it seems to have been ignored by most. Few wrote about that matter in journals or letters. Perhaps that was because such a large percentage were in their twenties and in the prime of their lives. There were a few doctors who ventured to California in 1849, but probably the majority of them intended to seek gold in the goldfields rather than in a doctor's office or a hospital. A few of the male Argonauts wrote of the wretched conditions in the area called Happy Valley and the amount of illness that went untreated or was poorly treated there. A male passenger in the ship *America* thought Happy Valley was "a great 'misnomen'" and considered it the most "squalid unhealthy place" he had ever seen. He wrote there were "Hundreds of tents in and about it with vast numbers of sick lying in them on the ground and about them in all directions." It seemed to him many of those sick young men "must die from the melonekolly fact of having no one to do or take the least interest in them."

He felt that anyone who fell ill and had no money or friends to take care of him had "little or no chance of ever being better." A. Bailey, who arrived in the bark *Sarah Warren* in early April 1850, wrote about the "melancholy" sight of the "haggard, dejected and wan looking countenances" he saw around San Francisco. These were the people who believed all the glowing accounts about California that were published in the East Coast newspapers and "spent every cent they could muster to get here" only to become "sick and have not where to lay their heads and no money to get home again." He felt the "Scoundrels who have written the exaggerated letters ought to be sentenced to State Prison for ten years."

It was a female Argonaut, however, who wrote most eloquently about the overall health situation in San Francisco. Sophia A. Eastman went to San Francisco in the brig *Colorado* to teach school and chronicled her struggles to find employment. She arrived in June 1849 and reported there were between two and three hundred females in San Francisco. Eastman was the only Argonaut to report that every person entering San Francisco was charged two dollars for a health certificate and that the money went to "support the Hospital which is free for all." After a month of searching, she reported she had been offered two jobs. One was to teach in a school for "young ladies and small children" for forty dollars a month plus food and lodging; the other was to work in the hospital at seventy-five dollars per month without any mention of food or lodging. She appears to have taken the job in the hospital and wrote about the suffering she saw there and of the "risk of life, reputation, & health for one to come to California" and added that there was "more poverty, wretchedness, & misery existing in this place than" she had ever seen. Then she mentioned "Vice & dissipation!" and " Houses of ill fame!" She also indicated there was "more insanity" than she had seen anywhere in her life. The hospital at which she worked was "filled up with cases" of insanity. These people seemingly were "poor, foolish, silly wretches" who believed all the stories they had read in the newspapers about getting rich and arrived in California expecting to get rich without having to work. When that did not happen, they lost "heart & reputation, & are brought to the hospital to die." She indicated they would die "a miserable death." In spite of these reports, Eastman noted that a young woman who had energy and health and was "willing to run the risk" could do well. She might find a good husband if she chose or "remain single & return home rich" to her home in New England.[14]

The number of places that offered gambling, the number of people who gambled, and the amounts of money wagered at a time were astonishing to many who arrived in San Francisco in 1849, and many wrote about it. They were surprised to see women gamble along with the men and that gambling was done on Sunday. William F. Reed wrote that "Gaming houses carry on a great stroke of business the betters losing and winning thousands as cool as a cucumber." Charles Williams reported he heard of one captain who won seventy-five thousand dollars in one night. Moses Cogswell thought there was "no end to the Gambling" and that "Two thirds of the buildings" were "drinking and gambling establishments." He saw a pile of "silver dollars, gold pieces, gold dust and Bars" large enough to "fill a Bushel Basket" on one of the gambling tables he passed on a visit to the city on a Sunday morning shortly after arriving in California. Charles S. Putnam also saw piles of "gold and silver . . . as big as a bushel basket" and concluded there was more money in San Francisco than in New York. Although Eugene Howard could not identify the various forms of gambling he witnessed, he saw "many hundred thousand dollars bet on a wheel of fortune and cards." Alexander F. Spear observed a gambling table only a few minutes but saw "hundreds of dollars change hands." He also noted there were boys and women as well as men at the gambling tables. Henry H. Hyde Jr. saw gamblers handle "dubbloons and Mexican dollars with a perfect looseness" and "Thousands of dollars exchange hands in a few minutes." James F. Caine was satisfied that there was "money enough in the country" when he saw the size of the "stacks of money . . . on the gamblers tables." Christian Miller wrote that San Francisco exceeded "al places in the world for" gambling. Many buildings were "crowded with gambling tables of all kinds of games continually, Sunday not excepted." He saw "many . . . gamblers have banks of $20,000 at once on the table." This led him to conclude that "Gold is as plenty here as coppers are with you." Quite possibly the most famous gambling house in San Francisco was the Parker House. It was constructed before July 1849 from materials sent for that purpose from New York. It may possibly have been partially prefabricated. The original cost was reported at $120,000, but the several rooms used for gambling rented for a total of $160,000 per year. There were two billiards rooms, each containing four tables, which rented for $12,000 per year; two gaming rooms that rented for $12,000 per year; and "several" smaller rooms for gaming that rented for $6,000 per year. In addition there was at least one dining room, lodging rooms, and offices that rented "at enormous prices." Although William S. Hull did not identify the building as the Parker House, he mentioned "the principal Hotel, a large two story frame building devoted to Gambling from one end to the other" and said it rented for $135,000 per year. C. W. Haskins noticed that numerous miners who returned from the mines and headed toward the Adams & Company Express office to send their money home often stop at a gambling hall "to discover upon which end of the tiger its tail was hung" and lose all their hard-earned gold. They would then had to return to the mines to start the cycle all over again. Thomas Reid recognized a number of professional gamblers and noted that "most all the hardest gamblers are busy . . . with their gambeling tools." He noted especially "Cris Lilly, the man that killed Macoy" and reported he was "worth forty thousand dollars . . . owns a splendid house . . . keeps a house of prostitution and makes a great deal of money at this business." He was also "banker at a gambeling game called monte." Reid saw fortunes "made and lost here in a day" and the losers "go to the diggings to get more" and witnessed little "respect for the Sabbath" in San Francisco. Henry Green, who had just arrived in the ship *Sabina*, wrote, "this is a very bad place for all kinds of gambeling and other vices and but little respect for the Sabbath." Isaac Bowles seemed disgusted with the "Drunkenness & gamblin and Sabath breaking" and asked God to deliver him "from any of these damnable sins."[15]

Considering the number of individuals who wrote about church services on board their vessels, the detail with which some described the services, and the feelings of some when such services were discontinued because of bad weather and then resumed again, one might reasonably expect many Argonauts to write about attending church services in San Francisco once they arrived. This was not the case, however. Most seem to have been more involved and interested in how much gold was available and how much they could obtain, what other prospects there were besides mining, how much everything cost, what the surroundings were like, and the amount of gambling going on around them although several condemned the gambling, especially on Sunday. William S. Hull did not mention going to church when he went ashore on his first Sunday in San Francisco, but he found "the Inhabitants paying more general observance of the Sabbath than I expected. Stores were mostly shut up, but the Gambling shops all open, and doing a big business." Two passengers from the bark *Belvidera* wrote about going to church. James F. Caine mentioned there were "three societies, viz. Methodist, Presbyterian, and Baptist" and that he "attended Service at the Presbyterian Tent." J. Haskell Stearns mentioned that he found the Presbyterian church after "a long search" and noted that "there was no steeple to designate it," as it was located in a "tent capable of holding about 150 persons." Most in attendance were males although there were "perhaps ten or twelve women & children" present. Stearns noted that the ground had been "covered with a matting" and that they sat on "benches without backs." He felt the "congregation was composed of persons as intelligent and respectable in their appearance as those of any congregation in our large towns at home." He indicated it made him "very happy to be able to spend the Sabbath in this way and he could "hardly keep back the tears" when some "old recollections came over me."[16]

George K. Goodwin was a twenty-three-year-old carriage painter when he sailed from Boston to San Francisco in the ship *Sweden* in 1849. Three decades later he included an account of that voyage in his published reminiscences. At the end of his description of the voyage, he penned a brief account of the times, a portion of which seems to be an appropriate close for this study. Of those young men going to California, Goodwin wrote they were

> all flocking to the new Eldorado, whose valleys were described as a "perfect paradise," and whose rivers were literally checked with gold. Few came with the expectation of making permanent homes in California. They came burning with a sudden thirst for adventure, as I did, and the accumulation of sudden wealth, the "California fever" spread with fatality and rapidity of a true epidemic. Young men of ardent and enthusiastic temperament, fell its first victims; those who were foot-free, and possessed of the means to obtain an outfit, set off alone or in companies, by such routes as seemed to them most practicable; arriving in California they were exposed to all the hardships of a camp life, without the discipline of an army, or the comforts and care with which a commissary provides. The partial organization with which most of them started from home, fell in pieces as soon as they touched the auriferous soil; each man was thrown upon his resources, inexperienced in hardships, and ignorant of the dangers by which he was surrounded; disappointed in hopes and dejected in spirits, he fell victim to disease in a climate the most salubrious in the world. When the warm suns of the spring had again dried up the rain and covered the virgin fields with a carpet of flowers, one-fifth of that grand army was no more. Fevers, scurvy and bowel complaints had done their work.

Goodwin added that many of the survivors were eager to return to their homes, but few wanted to suffer the rigors of Cape Horn in a sailing vessel again.[17]

There is probably no reasonable way of knowing or determining how many of those who traveled to California in sailing vessels in 1849 actually achieved their goal of finding enough gold to support them throughout their future lives. It is probably safe to speculate the number was quite small. It is probably also impossible to determine how many of them stayed in California and how many returned to their original homes, but it seems safe to assume that more stayed than originally expected or intended to do so. Within three or four years the vast majority of the placer gold that could be gathered by hand was removed, but other methods of obtaining such gold were developed and were practiced where possible for many years although they caused considerable damage to the rivers and streams of California. Also hard-rock mining started as early as 1852. Likely some men obtained employment in those endeavors. Others obtained employment in businesses that developed in the towns and cities throughout California. Others became farmers and ranchers to produce the food needed by fellow citizens. Thus, in many ways, those adventuresome Argonauts who braved the ocean waves and experienced the rigors of Cape Horn helped begin the process that made California what it is today.

Notes

INTRODUCTION

1. Marx, *The Magic of Gold*, 1–37, 377–91.
2. Adjusted for inflation, the $344.75 is worth about $6,300 in 1999 dollars whereas the 14.43 ounces of gold would bring about $5,160 at the current price of gold.
3. Reynolds, *The Golden Dream of Francisco Lopez*, 1–8.
4. The Marshall nugget was displayed at the Oakland Museum in Oakland, California, during the spring of 1998 in a special exhibition to celebrate the sesquicentennial of the discovery of gold in northern California. It is somewhat smaller and thinner than a dime. One source reported it was about the size of a pea. The Wimmer nugget is owned by the Bancroft Library at the University of California, Berkeley, and is about the size and thickness of a modern half dollar. On January 18, 1998 the *Sacramento Bee* published a special sesquicentennial issue with a considerable amount of historical information on the California gold rush.
5. The classic account of the Panama route is John Haskell Kemble's *The Panama Route, 1841–1869* published by the University of California Press in 1943 and reprinted by the University of South Carolina Press in 1990. James P. Delgado includes a chapter on the isthmian route in his *To California by Sea: A Maritime History of the California Gold Rush* published by the University of South Carolina Press in 1990. Oscar Lewis has one chapter on the Cape Horn route and another on crossing Panama and Nicaragua in his *Sea Routes to the Gold Fields: The Migration by Water to California in 1849–1852* published by Alfred A. Knopf in 1949. He also has chapters on the places at which those who rounded Cape Horn stopped and on California when the Argonauts arrived. J. S. Holiday's *The World Rushed In: The California Gold Rush Experience* published by Simon and Schuster in 1981 is possibly the most thorough study of the overland route. Hundreds of accounts of individual overland journeys have been published beginning as early as 1850. Most of them are listed in L. W. Mintz's *The Trail: A Bibliography, 1841–1864* published by the University of New Mexico Press in 1987.

1: PREPARATIONS FOR THE VOYAGE

1. Dutka, "New York Discovers GOLD! In California: How the Press Fanned the Flames of Gold Mania." The *New York Daily Tribune* had a series of at least fourteen columns labeled "Golden Chronicles" between January 23 and June 1, 1849 that included extensive records of vessels sailed or about to sail from ports along the Atlantic coast and the Gulf of Mexico, joint stock companies formed throughout the country, and vessels purchased for voyages to California with prices paid.

That newspaper, and newspapers in all major ports, also had hundreds of other reports of vessels sailing to California and frequently provided names and/or numbers of passengers in those vessels.

2. Halsey, A Forty-Niner's Diary.

3. The length of voyages and distance sailed are derived from examination of a large number of journals, some of which contain daily records of distance sailed and others of which simply give total distance sailed upon arriving in San Francisco as well as of *The Key to the Goodman Encyclopedia of the California Gold Rush Fleet,* San Francisco: Zamorano Club, 1992, which includes a list 762 vessels that sailed to California in 1849 and gives the departure and arrival dates and the number of days of each vessel plus additional information. A tabulation of the daily miles sailed by the bark *Orion* in *Gold Rush Voyage of the Bark Orion,* 277–82, reveals she sailed 18,144 miles. Pierce W. Baker kept a record of miles traveled each day during his voyage in the ship *Nestor.* The total was 20,196 miles. Delgado, *To California by Sea,* 18, gives the figure of 13,328 miles calculated by Matthew Fountaine Maury from his examination of logbooks of vessels that sailed around Cape Horn to California.

4. Howe, *Argonauts of '49.* The alphabetical list of companies with brief descriptions is found on pages 187–213. Based upon company names provided in journals, notably the ship *Capitol,* it appears there were several other Massachusetts companies Howe did not discover.

5. That the members expected to live on board their vessel is indicative of the lack of information many of them had about California and the location of the gold they were going to seek. Some who went in small vessels were able to sail as far inland as Sacramento, but even that city was too far from the gold regions for miners to continue to live on board the vessel and seek gold.

6. Although there may well have been hundreds of bylaws written and adopted by companies, only a few seem to have survived. A printed copy of those of the New York and California Mutual Benefit Association is pasted on the third page of the original diary of Isaac S. Halsey of his journey to California in the ship *Salem,* the Bancroft Library, University of California, Berkeley. Halsey's original diary also contains a copy of the constitution and bylaws of the New York and Californian Excelsior Mining Company dated October 1, 1849, which was formed by nine members of the New York and California Mutual Benefit Association during the voyage. William Graves clipped a copy of the constitution of the Salem Mechanics Trading and Mining Association from an unidentified newspaper and pasted it into the back his journal of his voyage in the ship *Crescent,* Bancroft Library, University of California, Berkeley. James White included a copy of the constitution and bylaws of the Boston and California Mining and Trading Joint Stock Company in his journal of a voyage in the ship *Edward Everett,* J. Porter Shaw Library, National Maritime Museum. A printed copy of the constitution and bylaws of the Granite State Trading, Mining and Agricultural Company, which seems to have sailed in the ship *Sweden* of Boston, is in the New Hampshire Historical Society Library. Howe included a copy of the bylaws of the Essex County and California Mining and Trading Company as appendix 2 in *Argonauts of '49.*

7. A copy of the prospectus and drafts, including a signed one, of the agreement

are in the Warren Papers at the Bancroft Library at the University of California, Berkeley. There is a notation beside the names of the two who did not fulfill the agreement. Unfortunately there does not appear to be a copy of the final accounting with Warren and the other men so it is impossible to know if the venture was a financially successful one for either the owners or the members of the Ship *Sweden* Company. Based upon a few letters in the Warren Papers, it appears it was not a successful venture. Although Warren was not one of those who failed to fulfill his contract, he seems not to have returned to Boston but rather went into business on his own in California.

8. Announcements and advertisements for the California Mutual Benefit and Joint Stock Association and the ship *Arkansas* appeared regularly in the *New York Daily Tribune* between January 23 and June 27, 1849. Occasional advertisements also appeared in the *Christian Advocate* (New York) during this period. During all of this time the members seem to have met two or three evenings a week at various Methodist churches and hotels or other buildings in which they reportedly had offices. The voyage of the *Arkansas* is described in the journals of Benjamin H. Deane and Robert N. Ferrell, Bancroft Library, University of California, Berkeley.

9. *New York Daily Tribune*, February 14, March 30, April 12 and 17, and May 21, 1849.

10. Doten, *Journals*. The first volume contains Doten's journal of the voyage of the *Yeoman* and additional information about the enterprise. Doten's father was one of the investors.

11. Delgado, *To California by Sea*, 19. The *Key to the Goodman Encyclopedia of the California Gold Rush Fleet* lists a total of 762 vessels that sailed to California between late 1848 and early 1850. I have encountered journals or letters from a couple of vessels not in the *Key*.

12. The list of companies sailing in the ship *Capitol* is in the Moses Chase Papers. His ticket for the *Capitol* in also included. Judging from the names, it would seem that most of them were Massachusetts companies, but only the Naumkeag Mining and Trading Company is included in the list of Massachusetts companies in Howe's *Argonauts of '49*. These are abbreviated names, or they were companies never discovered by Howe, who lists only the Naumkeag Company as sailing in the *Capitol*. Abraham Schell lists sixteen companies sailing in the ship *Tarolinta* out of New York. He provides drawings and descriptions of the flag of each company. This is the only reference I have seen to company flags.

13. Advertisements for vessels and companies in the *New York Daily Tribune*, January–September 1849, and the *Baltimore Sun*, January–June 1849; *The Key to the Goodman Encyclopedia of the California Gold Rush Fleet* and journals kept by passengers on a few of these vessels provided the information included in the several paragraphs about these vessels.

14. Advertisements for gold washers are found multiple times virtually every week in the *New York Daily Tribune* between the mid-December 1848 and the beginning of September 1849, by which time news had returned from California that they were of little or no use in that place. Advertisements for all of the commodities are also in the same paper for that period of time. The author has approximately seventy-five pages of notes on these matters collected for a paper titled "Selling the California

Gold Rush in the Big Apple," presented at the Mining History Conference in Nevada City, California, in June 1995.

15. Harvey, Journal, *Crescent,* October 14–December 5, 1849. Harvey was unusual in recording all of his activities and thoughts leading up to the departure of the ship *Crescent* on December 6, 1849. Most journalists started their record the day they departed or as soon thereafter as they recovered from seasickness.

16. Hull, Journal, ship *Jane Parker.*

17. Hollingsworth, Papers and journal, 1849, *Daniel Webster.* The company outfits are listed in the introduction to the journal, and the personal outfits are on a loose sheet removed from the journal. Primage is a fee paid to the captain and crew for loading and taking care of freight.

18. Lewis, Journal, ship *Charlotte,* 1849. The list is on page 4 of the journal. His "prayer book Episcopal Church" is undoubtedly the Book of Common Prayer. What he meant by "sea shirts" is unknown.

19. Dornin, Reminiscences.

20. According to the 1851 *New York City Directory* produced by Doggett and Rode, D. & J. Devlin Clothiers was located at 53 John Street. Both Daniel and Jeremiah resided at 33 John Street.

21. Browne, *Letters, Journals and Writings,* 64–69. Browne took a leading role in the campaign to have Capt. Hall J. Tibbits removed as commander of the ship *Pacific.* It was probably this action that led the secretary of the treasury to send a letter to Browne before he actually arrived in California informing him that his appointment was terminated. What he meant by "a light summer shad-sack" is uncertain.

22. Stearns, Journal, bark *Belvidera,* 1849. Passengers who kept journals in this vessel spelled the name various ways including *Belvidere* and *Bilvedere,* but *Belvidera* seems to be correct. Most other vessels had six-by-six-feet staterooms that housed only two men. Having four men in that same amount of space made quarters quite cramped. "Switchel" was a mixture of water, molasses, and vinegar, which passengers sometimes concocted when their water was particularly bad.

23. Harvey, Journal, ship *Crescent,* 1849.

24. Coffin, *A Pioneer Voyage,* 10, 15–16. A plan of the between decks areas is included facing page 10.

25. Stillman, *Seeking the Golden Fleece,* 81–82. Pages 35–177 contain an account of his voyage in 1849 in the ship *Pacific.*

26. The petitions filed by those passengers (Frank Cheney, Charles D. Cleveland, Elijah B. Galusha, Elon C. Galusha, Judson Galusha, Henry D. Kingsbury, Anson A. Nicholson, and Owen Spencer) are in the National Archives, Northeast Region, Bayonne, New Jersey, case numbers 7-224, 6-227, 6-239, 6-232, 6-236, 6-237, and 1-47. A description of the tempestuous voyage of the *Pacific* is given in Schultz, "The Gold Rush Voyage of the Ship *Pacific:* A Study in Vessel Management."

27. Woodbury, Journal, ship *Argonaut,* November 5, 1849.

28. The description is on a loose section of paper at the front of Woodbury's journal. Why he wrote two such conflicting descriptions remains a mystery. "Picking raisins" was a common practice to remove those with worms.

29. Ewer, Journal, ship *York,* May 12, 1849. Bancroft Library, University of California, Berkeley. Rats, bed bugs, and roaches were common pests on sailing vessels

bound for California. Ants and moths were rarely mentioned in other journals.

30. Upham, *Notes of a Voyage,* 32.

31. *Ibid.,* 36–37.

32. Brown, Journal, bark *Selma,* April 16, 1849. The information that Brown and Coe were both physicians comes from the list of passengers with age, place of residence, and occupation of each in the logbook for the *Selma.*

33. Bee, Journal, ship *South Carolina,* May 1, 1849.

34. Cogswell, "Gold Rush Diary," 1–50. In many other vessels passengers slept on deck in the tropical latitudes.

35. Jones, Journal, bark *Nautilus,* February 23, 1849.

36. McCrackan, Letter to his sister Lottie, April 30.

37. *Ibid.,* Letter to his mother and sisters, July 22, 1849.

38. Graves, Journal, *Crescent,* March 18, 1850.

39. Woodbury, Journal, ship *Argonaut,* 1849. This information appears in a loose section at the front of the journal.

40. Wheeler, Journal, bark *Hannah Sprague,* June 25, 1849.

41. Corneilson, Journal, bark *Hannah Sprague,* August 17, 1849.

42. Taylor, Journal, ship *Orpheus,* February 10 and March 25, 1849.

43. Farwell, "Cape Horn and Cooperative Mining in '49," 579–94. King's original records are currently available in the Society of California Pioneers Library.

44. Graves, Journal, ship *Crescent,* 1849.

45. White, Journal, ship *Edward Everett,* 1849.

46. Woodbury, Journal, ship *Argonaut,* 1849.

47. Graves, Journal, ship *Crescent,* 1849. Cross also included the occupations of the passengers in his journal, but Harvey did not.

48. Hollingsworth, Journal, ship *Daniel Webster,* 1849.

49. White, Journal, ship *Edward Everett,* 1849.

50. Stevens, Journal, bark *Emma Isadora,* 1849.

51. Logbook, bark *Selma,* 1849. A Brittanner was probably one who made tableware from Brittania metal, an alloy of tin, copper, and antimony.

52. Bailey, Journal, ship *Sweden,* 1849, and James L. L. F. Warren Papers.

53. Williams, Journal, ship *Regulus,* 1849.

2: UNDERWAY AT LAST

1. *New York Daily Tribune,* March 19 and 30, April 10, May 17, and June 9, 1849. Her sailing day is given as May 21 in *The Key to the Goodman Encyclopedia of the California Gold Rush Fleet.*

2. *Baltimore Sun* and *Baltimore American and Commercial Daily Advertiser,* February 7–April 19, 1849. For information about all of the vessels that sailed from Baltimore and a complete account of the voyage of the *Andalusia,* see Schultz, "Ship *Andalusia:* Queen of the Baltimore Gold Rush Fleet."

3. *New York Daily Tribune,* March 20, April 17, and May 21, 1849.

4. *New York Daily Tribune,* January 23, 25, and 30; February 5, 8, 13, 20, and 26; March 20; April 3, 13, and 23; May 4, 9, 17, and 30; and June 7 and 12, 1849.

5. *New York Daily Tribune,* January 25, February 6, and April 18, 1849.

6. *New York Daily Tribune,* January 26, February 6 and 8, and March 20, 1849.

7. *New York Daily Tribune,* January 15, February 5 and 14, March 7, and April 3. The name of the captain is given as I. Thatcher in *The Key to the Goodman Encyclopedia of the California Gold Rush Fleet.* It is possible that the newspaper was incorrect in initially giving the name as I. Thurston and later corrected it to Thacher. The papers of the day and others often erred in the names of both captains and passengers.

8. *New York Daily Tribune,* January 10 and 10, and February 28, 1849.

9. *New York Daily Tribune,* December 28, 1848, and January 19 and February 13, 1849.

10. *Baltimore Sun,* January 25 and February 1, 15, 24, and 26, 1849.

11. *Baltimore Sun,* April 16, May 8, June 1 and 14, and July 1, 11, 12, and 13, 1849. The term "Three times three" was used often and meant three series of three cheers, making a total of nine cheers. Included in her cargo was a packaged structure twenty-five by eighty feet to be erected in San Francisco and used as a warehouse and store by James Weathered and a small steamer named *Mt. Vernon* to be used in navigating the small streams of the gold region.

12. *Baltimore Sun,* July 9, 15 (and many days thereafter), and 31, and August 22, 1849.

13. *New York Daily Tribune,* various dates, May 22–August 15, 1849. Judging from the change in the names of masters of this and other vessels discussed previously, it appears that captains seem to have been free to change their minds if a vessel was too slow to sail or if they got a better offer from the owners of another vessel.

14. *New York Daily Tribune,* February 8, 17, and 27, and March 1, 9, and 31, 1849.

15. *New York Daily Tribune,* Feb. 1, 15, and 21, and March 5, 15, and 26, 1849. The change from "a limited number of passengers" in the initial advertisement to "the number will be limited to 150" three weeks later certainly seems a significant alteration in plans. The projected sailing time of 100 days was likely an exaggeration, considering the total sailing time of 175 days, but predicting sailing time for a voyage (especially a voyage as long as the one to California) around Cape Horn was certainly not a scientific matter in the age of sail. The predicted rapid voyage was probably a ploy to entice passengers to choose her over other vessels.

16. *New York Daily Tribune,* February 27; April 9, 23, and 25; and June 4, 1849. The lengths of the voyages in this instance and some others above come from *The Key to the Goodman Encyclopedia of the California Gold Rush Fleet.* In some instances this source has a different number of passengers than is given in the *New York Daily Tribune.* For example, the *Tribune* reports 174 passengers in the *Susan G. Owens* whereas the *Key* gives the number as 191. Differences in numbers of passengers and variances in names of passengers is quite common in different sources during this period.

17. The information on the length of the voyages of the several vessels discussed is all available in *The Key to the Goodman Encyclopedia of the California Gold Rush Fleet.*

18. Taylor, Journal, ship *Orpheus,* January 30, 1849.

19. Dornin, Reminiscences, 5–6.

20. *Friendship* (ship), Series of anonymous and mostly undated episodes during a voyage from Fairhaven, Massachusetts, 1849. Because the passage lasted 178 days,

one might conclude that only modestly good fortune fell upon the passengers who sailed in the *Friendship,* as many vessels made quicker passages, but many others made longer ones.

21. *Boston Journal,* February 27, 1849.

22. Cogswell, "Gold Rush Diary," 9; Fuller, Journal, ship *Sweden,* March 1, 1849; Tolman, Journal, ship *Sweden,* March 1, 1849.

23. Johnson, *California: A Sermon Preached in St. John's Church, Brooklyn, N.Y. on Sunday, February 11, 1849,* 4–13.

24. Shepard and Caldwell, *Addresses.*

25. Schaeffer, *Sketches of Travels,* 7–10.

26. Graves, Journal, ship *Crescent,* December 6, 1849; Harvey, Journal, ship *Crescent,* December 6, 1849; and Cross, Journal, ship *Crescent,* December 6, 1849.

27. Denham, Journal, schooner *Rialto,* February 7, 1849. Holmes Hole is currently called Vineyard Haven.

28. Reed, Journal, ship *Magnolia,* December 8, 1849; Collins, Journal, ship *Magnolia,* December 8, 1849; [George Payson], *Golden Dreams and Leaden Realities,* 15.

29. Ferrell, Journal, ship *Arkansas,* June 26, 1849; Deane, Journal, ship *Arkansas,* June 26, 1849.

30. Baker, Journal, bark *San Francisco,* August 15, 1849.

31. Kingsley, "Diary of Nelson Kingsley," 242.

32. Jones, Journal, bark *Nautilus,* February 23 and March 1, 1849. The quantity of gunpowder some of the men took is an indication of how little they knew about California and the mining process there or what they would face once they arrived. Gunpowder was not needed for the placer mining that was done in 1849. Hard-rock mining, for which gunpowder was used, was not started until two or three years later. Many who went out thought they would have to fight to protect themselves from Indians, Spaniards, and Mexicans. Although there were minor problems with them, the Argonauts did not have war with any of them.

33. Lyman, *Journal of a Voyage,* 9–10. Hanks was likely an officer of the company or someone who had previously served as a captain of a vessel, as Charles A. Falkenberg was captain of the *General Morgan.*

34. Anonymous, Journal, bark *Gold Hunter,* October 3–13, 1849.

35. Gager, Journal, ship *Pacific,* January 22–23, 1849; Anonymous, Journal, ship *Pacific,* January 22, 1849; Williams, Journal, ship *Pacific,* January 22, 1849; Clark, Journal, ship *Pacific,* January 22, 1849; Stillman, *Seeking the Golden Fleece,* 35–36; and Browne, *Letters, Journals and Writings,* 70–71.

36. Anonymous, Journal, ship *America,* April 2, 1849, Bancroft Library.

37. Halsey, A Forty-Niner's Diary, 10–12.

38. Brannan, Letters to his wife, Mary, May 9 and 11, 1849.

39. Gager, Journal, ship *Pacific,* February 5 and July 10, 1849.

40. Hollingsworth, Journal, ship *Daniel Webster,* February 3, 1849.

41. Hyde, Journal, ship *Lenore,* February 3, 1849.

42. Denham, Journal, schooner *Rialto,* February 10, 1849.

43. Ewer, Journal, ship *York,* April 4, 1849.

44. Christman, *One Man's Gold,* 10–11.

45. Sheppard, Journal, ship *Morrison,* April 3, 9, and 12, 1849.

46. Anonymous, Journal, *Pharsalia,* February 23, March 12 and 29, and April 27, 1849.

47. Cooledge, Journal, bark *Oxford,* January 11, 1849.

48. *Ibid.,* March 6 and 8, 1849.

49. Gager, Journal, ship *Pacific,* January 24, 25, and 30; February 7; and April 3, 8, and 10, 1849, and Williams, Journal, ship *Pacific,* January 23–26, February 1, and April 3, 1849.

50. Lyman, *Journal of a Voyage,* 10–15 and 44.

51. Fletcher, Journal, bark *Elvira,* January 2–7 and March 6–8, 1849.

52. Overton, Journal, bark *Keoka,* February 7 and 9, and July 10, 1849.

53. Collins, Journal, ship *Magnolia,* February 9–15; April 13–16; and June 20–21, 1849.

54. Meredith, Journal, bark *Strafford,* February 8 and 13, 1849.

55. Woodbury, Journal, ship *Argonaut,* October 31, 1849.

56. Schaeffer, *Sketches of Travels,* 10.

57. Anonymous, Journal, ship *America,* April 2, 1849, Bancroft Library.

58. Hutchinson, Journal, bark *Belgrade,* November 27, 1849.

59. Christman, *One Man's Gold,* 24.

60. Baker, Journal, bark *San Francisco,* August 18, 1849.

61. Dornin, Reminiscences, 8.

62. Hollingsworth, Journal, ship *Daniel Webster,* February 4, 1849.

63. Taylor, Journal, ship *Orpheus,* March 22, 1849.

64. Davis, *Reminiscence,* 31–33.

65. Goodwin, *Reminiscence,* 5–6.

3: FOOD AND DRINK

1. Denham, Journal, schooner *Rialto,* March 3, 1849.

2. Although commercial canning of foods in metal containers was practiced in 1849 and had been possible for about half a century, few of those bound for California appear to have taken any of it with them. It was certainly heavily advertised by merchants in New York in the *New York Daily Tribune* and was likely also advertised in other major ports. Canning and otherwise preserving foods at home in glass jars was practiced by the mid-nineteenth century, but taking large quantities of such containers was not practical to take on a long sea voyage or in the gold fields of California. Some passengers did take a few such containers among their personal luxuries. Collins, Journal, ship *Magnolia,* March 13, 1849, notes that they had "one of our boxes of preserved meats cooked. They were first rate." Gould, Journal, ship *Maria,* May 6, 16, and 20, 1849, mentions having canned roast turkey. In one instance he referred specifically to Underwood's and on June 25, 1849 referred to drinking canned milk. Williams, Journal, ship *Regulus,* August 14–27, 1849, in a lengthy account of problems within the Bunker Hill Trading and Mining Association, notes that they had taken on board twelve dozen cans of milk and between four hundred and five hundred dollars in preserved fowl, sausages, and other meats that were to be shared by all but seem to have all been consumed by the officers and directors. Fuller's journal in the ship *Sweden* con-

tains references to preserved meats and "fresh meats" on several Sundays at times during the voyage when it could have been only canned meats.

3. Tickets for the *Crescent* were mentioned by some of the passengers in their journals. The Archives and Collections office of the City of Sacramento and the Bancroft Library at the University of California, Berkeley, have tickets for the *Capitol*. J. Wells Henderson of Philadelphia had a ticket for the *Orion* in 1986 and kindly furnished the author with a photocopy. The printed bill of fare on the back of the ticket is the only such item I have seen during my research. *Gold Rush Voyage on the Bark Orion* contains daily excerpts from four accounts of the voyage of this vessel. None of them make any reference to a bill of fare. Foster Hooker Jenkins, whose original journal is in the library of the California State University, Northridge, records complaints about how the food was cooked early in the voyage, but unfortunately does not identify what was cooked. None of the other accounts as published provide any information about food or give any indication that the bill of fare published on the ticket was followed. There are references in some of the journals to bills of fare being posted by captains during a few voyages, but this happened most often after there had been a conflict about the quantity and quality of foods served the passengers.

4. Randle, Letters, March 29 and April 17, 1849, to "Dear Friends" and "Dear Sisters"; Stearns, Journal, bark *Belvidera*; and Shepard, Journal, bark *Belvidera*, March 11, 1849. It was quite common in gold rush ships to give each person a weekly allowance of things such as butter, cheese, sugar, molasses, vinegar, and a few other things rather than have them out for each meal and allow individuals to use all they wanted. Duff was sometimes a very popular commodity and sometimes a very lowly regarded one. It was made of flour, "slush" (the grease skimmed from boiling salt meat), water, seasoning, and raisins (or sometimes plums or apples and occasionally a combination of them) mixed together in a tight canvass bag and boiled in salt water for four hours. Locke, a passenger in the brig *Sea Eagle* from Boston, provides a more detailed and elaborate recipe for duff in a letter to his wife on April 16, 1849: "1 cup of milk, 1 cup molasses, half a cup melted butter, teaspoon salaratus [baking powder], five cups of flour, a pound of raisins, and nutmeg and cloves." Locke simply notes to boil it four hours. Even though he did not indicate it, this would have to be enclosed in a cloth and emersed in boiling water. He also provided a recipe for a sauce: "Half a cracker, 1 cup sugar, 1 lemon, cup of cold water." Although he did not indicate it, this would undoubtedly have to be cooked. "Lobscouse," sometimes spelled "lobskouse" and sometimes referred to simply as "scouse" or "skouse," was a stew consisting of onions, meat (usually salt pork), potatoes, crushed sea biscuits or hard bread, seasonings of pepper and perhaps salt, and some sort of thickening if it were available, all boiled together in water. Fresh water was used unless water rationing existed in the ship. Passengers in the ship *Magnolia* had a disagreement over whether or not there should be onions in their lobscouse and held a meeting to decide the issue. It eventually came to a vote in which the "no onions" faction won. Collins, Journal, ship *Magnolia*, February 28, 1849, and Reed, Journal, ship *Magnolia*, March 1, 1849. [George Payson], *Golden Dreams and Leaden Realities*, 26–27, indicates the vote was taken by having those in favor of onions go to one side of a seam in the deck

and those opposed go to the other side of the seam. He said the "disonionists" won by one vote. Dunderfunk is a dish made from soaked or boiled hard bread (that has first been pounded) mixed with molasses, spice (either cinnamon or allspice), and grease saved from boiling beef and pork, and baked for an unspecified time. *Gold Rush Voyage on the Bark Orion,* 90; Howe, *Argonauts of '49,* 52.

5. Cross, Journal, ship *Crescent,* April 1, 1850; Graves, Journal, ship *Crescent,* April 15, 1850; and Harvey, Journal, ship *Crescent,* April 1, 1850. The first item listed for dinner on Tuesday is difficult to read in all three journals. Sago, as it appears in Graves, is a powdery starch from the trunks of sago palm trees and is used to thicken foods. Sego, as it appears in Harvey, is the succulent edible bulb from the sego lily. In Cross it appears to read "legs." None of the three seem logical.

6. Williams, Journal, ship *Pacific,* February 16, 1849; Clark, Journal, ship *Pacific,* undated note at the end of the journal; and Stillman, *Seeking the Golden Fleece,* 44–45. Gager does not mention a bill of fare in his journal.

7. Bailey, Journal, ship *Sweden,* April 5, 1849. Tolman, Journal, ship *Sweden,* July 16, 1849, provided an abbreviated version of the bill of fare near the end of the voyage. Cassia is a spice of inferior quality made from the bark of the *Cinamonmum cassis* tree found in tropical Asia.

8. Taylor, Journal, ship *Orpheus,* February 9, 1849.

9. Child, Letter to Sophia A. Eastman, October 31–December 21, 1849, Maria M. Child Correspondence.

10. Josiah Griswold, Letter, May 17, 1849, to Benjamin S. Hill, Benjamin S. Hill Correspondence.

11. Woodbury, Journal, ship *Argonaut,* November 25, 1849.

12. Extract from an anonymous journal, brig *Forest,* probably between February 19 and March 11, 1849.

13. Booth, Journal, ship *Andalusia,* June 28, 1849.

14. Baker, Journal, bark *San Francisco,* September 9, 16, and 23, and December 16, 1849. On December 9, 1849 Baker records words to a song that was to be chanted or sung to the tune of "Troubadour." The cook, especially if he was black, was commonly called Doctor in nineteenth-century sailing vessels. The alternating gender in referring to the pig is a mystery.

> Gaily the "Doctor" now sharpened his knife,
> While he was thinking of "taking a life"
> Gazing mysteriously, with evil eye.
> Grunting pig, grunting pig, you've got to die!
>
> "Slam" went the Galley door, out came the cook.
> Steadily he traveled aft, with "darkened look."
> "Come, let us haul her out" that was his cry.
> Grunting pig, grunting pig, this day you must die!
>
> Hark, 'twas the grunting pig, squealing most dire
> As he was dragged along, towards the fire
> "Catch hold and throw him down, there make him lie
> Grunting pig, grunting pig, now you must die!

Down fell the grunting pig, thrown flat on deck.
<u>Slash</u> went the carving knife into her neck
Swift flows the bloody stream. See—See it fly!
Grunting pig, grunting pig, now you <u>must</u> die!

Slush goes the water hot, scalding his hair,
Quick fly the Darkey's fists, scrubbing him bare.
Soon then they cut him up and now ends the cry
Grunting pig, grunting pig, you've got to die!

15. Fletcher, Journal, bark *Elvira*, March 24, April 7 and 21, and May 19, 1849.

16. Teller, Journal, brig *Mary Stuart*, February 25, 1849.

17. Baker, Journal, ship *Nestor*, December, 1849.

18. Palmer, *A Voyage Round Cape Horn*, 5.

19. Harvey, Journal, ship *Crescent*, February 15, 1850.

20. *Gold Rush Voyage on the Bark Orion*, 101.

21. Green, Journal, ship *Sabina*, March 4, 1849.

22. Spear, *Memorandum Book*, November 24 and 29; December 2, 9, 15, and 30, 1849; January 13, 16, and 31; February 2, 3, 6, and 9; and March 2 and 3, 1849.

23. Whaley, *Consignments to El Dorado*, 163.

24. Barker, Journal, ship *Nestor*, January 24, March 17, and April 9, 1850.

25. Spear, *Memorandum Book*, January 2–3, 1850.

26. *Ibid.*, March 4, 1849.

27. Booth, Journal, ship *Andalusia*, September 9 and 15, 1849.

28. Keeler, Journal, bark *Anna Reynolds*, May 2–3, 1849.

29. Spear, *Memorandum Book*, November 28 and 29, and December 4, 5, 24, and 25, 1849; January 3 and 4, February 14, and March 4, 1850.

30. Booth, Journal, ship *Andalusia*, August 1, 1849.

31. *Gold Rush Voyage on the Bark Orion*, 143–44.

32. Hale, *Log of a Forty-Niner*, 53.

33. Harvey, Journal, ship *Crescent*, March 22–29 and April 15 and 26, 1850.

34. Haskins, *Argonauts of California*, 23.

35. Young, Journal, bark *Helen Augusta*, July 25, 1849.

36. Reed, Journal, ship *Magnolia*, April 21 and 24, and May 8, 1849.

37. Keeler, Journal, bark *Anna Reynolds*, May 2–3, 1849.

38. Van Dyke, Journal, ship *Tahmaroo*, February 3, 1849.

39. Booth, Journal, ship *Andalusia*, April 21, May 16, and June 9, 1849. What she referred to as plum pudding might possibly have been duff, which was sometimes called plum duff.

40. Baker, Journal, ship *Nestor*, January 19, 1850.

41. Lyman, *Journal of a Voyage*, 14.

42. Swain, Journal, bark *Belvidera*, April 11 and 21, 1849.

43. Meredith, Journal, bark *Strafford*, February 14–June 3, 1849. "Role Poles" are probably roly-polies, puddings made by rolling up jam or fruit in pastry dough and cooking them.

44. Whaley, *Consignments to El Dorado*, 123 and 163.

45. McCrackan, Letters to his sisters, Mary, May 24–29, 1849, and Lottie,

August 1–7, 1849. Based on what other passengers wrote about porpoises they caught, twelve feet seems quite long, especially for a young porpoise.

46. Bailey, Journal, ship *Sweden*, July 17, 1849; Cogswell, "Gold Rush Diary," 41; and Tollman, Journal, ship *Sweden*, July 16, 1849.

47. Hale, *Log of a Forty-Niner*, 35; Hall, *Around the Horn in '49*, 111; Lyman, *Journal of a Voyage*, 22; and Akerman, Journal, bark *Daniel Webster*, December 20, 1849 and January 6, 1850.

48. Anonymous, Journal, ship *Plymouth*, April 15, 1850; Childs, Journal, ship *Reindeer*, January 25, 1850; Ewer, Journal, ship *York*, July 14 and 16, 1849.

49. Wheeler, Journal, bark *Hannah Sprague*, July 13, 1849; Christman, *One Man's Gold*, 47–48.

50. Anonymous, Journal, ship *Plymouth*, February 18, 1850; Hale, *Log of a Forty-Niner*, 20–21; and Nash, *To the Goldfields*, 4.

51. Booth, Journal, ship *Andalusia*, May 21, 1849.

52. Ewer, Journal, ship *York*, June 6, 1849; Whaley, *Consignments to El Dorado*, 78; Overton, Journal, bark *Keoka*, March 28, 1849; Woodbury, Journal, ship *Argonaut*, December 3, 1849; Harvey, Journal, ship *Crescent*, January 30, 1850; and Stearns, Journal, bark *Belvidera*, May 2, 1849.

53. Stevens, Journal, bark *Emma Isadora*, April 24, 25, and 27, 1849 (the flying fish wings are still in the journal); Ship *Friendship*, undated episode while on a voyage, 1849; La Motte, Letter to his mother, August 22–October 12, 1849, La Motte Family Letters; Bailey, Journal, ship *Sweden*, June 28, 1849; Jessup, Journal, ship *Sheffield*, January 24, 1850; and Keeler, Journal, bark *Anna Reynolds*, May 31, 1849.

54. Kendall, *A Landsman's Voyage*, 119–20; Doten, *Journals*, 1:19; and Denham, Journal, schooner *Rialto*, March 24, 1849.

55. "Rhyme of the Ancient Mariner" was first published in *Lyrical Ballads* in 1798 and has been reprinted and interpreted numerous times. The part of the ballad of over 650 lines that is pertinent here is what happened when one of the sailors killed an albatross. Many high school students in English classes have had to memorize these often quoted lines that illustrate the punishment all suffered as their ship was stalled and the supply of drinking water dwindled:

> Water, water, every where,
>   And all the boards did shrink
> Water, water, every where,
>   Nor any drop to drink.

It is noteworthy that none of the vessels in which passengers killed albatross appear to have suffered severe consequences because of that action.

56. Christman, *One Man's Gold*, 44–45; Upham, *Notes of a Voyage*, 126; Akerman, Journal, bark *Daniel Webster*, December 11 and 17, 1849; Anonymous, Journal, ship *Pharsalia*, March 18, 1849; Anonymous, Journal, ship *Plymouth*, March 3, 1850; and Wilson, Journal, brig *Oriental*, December 28, 1849.

57. Dornin, Reminiscences; Upham, *Notes of a Voyage*, 116–17.

58. Keeler, Journal, *Anna Reynolds*, July 23–August 11, 1849; Kingsley, "Diary," 278–81.

59. Van Dyke, Journal, ship *Tahmaroo*, February 2, 1849.

60. Williams, Journal, ship *Pacific*, January 22–March 26, 1849; Stillman, *Seeking the Golden Fleece*, 39–53; Browne, *Letters, Journals and Writings*, 73–77; National Archives, U.S. Consular Dispatches from Rio de Janeiro, 5 June 1849–27 December 1850. More than half of the information is about the conflict between Captain Tibbits and the passengers. The conflict is discussed at length in Schultz, "The Gold Rush Voyage of the Ship *Pacific*: A Study in Vessel Management, 190–200.

61. Fuller, Journal, ship *Sweden*, March 1–August 5, 1849, especially the entries for each Sunday; Tolman, Journal, ship *Sweden*, March 18, April 26, and June 11, 1849; Cogswell, "Gold Rush Diary," 10–13, 16–17, 21, 34, and 43; Goodwin, *Reminiscence*, 9, 11, 13, and 27–30.

62. Childs, Journal, ship *Reindeer*, November 29 and December 6, 1849, and January 9 and February 2, 1850; Farren, Journal, ship *Reindeer*, February 6–10, 1850.

63. Van Dyke, Journal, ship *Tahmaroo*, April 26, 1849.

64. Snow, Journal, ship *Euphrasia*, December 10, 12, 17, and 19, 1849, and January 21, 1850.

65. Towne, Journal, ship *Capitol*, February 5 and 12, 1849. There are references to the meeting on these dates, but the petition and the captain's response are actually in the back of the journal.

66. Bailey, Journal, bark *Sarah Warren*, October 21 and 26; November 5, 10, 11, 12, 13, 23, and 30; December 6, 13, and 24, 1849; and March 26, 1850.

67. Williams, Journal, ship *Regulus*, September 17, 1849.

68. Bailey, Journal, bark *Sarah Warren*, November 30, 1849.

69. Williams, Journal, ship *Pacific*, July 17, 1849; Kendall, *A Landsman's Voyage*, 26 and 29–30; and Anonymous, Journal, the ship *America*, April 19, 1849, Bancroft Library.

70. Kendall, *A Landsman's Voyage*, 27–30 and 36; Howard, Journal, bark *Midas*, December 4, 1849; Gould, Journal, bark *Maria*, May 8–9, 1849; Reid, Journal, bark *Velasco*, April 29, 1849; Martin, Journal, bark *Elvira*, February 13, 1849; Davis, *Reminiscences*, 89; and Marchant, Poetic journal, ship *Magnolia*.

71. Christman, *One Man's Gold*, 36–37, 41, and 44–45; Upham, *Notes of a Voyage*, 30, 36, 130, and 207; Carder, Journal, ship *Hopewell*, May 5, 1849; Taylor, Journal, ship *Orpheus*, April 20 and 23, and June 24, 28, 29, and 30, 1849; Stevens, Journal, bark *Emma Isadora*, August 31 and September 1 and 2, 1849; Reed, Journal. ship *Magnolia*, May 15, July 29, and August 7, 13, and 22, 1849; and Collins, Journal, ship *Magnolia*, August 13, 1849.

4: AMUSEMENT AND ENTERTAINMENT

1. Hall, *Around the Horn in '49*, 111–13.

2. Ewer, Journal, ship *York*, July 27, 1849.

3. Spear, *Memorandum Book*, December 6, 1849; January 2, 10, and 16, February 22, and most days of March 1–26, 1850.

4. Fletcher, Journal, bark *Elvira*, January 2–July 26, 1849.

5. Randall, Journal, ship *Hannibal*, January 3, 1850; Collins, Journal, ship *Magnolia*, February 19 and May 20, 1849; Goodwin, *Reminiscence*, May 27 and July 25, 1849; and Whaley, *Consignments to El Dorado*, February 15, April 23, and May 1 and 6, 1849.

6. Upham, *Notes of a Voyage,* 34; Deane, Journal, ship *Arkansas,* August 10, 1849; Stearns, Journal, bark *Belvidera,* April 2, 1849; Gager, Journal, ship *Pacific,* April 19, 1849; Cooledge, Journal, bark *Oxford,* January 28, 1849; and Gould, Journal, bark *Maria,* May 11, 1849.

7. Anonymous, Journal, ship *Pharsalia,* March 8, 1849; Cross, Journal, ship *Crescent,* March 7, 1849; Gould, Journal, bark *Maria,* May 10, 1849; Williams, Journal, ship *Pacific,* July 29, 1849; Stearns, Journal, bark *Belvidera,* March 21 and 24, 1849; Cooledge, Journal, bark *Oxford,* June 3, 1849, and Randall, Journal, ship *Hannibal,* December 11, 1849.

8. Cross, Journal, ship *Crescent,* February 16, 1850; Harvey, Journal, ship *Crescent,* February 18, 1850; Gager, Journal, ship *Pacific,* February 22, 1849; Cooledge, Journal, bark *Oxford,* June 17, 1849; and Cooledge, *Off to the Goldfields,* 5.

9. Anonymous, Journal, ship *Pharsalia,* March 2, 1849; Williams, Journal, ship *Pacific,* April 30 and July 25 and 26, 1849; Stillman, Letter to his brother, February 1849; Collins, Journal, ship *Magnolia,* July 7, 1849; Whaley, *Consignments to El Dorado,* 121; and Anonymous, Journal, ship *Plymouth,* January 1 and 3, 1850.

10. Deane, Journal, ship *Arkansas,* September 15 and 18, and October 29, 1849; McCrackan, Letter to his mother, June 29–July 6, 1849; Cogswell, "Gold Rush Diary," 14 and 37; Williams, Journal, ship *Pacific,* April 16; May 4, 9, 10, and 24; June 13 and 18; and July 19, 1849; Clark, Journal, ship *Pacific,* April 10, 1849; Sheppard, Journal, ship *Morrison,* April 5 and 16, 1849; Randall, Journal, ship *Hannibal,* January 5 and 20, 1850; Anonymous, Journal, ship *Plymouth,* January 5, 9, and 11; February 4, 9 and 19; and March 20, 1850; and Anonymous, Journal, bark *Gold Hunter,* April 17 and May 18 and 23, 1849.

11. Kendall, *A Landsman's Voyage,* 51; Cogswell, "Gold Rush Diary," 36; Benton, Journal, ship *Edward Everett,* May 10, 14, and 15, 1849; [George Payson], *Golden Dreams and Leaden Realities,* 33; Booth, Journal, ship *Andalusia,* May 7, June 5 and 13, and August 14 and 16, 1849; Ewer, Journal, ship *York,* July 27, 1849; La Motte, Letter, August 22, 1849; Snow, Journal, ship *Euphrasia,* December 4, 8, and 11, 1849; Kingsley, "Diary," 245–46; and Hatch, Journal, schooner *Damariscove,* January 21, 1850.

12. Cogswell, "Gold Rush Diary," 16–17; Anonymous, Journal, ship *Plymouth,* January 10 and 30 and May 6 and 11, 1850; Benton, Journal, ship *Edward Everett,* May 24, 1849; Doten, *Journals,* 1: 9; Cooledge, Journal, bark *Oxford,* March 19, 1849; Whaley, *Consignments to El Dorado,* 96–97, 100, and 123; Hyde, Journal, ship *Lenore,* March 17, 1849; Van Dyke, Journal, ship *Tahmaroo,* February 9, 1849; Caine, Journal, bark *Belvidera,* July 10, 1849; and Booth, Journal, ship *Andalusia,* September 2, 6, and 7, 1849.

13. Booth, Journal, ship *Andalusia,* August 13, 17, 21, 22, 24, 27, 30, and 31 and September 3 and 5, 1849.

14. Cogswell, "Gold Rush Diary," 13 and 45; Goodwin, *Reminiscence,* 12; Benton, Journal, ship *Edward Everett,* June 6 and 20, 1849; and Hyde, Journal, ship *Lenore,* May 30, 1849.

15. Swain, Journal, bark *Belvidera,* July 15, 1849, and Anonymous, Journal, ship *America,* April 12, 1849, Bancroft Library.

16. Brannan, Letter to his wife, May 20–June 3, 1849; Browne, *Letters, Journals and Writings,* 79; Deane, Journal, ship *Arkansas,* July 30 and August 6, 1849; Towne, Jour-

nal, ship *Capitol,* February 20 and 24, 1849; Van Dyke, Journal, ship *Tahmaroo,* January 30, 1849; Green, Journal, ship *Sabina,* March 14, 1849; Stevens, Journal, bark *Emma Isadora,* April 28 and August 8, 1849; Hall, *Around the Horn in '49,* 29–30 and 72; Childs, Journal, ship *Reindeer,* February 8, 1849; Farren, Journal, ship *Reindeer,* January 17 and March 7 and 14, 1849; and Kingsley, "Diary," 253–57.

17. *Gold Rush Voyage on the Bark Orion,* 73–74 and 77; Kingsley, "Diary," 245–57; Deane, Journal, ship *Arkansas,* July 17, 1849; Sophia A. Eastman, Letter, October 21–December 23, 1849, Maria M. Child Correspondence; Benton, Journal, ship *Reindeer,* February 21 and 24; March 10, 17, and 24; May 19 and 26; and June 2, 9, and 16, 1849; Browne, *Letters, Journals and Writings,* 80; Gager, Journal, ship *Pacific,* February 10 and 15, 1849; Stillman, *Seeking the Golden Fleece,* 44; Williams, Journal, ship *Pacific,* February 14 and 22, 1849; Sheppard, Journal, ship *Morrison,* June 7, 8, 9, 12, and 17, 1849; Coffin, *A Pioneer Voyage,* 41–52; Booth, Journal, ship *Andalusia,* August 13–17, 20–25, and 27, 1849; *The Petrel;* and *The Barometer.*

18. McCrackan, Letter to his sister Lottie, April 30, 1849; Booth, Journal, ship *Andalusia,* May 16, 1849; Gould, Journal, ship *Maria,* May 30, 1849; Anonymous, Journal, ship *Plymouth,* June 8, 1849; and Taylor, Journal, ship *Orpheus,* May 17, 1849.

19. Anonymous, Journal, ship *Plymouth,* April 12, 1850.

20. Smith, *Historical Sketch of the Lives of William Wiggin Smith and Joseph Hiram Smith,* 31–32.

21. Whaley, *Consignments to El Dorado,* 141, and Haskins, *Argonauts of California,* 28.

22. McCrackan, Letter to his sister Lottie, August 1–6, 1849.

23. McCrackan, Letter to his mother and sisters, July 23–27, 1849.

24. Palmer, *A Voyage round Cape Horn,* 12–13.

25. Anonymous, Journal, ship *Pacific,* June 14, 1849, and McCrackan, Letter to his sister Mary, April 30–May, 10, 1849.

26. Davis, *Reminiscences,* 95–96.

27. Taylor, Journal, ship *Orpheus,* March 8, 1849, and Meredith, Journal, bark *Strafford,* March 9, 1849.

28. Fuller, Journal, ship *Sweden,* March 7 and 8, 1849; Cogswell, "Gold Rush Diary," 11; Goodwin, *Reminiscence,* 10–13; Stillman, *Seeking the Golden Fleece,* 42; Gager, Journal, ship *Pacific,* February 6 and April 21, 1849; Williams, Journal, ship *Pacific,* February 6 and April 19, 21, and 23, 1849; Reid, Journal, ship *Velasco,* April 7 and 24 and August 24, 1849; Taylor, Journal, ship *Orpheus,* February 15 and 17 and April 26, 1849; and Stearns, Journal, bark *Belvidera,* March 21, 1849.

29. Cogswell, "Gold Rush Diary," 43; Harry G. Brown, Journal, bark *Selma,* April 20, 1849; Cross, Journal, ship *Crescent,* February 5, 1849; Graves, Journal, ship *Crescent,* February 5, 1849; Hollingsworth, Journal, ship *Daniel Webster,* April 6, 1849; Cooledge, *Off to the Goldfields,* 11; and Benton, Journal, ship *Edward Everett,* June 22, 1849.

30. Bailey, Journal, ship *Sweden,* July 13, 1849; Whaley, *Consignments to El Dorado,* 75 and 78; Williams, Journal, ship *Pacific,* February 20, 1849; Doten, *Journals,* 1: 8; Anonymous, Journal, ship *Pacific,* May 19–23, 1849; Gager, Journal, ship *Pacific,* May 19–23, 1849; Browne, *Crusoe's Island,* 11–22, 25–27, 91–92, and 141–44; and *New York Daily Tribune,* August 8, 1849, letter probably by Philip E. Walden of Brooklyn, who was a passenger in the ship.

31. Dougal, *Off for California*, 38; Lyman, *Journal of a Voyage*, 82; and Taylor, Journal, ship *Orpheus*, February 24, 1849.

32. Anonymous, Journal, ship *Plymouth*, January 2–March 28, 1850. When the California-bound sailing vessels put into a port, many of the passengers made up for the limited walking facilities on board their vessel by walking many miles through such cities as Rio de Janeiro, Talcahuano, Lima, and Valparaiso and on into the outlying regions of those cities. On the island of Juan Fernandez many of them climbed up into the mountains to visit the cave of Robinson Crusoe. In addition nearly all wrote long and detailed descriptions of what they did and saw in those places and their reactions to the land and the people. Many compared the places and the people with that of their homelands. Invariably they saw their friends and families at home as being much more industrious and advanced technologically than the peoples of the foreign countries they visited. These commentaries by passengers in sailing vessels bound for California provide prime but little-used resource materials on North American citizens' opinions of their neighbors and countries to the south.

33. Meredith, Journal, bark *Strafford*, May 9 and June 1, 1849, and Howard, Journal, bark *Midas*, December 26, 1849.

34. Anonymous, Journal, bark *Gold Hunter*, December 1, 1849; February 18 and March 12, 1850; Locke, Journal, brig *Sea Eagle*, May 31 and June 15, 1849; and Hall, *Around the Horn in '49*, 39.

35. Cooledge, *Off to the Goldfields*, 5; Randle, Letter, May 1–5, 1849; Keeler, Journal, bark *Anna Reynolds*, May 11, 1849; Kingsley, "Diary," 58; Gould, Journal, bark *Maria*, May 29, 1849; Graves, Journal, ship *Crescent*, April 17, 1849; Howard, Journal, bark *Midas*, November 17, 1849; Nash, *To the Goldfields*, 5; Upham, *Notes of a Voyage*, 40; Meredith, Journal, bark *Strafford*, March 17, 1849; Hale, *Log of a Forty-Niner*, 33; Ewer, Journal, ship *York*, June, 1849; Anonymous, Journal, ship *Plymouth*, February 6, 1849; and Baker, Journal, ship *San Francisco*, September 26, 1849.

36. Childs, Journal, ship *Reindeer*, December 4, 1849; Overton, Journal, bark *Keoka*, March 17 and August 8, 1849; Kendall, *Landsman's Voyage*, 24; Fletcher, Journal, bark *Elvira*, January 30, 1849; and Martin, Journal, bark *Elvira*, January 30, 1849.

37. McCrackan, Letter to his sister Lottie, May 10–12, 1849.

38. Coleman, Journal, bark *Russell*, April 4, 1849.

39. Reed, Journal, ship *Magnolia*, March 17, 1849, and Booth, Journal, ship *Andalusia*, May 21, 1849.

40. Anonymous, Journal, ship *Pacific*, April 11, 1849; Stillman, *Seeking the Golden Fleece*, 76–78; Williams, Journal, ship *Pacific*, April 5, 1849; and Gager, Journal, ship *Pacific*, April 5, 1849.

41. Hale, *Log of a Forty-Niner*, 59; Upham, *Notes of a Voyage*, 180; Baker, Journal, bark *San Francisco*, August 18, 1849; Anonymous, Journal, ship *America*, April 3, 1849 and several other entries in April, May, and June 1849, Bancroft Library; and Williams, Journal, ship *Pacific*, January 24, 1849.

42. Bailey, Journal, ship *Sweden*, June 14, 1849; Baker, Journal, bark *San Francisco*, August 18, 1849; Ewer, Journal, ship *York*, June 3, 1849; Meredith, Journal, bark *Strafford*, August 9, 1849; and *Gold Rush Voyage on the Bark Orion*, 91.

43. Cogswell, "Gold Rush Diary," 24; Williams, Journal, ship *Pacific*, February 5 and 15, 1849; Hollingsworth, Journal, ship *Daniel Webster*, April 10, 1849; Barker, Jour-

nal, ship *Nestor,* December 24, 1849 and March 30, 1850; Meredith, Journal, bark *Strafford,* February 19 and 22 and March 2 and 25, 1849; Sheppard, Journal, ship *Morrison,* March 27, 1849; and Hull, Journal, ship *Jane Parker,* February 22, 1849.

44. Brown, *Letters, Journals and Writings,* 105; Cogswell, "Gold Rush Diary," 33; Childs, Journal, ship *Reindeer,* January 25, 1850; Bailey, Journal, ship *Sweden,* April 17, and May 11, 1849; Williams, Journal, ship *Pacific,* April 26, 1849; Hall, *Around the Horn in '49,* 69–70; Kendall, *Landsman's Voyage,* 86; Overton, Journal, bark *Keoka,* May 8, 1849; Fitch, Journal, ship *Florida,* September 27, 1849; and Anonymous, Journal, bark *Gold Hunter,* January 19 and March 23, 1850.

45. Cogswell, "Gold Rush Diary," 15; Doten, *Journals,* 1: 13; McCrackan, Letter to sister Mary, May 24–29, 1849; and Williams, Journal, ship *Pacific,* February 17, 1849.

46. Fowler, Account of a voyage, 5 and 7; Christman, *One Man's Gold,* 34; *Gold Rush Voyage on the Ship Orion,* 110–11; Williams, Journal, ship *Pacific,* March 1, 1849; Barker, Journal, ship *Nestor,* February 23, 1850; Upham, *Notes of a Voyage,* 52, 128–32, 175–76, and 179; Sheppard, Journal, ship *Morrison,* April 15 and 16, 1849; Anonymous, Journal, ship *Pharsalia,* April 30, 1849; and Howard, Journal, bark *Midas,* February 4, 1850.

47. Lyman, *Journal of a Voyage,* 13; Deane, Journal, ship *Arkansas,* July 21, 1849; Tolman, Journal, ship *Sweden,* July 6, 1849; Christman, *One Man's Gold,* 19; Anonymous, Journal, ship *Gold Hunter,* March 20, 1850; Doten, *Journals,* 1: 14–15 and 17–20; Kendall, *Landsman's Voyage,* 78; Kingsley, "Diary," June 5 and October 17, 1849; Reed, Journal, ship *Magnolia,* March 29, May 3, June 19, and August 6 and 19, 1849; Collins, Journal, ship *Magnolia,* March 28; and Anonymous, Journal, ship *America,* April 28–29, May 4, April 30, and June 29, 1849, Bancroft Library.

48. Anonymous, Journal, ship *Plymouth,* May 2 and 3, 1849; Wilson, Journal, brig *Oriental,* December 17, 1849; Fitch, Journal, ship *Florida,* August 10, 1849; Morgan, Gold Dust: The Log of a Forty-Niner, 5; and Anonymous, Journal, ship *America,* May 23 and 24, 1849, Bancroft Library.

49. Anonymous, Journal, ship *Plymouth,* May 2 and 28, 1849; and Kendall, *Landsman's Voyage,* 78.

50. Baker, Journal, ship *San Francisco,* August 17, 1 and 29–30, and September 27, 1849.

51. Upham, *Notes of a Voyage,* 96, 96, and 111.

52. Anonymous, Journal, bark *Gold Hunter,* October 18 and December 23, 1849 and March 2, 1850.

53. Locke, Journal, brig *Sea Eagle,* October 7, 1849; Ewer, Journal, ship *York,* June 6, 1849; Hatch, Journal, schooner *Damarsicove,* February 2, 1850; Logbook, bark *Selma,* August 28, 1849; Coleman, Journal, bark *Russell,* July 14 and 17, 1849; Whaley, *Consignments to El Dorado,* 96–98 (The three persons listed as being impersonated were well-known actors who appeared at the Astor Place Opera House in New York.); Baker, Journal, bark *San Francisco,* August 24, 1849; Tollman, Journal, ship *Sweden,* May 16, 1849; Cogswell, "Gold Rush Diary," 25 and 28–28; Fuller, Journal, ship *Sweden,* May 9, 1849; Goodwin, *Reminiscence,* 24, 26, and 31; Christman, *One Man's Gold,* 29; Stearns, Journal, bark *Belvidera,* May 3, 1849; Williams, Journal, ship *Pacific,* July 18, 1849; and Booth, Journal, ship *Andalusia,* August 21 and 23, 1849.

54. Harvey, Journal, ship *Crescent*, February 22 and 23, 1850; Upham, *Notes of a Voyage*, 112–13; Christman, *One Man's Gold*, 33. The excessive use of alcohol by some passengers in these celebrations was in keeping with other celebrations such as Washington's birthday and Fourth of July observances held in a great many vessels. This might be indicative of the way these men were accustomed to celebrating such events at home. On the other hand, they might have been doing the exact opposite of what they did at home since they were far from home and might have felt news of their activities would never reach home.

55. Kendall, *Landsman's Voyage*, 60; Hall, *Around the Horn in '49*, 71,116–17, and 121; Booth, Journal, ship *Andalusia*, August 15, 1849; Anonymous, Journal, bark *Gold Hunter*, December 7, 1849; Bowles, Journal, ship *Mount Vernon*, July 18, 1849; Hollingsworth, Journal, ship *Daniel Webster*, May 8 and 27 and June 28, 1849; Anonymous, Journal, ship *Plymouth*, January 15 and May 7, 8, and 11, 1850; Cogswell, "Gold Rush Diary," 36; Kingsley, "Diary," 152–53; and Brannan, Letters to his sister Mary, July 11–21, August 7–15, and November 15–18, 1849.

56. Fletcher, Journal, bark *Elvira*, various dates between January 16 and March 10, 1849; Meredith, Journal, bark *Strafford*, June 4, 1849; Chittenden, Journal, bark *Croton*, June 14, 1849; Stearns, Journal, bark *Belvidera*, June 28, 1849; Howard, Journal, bark *Midas*, November 10 and 25 and December 1, 1849, and January 17 and March 2, 1850; and Hatch, Journal, schooner *Damariscove*, January 20 and 21, February 2, and June 3, 1850.

57. Martin, Journal, bark *Elvira*, March 12, 1849; Stevens, Journal, bark *Emma Isadora*, July 3, 1849; Sophia A. Eastman, Letter to Maria M. Child, October 31–December 23, 1849; and Hollingsworth, Journal, ship *Daniel Webster*, February 20, 1849. Similar information is available in many of the other journals of passengers bound for California.

58. Cross, Journal, ship *Crescent*, March 9, 1850.

5: SUNDAYS, HOLIDAYS, AND SPECIAL DAYS

1. Badger, Journal, brig *Triumph*, November 18, 1849.

2. Kingsley, "Diary," entries for all Sundays, March 25–November 11, 1849. He did not identify the source from which the sermons were taken.

3. Booth, Journal, ship *Andalusia*, April 21 and 28, May 6, June 3 and 17, July 8, August 5, 11, 12, 19, and 26, and September 2, 1849.

4. Denham, Journal, schooner *Rialto*, February 11 and 18, April 15 and 29, May 13, and June 3 and 24, 1849. Holmes Hole is now called Vineyard Haven.

5. Benton, Journal, ship *Edward Everett*, entries for all Sundays between January 14 and July 1, 1849.

6. Snow, Journal, ship *Euphrasia*, entries for all Sundays between November 25, 1849 and May 19, 1850.

7. Sheppard, Journal, ship *Morrison*, entries for all Sundays between February 17 and September 23, 1849.

8. Hyde, Journal, ship *Lenore*, entries for all Sundays between February 10 and July 1, 1849.

9. Gager, Journal, ship *Pacific*, entries for all Sundays between January 28 and

August 5, 1849, and Williams, Journal, ship *Pacific,* entries for all Sundays between January 28 and August 5, 1849.

10. Stearns, Journal, bark *Belvidera,* entries for all Sundays between March 11 and October 1, 1849; Caine, Journal, bark *Belvidera,* entries for all Sundays between March 4 and October 14, 1849; and Swain, Journal, bark *Belvidera,* March 18 and 25, April 1, 8, and 22, and August 12 and 19, 1849.

11. Graves, Journal, ship *Crescent,* entries for all Sundays between December 9, 1849 and May 26, 1850; Harvey, Journal, ship *Crescent,* entries for all Sundays between December 16, 1849 and May 19, 1850; Cross, Journal, ship *Crescent,* entries for all Sundays between December 9, 1849 and May 26, 1850; and Hutchinson, Journal, bark *Belgrade,* March 24, 1850.

12. Meredith, Journal, bark *Strafford,* entries for all Sundays between February 4 and August 26, 1849 (long quote on July 22).

13. Tolman, Journal, ship *Sweden,* March 11, 1849; Bailey, Journal, ship *Sweden,* entries for all Sundays between March 11 and April 22, 1849 (words to one song on March 11); Fuller, Journal, ship *Sweden,* entries for all Sundays between March 4 and May 8, 1849 (words to songs on March 25, April 8, 22, and 29, and May 8); Cogswell, "Gold Rush Diary," entries for all Sundays between March 4 and July 29, 1849; and Goodwin, *Reminiscence,* entries for all Sundays between March 4 and July 29, 1849 (words for hymns on March 18 and 25, 1849).

14. Anonymous, Journal, ship *America,* entries for all Sundays between April 8 and September 16, 1849, Bancroft Library.

15. Chittenden, Journal, bark *Croton,* entries for all Sundays between January 21 and July 29, 1849; Fletcher, Journal, bark *Elvira,* entries for all Sundays between January 14 and June 26, 1849; Martin, Journal, bark *Elvira,* entries for all Sundays between January 7 and June 24, 1849; Towne, Journal, ship *Capitol,* entries for all Sundays between January 23 and July 23, 1849; Overton, Journal, bark *Keoka,* entries for all Sundays between February 5 and September 17, 1849; and Cooledge, Journal, bark *Oxford,* entries for all Sundays between January 22 and August 21, 1849.

16. Anonymous, Journal, bark *Gold Hunter,* January 1, 1850; Barker, Journal, ship *Nestor,* January 1, 1850; Goodall, Journal, schooner *St. Mary,* January 1, 1850; Spear, *Memorandum Book,* January 1, 1850; Woodbury, Journal, ship *Argonaut,* January 1, 1850; Christman, *One Man's Gold,* 69; Howard, Journal, bark *Midas,* January 1, 1850; Akerman, Journal, bark *Daniel Webster,* January 1, 1850; and Nash, *To The Goldfields,* 4.

17. Meredith, Journal, bark *Strafford,* February 14, 1849; Bee, Journal, ship *South Carolina,* February 14, 1849; Whaley, *Consignments to El Dorado,* 96; Benton, Journal, ship *Edward Everett,* February 14, 1849; Taylor, Journal, bark *Isabel,* February 14, 1849; and Anonymous, Journal, ship *Plymouth,* February 14, 1850.

18. Teller, Journal, brig *Mary Stuart,* February 22, 1849; Benton, Journal, ship *Edward Everett,* February 21 and 22, 1849; Cross, Journal, ship *Crescent,* February 22 and 23, 1849; and Graves, Journal, ship *Crescent,* February 22, 1849.

19. Taylor, Journal, bark *Isabel,* February 21 and 28, 1849.

20. Taylor, Journal, ship *Orpheus,* February 22, 1849.

21. Hull, Journal, ship *Jane Parker,* February 22, 1849, and Carson, Journal, ship *Jane Parker,* February 20 and 22, 1849.

22. Anonymous, Journal, ship *Pharsalia*, February 22, 1849.

23. Meredith, Journal, bark *Strafford*, February 22, 1849.

24. Chittenden, Journal, bark *Croton*, March 5, 1849; Meredith, Journal, bark *Strafford*, March 5 and June 17, 1849; Benton, Journal, ship *Edward Everett*, March 5, 1849; Collins, Journal, ship *Magnolia*, March 5, 1849; and Reed, Journal, ship *Magnolia*, March 5, 1849.

25. Hall, *Around the Horn in '49*, 38; Gould, Journal, bark *Maria*, April 27, 1849; and Hyde, Journal, ship *Lenore*, March 5, 1849.

26. Whaley, *Consignments to El Dorado*, an illustration of the invitation appears between pages 62 and 63; Martin, Journal, bark *Elvira*, March 5, 1849; Fletcher, Journal, bark *Elvira*, March 3, 5, and 6, 1849; Cooledge, Journal, bark *Oxford*, March 4, 1849.

27. Meredith, Journal, bark *Strafford*, April 1, 1849; Collins, Journal, ship *Magnolia*, April 1, 1849; Spear, *Memorandum Book*, April 1, 1849; Fuller, Journal, ship *Sweden*, April 1, 1849; Sheppard, Journal, ship *Morrison*, April 1, 1849; and Upham, *Notes of a Voyage*, 102–3.

28. Gager, Journal, ship *Pacific*, June 19, 21, 23, 26, and 29, and July 3, 4, and 5, 1849; Anonymous, Journal, ship *Pacific*, June 25 and July 2 and 4, 1849; Clark, Journal, Ship *Pacific*, July 4, 1849; Williams, Journal, ship *Pacific*, June 19, 21, and 27, and July 4, 1849; and Stillman, *Seeking the Golden Fleece*, 103–7. A more complete description of Fourth of July celebrations is found in Schultz, "A Forty-Niner Fourth of July," 3–13.

29. Doten, *Journals*, 1: 26–27; Booth, Journal, ship *Andalusia*, July 4, 1849; Hall, *Around the Horn in '49*, 100–102; Uphan, *Notes of a Voyage*, 193–95; Kendall, *A Landsman's Voyage*, 111–12; Meredith, Journal, bark *Strafford*, July 4, 1849; *Celebration . . . Barque "Hannah Sprague,"* 13–16 (pages 5–12 contain the oration given by Alfred Wheeler); and Cowley, Journal, bark *Canton*, July 4, 1849.

30. Benton, Journal, ship *Edward Everett*, July 4, 1849; Swain, Journal, bark *Belvidera*, July 4, 1849; Caine, Journal, bark *Belvidera*, July 4, 1849; Stearns, Journal, bark *Belvidera*, July 4, 1849; Anonymous, Journal, ship *Pacific*, June 30, 1849; Stillman, *Seeking the Golden Fleece*, 105; Cooledge, Journal, bark *Oxford*, July 4, 1849; Fowler, Account of a Voyage, 2–5; and Jacobs, Journal, ship *Edward Everett*, July 4, 1849. *Celebration . . . Bark "Hannah Sprague"* contains a program for the day including references to the songs "Hail Columbia," "Star Spangled Banner," and "Old Grey Mare." The last one was sung after the toasts were completed.

31. Williams, Journal, ship *Regulus*, June 25–July 10, 1849, and Sheppard, Journal, ship *Morrison*, July 3 and 4, 1849.

32. Howard, Journal, bark *Midas*, November 28 and 29, 1849; Woodbury, Journal, ship *Argonaut*, November 29, 1849; *Gold Rush Voyage on the Bark Orion*, 77–79; Ferrell, Journal, ship *Arkansas*, November 29, 1849; Deane, Journal, ship *Arkansas*, November 22, 23, 27, 28, and 29, 1849; Spear, *Memorandum Book*, November 29, 1849; Childs, Journal, ship *Reindeer*, November 29, 1849; Snow, Journal, ship *Euphrasia*, November 29, 1849; and Baker, Journal, ship *San Francisco*, November 9 and 29, 1849.

33. McCrackan, Letter to Nathan Smith, July 20, 1849; Barker, Journal, ship

Nestor, December 25, 1849; Christman, *One Man's Gold,* 66–67; Graves, Journal, ship *Crescent,* December 24 and 25, 1849; Akerman, Journal, bark *Daniel Webster,* December 25, 1849; Woodbury, Journal, ship *Argonaut,* December 25, 1849; Hutchinson, Journal, bark *Belgrade,* December 25, 1849; Randall, Journal, ship *Hannibal,* December 25, 1849; Nash, *To the Goldfields,* 3; Baker, Journal, bark *San Francisco,* December 25, 1849; Wilson, Journal, brig *Oriental,* December 25, 1849; Bailey, Journal, ship *Sarah Warren,* December 25, 1849; and Howard, Journal, bark *Midas,* December 25, 1849.

34. Stevens, Journal, bark *Emma Isadora,* May 1, 1849; Anonymous, Journal, ship *Pharsalia,* May 1 and 8, 1849; Hall, *Around the Horn in '49,* 46–47; Lyman, *Journal of a Voyage,* 25–26 and 49 (he mentions the election on both April 2 and May 2); Ewer, Journal, ship *York,* June 25, 1849; Locke, Journal, brig *Sea Eagle,* June 17, 1849; Martin, Journal, bark *Elvira,* June 16 and 17, 1849; Anonymous, Journal, ship *Plymouth,* June 19, 1849; Cooledge, Journal, bark *Oxford,* June 17, 1849; Cogswell, "Gold Rush Diary," 36; Booth, Journal, ship *Andalusia,* September 10 and 12, 1849; and *Baltimore American & Commercial Daily Advertiser,* September 13, 1849.

35. Reed, Journal, ship *Magnolia,* May 31, 1849; Cooledge, Journal, bark *Oxford,* April 3, 1849; Bowles, Journal, ship *Mount Vernon,* May 9, 1849; Floyd Jones, Letter to his parents, May 2, 1849, Floyd-Jones Family Correspondence; Doten, *Journals,* 1: 22 and 29; Upham, *Notes of a Voyage,* 131; Morgan, Gold Dust: The Log of a Forty-Niner, 6; Deane, Journal, ship *Arkansas,* September 24, 1849; Lewis, Journal, ship *Charlotte,* July 26, 1849; Carson, Journal, ship *Jane Parker,* February 5, 1849; McCrackan, Letter to his mother, April 4–22, 1849; Fuller, Journal, ship *Sweden,* March 20, 1849; Gager, Journal, ship *Pacific,* June 26, 1849; and McCrackan, Letter to sister Lottie, May 30–June 7, 1849.

6: WEATHER PROBLEMS

1. Booth, Journal, ship *Andalusia,* June 26 and July 9, 1849; Kendall, *A Landsman's Voyage,* 92–93; Snow, Journal, ship *Euphrasia,* March 9, 1850; and McCrackan, Letter to his mother, April 4–22, 1849.

2. Cogswell, "Gold Rush Diary," 9; Snow, Journal, ship *Euphrasia,* February 28, 1850; Howard, Journal, bark *Midas,* January 1, 1850; and Booth, Journal, ship *Andalusia,* July 18, 1849.

3. Bailey, Journal, bark *Sarah Warren,* November 14, 1849; Meredith, Journal, bark *Strafford,* March 25, 1849; Anonymous, Journal, ship *America,* June 14, 1849, Bancroft Library; and Booth, Journal, ship *Andalusia,* June 19, 1849.

4. Anonymous, Journal, ship *American,* Bancroft Library.

5. Nash, *To the Goldfields,* 10; Anonymous, Journal, bark *Gold Hunter,* January 7, 10, and 11, 1849; Collins, Journal, ship *Magnolia,* March 26 and 27, 1849; McCrackan, Letter to his sister Lottie, June 8–11, 1849; Meredith, Journal, bark *Strafford,* March 24, 1849; Corneilson, Journal, bark *Hannah Sprague,* October 11, 1849; Harry G. Brown, Journal, bark *Selma,* September 17, 1849; Bailey, Journal, bark *Sarah Warren,* February 24, 1850; and Teller, Journal, brig *Mary Stuart,* January 28–July 4, 1849.

6. Bell, Journal, schooner *Gager,* March 3 and 29, 1849; Cogswell, "Gold Rush Diary," 14–16; Stevens, Journal, bark *Emma Isadora,* May 13, 1849; Nash, *To the Goldfields,* 4–5; Kendall, *A Landsman's Voyage,* 25 and 27; Wheeler, Journal, bark *Hannah Sprague,* June 21, 1849; Upham, *Notes of a Voyage,* 42 and 50; Barker, Journal, ship *Nestor,* January 11 and 12, 1850; Gould, Journal, bark *Maria,* April 27, 1849; Harvey, Journal, ship *Crescent,* January 16 and April 11, 12, 14, and 16, 1850; and Taylor, Journal, ship *Orpheus,* February 25 and June 10 and 11, 1849.

7. Taylor, Journal, ship *Orpheus,* April 8, 1849; Butler, Journal, ship *America,* June 26 and July 3, 1849; Harry G. Brown, Journal, bark *Selma,* July 21, 1849; Taylor, Journal, bark *Isabel,* June 18, 1849; Kingsley, "Diary," 284–85; Keeler, Journal, bark *Hannah Sprague,* August 20, 1849; Stevens, Journal, bark *Emma Isadora,* June 15–30, 1849; and Dougal, *Off for California,* 43–45.

8. Cogswell, "Gold Rush Diary," 23 and 30. Cogswell noted on May 20 that it was "quite a curious coincidence" that the *Sweden* was then in the exact same place she had been a year earlier carrying troops to California.

9. Wilson, Journal, brig *Oriental,* December 12–25, 1849; Stevens, Journal, bark *Emma Isadora,* June 15–30, 1849; Teller, Journal, brig *Mary Stuart,* April 3–24, 1849; Anonymous, Journal, ship *Pacific,* April 17–May 9, 1849; Anonymous, Journal, bark *Gold Hunter,* January 20, 1850; Locke, Journal, brig *Sea Eagle,* June 25–August 1, 1849; Bell, Journal, schooner *Gager,* April 30–June 25, 1849; Hollingsworth, Journal, ship *Daniel Webster,* April 10–17, 1849; Meredith, Journal, bark *Strafford,* June 1, 1849; Van Dyke, Journal, ship *Tahmaroo,* June 30, 1849; Goodall, Journal, schooner *St. Mary,* September–October, 1849; and Lewis, Journal, ship *Charlotte,* June 7, 1849.

10. Caine, Journal, *Belvidera,* May 26–June 27, 1849, and Stearns, Journal, bark *Belvidera,* May 26–June 24, 1849.

11. Ferrell, Journal, ship *Arkansas,* September 25–October 21, 1849.

12. Anonymous, Journal, ship *Plymouth,* March 26, 1849. What he meant by "chasser" is uncertain, but it might have been chasseur, French troops trained for rapid maneuvers.

13. La Motte, Letter to his mother, August 22–October 12, 1849, and Doten, *Journals,* 1: 22–23.

14. Sheppard, Journal, ship *Morrison,* February 11–15, 1849.

15. Anonymous, Journal, ship *America,* April 6, 1849, Bancroft Library.

16. Bell, Journal, schooner *Gager,* February 22, 1849.

17. Bailey, Journal, bark *Sarah Warren,* December 18, 1849.

18. Anonymous, Journal, ship *America,* June 18–21, 1849, Bancroft Library.

19. Stearns, Journal, bark *Belvidera,* May 19, 1849.

20. Overton, Journal, bark *Keoka,* June 8–10, 1849.

21. Chittenden, Journal, bark *Croton,* June 21–23, 1849.

22. Hatch, Journal, schooner *Damariscove,* March 2, 1850.

23. Anonymous, Journal, ship *Pacific,* April 18, 1849.

24. Deane, Journal, ship *Arkansas,* October 17–18, 199; Bailey, Journal, ship *Sarah Warren,* November 17, 1849; Barker, Journal, ship *Nestor,* March 5, 1850; Taylor, Journal, ship *Orpheus,* February 18 and April 21, 1849; Locke,

Journal, brig *Sea Eagle*, April 20, 1849; and Cogswell, "Gold Rush Diary," 39–40.

25. Gager, Journal, ship *Pacific*, July 20, 1849.

26. Chittenden, Journal, bark *Croton*, July 10, 1849.

27. Van Dyke, Journal, ship *Tahmaroo*, June 19–July 1, 1849.

28. Caine, Journal, bark *Belvidera*, October 2–12, 1849, and Stearns, Journal, bark *Belvidera*, October 2–12, 1849. The price quoted for carrying passengers is more than double what other passengers reported in their journals. A. Henry Stevens, a passenger in the bark *Emma Isadore*, reported on September 12, 1849 they were quoted a price of one dollar to be rowed ashore. He added that in Rio de Janeiro and Valparaiso the price was ten cents although the distance was twice that of San Francisco.

29. Williams, Journal, ship *Pacific*, July 26–August 4, 1849.

30. Stevens, Journal, bark *Emma Isadora*, September 2–12, 1849.

7: PEOPLE PROBLEMS

1. Reed, Journal, ship *Magnolia*, March 6, 1849; Meredith, Journal, bark *Strafford*, June 28, 1849; and Anonymous, Journal, ship *Pharsalia*, April 23, 1849.

2. Williams, Journal, ship *Regulus*, July 25–September 17, 1849. The Bunker Hill Trading and Mining Association was only one of a large number of such companies dissolved before the groups ever arrived in California. Most, if not all, of the others dissolved soon after they arrived. Many miners, however, did work together with one or more friends from home or ones they made after they arrived in California. They could work more effectively and efficiently as pairs or in groups than they could alone.

3. Ferrell, Journal, ship *Arkansas*, December 1, 1849.

4. Upham, *Notes of a Voyage*, 174–75.

5. Wheeler, Journal, bark *Hannah Sprague*, June 29, 1849, and Corneilson, Journal, bark *Hannah Sprague*, July 2, 1849.

6. Farren, Journal, ship *Reindeer*, January 22, 1849, and Reid, Journal, *Velasco*, August 27, 1849.

7. Hollingsworth, Journal, ship *Daniel Webster*, May 23 and July 2 and 4, 1849.

8. Akerman, Journal, bark *Daniel Webster*, January 4 and February 8, 1850.

9. Upham, *Notes of a Voyage*, 28, 37–38, 45, 60, 119, 125–26, 135–37, 171–73, 180–81, and 204–5, and Folwell, Journal, brig *Osceola*, June 8 and 29–30 and July 1–2, 1849.

10. Jessup, Journal, ship *Sheffield*, December 23–27, 1849 and February 8–23, 1850. The *Sheffield* was on a combined gold rush and whaling voyage. She carried a cargo of lumber and wheels to San Francisco and then proceeded on a whaling voyage that lasted until 1854. Contrary to the experience of many vessels that arrived in San Francisco at the time, the *Sheffield* did not lose any crew members other than those six turned over to the sloop of war *Warren*.

11. *New York Daily Tribune*, July 26, 1849, and *Baltimore Sun*, July 27 and August 13, 1849.

12. *Baltimore Sun*, August 25, 1849.

13. Sheppard, Journal, ship *Morrison,* April 2, May 2, and June 1, 1849.

14. Bailey, Journal, bark *Sarah Warren,* January 14 and 16, 1850.

15. Taylor, Journal, ship *Orpheus,* May 16–17, 1849.

16. Teller, Journal, brig *Mary Stuart,* May 2, 1849, and Anonymous, Journal, ship *Pacific,* May 5 and 6, 1849.

17. Upham, *Notes of a Voyage,* 28–29; McHenry, Letter to his father, April 4, 1849; and Graves, Journal, ship *Crescent,* January 23, 1850.

18. United States. Department of State. Consular Despatches, Valparaiso, Chile, 1844–1957.

19. Schultz, "Gold Rush Voyage of the Ship *Pacific:* A Study in Vessel Management," 190–200; *New York Daily Tribune,* July 21, 1849; and *Baltimore Sun,* April 3 and May 22, 1849. No letter directly to Gorham Parks notifying him of his dismissal has been found in the National Archives. Edward Kent of Bangor, Maine, wrote Secretary of State John M. Clayton on June 27, 1849 that he was accepting the position as consul at Rio de Janeiro. Parks wrote Clayton on October 1, 1849 that he had turned the archives of the consulate over to Kent. Both of these letters are in the National Archives, Department of State, Consular Despatches, Rio de Janeiro, Brazil.

20. Tolman, Journal, ship *Sweden,* May 31, 1849, and Bell, Journal, *Gager,* August 3, 1849.

21. Reed, Journal, ship *Magnolia,* March 23, 1849, and Collins, Journal, ship *Magnolia,* April 24, 1849. Both men seem to describe the same incident. Why they have them dated a month a part remains a mystery.

22. Reynolds, Reminiscence. His spelling the captain's name as Poisers seems incorrect.

23. Whaley, *Consignments to El Dorado,* 172–73 and 189–90.

24. Taylor, Journal, bark *Isabel,* March 19 and June 16, 1849.

25. Deane, Journal, ship *Arkansas,* August 13, 1849; Wheeler, Journal, bark *Hannah Sprague,* November 12, 1849; and Booth, Journal, ship *Andalusia,* September 1, 3, and 17, 1849.

8: MISCELLANEOUS PROBLEMS

1. Deane, Journal, ship *Arkansas,* June 29–July 9, 1849; Bowles, Journal, ship *Mount Vernon,* August 13 and 16, 1849; Jessup, Journal, ship *Sheffield,* September 1, 1849; Anonymous, Journal, bark *Gold Hunter,* November 12–17, 1849; Corneilson, Journal, bark *Hannah Sprague,* June 1–24, 1849; Baker, Journal, bark *San Francisco,* November 29, 1849; Bailey, Journal, bark *Sarah Warren,* October 21–31, 1849; and Spear, *Memorandum Book,* December 29–31, 1849.

2. Upham, *Notes of a Voyage,* 124; Hollingsworth, Journal, ship *Daniel Webster,* May 8, 1849; Reid, Journal, bark *Velasco,* June 25 and 27, 1849; Christman, *One Man's Gold,* 37 and 47; Anonymous, Journal, ship *Pharsalia;* Bailey, Journal, bark *Sarah Warren,* December 9, 1849 and January 21 and 26, 1850; and Fowler, Account of the voyage, 5–6 and 11.

3. Kingsley, "Diary," 268; Ewer, Journal, ship *York,* July 12, 1849; Overton, Journal, bark *Keoka,* March 26, 1849; Gager, Journal, ship *Pacific,* February

16–27, 1849; Spear, *Memorandum Book,* January 7–13, 1850; and Teller, Journal, brig *Mary Stuart,* February 21–23, 1849.

4. Booth, Journal, ship *Andalusia,* May 16 and July 22–24, 1849; Anonymous, Journal, ship *George Washington,* May 7–8, 1849; Baker, Journal, bark *San Francisco,* August 29–30, 1849; Caine, Journal, bark *Belvidera,* April 30–August 15, 1849; and Hatch, Journal, schooner *Damariscove,* January 22–June, 3, 1850.

5. Fuller, Journal, ship *Sweden,* March 7 and 8, April 6, May 31, July 9, and August 2, 1849; Bailey, Journal, ship *Sweden,* July 11, 1849; Cogswell, "Gold Rush Diary," 12, 14, 34, and 38–40; Anonymous, Journal, ship *Pharsalia,* February 3, 20, and 24, 1849; Goodwin, *Reminiscence,* 9, 12, and 23; Van Dyke, Journal, ship *Tahmaroo,* February 20, 22, 24, and 27, 1849; Chittenden, Journal, bark *Croton,* February 27–28, March 1, 3, and 22–23, 1849; and *Baltimore Sun,* March 1, 1849.

6. Harvey, Journal, ship *Crescent,* January 17 and 19, 1850; Collins, Journal, ship *Magnolia,* March 10, 1849; Jessup, Journal, ship *Sheffield,* August 22, 1849; Spear, *Memorandum Book,* November 19, 1849; and Teller, Journal, brig *Mary Stuart,* February 20–22, 1849.

7. Collins, Journal, ship *Magnolia,* March 10–July 21, 1849 and Reed, Journal, ship *Magnolia,* March 11–July 17, 1849.

8. Coffin, *A Pioneer Voyage,* 28–29; Ferrell, Journal, ship *Arkansas,* July 5–6, September 22–23 and October 5, 1849; and Deane, Journal, ship *Arkansas,* July 5–6 and September 20–24, 1849.

9. Fowler, Account of a voyage, 7, 10, and 12–17; Christman, *One Man's Gold,* 64–65; Reed, Journal, ship *Magnolia,* June 20, 1849; Davis, *Reminiscences,* 58–62; and Miller, Letter to his parents, October 29, 1849.

10. Taylor, Journal, ship *Orpheus,* June 14, 1849; Whaley, *Consignments to El Dorado,* 27–28; Tolman, Journal, ship *Sweden,* May 6–7, 1849; Bailey, Journal, ship *Sweden,* April 30, 1849; Fuller, Journal, ship *Sweden,* April 22–30, 1849; and Van Dyke, Journal, ship *Tahmaroo,* January 30–31, 1849.

11. Hutchinson, Journal, bark *Belgrade,* February 11–April 15, 1850; Nash, *To the Goldfields,* Letter from Nash to his wife, May 27, 1850; Shepard, Journal, bark *Belvidera,* August 29, 1849; Swain, Journal, bark *Belvidera,* August 25 and 28, 1849; Caine, Journal, bark *Belvidera,* August 29, 1849; and Stearns, Journal, bark *Belvidera,* August 24–29, 1849.

12. Chittenden, Journal, bark *Croton,* July 4, 9, and 27–29, 1849; Morgan, Gold Dust: The Log of a Forty-Niner, July 21, 1849; Brannan, Letter to his wife, Mary, June 15–21, 1849; *Gold Rush Voyage on the Bark Orion,* 153–57 and 160–61; Reid, Journal, bark *Velasco,* April 16, May 26, June 13 and 15–18, and September 11, 1849; and Locke, Journal, brig *Sea Eagle,* October 7, 1849. "Consumption" is the term used for tuberculosis in the nineteenth century.

13. Teller, Journal, brig *Mary Stuart,* March 8 and April 16 and 28, 1849; Barker, Journal, ship *Nestor,* February 8, 1850; Jessup, Journal, ship *Sheffield,* November 9, 1849; *Gold Rush Voyage on the Bark Orion,* 90–91; Ewer, Journal, ship *York,* August 16, 1849; Bailey, Journal, bark *Sarah Warren,* January 7–8, 1850; Van Dyke, Journal, ship *Tahmaroo,* April 1, 1849; Spear, *Memorandum*

Book, November 30, December 4, 6, 7, and 9, 1849; Gager, Journal, ship *Pacific,* April 24–25, 1849; Williams, Journal, ship *Pacific,* April 24, 1849; and Overton, Journal, bark *Keoka,* February 6, 15, and 21, 1849.

14. Fletcher, Journal, bark *Elvira,* June 2, 1849; Martin, Journal, bark *Elvira,* June 2, 1849; [George Payson], *Golden Dreams and Leaden Realities,* 53; Collins, Journal, ship *Magnolia,* May 23, 1849; Reed, Journal, ship *Magnolia,* May 23, 1849; and Meredith, Journal, bark *Stratford,* June 27, 1849.

15. Anonymous, Journal, ship *George Washington,* May 2, 1849; Whaley, *Consignments to El Dorado,* 133–36; Smith, *Historical Sketch of the Lives of William Wiggin Smith and Joseph Hiram Smith,* 27–30; and Denham, Journal, schooner *Rialto,* May 22, 1849. Despite the differences in the number of people involved, the two incidents involving the brig *Forrest* are probably one and the same.

16. Benton, Journal, ship *Edward Everett,* February 9, 1849; Taylor, Journal, ship *Orpheus,* June 11, 1849; Whaley, *Consignments to El Dorado,* 191 and 199; Stearns, Journal, bark *Belvidera,* inventory of the contents of his stateroom in September 1849; Swain, Journal, bark *Belvidera,* April 16–26, May 10, and September 4–21, 1849; Kendall, *A Landman's Voyage,* 27, 31, and 43; Doten, *Journals,* 1: 7; Collins, Journal, ship *Magnolia,* August 12–21, 1849; Reid, Journal, bark *Velasco,* May 19, July 12, and August 2, 19, 27, and 30, 1849; Christman, *One Man's Gold,* 73; Carder, Journal, ship *Hopewell,* May 22, June 1 and 7, and July 11, 1849; Howard, Journal, bark *Midas,* November 17 and December 8, 1849; Upham, *Notes of a Voyage,* 191; Spear, *Memorandum Book,* January 2 and February 21, 1850; Reed, Journal, ship *Magnolia,* June 5 and August 5, 1849; Farren, Journal, ship *Reindeer,* March 2, 1850; Overton, Journal, bark *Keoka,* August 6, 1849; Gould, Journal, bark *Maria,* May 11, 1849; Booth, Journal, ship *Andalusia,* August 16, 189; Ferrell, Journal, ship *Arkansas,* December 1, 1849; Fitch, Journal, ship *Florida,* December 19, 1849; Stillman, *Seeking the Golden Fleece,* 111–12 and 115; Stillman, Letter to his brother, February 26, 1849; Browne, *Letters, Journals, and Writings,* 116; Williams, Journal, ship *Pacific,* January 29, February 26, and July 17, 189; Hollingsworth, Journal, ship *Daniel Webster,* May 23, 1849; Anonymous, Journal, ship *Plymouth,* May 28, 1849; Williams, Journal, ship *Regulus,* August 9, 1849; Ewer, Journal, ship *York,* August 24, 1849; Baker, Journal, bark *San Francisco,* December 18–22 and 27, 1849; Kingsley, "Diary," 277; and Beach, Excerpts from a journal, ship *Apollo.*

17. Williams, Journal, ship *Pacific,* April 16, 1849; Meredith, Journal, bark *Stratford,* March 14, 1849; Chittenden, Journal, bark *Croton,* March 2 and April 8, 1849; Teller, Journal, brig *Mary Stuart,* April 2, 1849; Booth, Journal, ship *Andalusia,* May 27, 1849; Cogswell, "Gold Rush Diary," 16; Tolman, Journal, ship *Sweden,* July 11, 1849; Christman, *One Man's Gold,* 20–21, 39–40, and 66; Upham, *Notes of a Voyage,* 26 and 42; Harry G. Brown, Journal, bark *Selma,* July 9, 1849; Samuel Brown, Journal, bark *Selma,* July 10, 1849; Logbook, bark *Selma,* July 10 and August 8–10, 1849; Hull, Journal, ship *Jane Parker,* February 27, 1849; Carson, Journal, ship *Jane Parker,* February 7 and 27 and March 18–19, 1849; and *Gold Rush Voyage on the Bark Orion,* 71.

18. Snow, Journal, ship *Euphrasia,* December 2, 22, and 29, 1849 and January 1 and 2, 1850; *Gold Rush Voyage on the Bark Orion,* 159; Anonymous, Journal,

bark *Gold Hunter,* February 28, 1850; Woodbury, Journal, ship *Argonaut,* March 8 and 10, 1849; and Whaley, *Consignments to El Dorado,* 75–76, 79, 95, and 98.

19. McCrackan, Letter to his mother and sisters, July 22, 1849; Booth, Journal, ship *Andalusia,* April 27, 1849; Ewer, Journal, ship *York,* June 3, 1849; Barker, Journal, ship *Nestor,* January 23, 1850; Butler, Journal, ship *America,* May 29, 1849; Van Dyke, Journal, ship *Tahmaroo,* May 6, 1849; Young, Journal, bark *Helen Augusta,* June 1, 1849; Farren, Journal, ship *Reindeer,* February 27, 1849; Gager, Journal, ship *Pacific,* February 10, 18, and 19, 1849; Taylor, Journal, ship *Orpheus,* May 16 and 19, 1849; Woodbury, Journal, ship *Argonaut,* December 21–23, 1849; Benton, Journal, ship *Edward Everett,* April 5–7, 1849; Bailey, Journal, ship *Sweden,* April 1, 1849; Tolman, Journal, ship *Sweden,* April 11 and May 24, 1849; Cogswell, "Gold Rush Diary," 18–19 and 29; Goodwin, *Reminiscence,* 19 and 26; Locke, Journal, brig *Sea Eagle,* May 20, 1849; and Christman, *One Man's Gold,* 23.

20. Green, Journal, ship *Sabina,* February 13 and 15 and March 30, 1849; Barker, Journal, ship *Nestor,* February 14 and 18, 1850; Upham, *Notes of a Voyage,* 109–10; and Taylor, Journal, ship *Orpheus,* February 18, 1849.

21. Christman, *One Man's Gold,* 76–77; Barker, Journal, ship *Nestor,* March 29 and April 21, 1850; and Corneilson, Journal, bark *Hannah Sprague,* November 6, 1849.

22. Meredith, Journal, bark *Strafford,* February 6, 1849; Van Dyke, Journal, ship *Tahmaroo,* February 13 and 18, 1849; Anonymous, Journal, bark *Gold Hunter,* February 7, 1850; Farren, Journal, ship *Reindeer,* February 23, 1850; Snow, Journal, ship *Euphrasia,* March 26, 1850; Cooledge, Journal, bark *Oxford,* May 21–22, 1849; and Hull, Journal, ship *Jane Parker,* June 1, 1849.

23. [George Payson], *Golden Dreams,* 23–24; Stevens, Journal, ship *Trescott,* no date given (the entire journal is written in rhyming couplets with no dates); Barker, Journal, ship *Nestor,* January 25, 1850; Ferrell, Journal, ship *Arkansas,* July 30, 1849; and Deane, Journal, ship *Arkansas,* October 29, 1849. Joanne Levy devotes one chapter to women traveling by sea via both Cape Horn and the isthmian route and another chapter to those on the overland route in her *They Saw the Elephant: Women in the California Gold Rush.* The remainder of the book describes activities of women after they arrived in California. She used some of the same sources I have used. Her study extends beyond the time period considered here.

24. Sophia A. Eastman, Letter to Maria M. Child, March 14–April 7, 1849, Maria M. Child Correspondence; Coffin *Pioneer Voyage,* 23 and 25–26; and Wheeler, Journal, bark *Hannah Sprague,* October 28, 1849.

25. Randall, Journal, ship *Hannibal,* April 24, 1849; Wheeler, Journal, bark *Hannah Sprague,* October 28, 1849; Booth, Journal, ship *Andalusia,* June 21 and July 21, 1849; Collins, Journal, ship *Magnolia,* August 17, 1849; Reed, Journal, ship *Magnolia,* August 17, 1849; Deane, Journal, ship *Arkansas,* October 3 and November 4, 1849; Ferrell, Journal, ship *Arkansas,* October 5, 1849; Corneilson, Journal, bark *Hannah Sprague,* October 28, 1849; McCrackan, Letter to his mother, July 10–12, 1849; Tolman, Journal, ship *Sweden,* July 13, 1849; Fuller, Journal, ship *Sweden,* July 14, 1849; and Goodwin, *Reminiscence,* 33.

26. *Baltimore Sun,* November 22, 1849; Anonymous, Journal, ship *America,* April 2 and 22, 1849, Bancroft Library; Taylor, Journal, ship *Orpheus,* April 6 and May

16, 1849; Benton, Journal, ship *Edward Everett,* January 14, 1849; Morgan, Gold Dust: The Log of a Forty-Niner, September 18–25, 1849; Stillman, Letter to his brother, February 26, 1849; Anonymous, Journal, ship *Pacific,* May 16, 1849; Browne, *Letters, Journals and Writings,* 78–79; and Lapp, *Blacks in the Gold Rush* (includes little information on how most of the African Americans arrived in California but does provide considerable information on what they accomplished there).

9: DUTIES AND RESPONSIBILITIES

1. Williams, Journal, ship *Pacific,* February 15 and June 25 and 26, 1849.

2. Christman, *One Man's Gold,* 15 and 69.

3. Barker, Journal, ship *Nestor,* January 4, 1850.

4. Hale, *The Log of a Forty-Niner,* 47; Meredith, Journal, bark *Strafford,* February 28, 1849; and Akerman, Journal, bark *Daniel Webster,* January 7, 1850.

5. Snow, Journal, ship *Euphrasia,* December 10, 1849; Howard, Journal, bark *Midas,* November 26 and December 4, 1849 and February 26, 1850; Anonymous, Journal, ship *Plymouth,* February 25, 1850; and Stearns, Journal, bark *Belvidera,* April 3 and 9, 1849.

6. Taylor, Journal, ship *Orpheus,* May 21, 1849.

7. Woodbury, Journal, ship *Argonaut,* November 22, 1849.

8. Fuller, Journal, ship *Sweden,* March 9 and 26, April 4, June 3, 6, 7, 11, and 18, and July 3, 1849.

9. Booth, Journal, ship *Andalusia,* August 22, 23, and 25, 1849.

10. Akerman, Journal, bark *Daniel Webster,* December 11, 1849; Benton, Journal, ship *Edward Everett,* May 25, 1849; Brannan, Letter to his wife, Mary, July 11–21, 1849; Hatch, Journal, schooner *Damariscove,* various entries in January and February, 1850; and Christman, *One Man's Gold,* 72.

11. Locke, Letter to his wife, Mary, April 22, 1849, and Journal, *Sea Eagle,* June 13 and October 7, 1849; Nash, *To the Goldfields,* 3 (although the vessel is identified as a schooner in the title, she was actually a bark); and Van Dyke, Journal, ship *Tahmaroo,* January 31, 1849.

12. Lyman, *Journal of a Voyage,* 20 and 26; Cogswell, "Gold Rush Diary," 36; Benton, Journal, ship *Edward Everett,* January 27 and 30, February 2 and 10, March 18, April 4, May 27, and June 14, 1849; Meredith, Journal, bark *Strafford,* February 14 and March 5, 1849; Cross, Journal, ship *Crescent,* April 13, 1850; and Booth, Journal, ship *Andalusia,* August 3–10, 1849.

13. Reid, Journal, ship *Velasco,* March 24 and 28; April 3; May 26; June 8, 9, 24, 26, and 30; July 3, 16, 17, 18, and 29; August 6, 8, 9, 11, 16, 17, 18, 19, 27, 30, and 31; and September 3, 4, 7, 9, 10, 11, 12, 13, 14, and 15, 1849.

14. Harvey, Journal, ship *Crescent,* December 1, 17, 26, and 28, 1849; January 7 and 26; February 7, 8, and 22; March 4, 12, and 13; April 1, 8, 9, and 10; and May 6, 1850; Graves, Journal, ship *Crescent,* January 26; February 8 and 22; March 11, 12, 13, and 20; April 1 and 8; and May 6, 1850; and Cross, Journal, ship *Crescent,* April 1; May 28, 29, and 30; and June 3, 6, 7, and 8, 1850.

15. Benton, Journal, ship *Edward Everett,* January 27, April 6 and 7, and May 16, 17, and 18, 1849.

16. Meredith, Journal, bark *Strafford,* February 14 and 15; March 5, 19, 27, and 31; April 2; June 4, 14, 20, 29, and 30; and July 2, 1849.

17. Hyde, Journal, ship *Lenore,* June 4–5 and 11, 1849.

18. Wheeler, Journal, bark *Hannah Sprague,* May 21–November 12, 1849; Corneilson, Journal, bark *Hannah Sprague,* November 1 and December 22, 1849.

19. Bowles, Journal, ship *Mount Vernon,* September 11, 25, and 26, 1849; Harvey, Journal, ship *Crescent,* April 9 and 18, 1850; Kingsley, "Diary," 304–8; Young, Journal, bark *Helen Augusta,* September 14, 15, 17, 18, 19, 20, 26, and 27, and October 22, 1849; and Benton, Journal, ship *Edward Everett,* May 8, 21, 23, 24, 25, 28, 30, and 31, and June 1, 2, 5, 7, 8, 12, 16, 18, 20, and 21, 1849.

10: FIRST IMPRESSIONS

1. Baker, Journal, bark *San Francisco,* January 11, 1850.

2. Browne, *Letters, Journals and Writings,* 125–26. The *Pacific* arrived on August 5, and Browne wrote on August 22, 1849. Browne had earlier been on a whaling voyage and written an unfavorable account of whaling after the conclusion of that experience.

3. Bailey, Journal, ship *Sweden,* August 3, 1849; Locke, Letter to his wife, November 15, 1849; Kingsley, "Diary," 319–20; Anonymous, Journal, bark *Gold Hunter,* March 26, 1850; Stillman, *Seeking the Golden Fleece,* 116; Spear, *Memorandum Book,* April 17, 1850; Hollingsworth, Journal, ship *Daniel Webster,* July 20, 1849; and Hale, *Log of a Forty-Niner,* 62–63.

4. McCrackan, Letter to his family, November 19 24; Hollingsworth, Journal, ship *Daniel Webster,* July 20, 1849; Chittenden, Journal, bark *Croton,* July 29, 1849; Hull, Journal, ship *Jane Parker,* July 21, 1849; and Corneilson, Journal, bark *Hannah Sprague,* November 12, 1849.

5. Ewer, Journal, ship *York,* September 16, 1849; Stillman, *Seeking the Golden Fleece,* 116; Hull, Journal, ship *Jane Parker,* July 21, 1849; La Motte, Letter to his father, November 29–December 30, 1849; McCrackan, Letter to his family, November 19–24, 1849; Locke, Letter, November 15, 1849; Corneilson, Journal, bark *Hannah Sprague,* November 12, 1849; Bailey, Journal, bark *Sarah Warren,* April 7, 1850; Anonymous, Journal, ship *America,* Bancroft Library, September 21, 1849; and Hale, *Log of a Forty-Niner,* 62–63.

6. Williams, Journal, ship *Pacific,* August 5, 1849; Reid, Journal, bark *Velasco,* October 7, 1849; Stearns, Journal, bark *Belvidera,* October 12, 1849; Corneilson, Journal, bark *Hannah Sprague,* November 12, 1849; and Hull, Journal, ship *Jane Parker,* July 27, 1849.

7. Stillman, *Seeking the Golden Fleece,* 116–17; Hollingsworth, Journal, ship *Daniel Webster,* July 23, 1849; Gould, Journal, bark *Maria,* July 1 and 2, 1849; McCrackan, Letter to his family, November 19–24, 1849; Williams, Journal, ship *Pacific,* August 5, 1849; Reid, Journal, bark *Velasco,* October 7, 1849; and Cogswell, "Gold Rush Diary," 49–50.

8. Hyde, Journal, ship *Lenore*, July 5, 1849; Browne, *Letters, Journals and Writings*, 125–26; Cogswell, "Gold Rush Diary," 53; Goodall, Journal, schooner *St. Mary*, January 25, 1850; Wilson, Journal, brig *Oriental*, March 3, 1850; La Motte, Letter to his father, December 15, 1849, and Letter to his mother, December 30, 1849; and Haskins, *Argonauts of California*, 48 and 50.

9. Randall, Letters to his family, September 12 and November 29–December 24, 1849; Putnam, Letter to his sister, September 22–October 14, 1849; Hyde, Journal, ship *Lenore*, July 5, 1849; Miller, Letter to his family, October 29, 1849; and Spear, *Memorandum Book*, September 21, 1849.

10. Lyman, *Journal of a Voyage*, 96–98; Stearns, Journal, bark *Belvidera*, October 13, 1849; and Bailey, Journal, bark *Sarah Warren*, April 7, 1850.

11. Hull, Journal, ship *Jane Parker*, July 21, 1849; Ferrell, Journal, ship *Arkansas*, December 19, 1849; Fowler, Account of a voyage, August 13, 1849; Anonymous, Journal, ship *America*, September 27, 1849, Bancroft Library; Kingsley, "Diary," 319–20; and Gould, Journal, bark *Maria*, July 3, 1849.

12. La Motte, Letters to his father and mother, December 15 and 30, 1849; McCrackan, Letter to his family, November 23–December 9, 1849; Anonymous, Journal, ship *America*, September 27, 1849, Bancroft Library; and Bailey, Journal, bark *Sarah Warren*, April 10, 1850.

13. La Motte, Letters to his father, mother, and brother Dan, December 15 and 30, 1849 and January 13, 1850; Robert N. Ferrell, Journal, ship *Arkansas*, December 19, 1849; Lyman, *Journal of a Voyage*, 96–98; Sheppard, Journal, ship *Morrison*, September 21, 1849; Hollingsworth, Journal, ship *Daniel Webster*, July 24, 1849; Benton, Journal, ship *Edward Everett*, July 6, 1849; Cross, Journal, ship *Crescent*, May 27, 1850; Fuller, Journal, ship *Sweden*, August 3, 1849; and Caine, Journal, ship *Belvidera*, October 18, 1849.

14. Anonymous, Journal, ship *America*, September 23, 1849, Bancroft Library; Bailey, Journal, bark *Sarah Warren*, April 20, 1850; Sophia A. Eastman, Letters to Maria M. Child, June 15 and 30 and July 15, 1849, Maria M. Eastman Child Correspondence.

15. Reed, Journal, ship *Magnolia*, September 9, 1849; Williams, Journal, ship *Pacific*, August 5, 1849; Cogswell, "Gold Rush Diary," 46–47; Putnam, Letter to his sister, September 22–October 1, 1849; Howard, Letter to Franklin R. Miller, August 30 and October 2, 1849; Spear, *Memorandum Book*, April 9, 1850; Hyde, Journal, ship *Lenore*, July 6, 1849; Caine, Journal, ship *Belvidera*, October 13, 1849; Miller, Letter to his parents, October 29, 1849; Anonymous, Journal, ship *America*, September 27, 1849, Bancroft Library; *New York Daily Tribune*, July 30, 1849, article titled "A Credit to California" by E. G. B.; Hull, Journal, ship *Jane Parker*, July 27, 1849; Haskins, *Argonauts to California*, 50; Reid, Journal, bark *Velasco*, October 7, 1849; Green, Journal, ship *Sabina*, August 9, 1849; and Bowles, Journal, ship *Mount Vernon*, October 4, 1849.

16. Hull, Journal, ship *Jane Parker*, July 27, 1849; Caine, Journal, bark *Belvidera*, October 14, 1849; and Stearns, Journal, bark *Belvidera*, October 14, 1849.

17. Goodwin, *Reminiscence*, 35–36.

Bibliography

PRIMARY SOURCES

Manuscripts

Abbe, Edward Payson. Journal, January 17–July 7, 1849, of a voyage from Boston to San Francisco in the ship *Edward Everett* under the command of Capt. Henry Smith. Huntington Library, San Marino, California, HM 20111. There is a skip in entries from March 1 to May 21 with a note that the entries for that period of time were kept in a second book because of the boisterous weather around Cape Horn and would be copied and enlarged upon at the back of this book. The entries do not appear there.

An Account of the Baxter Association's Voyage from New York to San Francisco, January 12–August 12, 1849. California State Library, Sacramento, California. Typescript copy. Voyage was made in the ship *Brooklyn* under the command of Capt. Joseph W. Richardson.

Adams, Louis K. Journal, January 23–July 19, 1849, of a voyage from Boston to San Francisco in the ship *Capitol* under the command of Capt. Thorndike Proctor. Peabody/Essex Museum, Salem, Massachusetts. Small pocket diary written in pencil. Entries are very short. Made stops at Rio de Janeiro and Valparaiso. Longest entries are during those stops.

Akerman, J. L. Journal, September 23, 1849–April 29, 1850, of a voyage from Boston to San Francisco in the bark *Daniel Webster* under the command of Capt. Joseph C. Higgins. Bancroft Library, University of California, Berkeley, 77/156 c. Journal was continued after arriving until early 1854. Includes a list of names of other 54 passengers, including 4 women and 2 children. Lists passengers' residences. Also a list of names of the crew. Most of the passengers were from the Boston area, but a few were from New Hampshire and New York State. One passenger and his wife were identified only as Germans. The age is given only for R. Saunders, who was 76, and it was noted that he returned home one week after arriving. Two of the women—Mrs. Fowler and Mrs. Sypp—were wives of other passengers while the other two—Mrs. C. Hall and Mrs. C. Abbott—seemingly were not accompanied by husbands. There is also reference to a Miss Hall, who was possibly one of the children. There are large gaps between entries in the early part of the journal. Only five entries exist for the leg between Boston and Rio de Janeiro. Between Rio, which they left on December 4, 1849, and the arrival at Valparaiso on April 29, 1850, the entries are much more regular. Between Valparaiso and San Francisco the entries are once again scattered and quite short. Akerman assumed the position of steward when they left Valparaiso. He shared the duties with his friend Dan, who is mentioned quite frequently and is probably D. Richard, who was from Ipswich, as was Akerman. Has an extensive description of Rio de Janeiro. Latter part of the journal deals with experiences in mining and other activities in California.

Andrews, James Harvey. Journal, December 2, 1849–June 17, 1850, of a voyage from Boston to San Francisco in the ship *Cheshire* under the command of Capt. John W. Dicks. Society of California Pioneers, San Francisco. Made stops in Rio de Janeiro and Valparaiso. Arrived in San Francisco June 17, 1850. Journal continues after their arrival until September 11, 1850. Most entries quite short. Longest entries are during stops.

Anonymous. Journal, April 1–September 21, 1849, of a voyage from New Bedford, Massachusetts, to San Francisco in the ship *America* under the command of Capt. Charles P. Seabury. Whaling Museum, New Bedford. Judging from the entry of June 4, 1849, this may well be the journal of Captain Seabury, for on that date the entry reads, "At daylight went on shore and paid my bills and came on board, took our anchors and stood out to sea with a light land breeze." No entries exist during the stops at St. Catherines Island, May 27–June 3, or at Callao, August 5–8. The entries are very short, and there are numerous gaps between entries. The volume also contains a record of the voyage back to Boston from Valparaiso and of a whaling voyage in 1850–1851.

Anonymous. Journal, April 1–September 27, 1849, of a voyage from New Bedford, Massachusetts, to San Francisco in the ship *America* under the command of Capt. Charles P. Seabury. Bancroft Library, University of California, Berkeley, 77/155 c. It seems that numbers of the passengers were whaling captains and mates from New Bedford, and the diarist frequently refers to individuals as captain. There appear to have been at least four companies on board as well as some passengers who were not members of companies. The diarist makes reference to "my color boy Henry" being seasick on April 2 and describes in some detail the sermon of a black preacher on April 8 and notes that most of those attending religious services that day were "Darkies." Short and long poems are scattered throughout the journal. Some were copied from other works, but others appear to be original works. Has detailed descriptions of activities and scenery at St. Catherines Island, Callao, and Lima. For several days after leaving the latter port, the diarist provides lengthy descriptions of the irreverent activities of many fellow passengers, some of whom he names. He consistently takes them to task for being Sunday Christians.

Anonymous. Journal, February 25, 1849–January 13, 1850, of a voyage from New York to San Francisco in the bark *Eliza Ann* under the command of Captain Cortin or Corwin. Peabody/Essex Museum, Salem, Massachusetts. Journal kept in the printed "Seaman's Journal" form with brief entries. Made stops in Valparaiso, Callao, Payta, and Panama, which caused the unduly lengthy voyage.

Anonymous. Extracts from an anonymous journal, January 11–July 6, 1849, of a voyage from Boston to San Francisco in the brig *Forest* under the command of Capt. N. Varina. Bancroft Library, University of California, Berkeley, C-F 150. These extracts were made with commentary by Malcolm B. Jones in 1936 from an original then in his possession. A negative photostat of one page of the original journal is bound with the typed extracts.

Bibliography

Anonymous. Journal, March 30–May 18, 1849, of a voyage from New York to San Francisco in the ship *George Washington* under the command of Capt. John Holdridge. California Historical Society, San Francisco. California State Library, Sacramento, has a photocopy of the original journal and a typescript copy. Actual dates of the voyage were February 2–May 28, 1849. This appears to be the second part of a three-part set.

Anonymous. Journal, October 3, 1949–March 26, 1850, of a voyage from Bangor, Maine, to San Francisco in the bark *Gold Hunter* under the command of Capt. Joseph Jackson. Bancroft Library, University of California, Berkeley, 77/160 c. The journal continues to March 13, 1851. Made stops in Rio de Janeiro and Valparaiso. This vessel carried a load of lumber for the government to be used in constructing buildings at Benecia near San Francisco. It also carried twenty-seven mechanics employed by the government and thirteen additional passengers. The names of all the passengers and the captain and two mates are provided in the first entry. The writer appears to have been one of the twenty-seven mechanics.

Anonymous. Journal, January 10–July 31, 1849, of a voyage from New York to San Francisco in the bark *Harriet Newell* under the command of Capt. E. Lockwood. Huntington Library, San Marino, California, HM 251. Has no entries between January 19 and February 4. Made stops in Rio de Janeiro and Callao. Entries are usually a full page and contain good descriptions of happenings.

Anonymous. Journal, February 12–August 4, 1849, of a voyage from New York to San Francisco in the bark *Isabel* under the command of Capt. Nicolas R. Brewer. Rutgers University Library, New Brunswick, New Jersey. Entries are brief and limited mostly to weather conditions, latitude and longitude, wind direction, and temperature. Has a list of passengers and crew, who were members of the New Brunswick and California Mining and Trading Company.

Anonymous. Journal, April 25–December 4, 1849, of a voyage from New York to San Francisco in the bark *Magdala* under the command of Capt. George Mason. Huntington Library, San Marino, California, HM 1060. Kept in logbook style. Information limited mostly to courses sailed, wind directions, and latitude and longitude through June 28. From then until July 13, while they were in Rio de Janeiro, the entries are even shorter, which is the opposite of many journals. Beginning July 14 the writer reverts to the logbook style of entries. They were in Valparaiso between September 27 and October 10.

Anonymous. Journal, January 22–August 5, 1849, of a voyage from New York to San Francisco in the ship *Pacific* under the command of Capt. Hall J. Tibbits from New York to Rio and Capt. George Easterbrook from Rio to San Francisco. Bancroft Library, University of California, Berkeley, C-F 216. On the basis of the type of paper used and the uniformness and quality of the writing, it is probable that this is a holograph copy rather than the original journal. There is no indication of when or by whom the copy might have been made. When they stopped at Rio de Janeiro, a large portion of the first-class passengers protested to the U.S. consul Gorham D. Parks that Captain Tibbits was insane and intemperate. After a delay of several days Parks removed Tibbits from command and appointed Easterbrook in his place. Easterbrook refused to allow Tibbits to continue in the vessel to San Francisco even though Tibbits was half owner of the vessel. Tibbits returned to New York, where he created a stir among the shipping and insurance interests, arranged for transportation to San Francisco via Panama, and met the *Pacific* to resume command when she arrived.

Anonymous. Journal, February 1–May 14 and July 6–23, 1849, of a voyage from Boston to San Francisco in the ship *Pharsalia* under the command of Capt. G. W. Allen. Bancroft Library, University of California, Berkeley, 91/145 c. Most entries are quite brief with little elaboration on incidents mentioned such as the captain and someone else having a row without any information on the subject or the result. The first portion is maintained in normal journal style whereas the July portion is written on loose sheets and scraps of paper. Cause of the large gap is unknown. Catalog records indicate that internal evidence suggests the author may have been from New Hampshire. My reading of the journal leads me to believe it was equally possible the author was from Maryland. This is based upon his several references to that state and to Baltimore and some derogatory remarks about New Englanders.

Anonymous. Journal, December 28,1849–June 28, 1850, of a voyage from Boston to San Francisco in the ship *Plymouth* under the command of Capt. William Portland. Bancroft Library, University of California, Berkeley, 77/17 c. First entry is January 1, 1850, and is a summary of the first four days of the voyage. The author noted it was too rough to write earlier. This appears to be a copy of his original journal he sent home. It is written on loose sheets. In the first entry he lists the names of the other passengers in his cabin. That list includes a Mrs. Parsons of Lynn, Massachusetts, who was traveling with her husband. They made one stop in Valparaiso, where they picked up fresh water and provisions and a Capt. H. G. McComas of Baltimore, who had commanded an unnamed schooner until his illness forced him to leave the vessel. On May 6, 1850, the author noted that he thought another passenger was writing letters about the voyage to a paper, perhaps in Boston.

Anonymous. Journal, February 6–August 23, 1849, of a voyage from New York to San Francisco in the ship *Robert Bowne* under the command of Capt. F. G. Cameron. Huntington Library, San Marino, California, HM 519. Had 160 passengers, all of whom are listed with their name, residence, occupation, and age. The list is divided into shareholders (122), passengers (42), cooks, etc. (7), stewards, etc. (10), sailors (18), and officers (6). Has long and detailed descriptions of Rio de Janeiro, Valparaiso, and Lima but very little about the voyage. All of the voyage is in summary form.

Anonymous. Journal, March 4–November 1, 1849, of a voyage from Boston to San Francisco in the brig *Sea Eagle* under the command of Captain Hammond. Huntington Library, San Marino, California.

Anonymous. Journal, March 17–September 16, 1849, of a voyage from New York to San Francisco in an unnamed bark. New Jersey Historical Society, Newark. Written in a small pocket diary with three days per page. Entries are very short and deal primarily with weather, direction sailed, speed, wind direction, etc.

Appelton, Horatio. Adventures of Horatio Appelton of Sonoma, California, 1874. Bancroft Library, University of California, Berkeley, C-E 65:11. Written for

Bibliography

Hubert Howe Bancroft. Contains information about his voyage from Boston to San Francisco in the ship *Edward Everett* and his experiences mining. The ship was owned by the 151 members of the Boston and California Mining and Trading Joint Stock Company.

Ark (Brig). List of officers, passengers, and crew of the brig *Ark,* which sailed from Newburyport, Massachusetts, bound for San Francisco, October 31, 1849. Bancroft Library, University of California, Berkeley. Gives name and residence of each person. There were 3 officers—a captain (Charles Marsh) and 2 mates; 9 cabin passengers; 112 steerage passengers; and a crew of 9. Three of the passengers were female.

Badger, Charles L. Journal, November 11, 1849–June 6, 1850, of a voyage from Boston to San Francisco in the brig *Triumph* under the command of Capt. Hiram Burt. Houghton Library, Harvard University, Cambridge. Has a list of the 4 passengers and 14 officers and crew on board. Information is recorded in a printed "Seaman's Journal" form and is kept in sea time with each day beginning at noon. Gives the latitude and longitude each day and concentrates primarily upon the weather. Made stops at Rio de Janeiro and Juan Fernandez Island.

Bailey, A. Journal, October 13, 1849–April 22, 1850, of a voyage from Portland, Maine, to San Francisco in the bark *Sarah Warren* under the command of Capt. Reuben Curtis. Bancroft Library, University of California, Berkeley, 85/42 c. Contains lists of names of the passengers, officers, and crew, vessel information, numerous strong complaints about the food and water, and descriptions of Valparaiso and San Francisco as well as some islands in the Pacific Ocean. Also has small sketches of Pacific islands as well as the harbor and city of Valparaiso.

Bailey, Benjamin. Journal, March 1–August 3, 1849, of a voyage from Boston to San Francisco in the ship *Sweden* under the command of Capt. Jesse G. Cotting. G. W. Blunt White Library, Mystic Seaport Museum, Inc., Mystic, Connecticut, Log 395. Bailey was a 23-year-old clerk from Boston. His journal contains a list of passengers with occupation, age, and residence for each. Also contains a list of the crew with positions in the vessel and residences. There were 210 people in the vessel. Included among the passengers were members of the Mt. Washington Mining and Trading Company, Roxbury Sagamore Company, Traders & Mechanics Mining Company, Cheshire Company, an unnamed company of 25 from Cambridge, and some who were not members of any company.

Baker, Isaac W. Journal, August 13, 1849–January 11, 1850, of a voyage from Beverly, Massachusetts, to San Francisco in the bark *San Francisco* under the command of Capt. Thomas Redmonds. Bancroft Library, University of California, Berkeley. The journal continues to November 8, 1850. The remainder of the volume contains a record of activities in the gold fields and his return home via the isthmian route. Baker included numerous illustrations. The forty members of the Beverly Joint Stock San Francisco Company were among the passengers. Their names are listed on the first page. Cargo included sixty-three thousand feet of planed boards, ten thousand bricks, and provisions for two years.

Barker, Isaac. Journal, September 18, 1849–February 25, 1850, of a voyage from Boston to San Francisco in the ship *Harriet Rockwell* under the command of Capt. S. Hawes. Huntington Library, San Marino, California, HM 19366.

Entries are brief and are kept in a small pocket diary with three entries on each page. Made stops at St. Catherines Island, where they spent several days in quarantine, as did all vessels that stopped there, and at Valparaiso.

Barker, Pierce W. Journal, November 30, 1849–May 6, 1850, of a voyage from Boston to San Francisco in the ship *Nestor* under the command of Capt. Nathan Pool. University of Washington Libraries, Seattle. Barker was a 24-year-old bachelor from Stratham, New Hampshire. Based upon a number of factors, this appears to be a copy of Barker's original journal, but there is no indication of who might have made the copy and when it was made. The journal ends twenty-nine days before they arrived at San Francisco. Contains a list of officers with name, rank, age, residence, and marital status; list of members of the M.U.C. Association of Salem, Massachusetts, who were among the passengers, with name, residence, age, and marital status as well as names and ages of a few wives; list of other passengers with name, residence, age, and marital status; and list of stewards and cooks. Also includes a record of the number of miles sailed each day. The total miles sailed was 20,296.

The Barometer. 1850. California State Library, Sacramento. Issues 1, 2, 3, 5, 6, 7, and 8 of a weekly manuscript paper "published" on board the ship *Mary Waterman* on a voyage to California in 1850. Issues contain letters to the editor, editorials, essays, poetry, riddles, etc. Issue number 8 contains excerpts from a diary kept on board the ship *Edward Everett* in 1849 in which mention is made of *The Barometer and Gold Hunter's Log,* the paper published on that vessel. Issue number 2 contains a long description of the celebration of George Washington's birthday on board the *Mary Waterman.*

Bartlett, Washington. Statement of a Pioneer of 1849, 1877. Bancroft Library, University of California, Berkeley, C-D 39. Recollections of his passage from Charleston, South Carolina, to San Francisco in the ship *Othello* in 1849 and impressions of San Francisco and other later activities. Bartlett had decided to go to California to establish a printing business before the discovery of gold was officially announced and had shipped equipment there early in 1848. He was the publisher of the *Journal of Commerce,* which he established in February 1850.

Beach, Joseph Perkins. Excerpts from a journal, 1849–1850. G. W. Blunt White Library, Mystic Seaport Museum, Inc., Mystic, Connecticut. Typed copy. Beach was supercargo in the ship *Apollo* owned by Moses Y. Beach. The vessel made a voyage to San Francisco in 1849.

Beach, Joseph Perkins. Records, 1849. J. Porter Shaw Library, National Maritime Museum, San Francisco. California Historical Society has a photocopy of the journal. Includes three volumes of a rough log, January 16–November 12, 1849, of the ship *Apollo* on a voyage from New York to San Francisco under the command of Capt. Charles H. Coffin.

Bean, Hiram P. Journal, September 23, 1849–February 16, 1850, of a voyage from Boston to San Francisco in the ship *Flavius* under the command of Capt. P. Jenkins. Huntington Library, San Marino, California, HM 16531. Entries are brief and are recorded in a small volume with three entries per page. Gives latitude and longitude nearly every day.

Bibliography

Bee, Albert Wilson. Journal, January 24–June 30, 1849, of a voyage from New York to San Francisco in the ship *South Carolina* under the command of Capt. Joseph Hamilton. California Historical Society, San Francisco. Typescript copy.

Bell, John W. Journal, February 14–September 12, 1849, of a voyage from New York to San Francisco in the schooner *Gager* under the command of Capt. William G. Bullions. New York Public Library, New York. They stopped in Rio de Janeiro, Montevideo, and Callao. They returned to Montevideo for repairs after suffering damages and losing an anchor in the Straits of Magellan. Bell and some others considered leaving the vessel in Montevideo and traveling overland to the Pacific. He later noted they did not do that because the Indians and robbers in the land made such travel unsafe.

Bennett, J. H. Letter, February 24, 1849, to his parents written at sea on board the bark *Oxford* between New York and Rio de Janeiro. Bancroft Library, University of California, Berkeley. This letter is kept with the journal of Cornelius Cooledge and contains comments about the quality and quantity of food served to the steerage passengers. A bill of fare for a week is included. Bennett implies the same bill of fare was served throughout the voyage, but there is evidence in Cooledge's journal that there were some variations.

Benton, Joseph Augustine. Journal, January 11–July 6, 1849, of a voyage from Boston to San Francisco in the ship *Edward Everett* under the command of Capt. Henry Smith. California State Library, Sacramento. Journal is continued to December 31, 1849. Benton was a recent graduate of the Yale Divinity School and began to practice the ministry upon his arrival in California. A list of the 151 members of the Boston and California Mining and Trading Joint Stock Company is included at the end of the first of two volumes. For each person Benton gives the name, mess number, marital status, occupation, residence, place of birth, place of education, religious affiliation, and next of kin.

Biggs, Abel R. Journal, February 5–September 17, 1849, of a voyage from New York to San Francisco in the bark *Keoka* under the command of Capt. James McGuire. J. Porter Shaw Library, National Maritime Museum, San Francisco. Photocopy. Contains a list of passengers with their residences as well as a list of the eight members of the Patchogue Mining and Trading Company of which Biggs was a member.

Blackwood, Thomas. Journal, March–April 1849, of part of the voyage from New York to San Francisco in the ship *Loo Choo* under the command of Capt. D. Cushman. Clark Memorial Library, Eastern Michigan University, Mount Pleasant. Appears to have been a letter written in journal format on thin paper. Ink has bled through, making reading difficult. Most entries are brief.

Booth, Anne (Willson). Journal, April 19–November 6, 1849, of a voyage from Baltimore to San Francisco in the ship *Andalusia* under the command of Capt. F. W. Willson. Bancroft Library, University of California, Berkeley, C-F 197. This is the only journal of a female discovered in the research for this work. Mrs. Booth appears to have been the niece of Captain Willson. She makes frequent references to her husband, who apparently resided in a different cabin of the vessel than she did. There were at least two companies on board, one of thirty men from Kentucky and one from York, Pennsylvania. The most noteworthy passenger appears to have been Rev. William Taylor, who had been sent to California as a missionary by the Methodist Church. Materials for a church for Reverend Taylor were included in the cargo.

Bowles, Isaac. Journal, April 19–October 15, 1849, of a voyage from Mattapoisett, Massachusetts, to San Francisco in the ship *Mount Vernon* under the command of Capt. Joseph T. Atsatt. Bancroft Library, University of California, Berkeley, C-F 86. Brief excerpts from the journal and some background information about Bowles, the *Mount Vernon,* and the voyage were published by Lawrence D. Romaine in the *Amateur Book Collector* 5 (March 1955): 5–7. The *Mount Vernon* had been a whaling vessel before this voyage and returned to the whaling fleet afterward. All of the people on board appear to have been members of a joint stock company, the name of which was not given in the journal.

Bradford, William. Journal, November 22, 1849–May 5, 1850, of a voyage from New York to San Francisco in the brig *Reindeer* under the command of Capt. Levi L. Batchelder. California State Library, Sacramento. The entries are very short and consist primarily of matters relating to the weather, position of the vessel, direction sailed, and wind direction. There is a gap in entries between November 24 and December 7.

Brannan, John. Papers, 1839–1862, including fifteen letters to his wife, Mary. F. Brannan, during his voyage from Philadelphia to San Francisco in the bark *Norwich* under the command of Captain Anthony. Bancroft Library, University of California, Berkeley. It appears from the letters that Brannan had been a shipmaster prior to making this trip as a passenger. They left Philadelphia on or about April 23, 1849, but had to return to port (or at least appear to have done so at Brannan's insistence) because the deck load was not properly arranged for safety. Rather than throw that load overboard, they returned to Philadelphia and rearranged the load and sailed again on or about May 11. They made stops in Rio de Janeiro and Valparaiso. He noted in the first letter they had a total of twenty-seven passengers. In one of the letters he reported the death of one passenger. They arrived in San Francisco some time after November 15. His letters contain some of the most vivid descriptions of sunrises and sunsets.

Brown, Harry G. Journal, April 11–October 12, 1849, of a voyage from New York to San Francisco in the bark *Selma* under the Command of Capt. Orrin Sellow. G. W. Blunt White Library, Mystic Seaport Museum, Inc., Mystic, Connecticut, Log 310. Includes lists of passengers and crew with age, residence, and occupation or position in the vessel. Among the passengers were the eighty-four members of the Fremont Mining and Trading Company. Also includes a separate abstract containing the distance sailed and the latitude and longitude for each day.

Brown, Samuel W. Journal, April 15–November 2, 1849, of a voyage from New York to San Francisco in the bark *Selma* under the command of Capt. Orrin Sellow. California Historical Society, San Francisco. Brown was a physician from Hartford, Connecticut, and was a member of the Fremont Mining and Trading Company. Parts of the journal are written as letters.

Brown, William A. Journal, February 22–August 29, 1849, of a voyage from Boston to San Francisco in the ship *Regulus* under the command of Capt.

Bibliography

Daniel Bradford. Huntington Library, San Marino, California, HM 16957. Includes a note on the first page that he was on an "expedition to California in search of gold, that all absorbing topic, and want of mankind." Voyage actually started March 1. Stopped at Rio de Janeiro and Callao. Gives the latitude and longitude and the number of miles sailed each day. Does not give nearly as much information on the conflicts between the officers and members of the Bunker Hill Trading and Mining Association that Thomas Williams provides.

Burke, Martin J. San Francisco Police, 1887. Bancroft Library, University of California, Berkeley, C-D 322. Dictation recorded for H. H. Bancroft concerning his arrival in California via Cape Horn in 1850. Document deals exclusively with his vigilance committee and police work.

Butler, Thomas A. (Better say Thomas D. Kempton). Journal, April 2–September 15, 1849, of a voyage from New Bedford, Massachusetts, to San Francisco in the ship *America* under the command of Capt. Charles P. Seabury. Whaling Museum Library, New Bedford, Massachusetts. Includes lists of officers, cabin passengers, steerage passengers, and crew with residence of each person. Both Butler and Kempton are listed as steerage passengers. Why both names appeared in the journal as is given above is unclear. There does not appear to be a change in handwriting anywhere in the journal.

Caine, James F. Journal, February 28, 1849–January 27, 1850, of a voyage from New York to San Francisco in the bark *Belvidera* under the command of Capt. Samuel Barney. Bancroft Library, University of California, Berkeley, 69/90 c. Photocopy of typescript copy of an original in the DeWitt Historical Society, Tompkins County, New York. Passengers were members of the Cayuga Joint Stock Company. Actual dates of the voyage were March 2–October 12, 1849. The remainder of the journal deals with his activities in California. They made one stop at Callao.

Callbreath, John C. Letters, 1849, to his family regarding his voyage from New London, Connecticut, to San Francisco in the ship *Mentor* under the command of Capt. J. M. Howard. Bancroft Library, University of California, Berkeley, 79/93 c. Dates of the voyage were January 30–June 30, 1849. The letters contain very little information about the voyage but provide good descriptions of the situation in California.

Carder, James B. Journal, March 22–August 11, 1849, of a voyage from Warren, Rhode Island, to San Francisco in the ship *Hopewell* under the command of Capt. George Littlefield. Bancroft Library, University of California, Berkeley, C-F 79. The voyage actually began January 28. Journal begins off the coast of Brazil. Passengers included the members of the Providence Mining Company. Due to the illness of Captain Littlefield, for a period of time the vessel was under the command of a Captain Grinnell and the first mate and another captain who was among the passengers. Arrangements were made to leave Captain Littlefield in Talcahuano, but he decided to continue in the vessel.

Carpenter, Augustus D. Journal, February 14–December 15, 1849, of a voyage from Boston to San Francisco in the brig *Col. Taylor* under the command of Capt. C. J. Lovett. Society for California Pioneers, San Francisco. They arrived in San Francisco September 12, 1849. Most entries are quite short, some giving only their position. Longest entries are during the stop at Valparaiso.

Carson, William McKendree. Journal, February 1–March 19, 1849, of a portion of a voyage from Baltimore to San Francisco in the ship *Jane Parker* under the command of Capt. C. Jordan. California Historical Society, San Francisco. Negative photostat copy of a typescript. Bancroft Library, University of California, Berkeley, has a microfilm copy. The journal is kept in a small pocket diary and ends when they sailed from Rio de Janeiro.

Charles Herbert (schooner). Miscellaneous accounts, bills, receipts, and other documents relating to outfitting the vessel for her voyage from Warren, Rhode Island, to San Francisco in 1849–1850 under the command of Capt. Caleb Carr Jr. Bancroft Library, University of California, Berkeley, C-G 10. The vessel was owned by the Warren Mining and Trading Association. The documents provide useful information on the prices paid for material purchased for the voyage.

Chase, Moses. Papers, 1832–1849, including certificate of citizenship, ticket for voyage from Boston to San Francisco in the ship *Capitol,* passport issued in 1849, list of passengers, crew and officers in the ship *Capitol,* deeds for land in California, and a newspaper clipping about Chase from the *Oakland Tribune.* Bancroft Library, University of California, Berkeley. The Sacramento History Center in Sacramento, California, also has a ticket for the *Capitol.* For a time in 1849 individuals sailing to California were required to have a passport to enter San Francisco. The passports were issued by the governors of the passengers' home states.

Child, Maria M. (Eastman). Correspondence, 1849–1850. Bancroft Library, University of California, Berkeley, C-B 574. Includes letters from her sister, Sophia A. Eastman, concerning her voyage from Boston to San Francisco in the brig *Colorado.* Stopped at St. Catherines Island and at Valparaiso. Their stay at the latter port was longer than normal, as they had to make repairs because of damage suffered in storms off Cape Horn. Letters written after her arrival in San Francisco provide helpful information on the quality of life there and are more valuable than those written during the voyage. The *Colorado* arrived in San Francisco on or about June 15, 1849.

Childs, Willard C. Journal, November 21, 1849–April 1, 1850, of a voyage from Natick, Massachusetts, to San Francisco in the ship *Reindeer* under the command of Capt. John Lord. G. W. Blunt White Library, Mystic Seaport Museum, Inc., Mystic, Connecticut. The journal is continued to May, 1851, and contains information on activities in California.

Chittenden, H. W. Journal, January 15–July 19, 1849, of a voyage from New York to San Francisco in the bark *Croton* under the command of Capt. D. Soulliard. J. Porter Shaw Library, National Maritime Museum, San Francisco. Journal is continued to October 22, but the entries are scattered. Chittenden sent his journal home with an acquaintance in October 1849. Has a good illustration of the customhouse in Valparaiso. Made stops at St. Catherines Island and Valparaiso.

Christianson, C. H. Journal, March 24–September 26, 1849, of a voyage from New York to San Francisco in the bark *Linda* under the command of Captain Christianson. California State Library, Sacramento. Negative photostat. Entries are brief and devoted almost entirely to weather conditions, speed, course, and handling the sails.

Christy Family. Papers, 1846–1865. J. Porter Shaw Library, National Maritime Museum, San Francisco. Contains a journal, November 6, 1849–March 15, 1850, of a voyage from Philadelphia to San Francisco in the schooner *General George Cadwalader* under the command of Capt. John Washington Salman. Most of the pages are covered with clippings. Also includes three pages of an original letter and a typescript of the entire letter of James Christy in which he describes his voyage in the schooner.

Clark, Addison S. Journal, January 22–August 5, 1849, of a voyage from New York to San Francisco in the ship *Pacific* under the command of Capt. Hall J. Tibbits between New York and Rio de Janeiro and Capt. George Easterbrook between Rio de Janeiro and San Francisco. Rutgers University, New Brunswick, New Jersey. Journal is continued to December 5, 1849, and contains information on activities in the mines. Has frequent gaps between entries. Following the last entry is a good deal of information about the controversy between the first-class passengers and Captain Tibbits in Rio de Janeiro, but nothing is said about that controversy in the body of the journal. Also contains a daily record of the latitude and longitude during the entire voyage and a list of eighty-eight of the ninety-eight passengers.

Coleman, George P. Journal, March 8–July 18, 1849, of a voyage from New Bedford, Massachusetts, to San Francisco in the bark *Russell* under the command of Capt. Francis B. Folger. California Historical Society, San Francisco. Photocopy and a microfilm copy. Among the fifty-five passengers were the forty-seven members of the Nantucket Mining and Trading Company. A list of the members' names and two poems are included.

Collins, S. Mortimer. Journal, January 25–August 28, 1849, of a voyage from New Bedford, Massachusetts, to San Francisco in the ship *Magnolia* under the command of Capt. Benjamin Frank Simmons. Bancroft Library, University of California, Berkeley, 73/131 c. Carbon typescript. Copy was prepared by Collins for his family in 1892. Location of original unknown but likely lost, as Collins referred to its tattered condition in the 1892 typescript. The California State Library, Sacramento, has a negative photostat copy of a handwritten transcript made by Collins in 1892. Contains information concerning the conflict between the passengers and the supercargo, Mr. Pope, and other officers about the living conditions on board not being what had been promised. Has a list of most of the 127 passengers with some indication of what became of many of them.

Cooledge, Cornelius. Journal, January 11–August 21, 1849, of a voyage from Boston to San Francisco in the bark *Oxford* under the command of Capt. Suchet Mauran. Bancroft Library, University of California, Berkeley. Contains lists of officers and crew members with their positions and residences and lists of cabin and steerage passengers with residences. Stopped at Rio de Janeiro and Talcahuano.

Corneilson, John Henry. Journal, May 21–November 12, 1849, of a voyage from New York to San Francisco in the bark *Hannah Sprague* under the command of Capt. David F. Lansing. New York Public Library, New York. Journal is continued to January 14, 1850, and contains information on activities in California. Corneilson left California January 15, 1850, for New York. He noted at the front of the journal that the vessel was bought, provisioned, and outfitted for the voyage by the New York Commercial and Mining Company and that he had paid $600 for his membership in the company. A list of the thirty-one members is included. Corneilson notes that there were upwards of one hundred people on board so there obviously were some passengers who were not members of the company that owned the vessel.

Cowley, Richard Brown. Journal, March 29–October 5, 1849, of a voyage from New York to San Francisco in the bark *Canton* under the command of Capt. N. Haynes. Huntington Library, San Marino, California, HM 26652. Most entries are brief and deal mostly with latitude and longitude, temperature, and other aspects of the weather. Two exceptions are the long description of the visit from King Neptune on May 3, 1849, and the celebration of the Fourth of July. In the latter he recorded the traditional thirteen national toasts and fifty-three other toasts with the names of those who offered them. Stopped at the Chatham Islands. Some of the passengers, including Cowley, were members of the Island City Mining and Trading Association.

Crary, Oliver B. Statement of Oliver B. Crary on Vigilance Committees in San Francisco, 1877. Bancroft Library, University of California, Berkeley, C-D 183. Dictation recorded for H. H. Bancroft regarding his trip to San Francisco in 1849 as captain of a vessel, his other voyages up to 1852, his command of steamers, and his activities in the 1856 vigilance committee. Little was said about the 1849 voyage.

Cross, William Berry. Journal, December 6, 1849–May 16, 1850, of a voyage from Salem, Massachusetts, to San Francisco in the ship *Crescent* under the command of Capt. John Madison. California State Library, Sacramento, California. Journal starts September 26, 1849, and includes some account of his preparations for the voyage and continues to September 10, 1850, with descriptions of his activities in California. The vessel was owned by the Salem Mechanics Trading & Mining Association of which Cross was a member. Contains a list of members with birthplaces, ages, occupations, and marital status of each member. Also contains lists of other passengers, officers, stewards, and seamen on board.

Cudworth, Abel. Journal, November 11, 1849–June 6, 1850, of a voyage from Boston to San Francisco in the brig *Triumph* under the command of Capt. Hiram Burt. Society of California Pioneers, San Francisco. Has a list of 45 passengers giving residence of each. Also has list of twelve officers and crew giving residence of each. Some entries are long and descriptive, and most entries are longer than usual.

Curry, W. B. List of officers, crew, and passengers on board the ship *George Washington* on her voyage from New York to San Francisco in 1849 under the command of Capt. John Holdridge. Positive photostat copy, California State Library, Sacramento California. Passengers were divided into saloon, second cabin, and steerage.

Deane, Benjamin H. Journal, June 6–December 26, 1849, of a voyage from New York to San Francisco in the ship *Arkansas* under the command of Capt. Philip

Bibliography

W. Shepeard. Bancroft Library, University of California, Berkeley, C-F 106. Actual dates of the journal were May 28–March 22, 1851. Early portion of the journal contains information on preparations for the voyage while later part contains information on activities in California. Deane was a member of the California Mutual Benefit and Joint Stock Association, an association of Methodists who owned the vessel. The *Arkansas* was wrecked on Alcatraz Island a day after they arrived in San Francisco but was salvaged and used as a store ship for many years.

De Costa, William H. Journal, February 9–August 22, 1849, of a voyage from Boston to San Francisco in the ship *Duxbury* under the command of Capt. W. C. Varina. Huntington Library, San Marino, California, HM 234 and 249. In his first entry he indicated he was not going to California "filled with big hopes of a speedy return, bent down with a burden of gold" like his fellow passengers. Rather he was going with "a small hope of doing something— what, I may not tell." Made stops at Rio de Janeiro and the island of Juan Fernandez. He wrote long descriptions of both places although that of Rio de Janeiro was written after June 24 while the stop was in April. Has numerous long descriptions of happenings including the visit from King Neptune on March 25. Two days after arriving in San Francisco he "went to work in the office of the Pacific News intending by so doing to realize a fortune in a few days."

Denham, George. Journal, February 7–July 3, 1849, of a voyage from Holmes Hole (Vineyard Haven), Massachusetts, to San Francisco in the schooner *Rialto* under the command of Capt. Charles Downs. G. W. Blunt White Library, Mystic Seaport Museum, Inc., Mystic, Connecticut, Log 840. Denham was a homesick minister who went gold seeking. The vessel was owned by the Rialto Mining Company, most of whose sixteen members were whaling captains. Because he had no previous experience at sea, he was ranked as a "greenhand." This made his duties as the religious leader on the vessel quite difficult for him, and he became very disillusioned.

Denney, C. A. Journal, February 24–September 10, 1849, of a voyage from Boston to San Francisco in the bark *Orb* under the command of Capt. F. W. Moores. Huntington Library, San Marino, California, HM 40682. He was a member of the North Western Association. He stayed in California only fifty-three days and then sailed from San Francisco in the ship *Memnon* to Hawaii, China, and Boston.

Dole, Charles Augustus. Journal, March 17–November 3, 1849, of a voyage from Salem, Massachusetts, to San Francisco in the bark *LaGrange* under the command of Capt. Joseph Dewing. Peabody/Essex Museum, Salem, Massachusetts. Dole was a butcher from Danvers, Massachusetts. Entries are long and descriptive. Has numerous illustrations of the bark and ports entered in the Falkland Islands, where they did considerable hunting for fresh meat. The entry for August 14 includes a drawing of the *LaGrange* speaking to the U.S. Revenue Cutter Service brig *Lawrence*. The August 23 entry has a drawing of the *LaGrange* surrounded by whales. The journal was written on loose sheets, some of which are damaged at the edges, making certain words illegible. Many entries are long and descriptive.

Dornin, George. Reminiscences, 1849–1879. California State Library, Sacramento. Dornin sailed from New York to San Francisco in the ship *Panama* under the command of Capt. Russell L. Bodfish in 1849. His journal of that voyage was destroyed in 1855, when his residence burned. He prepared these reminiscences for his children.

Dougal, William H. Journal, April 7–November 22, 1849, of a voyage from New York to San Francisco in the bark *Galindo* under the command of Capt. P. B. Macy. Bancroft Library, University of California, Berkeley, C-F 181. The Dougal collection also includes a few letters and some sketches by Dugal during the voyage. The journal, letters, and sketches were published in 1949 as *Off for California.*

Eddy, John E. Journal, April 13–August 9, 1849, of a voyage from Warren, Rhode Island, to San Francisco in the ship *Hopewell* under the command of Capt. George Littlefield. Bancroft Library, University of California, Berkeley, 93/30 c. The journal starts when they are near Cape Horn and continues to their arrival in San Francisco. They stopped in Talcahuano because of the poor health of the captain and to obtain fresh supplies. The captain was taken on shore to attempt to recover his health. He told them he was leaving the ship in charge of the mate and Captain Grinnell and to obey them as they would him. In spite of his poor health, Captain Littlefield returned to the ship when they departed. His poor health continued during the remainder of the voyage.

Edmonston, Charles N. Levi Augustus Maxcy, undated. Bancroft Library, University of California, Berkeley, C-D 5200. Maxcy arrived in San Francisco at the end of 1849 in the bark *Velasco* with the Narragansett Trading and Mining Company of Providence, Rhode Island. The only information on the voyage is copied from Allen Taylor, *Memorial and Biographical History of the Counties of Merced, Stanislaus, Calaveras, Toulumne, and Mariposa,* published in 1892 by Lewis Publishing Company.

Edmunds, Elawson. Letter, November 4, 1849, to his brother, describing his "long and tegus voige" from Boston to San Francisco in an unnamed vessel. California Historical Society Library, San Francisco. Reports he was a member of the Eldorado Association, which broke up when they arrived or before then and that the same happened to all the companies that came to California. Also noted that "the officers tride to jew us out of our Rights" and that he would have been better off paying $125 for his passage rather than the $200 he paid for membership. He sold his share in the association for $100.

Edwards, John Robert. Abstract journal, March 9–September 17, 1849, of a voyage from New York to San Francisco in the bark *Henry Harbeck* under the command of Capt. T. G. Merwin. California State Library, Sacramento. Provides only dates, latitude, longitude, wind direction, barometric pressure, and air and water temperatures.

Ewer, Ferdinand Cartwright. Journal, April 4–September 16, 1849, of a voyage from Boston to San Francisco in the ship *York* under the command of Capt. George N. Cheever. Bancroft Library, University of California, Berkeley. Journal continues to November 23 and contains information on activities in California. The *York* was owned by the Pacific Mining Company, whose thirty-eight members each paid $1,000. The journal consists of five parts, which may have been mailed home separately. Three clippings included in the journal provide information on the company and a list of its members. There are many gaps between entries.

Farren, John Wilmot. Journal, November 22, 1849–April 2, 1850, of a voyage from Boston to San Francisco in the ship *Reindeer* under the command of Capt. John Lord. California Historical Society, San Francisco. On February 9, 1850, the passengers sent a petition to the captain expressing dissatisfaction with the provisions.

Fay, Caleb Taylor. Statement of Historical Facts on California, 1878. Bancroft Library, University of California, Berkeley, C-D 78. Dictation recorded for H. H. Bancroft concerning his arrival in San Francisco via Cape Horn in 1849 and his activities in California. Only the first three or four pages deal with the voyage from Boston, probably in the bark *Orb*. Fay and twenty-one other passengers were members of the Northwestern Association, which owned the vessel.

Ferrell, Robert N. Journal, June 26–December 19, 1849, of a voyage from New York to San Francisco in the ship *Arkansas* under the command of Capt. Philip W. Shepeard. Bancroft Library, University of California, Berkeley. The library has the original journal, a rough typescript copy, and a photostatic copy of the original, one of twenty made in 1930 by either Edward S. Clark or E. M. Francis. The Peabody/Essex Museum in Salem, Massachusetts, has another photostatic copy, and the California Historical Society in San Francisco has two photostatic copies of the original and a copy of the typescript. The *Arkansas* was owned by a group of Methodists organized under the name California Mutual Benefit and Joint Stock Association. There were also some passengers who were not members of the association. They made stops in Rio de Janeiro and Talcahuano. Both places are described in some detail.

Fitch, Henry W. Journal, August 1, 1849–January 3, 1850, of a voyage from Fairhaven, Massachusetts, to San Francisco in the ship *Florida* under the command of Capt. James E. Robinson. Whaling Museum Library, New Bedford, Massachusetts. The *Florida* was a whaling vessel purchased by the Acushnet Building and Mining Association, which consisted of forty members. They carried a large quantity of lumber and other building supplies as well as some small vessels to California. The *Florida* sailed for Callao on August 19 and continued to New York on November 20, 1850.

Flagg, Hiram B. Journal, January 11–July 6, 1849, of a voyage from Boston to San Francisco in the ship *Edward Everett* under the command of Capt. Henry Smith. Society of California Pioneers, San Francisco. Has a list 150 passengers in alphabetical order with occupation, residence, place of birth, and age for nearly all. Flagg was a 30-year-old iron founder from Lawrence, Massachusetts. Passengers were members of the Boston and California Mining and Trading Joint Stock Company. Entries are very short.

Fletcher, Warren. Journal, January 2–July 15, 1849, of a voyage from Boston to San Francisco in the bark *Elvira* under the command of Capt. George R. Nickerson. Bancroft Library, University of California, Berkeley, C-F 4:1. Includes a list of thirteen passengers, some of whom are identified as officers in the bark. From what is written in the last few entries, it appears that they never intended to seek gold in the mines but rather to start a business in Sacramento. They went there almost immediately and started constructing a building and unloading goods to sell.

Floyd-Jones. Family Correspondence, 1848–1878. Bancroft Library, University of California, Berkeley, C-B 625. Includes six letters from Edward Floyd Jones to his family describing his voyage from New York to San Francisco in the ship *Sara & Eliza*, February 14–September 6, 1849, as well as a hand-drawn chart of the voyage with a daily record of the latitude and longitude of the vessel.

Folwell, Thomas Iredell. Journal, January 16–August 5, 1849, of a voyage from Philadelphia to San Francisco in the brig *Osceola* under the command of Capt. James Fairfowl. California State Library, Sacramento. Photocopy of typescript. Volume also contains copies of three letters Folwell wrote to his wife and sons as well as excerpts from Samuel Upham's *Notes of a Voyage to California via Cape Horn*, which was also written in the *Osceola*.

Fowler, Stephen Lawrence. Journal, January 12–September 5, 1849, of a voyage from New York to San Francisco in the ship *Brooklyn* under the command of Capt. Joseph W. Richardson. Society of California Pioneers, San Francisco. Bancroft Library, University of California, Berkeley, has a typescript copy (C-F 144) made by the California Historical Survey Commission in 1916. First part of the journal is a brief summary of the voyage. Regular entries begin on August 9, shortly before they arrived in San Francisco. The journal continues into early 1852 and includes descriptions of activities in California. Several passengers suffered from scurvy, and some died from that malady after they arrived in San Francisco.

Fowler, Stephen L., and James E. Fowler. Account of a voyage from New York to San Francisco in the ship *Brooklyn* under the command of Capt. Joseph W. Richardson. Bancroft Library, University of California, Berkeley. Typescript copy. Prior to August 9, 1849, all of the information is in summary form centered around broad topics. After that date the entries are made regularly and contain information about sickness, especially scurvy, among the passengers and sailors. Several of them died after arriving in San Francisco. Some legal action was brought against Captain Richardson, which resulted in his being fined $2,000.

French, James P. Journal, May 14–November 2, 1849, of a voyage from Boston to San Francisco in the ship *Helen Augusta* under the command of Capt. F. Myrick. University of California, San Diego. Passengers included members of the Mechanics and Merchants Mining Company.

Friendship (ship). Series of mostly undated episodes on board the ship while on a voyage from Fairhaven, Massachusetts, to San Francisco under the command of Capt. William Stott. Whaling Museum Library, New Bedford, Massachusetts. Most of the officers and crew were members of the Friendship Mining Company. Mrs. Diana Stott, wife of the captain, was included among the four passengers. The vessel carried a cargo of lumber, houses, and provisions. All of the episodes occurred during the first two months of the voyage, which began September 2, 1849.

Fuller, Charles Herbert. Journal, March 1–August 5, 1849, of a voyage from Boston to San Francisco in the ship *Sweden* under the command of Capt. Jesse C. Cotting. Bancroft Library, University of California, Berkeley. Although this journal is catalogued under the name Fuller, there is some question about who the writer really was. In the entry for July 3, 1849, the author notes "One of my chums has just handed me a piece of poetry written for a young lady in Richmond, Va he said she is about 14 years old and is a smart and beautiful girl and he writes the following lines to her." This is followed by a copy of the poem titled "To Annie." At the bottom is written the name Charles Herbert Fuller. The author regularly wrote the name J. L. L. Warren at the bottom of the words to the several songs Warren wrote for Sunday services and a funeral. On May 31 the author also notes, "Mr Fuller one of my chums is sick with the mumps." On June 19 the author tells of an Irishman suffering from rheumatism in the morning. When he later sees him on deck and asks how he is doing, the Irishman responds "very weak Jim." Thus the journalist is probably someone named Jim or James. Since the lists of passengers in the *Sweden* in the Warren Papers and the Journal of Benjamin Bailey provide only the initials rather than first names, it has not been possible to identify anyone named Jim or James other than James L. L. F. Warren.

Gager, James H. Journal, January 22–August 5, 1849, of a voyage from New York to San Francisco in the ship *Pacific* under the command of Capt. Hall J. Tibbits from New York to Rio de Janeiro and Capt. George Easterbrook from Rio de Janeiro to San Francisco. Society of California Pioneers, San Francisco. Includes a list of passengers with age and residence of each. There were a few wives and children of officers and owners of the vessel among the passengers. Captain Tibbits was removed from command in Rio de Janeiro by U.S. consul Gorham D. Parks because of strong complaints by the first-class passengers that Tibbets was insane and intemperate.

Gambart, John E. Journal, January 30–August 2, 1849, of a voyage from New York to San Francisco in the bark *Cordelia* under the command of Captain Barker. Huntington Library, San Marino, California, HM 17013. The passengers were members of an association whose name is not given. Some of the members had contracted with substitutes to go to California in their places. The substitutes were obligated to give their principles half of whatever gold they found. The members of the association adopted bylaws on July 9. Most of the entries are brief and are limited to matters related to the weather. Exceptions are the entries for February 19–22, which include long descriptions regarding planning for and celebrating Washington's birthday, and the visit at Valparaiso where he recorded many rumors about California. They also stopped at Rio de Janeiro. Shortly after arriving in San Francisco, they sailed the bark to Sacramento, where the members of the association voted to disband.

Garniss, James R. The Early Days in San Francisco, 1877. Bancroft Library, University of California, Berkeley, C-D 189. Dictation recorded for H. H. Bancroft. Contains recollections of his voyage around Cape Horn to San Francisco in 1849 and as a merchant, auctioneer, and insurance underwriter in San Francisco. The men who sailed with Garniss went to California to engage in business rather than go to the mines.

Gold Rush Letters, 1849–1852. Bancroft Library, University of California, Berkeley. Includes two letters from Thomas Forbes to Hezekiah Branard (or Brainard) in Connecticut. One deals with the passage of the ship *Henry Lee* from New York to San Francisco, February 7–September 13, 1849. The other includes information on his mining experiences and the fate of the Hartford Union Mining and Trading Company, which sailed in the *Henry Lee*.

Goodall, Charles. Journal, March 7, 1849–January 25, 1850, of a voyage from New Orleans to San Francisco in the schooner *St. Mary* under the command of Captain Chasten (or Chastain or Chasteau). Bancroft Library, University of California, Berkeley, C-F 116. Front part of the volume contains Goodall's record of earlier trips in sailing vessels beginning in 1847. Because of severe gales and other problems, they put into port in Baltimore for repairs on April 5. The passengers made strong complaints to and demands of the owners that resulted in the removal of the captain, who they accused of drunkenness. He was replaced by George Chason. They sailed from Baltimore on May 14.

Gould, Walter Balfour. Journal, April 27–July 3, 1849, of a voyage from Boston to San Francisco in the bark *Maria* under the command of Capt. J. P. Baker. New York Historical Society, New York. The portion of the voyage between New York and Rio de Janeiro is covered in summary fashion and was written at a later time. Gould started regular entries when they were in the South Pacific. Includes a track chart, several drawings (including one of the *Maria*), and list of officers.

Gove, Enoch. Papers, 1849, including letters from Boston to his brother Amos W. Gove and Coridon B. Phelps; a list of the passengers in the ship *Edward Everett* with name, occupation, residence, place of birth, and age of each; and a daily record of latitude of the *Edward Everett*, January 13–July 5, 1849. Bancroft Library, University of California, Berkeley. Microfilm copy, C-F 117 film.

Graves, William. Journal, December 6, 1849–May 26, 1850, of a voyage from Salem, Massachusetts, to San Francisco in the ship *Crescent* under the command of Capt. John Madison. Bancroft Library, University of California, Berkeley, 77/148 c. The vessel was owned by the sixty-one members of the Salem Mechanics Trading and Mining Association. Volume includes a list of the members with name, place of birth, occupation, residence, age, marital status, and number of children for each. Also includes a list of officers and crew and a record of the cargo with prices. A copy of the constitution of the Salem Mechanics Trading and Mining Association clipped from a contemporary newspaper is pasted into the back of the volume.

Green, Henry. Journal, February 7–August 9, 1849, of a voyage from Sag Harbor, New York, to San Francisco in the ship *Sabina* under the command of Capt. Henry Green. G. W. Blunt White Library, Mystic Seaport Museum, Inc., Mystic, Connecticut, Log 754. Green was also president, treasurer, and a trustee of the Southampton and California Mining and Trading Company, which owned the *Sabina*. Includes lists of the members of the company with the amount of merchandise and cash to which each was entitled and of the officers and crew. Eight additional passengers paid $150 each for the voyage. Journal continues to May 11, 1850, and contains information on activities in California.

Halsey, Isaac S. A Forty-Niner's Diary. Copy number 24 of a transcript made in 1978 by Frank S. Halsey of part of the journal of Isaac S. Halsey's voyage from New York to San Francisco in the ship *Salem* under the command of Capt. Thomas A.

Bibliography

Eldridge. Bancroft Library, University of California, Berkeley, 79/130 c. The Bancroft Library also has what appears to be the original journal from October 10, 1849–June 1, 1851, as well as a holograph transcription for the period March 12–21, 1849. There were approximately 150 passengers in the *Salem*. Includes a printed copy of the bylaws of the California Mutual Benefit Association, the company that sailed in the *Salem*, as well as a holograph copy of the constitution and bylaws of the New York and California Excelsior Mining Company, which was formed during the voyage by a portion of the members of the California Mutual Benefit Association. Also includes mining records of the New York and California Excelsior Mining Company between December 1855 and August 1857.

Halsey, Isaac Sherwood. A Forty-Niner's Diary. Copy number 25 of photocopy or multilith publication by Frank S. Halsey. California State Library, Sacramento. A duplicate of the transcript held by the Bancroft Library but also has a reproduction of a drawing of the *Salem* by Isaac Sherwood Halsey.

Hamilton (ship). Logbook, 1849–1851, of a voyage from Boston to San Francisco, Honolulu, Hawaii, Bali, and Calcutta under the command of Capt. Peter C. Peterson. G. W. Blunt White Library, Mystic Seaport Museum, Inc., Mystic, Connecticut. Vessel carried passengers and a cargo of lumber, building materials, bricks, and coal to San Francisco.

Harrington, Augustus. Journal, March 17–September 23, 1849, of a voyage from Salem, Massachusetts, to San Francisco in the bark *LaGrange* under the command of Capt. Joseph Dewing. Peabody/Essex Museum, Salem, Massachusetts. California State Library, Sacramento has a typescript copy made by Frank C. Damon, historical editor of the *Salem Evening News* in 1928 and used by him as the basis for a serial in that newspaper. Passengers included the members of the Salem and California Mining and Trading Company or Expedition. Harrington used both terms. Includes a list of members of the company with occupation and residence of each. Entries are generally long and descriptive. Has a lengthy description of the celebration of July 4.

Harvey, Charles Henry. Journal, December 6, 1849–May 26, 1850, of a voyage from Salem, Massachusetts, to San Francisco in the ship *Crescent* under the command of Capt. John Madison. Library of Congress, Washington, D.C. Journal begins October 14, 1849 and continues through 1858 in several volumes. The early part of the diary has information on his preparations for the voyage while the later part describes mining in California. Passengers included sixty-one members of the Salem Mechanics Trading and Mining Company. Includes lists of the members, other passengers, officers and sailors. Also includes a record of expenses of the company prior to sailing as well as of the sources of funds. Under date April 1, 1850 there is a record of the weekly bill of fare adopted by the company. For the period February 9–March 27, 1850 there are two versions of the journal, the second being considerably more detailed than the first.

Hatch, William M. Journal, December 28, 1849–July 12, 1850, of a voyage from Damariscotta, Maine, to San Francisco in the schooner *Damariscove* under the command of Capt. G. W. Talbot. California Historical Society, San Francisco. Photocopy. They made stops at St. Catherines Island, where they spent six days in quarantine before they could get water and wood, and at Juan Fernandez

Island. Went through the Straits of Magellan rather than around Cape Horn. Had on board an unnamed company of twenty-one men. Includes a list of members of the company and crew with age and occupation of each.

Herbert, William A. Journal, January 2–June 26, 1849, of a voyage from Boston to San Francisco in the ship *Elvira* under the command of Capt. George R. Nickerson. Huntington Library, San Marino, California, HM 978. Stopped in Rio de Janeiro. Includes a list of twelve passengers at the front of the journal. Most entries quite brief and limited to latitude and longitude, number of days out, and weather conditions. Has original poems in the entries for April 15 and 25, May 1, 6, and 14, and June 1 and 10.

Hill, Benjamin S. Correspondence, 1849–1853. Bancroft Library, University of California, Berkeley, C-B 655. Includes both original letters and transcripts. Two of the letters are from Josiah Griswold to Benjamin S. Hill and contain a description of Griswold's voyage from New York to San Francisco in the bark *Salem*, March 12– October 12, 1849.

Hollingsworth, Anderson. Journal, January 1–August 1, 1849, of a voyage from New York to San Francisco in the ship *Daniel Webster* under the command of Capt. I. G. Pierce. Bancroft Library, University of California, Berkeley, 89/80 c. Library has both the original and a typescript copy. Actual dates of the voyage were February 3–July 20, 1849. Contains lists of cabin and steerage passengers including names, residences, ages, and occupations of the sixty passengers. Also includes a record of the names, residences, and ages of the officers and crew members. There were four organized companies among the passengers named the McPerines Company and the New York Bowery Mining Company of New York and the ABC & Company and another unnamed company from Boston.

Hopkins, Mark. Biographical sketch. Bancroft Library, University of California, Berkeley. Typescript with corrections by D. R. Sessions. Information was probably obtained from W. R. S. Foye. C. P. Huntington wrote a letter to W. R. S. Foye on October 21, 1886 introducing D. R. Sessions for the purpose of obtaining a sketch of the life and labors of Mark Hopkins for H. H. Bancroft. Hopkins was a passenger in the ship *Pacific*. The Bancroft Library has both a handwritten and a typed copy. Both have corrections by Sessions.

Howard, Eugene. Letter, August 30 and October 2, 1849, from Eugene Howard on board the bark *Mousam* on a voyage from New York to San Francisco under the command of Capt. Franklin R. Miller. Bancroft Library, University of California, Berkeley, 73/122 c, 190. Letter contains a brief summary of the voyage. On August 30 they were in the North Pacific Ocean, and on October 2 they were in San Francisco.

Howard, John T. Journal, October 30, 1849–March 24, 1850, of a voyage from Thomaston, Maine, to San Francisco in the bark *Midas* under the command of Capt. George Jordan. Bancroft Library, University of California, Berkeley, 76/10 c. First entry is a six-page introduction that contains information revealing that there were twenty-one passengers. Journal ends shortly before they arrived in San Francisco.

Howland, William. Journal, February 7–August 5, 1849, of a voyage from New York to San Francisco in the bark *Isabel* under the command of Capt. Nicolas R.

Bibliography

Brewer. Rutgers University Library, New Brunswick, New Jersey. Passengers were members of the New Brunswick and California Mining and Trading Association.

Hudson, Phinehas. Journal, February 3–July 22, 1849, of a voyage from New York to San Francisco in the ship *Daniel Webster* under the command of Capt. Jacob G. Pierce. Society of California Pioneers, San Francisco. Many entries are longer than usual. Between entries for May 12 and 13, 1849 there is a list of the fifty-nine passengers with name, occupation, residence, and age of each and a list of officers and crew with name, place of origin, and age of each. Hudson was a 45-year-old ship carpenter from Long Island.

Hull, William S. Journal, January 25–July 27, 1849, of a voyage from Baltimore to San Francisco in the ship *Jane Parker* under the command of Capt. C. Jordon. Maryland Historical Society, Baltimore. This is more of a narrative than a daily journal, as most entries are lengthy summary descriptions of activities over several days or even weeks. Contains copies of daily notes from the journal of B. Bales for the period January 25–May 24, 1849. There were seventy-nine passengers housed in two cabins below deck, one forward and one aft.

Hull, William S. Speech given by Hull as part of the July 4, 1849 celebration on board the ship *Jane Parker* of Baltimore. Maryland Historical Society, Baltimore.

Hutchinson, Robert. Journal, November 25, 1849–May 17, 1850, of a voyage from Cherryfield, Maine, to San Francisco in the bark *Belgrade* under the command of Capt. Horatio N. Palmer. California State Library, Sacramento. Original typescript copy. Bancroft Library, University of California, Berkeley, C-F 72, and Huntington Library, San Marino, California, both have carbon copies of the typescript. List of the forty-eight members of the Sacramento Navigation & Mining Company and ten other passengers who worked their passage are included in the first entry. Journal stopped shortly before their arrival in San Francisco.

Hyde, Henry H. Jr. Journal, February 2–September 19, 1849, of a voyage from Boston to San Francisco in the ship *Lenore* under the command of Capt. H. H. Greene. Bancroft Library, University of California, Berkeley, C-F 45. Holograph copy made by George E. Hyde in 1873, who noted that parts of the original were omitted or guessed at because of decay in the original. The California State Library, Sacramento, has a carbon typescript. Copy at the California State Library has a list of the officers and members of the New England and California Trading and Mining Association whose one hundred members sailed as passengers. Residence, age, marital status and occupation given for each member.

Ingalls, E. A. Journal, October 30, 1849–March 27, 1850, of a voyage from Boston to San Francisco in the ship *Henry Ware* under the command of Capt. M. Mason. Bancroft Library, University of California, Berkeley. Well-written journal with detailed descriptions of daily events during the voyage. Has a good description of San Francisco. Journal continues to October 1850 and includes an account of his disappointing efforts to find gold and a portion of his trip home by steamer to Panama and overland across the isthmus.

Jackson, Stephen. Letters to his mother and brother, 1849–1867. Bancroft Library, University of California, Berkeley, C-B 624. First letter relates his plans to sail to California in the ship *Hannibal* of Boston under the command of Capt. George H. Willis. Second letter contains a description of the voyage from Boston to San Francisco. Other letters include descriptions of his experiences in California.

Jacobs, Enoch. Journal, January 11–July 29, 1849, of a voyage from Boston to San Francisco in the ship *Edward Everett* under the command of Capt. Henry Smith. Huntington Library, San Marino, California. Passengers were members of the Boston and California Mining and Trading Joint Stock Company. Stopped in Valparaiso. Entries are usually long and full of descriptions of what was happening on board and thoughts about them and other matters. Has a long description of the Fourth of July celebration including a long poem composed for the day by Joseph Augustine Benton.

Jessup, Isaac M. Journal, August 17, 1849–June 16, 1850, of a voyage from Cold Spring Harbor, New York, to San Francisco in the ship *Sheffield* under the command of Capt. Thomas W. Roys. G. W. Blunt White Library, Mystic Seaport Museum, Inc., Mystic, Connecticut, Log 351. The *Sheffield* was actually on a whaling voyage to the Pacific Ocean but carried a cargo of lumber and wheels to San Francisco. They made little effort to take any whales during that part of the voyage, which lasted until 1854.

John G. Colley (bark). Records, 1849. J. Porter Shaw Library, National Maritime Museum, San Francisco. A rhyming verse account of the voyage of the bark *John G. Colley* from Norfolk, Virginia, to San Francisco. Titled "A tribute to those life-lasting feelings of Disgust, Contempt, & Scorn Unanimously entertained, by the Passengers, Officers and crew of the bark John G. Colley for Capt. William Smith, New York."

Jones, Dudley Emmerson. Papers, 1849–1906, including a journal, February 23–April 25, 1849, of a voyage from New York to San Francisco in the bark *Nautilus* under the command of Capt. S. G. Wilson and some later recollections containing expansion of what is in the journal. University of Arkansas Library, Fayetteville. Journal ends during their stay in Rio de Janeiro of which there is a long and detailed description. Some recollections provide detail on the organization of the Albany Company for California, the joint stock company that owned the bark.

Jones, Dudley Emmerson. Papers, including two long letters with some information added by Jones in 1908 and a typed essay titled "A Short Biographical Sketch with Facts Concerning the Early Life and Adventures of Dudley Emmerson Jones Together with Copies of His Letters to His Parents, Written While at Sea and after Having Reached California—The Land of Gold." Bancroft Library, University of California, Berkeley. Information was compiled from notes and data supplied at the request of Jones's grandson, Philip Sherman Bernays in Los Angeles in 1908. It is reported that each of the one hundred members of the Albany Company for California paid $300. Seventy-five members went to California while the remaining twenty-five stayed in New York to manage the affairs of the company. The company dissolved shortly after arriving. Jones returned to New York in 1852.

Keefe, Charles Norton. Journal, March 12–August 29, 1849, of a voyage from New York to San Francisco in the ship *Salem* under the command of Capt. Thomas

Bibliography

A. Eldridge. Bancroft Library, University of California, Berkeley, C-F 148. Microfilm copy. Provides the latitude and longitude on a daily basis to mid-April and then has a summary, between the entries for April 15 and 16, 1849, of the daily position until the end of the voyage. Entries are quite short at the beginning but get increasingly longer as he details a squabble between the passengers and the captain, who resigned his position on April 14. Thereafter the entries become short again. Made stops in Rio de Janeiro and Talcahuano.

Keeler, James P. Journal, March 12–October 28, 1849, of a voyage from New Haven, Connecticut, to San Francisco in the bark *Anna Reynolds* under the command of Capt. John Bottom. California Historical Society, San Francisco. There are a few gaps in the entries, and the period between March 23 and June 20 exists in two versions, one in ink and another in pencil. The entries are generally rather short. Made stops at Port au Grand Isle, St. Vincent, Port Praya, St. Iago, Port Stanley, Falkland Islands, and Talcahuano. Passengers did a good bit of hunting at the Falkland Islands.

Keeler, Julius M. Biographical Sketch, circa 1888. Bancroft Library, University of California, Berkeley, C-D 831. Includes some information about his voyage from New York to San Francisco in 1849 in the ship *Arkansas* as a member of the California Mutual Benefit and Joint Stock Association, which owned the vessel.

Kent, George F. Journal, February 8–September 16, 1849, of a voyage from Boston to San Francisco in the brig *Rodolph* under the command of Capt. Hartwell Walker. Huntington Library, San Marino, California, HM 524. Passengers included the sixteen members of the Shawmut & California Company, who purchased the 123-ton, four-and-a-half-year-old brig for $3,500. There were eighteen other passengers, two cooks and five stewards. Includes a detailed introduction to the journal in which he indicates he was secretary of the company. Entry for March 31 includes his long elegy on the death of one of their pigs the previous day. On May 10 he includes two poems by J. V. Sullivan of Boston, one of which is titled "A Galley Lyne." On May 26 he includes another poem by Sullivan about their visit to the island of Mocha, where they stopped for wood, water, and provisions. For June 18 he includes a long poem about celebrating the Battle of Bunker Hill on June 17. He provides a long description of their Fourth of July celebration that includes an ode by William K. Blanchard, the thirteen traditional national toasts by the toastmaster, and twenty-eight additional volunteer toasts by other individuals. Entry for August 31 includes a list of passengers and their residences. They stopped at Talcahuano for nearly two weeks.

King, Henry Louis. Statement, 1887. Bancroft Library, University of California, Berkeley, C-D 327. Dictation recorded for H. H. Bancroft. Has some information on his voyage from New York to San Francisco as a member of the California Mining and Trading Company in the bark *Palmetto*. Each of the forty-two members paid five hundred dollars.

Kitfield, A. E. Journal, March 17–September 17, 1849, of a voyage from Salem, Massachusetts, to San Francisco in the bark *LaGrange* under the command of Capt. Joseph Dewing. Peabody/Essex Museum, Salem, Massachusetts. Arrangement of the first part of the journal seems very confused. Contains a list of the ship's company with occupation and residence of each person. In the middle of the voyage there are words to a song written by someone named Barker and sung on the day the *LaGrange* sailed from Salem. There are actually two versions of the diary, the first of which consists of brief entries and the second of longer entries.

Kleinhans, Daniel W. Memoirs, undated. Bancroft Library, University of California, Berkeley, C-D 5056. Includes recollections of his voyage from New York to San Francisco in the brig *John Endors* in 1849 and descriptions of San Francisco and Sacramento. Has some good information about the gold hysteria in 1848.

Knoche, Johann Edward. Recollections of the Early Days of a Pioneer, written in 1901. Bancroft Library, University of California, Berkeley, C-D 5010. Includes some information about his voyage from New Orleans to San Francisco in the bark *Montgomery* in 1849.

La Motte Family. Letters, 1849–1872. Bancroft Library, University of California, Berkeley, C-B 450. Library has both original letters and typescript copies. Six letters by Robert and Harry La Motte to their family contain details of their voyage from Philadelphia to San Francisco in the bark *Maria* under the command of Capt. John J. Mattison. At least two letters are in journal form and contain entries for several days.

Leonard, Albert. Statement and Papers, 1888–1892. Bancroft Library, University of California, Berkeley, C-D 793. Includes a dictation by William J. Kerr for H. H. Bancroft concerning Leonard's voyage from New York to San Francisco in the bark *Strafford*. Makes mention of the company of one hundred that purchased the vessel. States that approximately half of them worked together until March 1850, when they dissolved the company and sold the vessel.

Lewis, Samuel C. Journal, March 4–September 16, 1849, of a voyage from Boston to San Francisco in the ship *Charlotte* under the command of Capt. Richard F. Savory. Bancroft Library, University of California, Berkeley, 77/154 c. Journal was started during February 1849 and continued to April 1850. Early entries contain information on preparations for the voyage. Contains lists of 17 cabin and 116 steerage passengers with residence and occupation of each. Also includes a list of all his outfits for the voyage and the price for each item.

Locke, Jonathan Frost. Journal, March 8–October 19, 1849, of a voyage from Boston to San Francisco in the brig *Sea Eagle* under the command of Captain Hammond. Bancroft Library, University of California, Berkeley, C-D 608. Journal ends shortly before they arrived in San Francisco. At least one leaf torn out following the entry of October 29, 1849.

Locke, Jonathan Frost. Letters, 1849, to his wife in Somerville, Massachusetts, while he was on a voyage from Boston to San Francisco in the brig *Sea Eagle* under the command of Captain Hammond. Bancroft Library, University of California, Berkeley, C-D 608. These letters supplement and duplicate information in his journal.

McCrackan, John. Letters, 1849, to his mother and sisters in New Haven, Connecticut, in which he describes his voyage from New York to San Francisco in the ship *Balance* under the command of Capt. E. Washborn Ruggles. Bancroft Library, University of California, Berkeley, C-B 444. Letters were written quite frequently and contain comments upon fellow passengers and crew members, extensive descriptions of bird and marine life, detailed accounts of life in the ship and the effect of weather on that life, and the long stay in Talcahuano. Voyage began April 1 and ended November 23, 1849. He notes that there were seventy-three people on board. That included the owners, Messrs. Brooks and Frye, who sold passage to San Francisco for $150.

McFarland, Horatio N. Journal, November 21, 1849–May 6, 1850, of a voyage from Boston to San Francisco in the ship *Carlo Mauran* under the command of Capt. Joseph H. Tillinghast. Peabody/Essex Museum, Salem, Massachusetts. Original and typescript copy.

McHenry, Charles Shewell. Letters, February 18–May 22, 1849, written during his voyage from Philadelphia to San Francisco in the ship *Grey Eagle* under the command of Capt. J. Powers. California State Library, Sacramento. Carbon typescript copy. Of the eight letters transcribed, only three relate to the voyage. The first was written at sea, the second at Valparaiso, and the third at San Francisco. All are long and descriptive.

Main, Charles. Journal, February 3–July 5, 1849, of a voyage from Boston to San Francisco in the ship *Lenore* under the command of Capt. H. H. Greene. Bancroft Library, University of California, Berkeley. Microfilm copy. Has a long description of their March 4 celebration including a dance at which some of the men dressed as females. At least some of the passengers were members of the New England and California Mining and Trading Association. Provides the latitude and longitude nearly every day and much information about the weather. Stopped in Talcahuano, which he describes in considerable detail. Includes a sketch of the country between Talcahuano and Conception.

Marchant, Abiah. Poetic journal written on board the ship *Magnolia* of her voyage to San Francisco, February–July, 1849. G. W. Blunt White Library, Mystic Seaport Museum, Inc., Mystic, Connecticut, VFM 1003. Each page contains one four-line poem about the events of the day. S. Mortimer Collins and William F. Reed both make references to a Miss Marchant in their journals. Collins includes a copy of at least one of her four-line poems.

Marshall, Robert. Journal, November 12, 1849–May 1, 1850, of a voyage from Boston to San Francisco in the schooner *Civilian* under the command of Capt. Thomas Dodge. Society of California Pioneers, San Francisco. Arrived in San Francisco on April 5, 1850. Has a complete bill of fare for a full week for the entry for November 30, 1849. Made stops at St. Catherines Island and Valparaiso. Marshall was one of fifty-eight members of the Cochituate Mining Company.

Martin, Benjamin Thomson. Journal, January 2–June 26, 1849, of a voyage from Boston to San Francisco in the bark *Elvira* under the command of Capt. George R. Nickerson. California State Library, Sacramento. Typescript copy. Contains a list of officers, crew, and twelve passengers. Includes copies of several letters written by Martin, mostly to the *Chelsea Pioneer*. There is evidence that the volume belonged to Charles A. Holbrook, another passenger from Boston, and some indications that he, rather than Martin, may have been the author of the journal.

Matthewson, T. D. Statement on California Affairs, 1878. Bancroft Library, University of California, Berkeley, C-D 124. Dictation recorded for H. H. Bancroft.

Includes information on his voyage from New York to San Francisco in the bark *Mallery*.

Mauran, J. Letters, January 25–July 28, 1849, written on board the ship *Oxford* during her voyage from Boston to San Francisco under the command of Capt. J. or S. Mauran to J. Dunbard & Co. of New Bedford, Massachusetts. University of California, San Diego.

Maxoy, A. E. Dictation and Letter, 1887. Bancroft Library, University of California, Berkeley, C-D 433. Dictation for H. H. Bancroft. Includes information on his voyage from Boston to San Francisco in the ship *Pharsalia* in 1849.

Meredith, Griffith. Journal, February 3–August 28, 1849, of a voyage from New York to San Francisco in the bark *Strafford* under the command of Capt. William L. Coffin. California State Library, Sacramento. Includes a list of the one hundred members of the New York Mining Company who were passengers in the bark and a record of the eighteen toasts offered during the Fourth of July celebration on board the vessel.

Miller, Christian. Letters, April 27 and October 19, 1849, to his family describing the voyage from Philadelphia to San Francisco in the ship *Mason* under the command of Capt. William Bell. Bancroft Library, University of California, Berkeley, 74/194 c. First letter has a brief account of the voyage between Philadelphia and Rio de Janeiro. The second deals with the remainder of the voyage but has more information on the situation in California than on the voyage. He notes that Captain Bell died on September 3. He also mentions that the distance from Philadelphia to San Francisco is computed to be seventeen thousand miles but estimated they had sailed twenty-five thousand miles.

Miller, Edward H. Notes regarding Mark Hopkins and related material, 1878–1888. Bancroft Library, University of California, Berkeley, C-D 749. Recollections of their voyage to California in 1849 in the ship *Pacific* and experiences in California. Includes some information on Hopkins's role in the dismissal of Captain Tibbits by the U.S. consul. Miller was involved in Hopkins's railroad businesses for many years.

Moore, Augustus. Pioneer Experiences of Augustus Moore written by himself for the Bancroft Library, 1878. Bancroft Library, University of California, Berkeley, C-D 129. Recalls his voyage from Boston to San Francisco in the ship *Nestor* under the command of Capt. Nathan Pool.

Morgan, William F. Journal, March 17–October 24, 1849, of a voyage from Salem, Massachusetts, to San Francisco in the bark *LaGrange* under the command of Capt. Joseph Dewing. Peabody/Essex Museum, Salem, Massachusetts. Contains two lists of passengers who were members of the Salem and California Mining and Trading Expedition. Gives occupation and residence of each in the first list. Second list indicates which ones had returned home and which were dead. Includes the words to "The California Song" written by Jesse Huchings and sung by him and the Barker family the day they left Salem. Has several drawings of the bark as well as of Eagle Harbor and Port Richard.

Morgan, William Ives. Gold Dust: The Log of a Forty-Niner. Bancroft Library, University of California, Berkeley, 70/190 c. Typescript copy of the journal,

June 27, 1849–1853, of Morgan during his voyage from New Haven, Connecticut, to San Francisco in the bark *John Walls, Jr.* under the command of Josiah Sanford Jr. Journal starts a month after their departure. Morgan was a member of the Brother's Mining and Trading Company. Other parts of the volume contain a record of a voyage to the Sandwich Islands and other islands in the Pacific and of Morgan's return to Connecticut via Nicaragua in 1853. Typescript was prepared by Florence Emlyn (Downs) Muzzy about 1930. She also provided some footnotes and biographical information on Morgan. Some excerpts from the journal were printed in *Harper's Magazine* 113 (November 1906): 920–926.

Morse, Ephriam W. Journal, February 3–July 5, 1849, of a voyage from Boston to San Francisco in the ship *Lenore* under the command of Capt. H. H. Greene. Huntington Library, San Marino, California, HM 26540. Passengers included the one hundred members of the New England and California Trading and Mining Association. Entries are short at the outset but become increasingly longer as the voyage progresses. Includes the latitude and longitude nearly every day. Stopped at Talcahuano and has long descriptions of activities and sights there.

Morse, Harry N. Biographical Sketch, 1888. Bancroft Library, University of California, Berkeley, C-D 761. Contains notes on his voyage to California in 1849 in the ship *Panama,* his experiences in the mines, enterprises in San Francisco and Oakland, and his career as sheriff and a detective in San Francisco.

Mulford, Thomas Whitehead. Journal, February 5–September 17, 1849, of a voyage from New York to San Francisco in the bark *Keoka* under the command of Capt. James McGuire. Society of California Pioneers, San Francisco. Many entries are long and descriptive. Journal seems well written. Has a copy of the constitution of the Patchogue Mining and Trading Company in the front. Includes a list of names and residences of the passengers.

Mullett, Charles T. Journal, February 3–August 31, 1849, of a voyage from Boston to San Francisco in the bark *Drummond* under the command of Capt. Thomas G. Pierce. Peabody/Essex Museum, Salem, Massachusetts. Journal was kept in a small pocket diary so entries are brief. Mentions celebrating Washington's birthday on February 22 with a thirteen-gun salute, singing, prayers, an address by Mr. Lindsey, and a dinner of roast pig, chicken, plum pudding, and pies. Has lists of twenty-one passengers in the forward cabin, most of whom were members of the Suffolk Mining Company, and twenty-two in the after cabin.

New Brunswick and California Mining and Trading Company. Minute Books, 1849–1851. Rutgers University Library, New Brunswick, New Jersey. Members of the company sailed from New York to San Francisco in the bark *Isabel.*

Noell, Charles P. Dictation, 1886. Bancroft Library, University of California, Berkeley, C-D 278. Recorded for H. H. Bancroft. Includes some information about his 1849 voyage around Cape Horn, but the name of the vessel is not given.

Osgood, Benjamin. Journal, March 6–September 30, 1849, of a voyage from Boston to San Francisco in the ship *Regulus* under the command of Capt. Daniel Bradford. Bancroft Library, University of California, Berkeley, 67/140 c. Journal continues to March 27, 1851. It was kept jointly with Charles W.

Richardson in a printed "Seaman's Journal" form but has additional pages bound in at the rear of the volume. Includes a list of 123 members of the Bunker Hill Trading and Mining Association, which owned the vessel. A second list of 125 names is included at the beginning of the extra pages and includes the residence and occupation of nearly every person.

Overton, Elias P. Journal, February 5–September 17, 1849, of a voyage from New York to San Francisco in the bark *Kooka* under the command of Capt. James McGuire. Bancroft Library, University of California, Berkeley, C-F 198. Includes a list of thirty-four passengers with the residence of each. Overton identified eight of the passengers as being members of "our company from Patchogue." Four of the passengers left the vessel in Rio de Janeiro because of a dispute with Captain McGuire. They took on many additional passengers at Valparaiso, including some Chileans and two women.

Pangborn, James Lamoureaux. Papers, 1849. J. Porter Shaw Library, National Maritime Museum, San Francisco. Includes a journal, February 23–October 3, 1849, of a voyage from New York to San Francisco in the bark *Nautilus* under the command of Capt. S. G. Wilson.

Peabody, B. R. Journal, April 4–September 17, 1849, of a voyage from Salem, Massachusetts, to San Francisco in the ship *Elizabeth* under the command of Capt. James S. Kimball. Peabody/Essex Museum, Salem, Massachusetts. Journal is kept in a printed "Seaman's Journal" form and provides little information other than weather conditions and speed of the vessel.

Pent, William. Journal, September 3, 1849–February 1, 1850, of a voyage from Edgartown, Massachusetts, to San Francisco in the ship *Sarah* under the command of Capt. Charles Worth. G. W. Blunt White Library, Mystic Seaport Museum, Inc., Mystic, Connecticut, Log 848. Contains a list of those who sailed in the *Sarah* with the residence of each. Journal ends before they arrived in San Francisco.

The Petrel. Manuscript newspaper published on board the ship *Duxbury* while on a voyage from Boston to San Francisco in 1849. Bancroft Library, University of California, Berkeley, C-F 147. A total of ten issues were produced by unknown persons. The first issue appeared on March 26, 1849 with a promise of an issue each Monday. Only the second issue is actually dated—April 2, 1849. The eighth issue contains an account of the celebration of the battle of Bunker's Hill. Issue 4 is missing.

Prime, Moses S. Journal, March 18–October 3, 1849, of a voyage from Salem, Massachusetts, to San Francisco in the bark *LaGrange* under the command of Capt. Joseph Dewing. California State Library, Sacramento. Journal is kept in logbook form and has little information other than time, speed, courses sailed, wind, weather, and sails set, furled, or taken in.

Putnam, Charles S. Letter, September 22–October 14, 1849, to his sister describing the latter part of his voyage from New York to San Francisco. Bancroft Library, University of California, Berkeley. Typescript copy, C-B 547, I:39. Letter was started in the Pacific Ocean and finished after his arrival in San Francisco. Includes some information about the voyage, news of friends and fellow gold seekers, and economic conditions in California. Does not give the name of the vessel.

Bibliography

Randall, Charles Henry. Letters, 1849, to his family in Providence, Rhode Island, describing his voyage from New York to San Francisco in the ship *Samoset* under the command of Capt. Louis G. Hollis. Bancroft Library, University of California, Berkeley, 68/40 c.

Randall, William Edgar. Journal, November 22, 1849–May 5, 1850, of a voyage from Boston to San Francisco in the ship *Hannibal* under the command of Capt. G. H. Willis. Bancroft Library, University of California, Berkeley, C-F 82. The library has both the original and a carbon typescript. The J. Porter Shaw Library at the National Maritime Museum in San Francisco has a photocopy. Passengers were housed in three locations—after cabin known as Revere House, forward cabin known as the Montgomery House, and between decks known as the United States Hotel. Contains lists of passengers in each area. Randall was seasick during much of the voyage. Sometimes his wife, Sara, wrote the entries. She also provided part of the list of passengers.

Randle, John T. Letters, 1849–1850, to his family prior to sailing from New York in the bark *Belvidera* under the command of Capt. Samuel Barney and after arriving in San Francisco. Bancroft Library, University of California, Berkeley, C-B 854. Rundle appears to have been a member of the Cayuga Joint Stock Company. Only two of the four letters were written during and about the voyage.

Reed, William F. Journal, February 8, 1849–August 1849, of a voyage from New Bedford, Massachusetts, to San Francisco in the ship *Magnolia* under the command of Capt. Benjamin Frank Simmons. Bancroft Library, University of California, Berkeley, C-F 214. Reed was a member of the crew. Journal continues to April 3, 1853 and contains records of experiences in the mines. Includes lists of cabin and steerage passengers, officers, and crew with residence of each. There were thirty-seven passengers in the cabin and fifty-seven in steerage.

Reid, Thomas. Journal, February 14–October 17, 1849, of a voyage from Boston to San Francisco in the bark *Velasco* under the command of Capt. E. B. Morgan. Bancroft Library, University of California, Berkeley, C-F 146. Passengers were members of the Naragansett Association. Includes a list of twenty-seven of the eighty-five members. The members voted to sell the vessel in Talcahuano and later to dissolve the association.

Reynolds, Benjamin Franklin. Reminiscences, undated. Bancroft Library, University of California, Berkeley, C-D 5118. Compiled in 1939 by Mattie V. Reynolds. Contains recollections of his 1849 voyage from Richmond, Virginia, to San Francisco in the ship *Glenmore*.

Richardson, Joel. Journal, November 1, 1849–April 28, 1850, of a voyage from Bangor, Maine, to San Francisco in the bark *Cantero* under the command of Capt. Joseph Saunders. California State Library, Sacramento and California Historical Society, San Francisco both have typescript copies. Contains a list of the fifty-five members of the Bangor Trading and Mining Company with residences, a list of other passengers with residences, and list of passengers taken on at Valparaiso with residences. Most entries provide primarily daily weather and courses sailed.

Rix, Timothy. Biography, 1872. Bancroft Library, University of California, Berkeley, C-D 277. Includes information about his membership in the company that purchased the ship *Edward Everett* and sailed her to San Francisco in 1849 and about the voyage around Cape Horn. The 151 members of the Boston and California Mining and Trading Joint Stock Company owned the ship.

Sanderson, George Henry. Journal, October 30, 1849–March 13, 1850, of a voyage from Boston to San Francisco in the ship *Henry Ware* under the command of Capt. H. Nason. Society of California Pioneers, San Francisco. Carbon typescript copy. Includes a good description of San Francisco. Often skips three to five days between entries, but entries sometimes long. Lists twenty-two passengers.

Saxon, William A. Journal, January 12–August 12, 1849, of a voyage from New York to San Francisco in the ship *Brooklyn* under the command of Capt. Joseph W. Richardson. Huntington Library, San Marino, California. Typescript copy, HM 17011. Passengers included 164 second cabin and steerage and 7 first cabin. Long descriptions of the celebrations of Washington's birthday and the Fourth of July. Stopped at the island of Juan Fernandez.

Scammon, Charles Melville. Letters, 1849–1850, to Otis Kimball, Bath, Maine, describing the voyage of the bark *Sarah Moers* from Bath, Maine, to San Francisco under the command of Capt. C. M. Scammon. Bancroft Library, University of California, Berkeley, 70/90 c.

Schell, Abraham. Journal, January 13–June 29, 1849, of a voyage from New York to San Francisco in the ship *Tarolinta* under the command of Capt. W. P. Cave. Bancroft Library, University of California, Berkeley. Microfilm copy of both the original and a typescript copy, CF 222 film. Eighty-five first-cabin and thirty-eight second-cabin passengers and a crew of twenty-seven. Journal ends seven days before they arrived. Made stops at Rio de Janeiro and Valparaiso. April 15 entry has a very long poem of sixty-one four-line stanzas about one passenger, possibly the one who produced a "scurrilous paper of a personal nature" called Frying Pan. Includes lists of members of the following companies on board with number of members for each: Albany and California Mining Company (of which Schell was a member), nineteen; Albany Eldorado Company, nineteen; Chelsea Adventurers, five; Leyon Winchester & Company, ten; Rail Road Company, three; Diamond Association, nine; Milne California Association, seven; Esperanza Company, four; Schoharie Association, five; Empire State Mining Association, nine; Fulton Mining Company, nine; Long Island Company, seven; Lafayette Company, six; and an unnamed company from Bridgeport, Connecticut, two. Includes a drawing of the flag for each company and residence of each person. There were also some independent passengers. Records a considerable amount of grumbling about the food and Captain Cave.

Selma (bark). Logbook, April 11–October 5, 1849, of the voyage from New York to San Francisco under the command of Capt. Orrin Sellow, kept by second mate Charles S. Bolles. Bancroft Library, University of California, Berkeley, 77/161 c. Two preliminary pages contain lists of members of the Fremont Mining and Trading Company and officers and crew. Age, residence, and occupation given for each person. "Left the Co. In Sacramento" is noted after many names.

Selover, Abia A. Statement and biographical sketch, 1886. Bancroft Library, University of California, Berkeley, C-D 362:2. Recorded for H. H. Bancroft.

Includes information on his 1849 voyage from New York to San Francisco in the ship *Loo Choo*.

Shepard, Isaac Jr. Journal, April 27, 1849–January 13, 1850, of a voyage from New York to San Francisco in the bark *Belvidera* under the command of Capt. Samuel Barney. California Historical Society, San Francisco. Journal starts nearly two months into the voyage. Passengers include members of the Cayuga Joint Stock Company.

Sheppard, Ebenezer. Journal, February 10–September 20, 1849, of a voyage from New York to San Francisco in the ship *Morrison* under the command of Capt. I. Spaulding. California Historical Society, San Francisco. Photocopy and typescript of the original in the Salem County Historical Society, Salem, New Jersey. Journal actually covers the period of autumn 1848 to May 10, 1851. The voyage to San Francisco is covered in the first 164 pages of the typescript. Contains a list of passengers. Sheppard and a young acquaintance went to California as an agent for Sheppard's uncle Johnson to sell $700 in goods, from which the two young men were to share the profits with the uncle. They each paid $150 for passage. There were one hundred male passengers. They made brief stops in Rio de Janeiro and Callao. Long poems are found in the entries for April 20, 21, 22, and 26 and June 3 and 8.

Sherman, Thomas Jr. Journal, November 7, 1849–May 26, 1850, of a voyage from Newburyport, Massachusetts, to San Francisco in the ship *Euphrasia* under the command of Capt. Charles Buntin. Peabody/Essex Museum, Salem, Massachusetts. Typescript copy. The passengers had extended conflicts about food with the captain and chose a committee to present grievances. Includes lists of officers, crew, and first-cabin, second-cabin, and steerage passengers—a total of 148 people. Gives the residence of each person. Stopped at Rio de Janeiro and Valparaiso. Includes two poems by Ezekiel B. Andrews, one of twenty-seven four-line rhyming stanzas about "our Living" and another of eight stanzas with eight lines each.

Skinner, Charles W. (comp.) Alfred Jamison, California Forty-Niner: His Life, Ancestry, Descendants. Compiled in San Francisco in 1941. Bancroft Library, University of California, Berkeley, C-D 5117. Includes biographical notes; copy of a letter by Jamison from Lima, Peru, in July 1849 describing his passage around Cape Horn; a copy of a letter written January 1851 from Feather River describing life in the mines; and a genealogical chart of the Jamison family. Does not give the name of the vessel, but Skinner suggests it might have been the schooner *A. Emery*. Bancroft Library also has the original letters cataloged under Jamison Family Papers.

Snow, Chester Joseph. Journal, November 8, 1849–May 26, 1850, of a voyage from Boston to San Francisco in the ship *Euphrasia* under the command of Capt. Charles Buntin. Bancroft Library, University of California, Berkeley, C-F 94. Lists 126 passengers with their residences. Also lists officers and crew. Journal continues to January 27, 1851 and includes information on his activities in the mines.

Spader, James V. Journal in the form of two long letters written February 7–August 18, 1849 during the voyage from New York to San Francisco in the bark *Isabel* under the command of Capt. Nicolas R. Brewer. Rutgers University Library, New Brunswick, New Jersey. Much of the second letter duplicates information in the first. Entries are brief, limited primarily to weather conditions, speed, latitude and longitude, temperature, sails set and taken in, etc. Passengers were members of the New Brunswick and California Mining and Trading Company.

Spear, Alexander F. *Alexander F. Spear, His Memorandum Book on a Voyage from Thomaston, Maine to California, 1849.* Photocopy of typescript probably done by T. A. Spear prior to 1973. J. Porter Shaw Library, National Maritime Museum, San Francisco. Includes an account of the voyage, November 12, 1849–April 7, 1850, from Thomaston, Maine, to San Francisco in the brig *Perfect* under the command of Capt. James Stackpole. Members of the California and Thomaston Protection Company were among the passengers. Also includes a summary of Spear's maritime and business career and a history of the California and Thomaston Protection Company by John B. Goodman III.

Stearns, J. Hascall. Journal, February 14–October 15, 1849, of a voyage from New York to San Francisco in the bark *Belvidera* under the command of Capt. Samuel Barney. California Historical Society, San Francisco. Stearns was one of the directors of the Cayuga Joint Stock Company, which was organized at the Western Hotel in New York City on February 15, 1849. Includes a list of the members of the company. There were seventy-nine members, each of whom paid five hundred dollars, which was used to purchase and outfit the vessel. A photocopy of the Articles of Association of the company copied from the Beinecke Library at Yale University is included in the volume.

Stevens, A. Henry. Journal, March 31–September 12, 1849, of a voyage from Boston to San Francisco in the bark *Emma Isadora* under the command of Capt. Sanford Henry. California State Library, Sacramento. Includes a printed copy of the "Rules and Regulations of the Mutual Protection Trading Company" and a list of members of the company with age, residence, and occupation of each. In a few cases there is indication of what became of the members. Also includes a separate record of temperature at sunrise, noon, and sunset between June 6 and July 10 as they rounded Cape Horn.

Stevens, Solomon. Fragmentary journal, December 15, 1849–May 26, 1850, of a voyage from Newburyport, Massachusetts, to San Francisco in the ship *Euphrasia* under the command of Capt. Charles Buntin. Peabody/Essex Museum, Salem, Massachusetts. First of the journal is missing. Starts in the middle of a sentence. The first page contains a letter of grievances to the captain, followed by the captain's response. These two items are among the few dated entries.

Stevens, William Lord. Journal in rhyming verse of the voyage, January 24–August 7, 1849, from Mystic, Connecticut, to San Francisco in the ship *Trescott* under the command of Capt. J. Mallory. G. W. Blunt White Library, Mystic Seaport Museum, Inc., Mystic, Connecticut, Log 401. One of three journals in rhyming verse discovered in this research project. Much of the information is hard to use, as the dates for the vast majority of information are difficult to determine.

Stickney, John J. Journal, December 25, 1849–May 3, 1850, of a voyage from Newburyport, Massachusetts, to San Francisco in the bark *Annah* under the command of Capt. G. W. Swasey. California Historical Society, San Francisco.

Bibliography

Library has both the original and a contemporary holograph copy. Copy extends about a week after the end of the original.

Stillman, Jacob Davis Babcock. Papers. California Historical Society, San Francisco. Includes a long letter/journal to his brother in which he describes the conflicts between the first-class passengers and Capt. Hall J. Tibbits of the ship *Pacific* in which they were sailing to San Francisco. Much of this information is included in his book *Seeking the Golden Fleece* (San Francisco: A. Roman Co., 1877).

Swain, H. F. W. Journal, March 1–October 13, 1849, of a voyage from New York to San Francisco in the bark *Belvidera* under the command of Capt. Samuel Barney. Bancroft Library, University of California, Berkeley, C-F 151. Seventy-four members of the Cayuga Joint Stock Company were among the passengers. Four women and a little girl were also on board. One of the women was the wife of Captain Barney. Another appears to have been the wife of Swain. Numerous gaps between entries near the end of the voyage and no entries during June as they rounded Cape Horn.

Taber, John H. Journal, November 27, 1849–May 11, 1850, of a voyage from New Bedford, Massachusetts, to San Francisco in the schooner *Abby P. Chase* under the command of Capt. William M. Bly. Whaling Museum Library, New Bedford, Massachusetts. Includes a list of passengers and crew clipped from an unidentified newspaper, possibly the *Whalemen's Shipping List* of December 4, 1849. There were thirty-four passengers.

Taylor, Augustus F. Journal, February 11–August 28, 1849, of a voyage from New York to San Francisco in the bark *Isabel* under the command of Capt. Nicolas R. Brewer. California State Library, Sacramento. Photocopy of typescript copy. Bancroft Library, University of California, Berkeley. Mimeograph copy, C-F 41. Among the passengers were forty-five members of the New Brunswick and California Mining and Trading Company. Includes one letter from Taylor to his wife dated August 17, 1849 and a copy of a letter to Taylor from J. R. Hardenbergh dated March 30, 1879 in which he discusses what had happened to some of the people on the voyage.

Taylor, Augustus FitzRandolph. Journal, February 7–August 6, 1849, of a voyage from New York to San Francisco in the bark *Isabel* under the command of Capt. Nicolas R. Brewer. Rutgers University Library, New Brunswick, New Jersey. Written in small pocket diary, three days per page. Entries very brief. Limited mostly to weather conditions, latitude and longitude, temperature, and wind directions. Passengers were members of the New Burnswick and California Mining and Trading Company.

Taylor, John. Journal, January 30–July 8, 1849, of a voyage from New York to San Francisco in the ship *Orpheus* under the command of Capt. Leander Freeman. Bancroft Library, University of California, Berkeley, C-F 43. Includes a typed list of some of the 198 passengers Taylor noted were on board in two cabins, 168 in the second, located between decks and 30 in the first, located on deck.

Teller, James M. Journal, January 27–July 4, 1849, of a voyage from New York to San Francisco in the brig *Mary Stuart* under the command of Captain Tucker. Bancroft Library, University of California, Berkeley, C-F 213. Based upon information for the July 1, 1849 entry, this seems to be a contemporary transcription by Teller himself. Teller seems to have been a member of an organized company but does not give the name of it. He also implies that there were other independent passengers on board.

Thompson, Celia May (Crocker). Crocker family history. Typescript copies. Bancroft Library, University of California, Berkeley, 76/191 c. Includes an interview with Charles G. Stumcke about his voyage from Boston to San Francisco in the ship *New Jersey* in 1849 and a history of the Crocker family's operation of Crocker's Station at Bronson, Tuolumne County.

Tolman, John. Journal, March 1–September 9, 1849, of a voyage from Boston to San Francisco in the ship *Sweden* under the command of Capt. Jesse G. Cotting. Bancroft Library, University of California, Berkeley, 82/9 c. Includes a list of members of the Roxbury Sagamore Company, of which Tolman appears to have been a member. That was one of a number of companies on board the vessel. Also includes a 1981 transcript of a letter he wrote to his mother during the voyage and sent from San Francisco.

Towne, William J. Journal, January 23–July 23, 1849, of a voyage from Boston to San Francisco in the ship *Capitol* under the command of Capt. Thorndike Proctor. Bancroft Library, University of California, Berkeley, 91/24 c. Includes lists of officers, crew, and passengers. Passengers are listed by the company of which they were members. There appears to have been 22 companies ranging in membership from 3 to 20. Also 29 independent passengers. Includes several resolutions passed and signed by 123 passengers on January 23, 1849 about their food and general conditions as well as a copy of Captain Proctor's response.

Tuttle, Henry A. Journal, March 17–September 17, 1849, of a voyage from Salem, Massachusetts, to San Francisco in the bark *LaGrange* under the command of Capt. Joseph Dewing. Peabody/Essex Museum, Salem, Massachusetts. Includes numerous illustrations and words to the song composed for the sailing of the vessel and sung by the Barkers. There is some confusion in the order of entries. The sequence of pages is 1–16, 27–42, 17–26, and 43 to the end. Contains a lengthy description of the celebration of the Fourth of July on pages 101–105. Stopped for several days at the Falkland Islands to hunt for provisions. Entries are generally long and descriptive. A drawing of the bark *LaGrange* is located at the entry for May 14.

Van Dyke, John. Journal, January 25–July 10, 1849, of a voyage from New York to San Francisco in the ship *Tahmroo* under the command of Captain Richardson. Bancroft Library, University of California, Berkeley, 89/14 c. Includes a list of sixty-five passengers and their residences in the first and second cabins. Van Dyke notes there were 210 people on board. The diary continues in summary form until March 1850, at which time Van Dyke apparently sent it home because he was tired of seeing it.

Varney, Jotham. Journal, October 31, 1849–May 30, 1850, of a voyage from Bath, Maine, to San Francisco in the bark *America* under the command of Capt. William Graves. California Historical Society Library, San Francisco. Photocopy of typescript copy. List of the officers and crew totaling eleven and a list of the ten members of the Brunswick Company and one additional passenger. Most entries are limited to dates, miles sailed, course, wind, and weather. Library also has eight letters to his wife. Six deal with the voyage.

Warren, James L. L. F. Papers, 1849–1889. Bancroft Library, University of California, Berkeley. Warren was a passenger in the ship *Sweden* that sailed from Boston to San Francisco on March 3, 1849 under the command of Capt. Jesse G. Cotting. Warren was active in the religious activities on board, having written several original hymns for early worship services, two hymns for a burial service for a passenger, and one for the service in Boston prior to their departure, but words to only one are in the papers. Words to most of the others are found in the journal of Charles H. Fuller at the Bancroft Library and in other journals kept on board the *Sweden*. The Warren Papers include letters; his passport from the governor of Massachusetts; a prospectus concerning the ship; agreements; a program for the departure ceremonies; a clipping about the departure; two copies of rules and regulations for the ship (one in the handwriting of Warren and one in the handwriting of Captain Cotting); a list of passengers with occupation, age, residence, and native state for each; words to a song titled "A Sabbath Song My Mother" composed by Warren; and a large quantity of accounts and bills for items purchased for the vessel prior to her departure from Boston as well as in California. These purchases apparently were for provisioning the members of the Ship *Sweden* Company, which Warren organized with the encouragement of the owners of the ship. Warren remained in California and engaged in various business ventures.

Welling, E. L. Journal, February 3–August 30, 1849, of a voyage from New York to San Francisco in the bark *Strafford* under the command of Capt. William L. Coffin. California State Library, Sacramento. Photocopy of typescript copy. Has a brief introduction and a few explanatory footnotes and editorial inserts by Jean (Romig) Kirkpatrick.

Wheaton, William R. Statement of Facts on Early California History, 1878. Bancroft Library, University of California, Berkeley. Dictation recorded for H. H. Bancroft. Includes information on his voyage in 1849 from New York to San Francisco in the bark *Strafford*.

Wheeler, Alfred. Journal, May 21–November 12, 1849, of a voyage from New York to San Francisco in the bark *Hannah Sprague* under the command of Capt. David F. Lansing. California Historical Society, San Francisco. Contains a copy of a resolution the passengers adopted thanking Captain Lansing and the first and second mates for the successful voyage. Among the 119 people on board were the 29 members of the California Mining Association. Wheeler was a practicing lawyer and took his law library with him, as he intended to practice law to make his gold rather than dig for it.

White, James. Journal, January 11–July 7, 1849, of a voyage from Boston to San Francisco in the ship *Edward Everett* under the command of Capt. Henry Smith. J. Porter Shaw Library, National Maritime Museum, San Francisco. Photocopy of original. Includes a list of passengers and the constitution and bylaws of the Boston and California Mining and Trading Joint Stock Company.

Williams, Charles. Journal, January 22–August 5, 1849, of a voyage from New York to San Francisco in the ship *Pacific* under the command of Capt. Hall J. Tibbits from

New York to Rio de Janeiro and Capt. George Easterbrook from Rio de Janeiro to San Francisco. Boston Public Library, K.1.9. Huntington Library, San Marino, California, has a typescript copy. Both versions include a list of the passengers in the first cabin. There are a number of transcription errors in the typescript.

Williams, F. Journal, October 30, 1849–April 7, 1850, of a voyage from Newburyport, Massachusetts, to San Francisco in the bark *Domingo* under the command of Capt. N. A. Dray. Bancroft Library, University of California, Berkeley, C-F 21. Journal is continued to October 27, 1859.

Williams, Henry. Statement, 1887. Bancroft Library, University of California, Berkeley, C-D 406. Dictation for H. H. Bancroft. Includes information on his voyage from New York to San Francisco in the ship *Panama*.

Williams, Thomas. Journal, March 1–September 30, 1849, of a voyage from Boston to San Francisco in the ship *Regulus* under the command of Capt. Daniel Bradford. Bancroft Library, University of California, Berkeley, 78/19 c. Includes a list of 125 members of the Bunker Hill Trading and Mining Association who were passengers in and owners of the ship. Gives residence and occupation of each member. There was considerable conflict among members and officers of the association about finances and privileges enjoyed by the officers.

Wilson, George H. Journal, July 1–November 16, 1849, of a voyage from New York to San Francisco in the ship *Tonquin* under the command of Capt. G. H. Wilson. Peabody/Essex Museum, Salem, Massachusetts. Entries are brief and limited mostly to wind, weather, sails set and taken in, and navigational calculations.

Wilson, George Osborne. Journal, September 15, 1849–March 6, 1850, of a voyage from East Machias, Maine, to San Francisco in the brig *Oriental* under the command of Capt. William C. Talbot. California Historical Society, San Francisco. Has a long description of cabin arrangement and general life and problems in the entry for January 27, 1850. Also has good descriptions of relationships between the passengers and crew. Most of the journal, however, deals with weather, directions sailed, and other routine stuff. Some pages appear to have been torn out. Contains lists of officers, crew, and passengers.

Winans, Joseph Webb. Statement of Recollections on the Days of 1849–52 in California, 1878. Bancroft Library, University of California, Berkeley. Library has both the original handwritten copy and a typed transcript, C-D 178. Includes some information on his voyage in 1849 from New York to San Francisco in the bark *Strafford*.

Woodbury, J. T. Journal, October 30, 1849–March 13, 1850, of a voyage from Boston to San Francisco in the ship *Argonaut* under the command of Capt. William Nott. Peabody/Essex Museum, Salem, Massachusetts. Includes a lengthy and detailed description of the ship and living conditions as well as lists of passengers in the after cabin, forward cabin, forward house, and steerage with age, profession, and residence for each with a note that the information on age and occupation has errors. Also a list of officers and crew.

Worden, G. B. Letter, April 23, 1849, from the ship *Dubury* in Rio de Janeiro to Ira Brown regarding the first portion of the voyage from Boston to San Francisco under the command of Capt. W. C. Varina. Bancroft Library, University of California, Berkeley, CB 547:138.

Bibliography

Yeatman, Anna M. D. Unknown to History Being the Cruise of the Good Ship Glenmore from Hampton Roads to San Francisco, Telling of the Adventures of the Virginia Argonauts to the Gold Fields in 1849. Photocopy of typescript. California State Library, Sacramento. Account of the voyage based upon the journal of Dr. James W. Claiborne and a narrative by Capt. Charles Edward Yeatman. Yeatman narrative apparently was written long after the voyage. William P. Poythress was in command of the vessel. Passengers were members of the Madison Mining and Trading Company.

Young, George W. Journal, May 15–October 31, 1849, of a voyage from Boston to San Francisco in the bark *Helen Augusta* under the command of Capt. Frederick W. Myrick. California Historical Society, San Francisco. Has some good descriptions, but main focus of the journal seems to be weather and the direction they were sailing. Young was a member of the Massachusetts Mining Company.

Archives

United States. Department of State. Consular Post Records. Callao, Peru. Letters Sent, 1840–1851; Letters Received, 1845–1850; and Arrivals and Departures of American Vessels; 1849–1854. Record Group 84. U.S. National Archives, Washington, D.C.

United States. Department of State. Consular Post Records. Rio de Janeiro, Brazil. Dispatches from the United States Consuls in Rio de Janeiro, 1811–1906. Record Group 84. U.S. National Archives, Washington, D.C. Microcopy T-172. Rolls 13 and 14 contain records for 1849. There is a wealth of material in these records regarding the dismissal of Hall J. Tibbits as captain of the ship *Pacific* of New York and Capt. J. Brown of the ship *Xylon* of Baltimore.

United States. Department of State. Consular Post Records. St. Catherines Island (Santa Catharina), Brazil. Marine Notes of Protest, 1833–1849 and Consular Register Record, 1849–1874. Record Group 84. U.S. National Archives, Washington, D.C.

United States. Department of State. Consular Post Records. Talcahuano, Chile. Account Book of Services to American Vessels and Seamen, 1846–1859; General Correspondence Received and Sent and Miscellaneous Records, 1846–1852; Arrivals and Departures of American Vessels, 1846–1857; and Despatches to the Department of State. Record Group 84. Microcopy T115. U.S. National Archives, Washington, D.C.

United States. Department of State. Diplomatic Instructions, Brazil, 1801–1906. U.S. National Archives, Washington, D.C. Volume 15 covers the years 1833–1862.

United States District Court. Southern District of New York. Petitions of Frank Cheney, Owen Spencer, Anson A. Nicholson, Charles D. Cleveland, Elijah B. Galusha, Henry D. Kingsbury, Elon C. Galusha, and Judson J. Galusha in lawsuits against the ship *Pacific* and owners, January 1849. National Archives and Records Administration. Federal Records Center, East Bayonne, New Jersey.

Newspapers

Baltimore American and Commercial Daily Advertiser, December 1, 1848–August 31, 1849.

Baltimore Sun, December 1, 1848–August 31, 1849.

Boston Journal, February 27, 1849.

New York Daily Tribune, December 1, 1848–August 31, 1849.

Sacramento Bee, January 18, 1998. Special sesquicentennial issue commemorating the discovery of gold at Sutter's Mill.

Published Accounts of Individual Voyages

Barra, Ezekiel I. *A Tale of Two Oceans; A New Story by an Old Californian: An Account of a Voyage from Philadelphia to San Francisco around Cape Horn, Years 1849–50, Calling at Rio de Janeiro, Brazil and Juan Fernandez in the South Pacific.* San Francisco: Press of Eastman & Company, 1893. In his *Sea Routes to the Gold Fields* Oscar Lewis indicates that parts of the voyage were made in the schooners *Samson and Urania.* Robert W. Weinpahl, who edited four accounts of the voyage of the bark *Orion,* notes that Barra joined the *Orion* in Rio de Janeiro. Barra gives the name of the vessel as *Urania* and also gives fictitious names for the captain and officers. Weinpahl asserts that the volume has numerous inaccuracies.

Christman, Enos. *One Man's Gold: The Letters and Journal of a Forty-Niner.* Edited by Florence M. Christman. New York: McGraw-Hill Book Company, Inc., 1930. Most of the volume is his journal of the voyage, July 3, 1849–February 12, 1850, from Philadelphia to San Francisco in the ship *Europe* under the command of Capt. Addison Palmer. The members of the California Gold Mining Association of Philadelphia occupied the second cabin in the between decks area of the vessel. He kept the journal at the request of his fiancée, Ellen Apple, whom he married after he returned from California. Several letters to Ellen are included in the publication. There are numerous gaps between entries, but it is unclear if they were in the original or if the editor omitted some entries.

Coffin, George. *A Pioneer Voyage to California.* Chicago: Privately printed, 1908. Coffin was an experienced shipmaster when he agreed to take charge of the ship *Alhambra* in New Orleans for a voyage to San Francisco with passengers and cargo in 1849. He first prepared the vessel by having deck houses constructed and installing state rooms and other sleeping bunks and tables and other facilities between decks. Based upon information in a brief preface, it appears that Coffin may have written the narrative in 1852, as he returned home after having spent a couple of years in California and another year sailing to various ports before returning to New York. In the brief preface Coffin indicates the narrative was based upon notes and memoranda made during the voyage and his recollection of events. The original narrative was passed on to his heirs, and his son Gorham B. Coffin published it in the summer of 1908. The voyage to California is described on pages 10–54. From his account Coffin appears to have had a good deal more trouble with his passengers and his crew than did most masters of California-bound vessels in 1849.

Cogswell, Moses. "The Gold Rush Diary of Moses Cogswell of New Hampshire." Edited by Elmer Munson Hunt. *Historical New Hampshire* (December 1949): 1–50. Cogswell was a member of the Roxbury Sagamore Mining Company, one of several companies that made the voyage, March 1–August 3, 1849, from

Boston to San Francisco in the ship *Sweden* under the command of Capt. Jesse G. Cotting. There are numerous gaps in the published diary, but it is unclear if they are the result of editing or if they also exist in the original diary, which is in the New Hampshire Historical Society.

Cooledge, Corneilus. *Off to the Gold Fields, 1849.* Edited by John Barton Hassler. N.p.: El Dorado County Historical Society, Publication No. 1, n.d. Contains excerpts from the journal, January 11–August 21, 1849, of a voyage from Boston to San Francisco in the bark *Oxford* under the command of Capt. Suchet Mauran. Includes lists of officers, crew, and cabin and steerage passengers. Contains words that appear to be an original composition to a song that was sung at the July 4 celebration.

Dore, Benjamin. *Journal of Benjamin Dore.* Berkeley: N.p., 1923. Reprinted, *California Historical Society Quarterly* 2 (1923–1924): 90–139. Contains an account of an 1849 voyage around Cape Horn to San Francisco in the bark *Cantero* under the command of Capt. J. Saunders. The original diary is in the Bancroft Library, University of California, Berkeley.

Doten, Alfred. *The Journals of Alfred Doten, 1849–1903.* Edited by Walter van Tilburg Clark. Reno: University of Nevada Press, 1973. 3 vols. The first volume contains his journal of the voyage, March 18–October 5, 1849, from Plymouth, Massachusetts, to San Francisco in the bark *Yoeman* under the command of Capt. J. M. Clark. Passengers included members of the Pilgrim Mining Company. The vessel was fitted out and provisioned by a group of investors in Plymouth that included Doten's father. The young men who went as passengers were to share their gold with the investors until such time as the investors recouped their investment.

Dougal, William H. *Off for California: The Letters, Log and Sketches of William H. Dougal, Gold Rush Artist.* Edited by Frank M. Stanger. Oakland, California: Biobooks, 1949. Contains Dougal's journal, April 7–November 22, 1849, of a voyage from New York to San Francisco in the bark *Galindo* under the command of Capt. P. B. Macy; letters he wrote to his family during the voyage; and reproductions of several sketches by him. The Bancroft Library at the University of California, Berkeley has a few of the original sketches.

Draper, Seth. *Voyage of the Bark Orion from Boston around Cape Horn to San Francisco, Cal., in the Year 1849, Touching at Rio de Janeiro and Juan Fernandez.* Providence, Rhode Island: Printed by H. O. Houghton & Co., Cambridge, 1870.

A Gold Rush Voyage on the Bark Orion from Boston around Cape Horn to San Francisco, 1849–1850. Edited by Robert W. Weinpahl. Glendale, California: Arthur H. Clark Company, 1978. Includes selections from the unpublished diary of Foster H. Jenkins, the logbook of the *Orion* kept by Henry S. Bradley, and the published accounts of the voyage by Ezekiel I. Barra and Seth Draper. The Jenkins diary is in the library of the California State University, Northridge, and the logbook is in the California Historical Society in San Francisco.

Goodwin, George K. *Reminiscence of George K. Goodwin, 1849–1881.* Philadelphia: Press of George F. Lasher, 1881. Pages 3–34 contain his journal, March 1–August 3, 1849, of the voyage from Boston to San Francisco in the ship *Swe-*

den under the command of Capt. Jesse G. Cotting. Goodwin and seven other young men organized the Traders and Mechanics Mining Company with Goodwin as president prior to leaving Boston.

Hale, Richard Hunt. *The Log of a Forty-Niner: Journal of a Voyage from Newbury-Port to San Francisco in the Brig* Genl. Worth *Commanded by Capt. Samuel Walton.* Edited by Carolyn Hale Russ. Boston: B. J. Brimmer Company, 1923. The first sixty-three pages contain the journal, November 28, 1849–May 6, 1850, of the voyage. Contains lists of passengers, officers, and crew and reproductions of a few drawings from Hale's original journal. Includes a few lengthy character sketches of some passengers.

Hall, John Linville. *Around the Horn in '49: The Journal of the Hartford Union Mining and Trading Company.* San Francisco: Book Club of California, 1928. Reprint of *Journal of the Hartford Union Mining and Trading Company.* J. L. Hall on board the *Henry Lee,* 1849. Account of the voyage, February 17–September 13, 1849, from New York to San Francisco in the ship *Henry Lee* under the command of Capt. David P. Vail. Hall was a printer from Hartford, Connecticut, and supposedly printed the journal during the voyage or after arriving in San Francisco and while still residing in the vessel. He reprinted the volume in 1898. Includes a list of the 122 members of the Hartford Union Mining and Trading Company with residences and occupations. See also George Gideon Webster below.

Haskins, C. W. *Argonauts of California Being the Reminiscences of Scenes and Incidents That Occurred in California in Early Mining Days.* New York: Fords, Howard & Hulbert, 1890. The first fifty pages contain an account of the voyage, April 1–September 19, 1849, from New Bedford, Massachusetts, to San Francisco in the ship *America* under the command of Capt. C. P. Seabury. An account of Haskins's experiences in the mining regions forms the second part of the book. The last part of the book consists of lists of passengers in many other vessels that sailed either around Cape Horn or on isthmian routes and lists of people who traveled overland to California. The volume also includes a number of illustrations, only a few of which are scenes from the voyage of the *America.*

Journal of a Voyage from Boston to San Francisco in 1849. Edited by Carroll D. Hall. Redwood City, California: N.p., 1933. An anonymous account of the voyage, January 12–July 6, 1849, of the ship *Edward Everett* under the command of Capt. Henry Smith.

Kendall, Joseph. *A Landsman's Voyage to California.* Edited by Wilbur Hall. San Francisco: Privately published, 1935. Account of part of the voyage, March 27–October 6, 1849, of the bark *Canton* from New York to San Francisco under the command of Captain Haynes. The journal published here covers only the period May 3–July 20, 1849. Also includes several letters written by Kendall. Includes a list of passengers and crew with occupation and residence for most of them. The sixty members of the Island City Mining and Trading Company were among the passengers.

Kingsley, Nelson. "Diary of Nelson Kingsley." Edited by Frederick J. Teggart. *Publications of the Academy of Pacific Coast History* 3 (December 1914): 237–413. Contains an account of his voyage, March 12–November 22, 1849, from New Haven, Connecticut, to San Francisco in the bark *Anna Reynolds* under the command of Capt. John Bottom. The original journal is in the Bancroft Library, University of California, Berkeley. Passengers included members of the California & New Haven Joint Stock Co. or New Haven & California Joint Stock Co. Kingsley used both names. The company removed Captain Bottom from command in Talcahuano in late September 1849 and elected a new captain named Webb along with two new mates.

Lyman, Albert. *Journal of a Voyage to California, and Life in the Gold Diggings. And Also of a Voyage from California to the Sandwich Islands.* Hartford, Connecticut: E. T. Pease; New York: Dexter & Bro.; Boston: Redding & Co., 1852. Pages 9–98 contain an account of a voyage, February 22–August 6, 1849, from New York to San Francisco in the schooner *General Morgan* under the command of Capt. Charles A. Falkenberg. Includes a list of members of the Connecticut Mining and Trading Company who were passengers in the vessel. Includes a few of the many pencil drawings Lyman did in his original journal.

Matteson, Thomas Jefferson. *The Diary of Thomas Jefferson Matteson.* San Andreas, California: Calaveras County Historical Society, 1954. Contains his journal, January 29–September 16, 1849, of the voyage from New York to San Francisco in the ship *George Washington* under the command of Capt. John Holdredge.

Stillman, Jacob D. B. *Seeking the Golden Fleece: A Record of Pioneer Life in California; to Which is Annexed Footprints of Early Navigators, Other Than Spanish, in California; With an Account of the Voyage of the Schooner Dolphin.* San Francisco: A. Roman & Co., 1877. Pages 11–34 contain an introduction to the times. Pages 35–117 contain an account of his voyage from New York to San Francisco in the ship *Pacific* under the command of Capts. Hall J. Tibbits (from New York to Rio de Janeiro) and George Easterbrook (from Rio de Janeiro to San Francisco). This account is based upon his original journal and letters sent home to members of his family. One letter to his brother is in the California Historical Society, San Francisco.

Underhill, George R. *Voyage to California and Return, 1849–1852.* N.p.: Underhill Society of America, [1980?]. Journal, March 8–September 17, 1849, of a voyage from New York to San Francisco in the bark *Palmetto* under the command of Captain Crocker. Passengers included members of the Greenwich and California Mining and Trading Company.

Upham, Samuel Curtis. *Notes of a Voyage to California via Cape Horn, together with Scenes in El Dorado, in the Years 1849–'50.* Philadelphia: Published by the Author, 1878. Reprinted, New York: Arno Press, 1973. The first 210 pages contain an account of the voyage, January 15–August 5, 1849, from Philadelphia to San Francisco in the brig *Osceola* under the command of Capt. James Fairfowl.

Whaley, Thomas. *Consignments to El Dorado: A Record of the Voyage of the Sutton.* Edited by June Allen Reading. New York: Exposition Press, 1972. Pages 67–234 contain Whaley's letters and journal, January 1–July 22, 1849, of his voyage from New York to San Francisco in the ship *Sutton* under the command of Capt. James H. Wardle. Includes lists of first- and second-class passengers with age, residence, and occupation for each.

Webster, George Gideon. *The Journal of a Trip Around the Horn, as Written and Printed on the Ship* Henry Lee. Ashland, Oregon: Lewis Osborne, 1970. This volume is virtually identical to Linville J. Hall, *Around the Horn in '49: The Journal of the Hartford Union Mining and Trading Company*. This 1970 volume includes an introduction to Hall's 1898 edition and some illustrations from the 1898 edition that do not appear in Hall's 1928 edition. This 1970 volume omits a few details included in both the 1898 and 1928 ones, most notably the several toasts offered at the July 4 celebration. The only evidence that Webster had anything to do with any of the editions is the statement on the 1970 edition title page: "as written and printed by Webster and Hall." Noted California gold rush researcher and author John B. Goodman III asserts that Webster was actually the author and Hall only the printer.

SECONDARY SOURCES

Adams, Elizabeth. "A Voyage to California." *More Books: Bulletin of the Boston Public Library* (January 1941): 3–10. Tells of the acquisition by the library of the journal of Charles H. Williams of his voyage from New York to San Francisco in the ship *Pacific* and briefly summarizes the turbulent voyage. Mentions a few other California-related items in the library.

Ament, William S. "By Sea to El Dorado," in *Oxcart to Airplane*. Edited by John Russell McCarthy. Vol. 6, 309–328. Los Angeles: Powell Publishing Company. Brief account of voyages around Cape Horn to California in 1849 and after based upon published accounts and manuscripts in the Huntington Library.

Bates, Morgan. *The Gold Rush: Voyage of the Ship* Loo Choo *Around the Horn in 1849*. Edited with an introduction by John B. Goodman III. Mt. Pleasant, Michigan: Cumming Press, 1977. Reproductions of letters of Morgan Bates, Thomas Blackwood, and Sylvester W. Higgins.

Baur, John E. "The Health Factor in the Gold Rush Era." *Pacific Historical Review* 18 (January 1949): 97–108. Reprinted in John Walton Caugly, *Rushing for Gold*. Berkeley: University of California Press, 1849. (American Historical Association, Pacific Coast Branch, Special Publication No. 1.)

Browne, J. Ross. *Crusoe's Island: A Ramble in the Footsteps of Alexander Selkirk. With Sketches of Adventure in California and Washoe*. New York: Harper & Brothers, 1864. The first 165 pages contain an account of the conflict between Capt. Hall J. Tibbits and the first-class passengers in the ship *Pacific*, which Browne calls the *Anteus,* and the removal of Captain Tibbits by the U.S. consul at Rio de Janeiro and a detailed account of the visit to Juan Fernandez Island by eleven passengers in the *Pacific.*

Browne, John Ross. *J. Ross Browne, His Letters, Journals and Writings*. Edited by Lina Fergusson Browne. Albuquerque: University of New Mexico Press, 1969. Contains writings by Browne between 1842 and 1875 including several long letters to his wife while he was a passenger on board the ship *Pacific* bound from New York to San Francisco in 1849.

California: Its Past History; Its Present Position: Its Future Prospects: Containing A History of the Country from Its Colonization by the Spaniards to the Present Time: A Sketch of the Geogrpahical and Physical Features and a Minute and Authentic Account of the Discovery of the Gold Region, and the Subsequent Important Pro-

ceedings Including a History of the Rise, Progress and Present Condition of the Mormon Settlements with An Appendix Containing the Official Reports Made to the Government of the United States. London: Printed for the Proprietors, 1850. There are two versions of this volume. The one cited here contains two illustrations of views of shipboard life in 1849. The illustration located opposite page 80 is titled "Tracing the Ships Progress," and the illustration located opposite page 136 is titled "Mid-Day Emigrants on Deck." This version also has a page preceding the title page bearing the inscription "The Emigrants Guide to the Golden Land, Shewing Him When to Go, Where to Go and How to Go." The other version lacks the two illustrations, and the 1850 date and has the inscription "California, Its Past History, Its Present Position, Its Future Prospects" on a page preceding the title page.

Celebration of the Seventy-Third Anniversary of the Declaration of Independence of the United States, on Board the Barque "Hannah Sprague." at Sea, July 4th, 1849. South Latitude 18° 28.'—Longitude 38° 10.' New York: Jennings & Co., Printers, 1849. Contains the order of the events of the day as well as the text of the patriotic address that Alfred Wheeler delivered on board the *Hannah Sprague* bound from New York to San Francisco. Among the passengers was at least one company of men known as the New York Commercial and Mining Company.

Davis, George. *Recollections of a Sea Wanderer's Life: Autobiography of an old-time seaman who has sailed in almost every capacity before and abaft the mast, nearly every quarter of the globe, and under the flags of four of the principal maritime nations.* New York: A. H. Kellogg, 1887. Pages 304–326 contain a brief account of the voyage in 1849 of the ship *Matilda* from New York to San Francisco under the command of Captain Land.

Davis, Raymond Cazallia. *Reminiscences of a Voyage around the World.* Ann Arbor, Michigan: D. D. Chase's Steam Printing House, 1869. Pages 15–176 contain an account of his voyage, September 8, 1849–February 28, 1850, from Bath, Maine, to San Francisco in the ship *Hampton.* These reminiscences were first published in the "Youths Department" of the *Peninsular Courier and Family Visitant,* a weekly paper the publisher of the book had been publishing for about five years.

Delgado, James P. *To California by Sea.* Columbia: University of South Carolina, 1990.

Donovan, Lynn Bonfield, "Day-by Day Records: Diaries from the CHS Library." *California Historical Quarterly* 54 (Winter 1975): 359–372 and 56 (Spring 1977): 72–81. An annotated bibliography of California gold rush journals in the collection of the California Historical Society, San Francisco.

Dutka, Barry L. "New York Discovers Gold! In California." *California History* 63 (Fall 1984): 313–319, 341. Based largely upon New York newspaper stories of 1848–1849.

Eagleston, John H. "Account of an Early California Voyage." *Essex Historical Collections* 12: 2 (1874): 124–31. An account of the voyage of the brig *Mary & Ellen.*

Evans, George W. B. "San Francisco in 1850." *Society of California Pioneers Quarterly* (December 1925): 191–214.

Farwell, Willard B. "Cape Horn and Cooperative Mining in '49." *Century Magazine* 42 (July 1891): 579–94. An account of the voyage from Boston to San Francisco in the ship *Edward Everett* in 1849. There were 150 members of the Boston and California Mining and Trading Joint Stock Company on board. Contains several good illustrations of shipboard life during such a voyage.

Flagg, Josiah Foster. "A Philadelphia Forty-Niner, Excerpts from His Diary." *Pennsylvania Magazine of History and Biography* 70 (October 1946): 390–122.

Frothingham, N. L. *Gold: A Sermon Preached to the First Church, on Sunday, Dec. 17, 1848.* Boston: Printed by John Wilson, 1849.

Goodman, John B. III. *The Key to the Goodman Encyclopedia of the California Gold Rush Fleet.* Edited by Daniel Woodward with an introduction by Neal Harlow. Los Angeles: The Zamorano Club, 1992. Contains an index to the 762 vessels included in Goodman's manuscript encyclopedia now at the Huntington Library in San Moreno, California. Includes name of vessel, rig or type, name of captain, dates of sailing and arrival, port of departure, places stopped during the voyage, when and where the vessel was built, disposition, and trade after arrival in San Francisco.

———. *The Schooner* Civilian *and the Cochituate Mining and Trading Company.* Los Angeles: Plantin Press, 1964. Brief account of the voyage, November 12, 1849–April 4, 1850, from Boston to San Francisco under the command of Capt. Thomas Dodge. Appears to be based in part upon the letters sent home by Josiah Hayward Jr.

———. "The 1849 California Gold Rush Fleet: The Schooner/Steamer *El Dorado*." *Southern California Quarterly* 68 (Spring 1986): 67–76. Account of the voyage from Philadelphia to San Francisco, May 7–November 23, 1849, under the command of Capt. Joseph C. Barnard. Includes drawings of the vessel as a schooner as she sailed from Philadelphia and as a sidewheel steamer to which she was converted soon after her arrival in San Francisco. Passengers included members of the El Dorado Association.

———. "The 1849 California Gold Rush Fleet: The Packet *Robert Bowne*." *Southern California Quarterly* 67 (Winter 1985): 447–63. Account of the voyage from New York to San Francisco, February 6–August 28, 1849, under the command of Capt. F. G. Cameron. Has a track chart for the voyage and a drawing of the ship entering San Francisco Bay, both by the author. Lists of officers, crew, and of passengers.

———. "The 1849 California Gold Rush Fleet: The Ship *Harriet Rockwell*." *Southern California Quarterly* 67 (Fall 1985): 311–20. Account of the voyage from Boston to San Francisco, September 8, 1849–February 24, 1850, under the command of Capt. Shubal Hawes. Has track chart of the voyage and drawing of the vessel entering San Francisco Bay, both by the author. Includes list of passengers.

———. "The 1849 California Gold Rush Fleet: The *Abby Baker*." *Southern California Quarterly* 67 (Summer 1985):199–206. Account of the voyage from Baltimore to San Francisco, November 7, 1849–July 24, 1850, in the bark *Abby Baker* under the command of Capt. Timothy Pratt until his death at sea on July 7, 1850, when he was succeeded by his son Timothy Augustus Pratt.

Bibliography

————. "The 1849 California Gold Rush Fleet: The *Magnolia*." *Southern California Quarterly* 67 (Spring 1985): 72–87. Account of the voyage from New Bedford, Massachusetts, to San Francisco, February 3–August 28, 1849, in the ship *Magnolia* under the command of Capt. Benjamin Frank Simmons. Has a track chart of the ship and a drawing of her nearing Cape Horn, both by the author.

Granite State Trading, Mining & Agricultural Company. N.p.: N.p., [1849]. It is possible that the members of this company sailed to San Francisco in the ship *Sweden*.

Harris, J. Morrison. *A Paper upon California; Read Before the Maryland Historical Society by J. Morrison Harris, Corresponding Secretary, March, 1849.* Baltimore: Printed for the Society by John D. Toy, 1849.

Hazelton, John Adams. *The Hazelton Letters: A Contribution to Western Americana.* Edited by Mary Geneva Bloom. Stockton, California: College of the Pacific, 1958. Reprinted from *The Pacific Historian* 1: 2, 3, 4. Contains six letters Hazelton wrote to members of his family in New Hampshire. The first two deal with his voyage from Boston to San Francisco in the brig *Randolph*.

Hotchkiss, Charles F. "California in 1849." *The Magazine of History, With Notes and Queries* Extra no. 191, 48 (No. 23): 133–52. Much of the article deals with an isthmian voyage to California, but it has some interesting observations on San Francisco and California in 1849.

Howe, Octavius Thorndike. *Argonauts of '49: History and Adventures of the Emigrant Companies from Massachusetts 1849–1850.* Cambridge: Harvard University Press, 1923.

Hunt, Rockwell D. "Pioneer Protestant Preachers in Early California." *Pacific Historical Review* 19 (January 1949): 84–96.

Ingalls, John. "California Letters of the Gold Rush Period: The Correspondence of John Ingalls, 1849–1851." *Proceedings of the American Antiquarian Society* (1937):145–82. First few letters contain information on his voyage in the ship *Pacific* from New York to San Francisco.

Johnson, Samuel Roosevelt. *California; A Sermon, Preached in St. John's Church, Brooklyn, N.Y., on Sunday, February 11, 1849, by Samuel Roosevelt Johnson, D.D., Rector.* New York: Stanford and Swords, 1849. Preached on the occasion of the departure of the bark *St. Mary* for California.

Kihn, Phyllis. "Connecticut and the California Gold Rush: The Connecticut Mining and Trading Company." *Connecticut Historical Society Bulletin* 28 (1963): 1–13. The company owned and sailed in the schooner *General Morgan*. Based in part upon the journal, February 22–August 5, 1849, of Albert Lyman during the voyage from New York to San Francisco.

Kull, Irving Stoddard. "The New Brunswick Adventurers of '49." *Proceedings of the New Jersey Historical Society* New Series 10 (January 1925): 12–28. Discusses formation of the New Brunswick & California Mining and Trading Company and the voyage of that group in 1849 from New York to San Francisco in the bark *Isabel*.

Latham, William B. "The Barque *Stafford*, the Record of Her Voyage to California. List of Passengers." *The Society of California Pioneers Publications* (1943): 51–60.

Levy, JoAnn. *They Saw the Elephant: Women in the California Gold Rush.* Hamden, Connecticut: Shoe String Press, 1990. The second chapter deals with traveling to California by sea by both the Cape Horn and the isthmian routes.

Lewis, Oscar. *Sea Routes to the Gold Fields: The Migration by Water to California in 1849–1852.* New York: A. A. Knopf, 1949.

———. "South American Ports of Call." *Pacific Historical Review* 18 (January 1949): 57–66. Brief descriptions of ports entered by vessels bound around Cape Horn to San Francisco in 1849.

Lorenz, Anthony J. "Scurvy in the Gold Rush." *Journal of the History of Medicine and Allied Sciences* 12 (1957). 473–510.

Marshall, Philip C. "New Jersey Expeditions to California in 1849." *Proceedings of the New Jersey Historical Society* 70 (January 1952): 17–36.

Marx, Jennifer. *The Magic of Gold.* Garden City, New York: Doubleday & Company, Inc., 1978. Contains two introductory chapters on gold in general and where and how it has been found and mined followed by thirteen chapters on the history of gold from the Pharaohs to the twentieth century. Chapter 14 contains a small amount of information on the California gold rush of 1849–1852.

Morgan, William Ives. "The Log of a Forty-Niner." *Harper's Magazine* 113 (February 1906): 920–26. Extracts from his diary, 1849–1853, including his account of sailing around Cape Horn in 1849 in the bark *John Walls, Jr.*

Morse, Edwin Franklin. "The Story of a Gold Miner: Reminiscences of Edwin Franklin Morse." *California Historical Society Quarterly* 6 (September 1927): 205–37. Pages 205–12 contain a brief account of his voyage, December 5, 1849–June 17, 1850, from Boston to San Francisco in the ship *Cheshire* under the command of Capt. J. W. Dicks.

Nash, Jared C. *To the Goldfields around the Horn from Maine to California in the Schooner* Belgrade. N.p.: N.p., circa 1956. Contains copies of two letters Nash sent home to his wife in 1850 and his journal, December 1, 1849–February 12, 1850, during part of the voyage of the bark (rather than schooner) from Cherryfield, Maine, to San Francisco under the command of Captain Plummer. Nash apparently became ill during the voyage and returned home to Maine without ever going into the mines.

Palmer, Robert H. *A Voyage Round Cape Horn.* Philadelphia: William S. Young, 1863. Pages 1–18 contain an account of the voyage, August 7–December 13, 1849, from Philadelphia to San Francisco in the bark *Maria* under the command of Captain Mattison.

Parsons, John E., ed. "Nine Cousins in the California Gold Rush." *New York Historical Society Quarterly* 47 (1963): 349–97. Nine cousins sailed from New York for California in 1849. Their adventures were recorded in the letters written home by William J. Emmet and Herman R. LeRoy. Some of the letters deal with the voyage of three of them in the ship *Christovol Colon* under the command of Capt. Francis C. Coffin.

[Payson, George]. *Golden Dreams and Leaden Realities.* New York: G. P. Putnam & Co., 1853. Has an introductory chapter by Francis Fogie Sr., Esq. Pages 15–75 contain an account of the voyage in 1849 of the ship *Magnolia* from New Bedford, Massachusetts, to San Francisco. The book was originally published as being by Ralph Raven. Payson called the ship *Leucothea* and used pseudonyms for many of the individuals. S. Mortimer Collins, who was also

Bibliography

a passenger in the *Magnolia*, provided the real names for those individuals in the transcribed copy of his journal.

Pomfret, John E., ed. *California Gold Rush Voyages, 1848–1849: Three Original Narratives*. San Marino, California: Huntington Library, 1954. Contains the journal of C. H. Ellis during the voyage from Boston to San Francisco in the brig *North Bend* under the command of Capt. R. G. Higgins, brief notes of John N. Stone of the voyage of the ship *Robert Bowne*, and journals kept on board the steamer *California* from New York to San Francisco.

Reynolds, Jerry. *The Golden Dream of Francisco Lopez*. Newhall, California: Santa Clara Valley Historical Society, n.d.

Richardson, Katherine Wood. "The Gold Seekers: The Story of the LaGrange and the California Pioneers of New England." *Essex Institute Historical Collections* 115 (1979): 73–122. Reconstruction of the voyage of the bark *LaGrange* from Salem, Massachusetts, to San Francisco, March–September 1849. Has a month-by-month record of the voyage and a roster of passengers including the members of the Salem and California Mining and Trading Company. Also has fourteen illustrations.

Richardson, William H. "The Argonauts of Jersey City." *Proceedings of the New Jersey Historical Society* New Series 11 (1926): 170–86, 369–77, 525–32. Brief accounts of various individuals, groups, and vessels that went from New Jersey to California in 1849.

Roberts, Sidney. *To Emigrants to the Gold Region. An Appeal to Citizens of the U.S., the Martyrdom of the Two Prophets, Joseph and Hiram Smith—Doctrines of the Latter Day Saints—on the Melchizadek Priesthood—the Materiality of the Soul. A Treatise Showing the Best Way to California, with Many Serious Objections to Going by Sea, Doubling the Cape, or Crossing the Isthmus, with the constitution and articles of Agreement, of the Joint Stock Mutual Insurance Merchandizing company. By Sidney Roberts, of Iowa City, Iowa, Traveling Agent for the Company*. New Haven: N.p., 1849.

Robinson, Warren T. *Dust and Foam; or, Three Oceans and Two Continents being Ten Year's Wandering in Mexico, South America, Sandwich Islands, the East and West Indies, China, Philippines, Australia, and Polynesia*. New York: Charles Scribner, 1859. Pages 11–142 contain an account of his 1849 voyage from New York to San Francisco in an unnamed bark to Rio de Janeiro and an unnamed steamer the remainder of the way.

Rydell, Raymond A. "The California Clippers." *Pacific Historical Review* 18 (January 1949):70–83. Reprinted in John Walton Caughey, *Rushing for Gold*. Berkeley: University of California Press, 1949. American Historical Association, Pacific Coast Branch, Special Publication No. 1.

"Sacramento's Prison Ship the *LaGrange*." *Golden Notes* 20 (October 1974): 1–12. Story about the bark that sailed from Salem, Massachusetts, in 1849.

Schaeffer, L. M. *Sketches of Travels in South America, Mexico, and California*. New York: James Egbert, Printer, 1860. Pages 7–31 contain an account of his voyage, March 24–September 17, 1849, from New York to San Francisco in the ship *Flavius* under the command of Capt. I. Thatcher.

Schultz, Charles R. "A Forty-Niner Fourth of July." *Log of Mystic Seaport* 38(Spring 1983):119–29.

———. "Ship *Andalusia:* Queen of the Baltimore Gold Rush Fleet." *Maryland Historical Magazine* 86 (Summer 1991):151–75.

———. "Gold Rush Voyage of the Ship *Pacific:* A Study in Vessel Management." *American Neptune* 53 (Summer 1993): 190–200.

Shepard, George, and S. L. Caldwell. *Addresses of Rev. Professor George Shepard and Rev. S. L. Caldwell, to the California Pilgrims, from Bangor, Maine.* Bangor: Smith & Sayward, printers, 1849. Reprinted by the Meriden Gravure Company and the Carl Purington Rollins Printing-Office of the Yale University Press, Christmas 1966, for Frederick W. Beinecke in a limited edition of 350 copies. These two sermons were preached at the Hammond Street Church in Bangor, Maine, on January 21, 1849 for the benefit of the passengers who were about to sail for San Francisco in the bark *Suliote* under the command of Capt. J. Simpson and the schooner *Eudorus* under the command of Capt. Charles L. Wiggin. Passenger lists for the two vessels are included in the reprint taken from the *Bangor Daily Whig and Courier.*

Smith, Charles H. *Historical Sketch of the Lives of William Wiggin Smith and Joseph Hiram Smith, a Pair of New England Twins Who Became California Pioneers in 1849.* Avalon, California: Privately printed, 1942. Pages 21–35 contain an account of their voyage, January 11–July 6, 1849, from Boston to San Francisco in the brig *Forest* under the command of Capt. N. Varina.

Taylor, William A. *California Life Illustrated.* New York: Published for the author by Carlton & Porter, 1860.

Thomas, Martin E. "Sea Voyages to El Dorado with a Descriptive Bibliography of Journals and Letters, 1848–1856," MA Thesis, University of California, Berkeley, 1937. Actually it is called a "Special Study" rather than a thesis. It is an extensively annotated bibliography of published and unpublished accounts of voyages, both Cape Horn and Isthmian, to San Francisco. Includes reference to twenty-five published and twenty-one, unpublished accounts.

Tibbits, Hall J. *Statement of Hall J. Tibbits, Master of the American Ship* Pacific, *as to His Removal from the Command of Said Ship, by Gorham Parks, U.S. Consul, at Rio de Janeiro.* New York: George F. Nesbitt, Stationer and Printer, 1849. This small pamphlet contains some introductory remarks by Captain Tibbits and copies of nineteen documents on file at the U.S. Consulate in Rio de Janeiro relating to the removal of Tibbits. All of the documents were selected by Tibbits to further his cause in having himself restored to command of the *Pacific.* He was successful in that campaign and met the ship in San Francisco and resumed command. An original exists at the California State Library, Sacramento.

Wells, Thomas Goodwin. "Letters of an Argonaut from August, 1849 to October, 1851." *Out West* 22 (January 1905): 48–54, (March 1905): 136–42, and (April 1905): 221–28. Wells was one of the founders of the Cheshire Company organized in southwestern New Hampshire late in 1849 to go to California. They sailed from Boston to San Francisco in the ship *Sweden* under the command of Capt. Jesse G. Cotting. None of the letters contain information on the voyage, but a couple of them contain early impressions of San Francisco.

Bibliography

Whidden, John D. *Ocean Life in the Old Sailing Ships Days. From Forecastle to Quarter-Deck by Captain John D. Whidden.* Boston: Little, Brown, and Company, 1912. Pages 78–83 contain brief mention of his voyage from Boston to San Francisco in the bark *Tiberias* under the command of Capt. Elisha Foster.

Winslow, Helen L. "Nantucket Forty-Niners: Gold Rush Voyages and a Passenger's Journal of a Voyage around the Horn." *Historic Nantucket* 4 (January 1956): 6–28.

Index

Index

Vessel Index

Vessel Index